All Things
Medieval

All Things

Medieval

An Encyclopedia of the
Medieval World

Volume 2

J–Z

Ruth A. Johnston

GREENWOOD

AN IMPRINT OF ABC-CLIO, LLC
Santa Barbara, California • Denver, Colorado • Oxford, England

Copyright 2011 by Ruth A. Johnston

All rights reserved. No part of this publication may be reproduced, stored in a
retrieval system, or transmitted, in any form or by any means, electronic, mechanical,
photocopying, recording, or otherwise, except for the inclusion of brief quotations in
a review, without prior permission in writing from the publisher.

Library of Congress Cataloging-in-Publication Data

Johnston, Ruth A.
  All things medieval : an encyclopedia of the medieval world / Ruth A. Johnston
     v. cm.
  Includes bibliographical references and index.
  ISBN 978-0-313-36462-4 (hard copy : acid-free paper) — ISBN 978-0-313-36463-1
(ebook) 1. Civilization, Medieval—Encyclopedias. I. Title.
  CB351.J675 2011
  909.07—dc22   2011004678

ISBN: 978-0-313-36462-4
EISBN: 978-0-313-36463-1

15 14 13 12 11   1 2 3 4 5

This book is also available on the World Wide Web as an eBook.
Visit www.abc-clio.com for details.

Greenwood
An Imprint of ABC-CLIO, LLC

ABC-CLIO, LLC
130 Cremona Drive, P.O. Box 1911
Santa Barbara, California 93116-1911

This book is printed on acid-free paper ∞

Manufactured in the United States of America

Contents

Introduction

This book is about the material culture, the things, of Europe in the Middle Ages. These things include nearly everything that could be seen, heard, touched, tasted, met, or experienced. The material culture's center is in the home and the workplace. All things in the home and at work are contained in the scope of this book. The church and the monastery had their things, as did the warriors. There are things in entertainment and the arts. Some people are counted as things, particularly if they were notable types throughout Europe who were defined by having a unique set of things. Two key events, the Crusades and the Black Death plague, are included because they shaped the material culture in dramatic ways and also had their own identifying things. The raw materials of the things are also included so that their nature and technology can be understood.

Europe is defined as broadly as can be useful. It includes Scandinavia, Spain, Europe's heartland of England, France, Germany, and Italy, and the Byzantine Empire that overlapped Europe and Asia. Information is not always available for all of these regions at all times, but where available, it has been included to give as broad a picture as possible.

Europe's Middle Ages span about 1,000 years, a time that transitions between antiquity and the modern world. Historians and authors have no exact dates for when the Middle Ages began and ended. It is the period between certain key events that clustered in the opening and closing centuries and seemed to mark a transition of culture and technology. This book uses roughly the years 550 and 1450 to define the Middle Ages.

The heartland of the Roman Empire, Italy, came under domination by the invading Goths at the end of the fifth century, and Roman rule shifted entirely to Constantine's eastern capital, Constantinople. Around the same time, the first Merovingian kings ruled the Franks; King Clovis I died in 511. Benedict of Nursia founded monasteries and wrote his Rule of Saint Benedict not long after 500. Around 550, the last Roman outposts in Britain fell to invading Anglo-Saxons. The Plague of Justinian carried off about one-third of Constantinople's (and Egypt's) population around 550. In Mecca, Mohammed saw visions and founded a new religion around 600.

These events define the effective beginning of Europe's Middle Ages, although the early years are often called, informally, the Dark Ages. Rome no longer towered over Europe with superior technology and culture and a strong government and army. The Goths in Italy, the Anglo-Saxons in England, the Franks in France and Germany, and the Visigoths in Spain were all relatively primitive and uncivilized compared to Rome and Constantinople. Europe's Middle Ages are the time when these Germanic tribes grew up, developing government, culture, and technology to match and surpass Rome's.

At the same time, the birth and growth of Islam also defined medieval Europe. Muslims were an aggressive force always pushing at Europe's borders. Defensive and aggressive action against Muslim armies was the heart of medieval warfare. The Muslim Caliphate, which spanned the southern shore of the Mediterranean Sea, was also a conduit for technology and products from far away. Gems, silk, spices, and ideas came from India and Persia through the Muslim Empire that united the Far East with Egypt and Spain. European culture imported products from Muslim traders while pushing back Muslim armies.

The most famous events in the Middle Ages were the Crusades, waves of defensive/aggressive war to take back territory from Islam. It was the age of the knight and his castle. Crusaders learned new construction methods and began building the classic castles of medieval Europe. Minstrels learned musical instruments from the East and sang "The Song of Roland" at tournament feasts. Spices from the East dressed meat, fish, and fruit in castle kitchens. The Byzantine story of Saint George and the dragon and travelers' stories populated Europe's imagination with knights, dragons, unicorns, lions, and sea monsters.

The medieval period in Europe was also the time when Latin dominated government, education, and literature. It was still the native language of Rome in 500, but Greek was already the native tongue in Constantinople. Latin was soon nobody's native language but everybody's common channel of communication. The Middle Ages were the time of Latin book production, Latin schooling, and Latin liturgy in the church. Lectures at the new universities of Bologna, Paris, and Oxford were taught in Latin.

It was the age of monasteries and the high-water mark of the Roman Catholic Church's influence. The Rule of Saint Benedict spread all over Europe. Both monasteries and convents dotted all regions thickly; they owned much of the land. Monks hand copied books and painted fanciful scenes and animals in the margins. Pilgrims venerated relics and donated to saints' shrines, and enormous cathedrals rose at these sites. Monastic choirs sang Latin plainchant under stone vaults and stained glass windows.

The governing system of medieval Europe was the Franks' feudalism. Designed as a way to create mini-kingdoms to support armed knights, feudalism assigned all land to men loyal to the king. Everyone who lived on the land was assigned to support these nobles with their labor, keeping only enough of their produce to live on. Towns began to grow, and peasants moved to the towns, but they needed to buy their freedom first, and towns had to be chartered by the king or count as free of feudal obligations. International commerce and technology grew within these free towns, but the countryside remained chained to feudalism.

The end of the Middle Ages was when, within a century, all these trends came to an end. By 1350, the Black Death plague had wiped out at least one-third of Europe's population, and feudalism stopped making sense not long after. By 1381, England's peasants staged a revolt. Gunpowder was coming into use around the same time, during the Hundred Years' War, and, by 1400, cannons were the key siege weapon. Armor and castles were quickly obsolete, and the arts of the knight became simply a rich man's sport. Restlessness and disillusionment from plague, famine, and war brought out dissent within the church, and the early Reformation came in the form of Lollards and Hussites. Latin was no longer anyone's native tongue, and reformers wanted the Bible to be in the vulgar languages, as secular books now were. Pilgrimages, monasteries, and relics lost influence, and many were destroyed in the 16th century. The modern world was being born.

The key date for the end of the Middle Ages is 1453—the fall of Constantinople to an army of Muslim Turks. The early Middle Ages had seen the fall of Rome and the birth of Islam; the period closed with a Muslim army triumphant in the remaining Roman capital. Gunpowder had breached the invincible walls. Scholars, artisans, and priests fled Constantinople as Roman scholars, artisans, and priests had fled Rome. They brought the learning of Greece back to Europe, and Europe's culture transitioned into the period we call the Renaissance.

List of Entries

List of Entries

Guide to Related Topics

Art
  Books
  Embroidery
  Glass
  Gold and Silver
  Heraldry
  Jewelry
  Painting
  Sculpture
  Tapestry

Buildings and Places
  Castles
  Cathedrals
  Cities
  Hospitals
  Houses
  Mills
  Monasteries
  Prisons
  Schools

Taverns and Inns
Universities

Business and Finance
  Banks
  Coins
  Fairs
  Gold and Silver
  Guilds
  Numbers
  Records
  Seals
  Weights and Measures

Clothing
  Armor
  Cloth
  Clothing
  Clothing Accessories
  Cosmetics
  Embroidery

Eyeglasses
Hair
Hats
Jewelry
Shoes

Customs and Events
Calendar
Funerals
Heraldry
Holidays
Hygiene
Magic
Tournaments
Weddings

Education
Alphabet
Books
Libraries
Schools
Universities

Entertainment
Animals
Arthur, King
Dance
Drama
Feasts
Games
Hood, Robin
Hunting
Minstrels and Troubadours
Music
Roland, Song of
Zoos

Food and Drink
Agriculture
Barrels and Buckets

Beverages
Fasts
Feasts
Fish and Fishing
Food
Gardens
Hunting
Kitchen Utensils
Poison
Salt
Spices and Sugar
Taverns and Inns
Water

Government
Castles
Church
Cities
Fairs
Guilds
Jews
Latrines and Garbage
Muslims
Prisons
Weights and Measures

The Household
Barrels and Buckets
Castles
Cities
Furniture
Gardens
Glass
Houses
Hygiene
Kitchen Utensils
Latrines and Garbage
Lights

Pottery
Tapestry

Medicine
Food
Gardens
Hospitals
Magic
Monasteries
Plague
Spices and Sugar
Universities

Natural Resources
Coal
Forests
Gold and Silver
Iron
Lead and Copper
Salt
Stone and Masons
Water

People
Babies
Beggars
Jews
Knights
Minstrels and Troubadours
Muslims
Pilgrims
Saints
Servants and Slaves
Women

Plants and Animals
Agriculture
Animals
Beekeeping
Fish and Fishing

Gardens
Horses
Hunting
Monsters
Poison
Zoos

Reading and Writing
Alphabet
Books
Libraries
Maps
Numbers
Parchment and Paper
Pens and Ink
Printing
Records
Schools
Universities

Religion
Bells
Books
Calendar
Cathedrals
Church
Crusades
Drama
Fasts
Feasts
Funerals
Holidays
Hospitals
Jews
Magic
Medicine
Monasteries
Music
Muslims

J

Jewelry

The word *jewelry* began as a term for a fancy gold centerpiece on a feast table, the *joyau* or *jouel*. It began to apply to personal adornment during the late 14th century, beginning at the splendid court of the duke of Burgundy. In medieval times, jewelry was not distinctively male or female, as it is today. Wealthy people wanted to show off what they could afford and reap the honor of high status. Men wore large jeweled brooches to hold their cloaks, and, when cloaks went out of use, they pinned brooches to their **hats.** The same heavy golden collar (necklace) or ring could be worn by either men or **women.**

During the 9th, 10th, and 11th centuries, European **clothing** styles were heavy and covered most skin. Brooches to clasp cloaks and belts to hold in all the layers were the most common jewelry. As fashion began to change more rapidly in the 13th century, necks, arms, and hair were more often exposed and could be decorated. Low-cut dresses allowed women to wear showy necklaces. Collars, necklaces, bracelets, rings, and headdresses were developed for use at court. By the 14th and 15th centuries, common people began wearing imitations of court jewelry using cheap materials.

Few medieval jewels have survived into modern times, and the ones that have are usually the largest and most historical, such as crowns kept safely in national museums. Other survivors were lost in their own time, either buried or sunk to the bottom of a river. The value of a piece of jewelry has always been in its materials and only secondarily in its design or workmanship. Jewels were inherited or sold, and the new owners often gave them to a goldsmith to recast them in the current style. The same gemstones were set over and over, and each age considered the old style unattractive and its own much better. Most of our knowledge of medieval jewelry comes from paintings and sculpture.

Gemstones and Beads

Gems, like anything from nature, had their own natural **magic.** They were believed to cure or ward off certain kinds of diseases or tragedies. Based on the *Natural History* of the Roman writer Pliny the Elder, medieval writers composed lapidaries, **books** about the properties of gems. Sapphires, for example, had cooling powers to cure headache and fever and made God more likely to answer prayer. Rubies were a charm against discord, and emeralds helped epilepsy. The popularity of lapidaries made them among the first books to be written in common tongues, as well as in Latin.

Amber, garnet, jet, and beryl were gems native to Europe. Amber was fossilized pinesap and occurred in abundance in the Baltic area, around modern Lithuania. The amber trade had been important since early medieval

Square-headed brooches were almost universal in early medieval Europe. The Franks and the Anglo-Saxons probably borrowed the form from Roman models. The square at the top held a hinged pin, while the cross shape at the bottom concealed the pin's clasp. The bridge between these parts held the gathered folds of a cloak or tunic. Brooches like these are found in many pagan graves. (Museum of London/ StockphotoPro)

times, as Scandinavian **ships** carried amber out of the Baltic Sea and traded it in France and England. Garnet is a mineral that came in a variety of colors. Its most common medieval form was dark red, as found in Bohemia, and some other forms came from Asia Minor and Russia. Jet is not a true mineral but is closer to petrified wood. It is pure black and can be polished to a glossy sheen. It occurred naturally in parts of England. Beryl is a transparent mineral that is colorless but often occurs with color tints. It had been known since classical times and occurred in many parts of Europe.

A few other minerals native to Europe made good jewelry. Rock crystal, a form of quartz, sparkled and could be used as itself or in imitation of other gems. It was not a real gemstone, but it was pretty and popular for many articles. It could be found easily in Germany and France. Pearls are not native to the Mediterranean Sea, and most pearls came to Europe from the Indian Ocean, but some river pearls came from Scotland (and later from Bohemia). A freshwater mussel that lived in Scottish rivers produced a small pearl that could be pierced and sewn onto clothing or mounted as a small gem. Toadstone was a fossilized fish tooth, but medieval people believed it came out of a toad's head. It was brown, and it polished well and was thought to bring good luck. Finally, Roman cameos were recycled into medieval jewelry. They had been left in Roman ruins, and people often found them. In Italy, where they had been made from native two-colored minerals, they were even more plentiful.

Coral reefs along the African shore of the Mediterranean Sea provided most of Europe's coral. Coral was considered protective against lightning; its growth in the ocean was thought to give it special properties. It was good for children's beads, since children needed special protection. Coral beads were popular for rosaries and other jewelry. Coral also made early buttons.

Fine gemstones had to be imported from the East, so they were very expensive. Medieval jewelers favored brightly colored stones: red, blue, and green. Eastern traders brought rubies from India, sapphires from Ceylon and Persia, emeralds from Egypt, amethyst from Russia, and turquoise from Persia and Tibet. Some amethyst also came from Germany. Diamonds were not as popular, or as common. Jewish and Arab traders imported diamonds from India and Africa during the late Middle Ages, and diamonds began to appear in some jewelry sets.

Gems were polished, not cut, until the late Middle Ages. The classic medieval gem was opaque, colored, round, and smooth. Sometimes they were engraved. In the 14th century, some jewelers were cutting simple planes on gems. Although diamonds were the most difficult to cut, they benefited most in appearance, and their natural crystalline shape lent itself well to cutting.

Beads are the mainstay of much personal ornament. In addition to the expensive gemstone or **gold** beads that royalty could afford, there were less expensive options. Venice's **glass** industry made glass beads in many colors, and these grew to be among the most common for less expensive jewelry. Amber, Northern Europe's traditional bead, came in yellow, orange, and a very pale yellow that was nearly white. Whitby jet made shiny black beads. Red coral was a very popular bead material because of its protective properties. Rock crystal made a clear, sparkling, expensive-looking bead. Cheap beads could be made of bone, stamped from a rib and polished into a round shape. Rosary beads were originally made of pressed rose petals picked in a special rose **garden** devoted to the Virgin Mary.

Early Medieval Jewelry

Byzantine jewelry blended traditions of Greece and Rome with art brought back from the East. Their goldsmiths used gold wire and gold plate; they set gems into place with fine wire claws, often shaped decoratively. They set emeralds, sapphires, rubies, and diamonds into gold jewelry. They drilled and threaded pearls into settings with gold wire. They also created mosaics in gold jewelry by setting stones such as garnets, or pieces of colored glass, into patterns.

Constantinople was a very rich manufacturing and trading **city** with longstanding aristocratic families, so the demand for jewelry was high. The highest art went into crowns, which became increasingly heavy and elaborate. Sixth-century crowns were heavy bands that encircled the head; they were decorated with gems and had strings of pearls hanging down over the ears. The next stage of crown was a heavy series of plates, each with a mosaic of jewels showing a **saint,** that also had strings of pearls. The next stage used an arch that went over the top of the head and was also heavily jeweled. The last evolution of the crown used two heavy bands of gold, one above the other, and, above these, a series of points standing up in the classic crown shape used by modern cartoonists.

Byzantine aristocratic women wore large, elaborate earrings. They had pierced ears and wore dangles, hoops, crescents, and crosses. Pearls and gems were threaded on gold wire. Other articles that demanded gold and gems were belts, bracelets, rings, and brooches used to pin cloaks. Religious symbols were also jeweled. A noble Byzantine woman might wear a highly decorated, large gold cross on her chest, hung as a necklace. One specific type was the reliquary: it looks to us like an ordinary large gold cross pendant, but it contained a small box, covered by a jewel, similar to a locket. Some tiny religious **relic** went into the reliquary, and it was worn like a charm.

Before the Franks, Anglo-Saxons, Danes, and Swedes converted to Christianity, they buried gold jewelry in graves. There are treasure hoards like the one found at Sutton Hoo, and there are more modest finds. Even after becoming Christians, Frankish royalty still went to the grave dressed in silk and gems. They favored arm rings for men and necklaces and rings for women. They viewed jewelry as wearable wealth and believed in flaunting it on **feast** days. Their jewelry was large and showy, but its workmanship was crude compared to the work produced in Constantinople at the same time.

The earliest jewelry from Northern Europe comes in the form of pins and brooches for cloaks. The Franks, Anglo-Saxons, and others made large gold pins for these practical purposes. Saucer brooches were large gold circles with a clasp on the back, probably for pinning a cloak to the wearer's tunic at the shoulders. They came in pairs, often connected by a string of amber beads. Quoit brooches were thick circles that fastened the pin through the hole. The other main kind of brooch is known as a square-headed brooch. A square (or rectangle) of **silver** or gold was connected to a decorative lobed cross by an arched bridge. A pin ran along the back; the bridge allowed space for a woolen cloak to run through the pin. Brooches were always very decorative. They had fine decorations of flowers, scrolls, dragons, and **animals,** and many had amber beads mounted in them.

Europe's medieval jewelry developed from these traditions. Italian jewelry was always more influenced by Byzantine fashions, while Northern

European work developed first from large pagan pieces. As travel increased trade in the 12th century, goldsmiths in the North began to learn from and copy the southern pieces. By the 15th century, it was difficult to tell where a piece had been made just by looking at it.

Crowns, Brooches, Necklaces, and Rings

Most medieval jewelry was made for royalty, and we have mainly these very expensive, large, showy pieces in museums. At the same time, clothing before the 14th century was usually ample and heavy, and their greatest need in jewelry was for pieces that fastened clothing together. Their jewelry often came in the form of pins, brooches, and belt fastenings. They were simple and large, with large, round gemstones. Cameos were popular and even appeared in some crowns, alternated with gems. Cameos associated the medieval wearer with the past glories of Rome.

By the close of the Middle Ages, Gothic-style jewelry had become elaborate and fanciful. A crown was a once-in-a-lifetime opportunity for a goldsmith to show all of his skills. Gold, silver, pearls, and glass went into this 15th-century Bohemian crown. (Digital Image © 2009 Museum Associates/Los Angeles County Museum of Art/Art Resource, NY)

After the 12th century, the elaborate Gothic style influenced jewelry styles. The 13th century was a generally prosperous time, and jewelry proliferated until kings began passing sumptuary laws. Only royalty, aristocrats, and large landowners and their families could wear jewels or gold. Royal jewelry inventories from the 14th century are sumptuous beyond modern imagination. Edward II owned 10 crowns. The mistress of his son, Edward III, had more than 20,000 pearls. Queen Isabella of England, married to the king in 1396, was given at least five crowns and as many brooches as gifts from the king and his lords, all covered with rubies, pearls, sapphires, and diamonds set in jeweled gold. A French duchess owned huge jeweled headdresses covered with pearls and every other costly gemstone.

Royal crowns grew ever more elaborate and delicate. At the same time, the late medieval period featured complicated headdresses for court ladies, which provided ladies the ability to wear imitation crowns without royal status. Bands like coronets encircled their veils and barbettes. The bands could be wide or narrow, and they gave large scope to the imaginations of the jewelers. The headdresses themselves, made of silk, were beaded with jewels, as were the pins, bands, and nets that held the **hair** tresses in place.

The classic ring brooch remained a common form for these new Gothic jewels. The ring was now elaborately worked in gold and set with smaller gems in pretty patterns, such as flowers or dragons. The brooch's clasp was a pin that fastened on the other side of the ring, as in Anglo-Saxon times. Ring brooches led to heart-shaped brooches and to lobed rings like cloverleafs or flowers.

When a new kind of clasp, called an ouch, was developed, the brooch no longer had to form its own way to catch the pin. New shapes were possible. Wheel brooches kept the ring shape but added gems in a center design held in place with spokes. Brooches could also be in other shapes, such as letters, usually *M* for Mary. Letter brooches were often enameled in bright colors. Cluster brooches could be shaped like a pair of birds or a bunch of flowers, of course heavily covered with gems and pearls. Gems lent themselves well to flowers, since one gem could be the center and the others the petals. **Hunting** motifs and animals, such as stags, dogs, lions, and falcons, were popular with royalty. As the Gothic period went on, brooch designs only grew more fanciful: griffins, unicorns, squirrels, doves, harps, the sun, eagles, swans, gardens, ladies, and even a dromedary.

Heraldic brooches came to function as badges for orders such as the knightly Order of the Garter. The use trickled down to lesser people, whose badges were made of lesser metals. The late Middle Ages had a fashion for livery, a uniform dress for all the servants of a great lord, and badges were often added, particularly in England. The earl of Norfolk's badge was a crowned ostrich feather, while the earl of Warwick had a bear and staff.

Badges could be made cheaply but impressively by using **lead,** gilding the outside to look like pure gold.

Necklaces began as either collars or rosary bead strings. Collars were wide, flat links of gold or silver designs. The links were fashioned as livery for each great lord's household, such as a string of *S* links for Lancaster. (This distinctive pattern is often called a "collar of SS.") French collars were made of links shaped like fleur-de-lis, as well as other shapes such as doves or leaves. The collar lay flat against the wearer's robes and had a pendant with some significant heraldic design, such as an order of knighthood. They were royal honors, not just jewelry, and were only worn by men.

Ladies' collars were more like flat, wide necklaces; they were smaller and fit closer around the neck than the men's and were more heavily jeweled or enameled. Ladies had been wearing beads as rosaries for some time, and the two styles began to blend. During the 15th century, necklaces, like brooches and rings, broke out of the aristocracy and were imitated in less costly style by the upper middle classes. While collars and rosaries both had a central pendant, the new 14th- and 15th-century necklaces could feature pendants prominently as the single ornament. The heart was a popular 15th-century pendant. For the wealthy, they were gold, set with diamonds or pearls. For the townspeople, they were silver or **copper,** perhaps gilded. Crosses were always the most common pendants—jewelry that passed as a mark of the wearer's devotion as well as affluence.

There were new types of jewelry at the close of the Middle Ages. Looser sleeves in the 15th century allowed for bracelets. As with other jewelry, they began as a fashion for royalty, set with pearls and gems. Pendants could be fastened to the new floppy or tall hats to secure the folded liripipe or to enliven plain black beaver.

In the 14th century, metalworkers refined and increased the production of wire. Wire was used in headdresses and jewelry, and it began a trend of plain gold or brass wire rings. Finger rings are ideal pieces of jewelry. They are easily noticed on hands, and they require only small quantities of precious materials. Their simple design allows for many different ways to decorate them. Plain bands can be engraved or decorated with enamel or niello to add colors or black to contrast with gold or silver. The bezel, the raised part on top of a ring, can be engraved or enameled or set with a gem or bead.

Although only aristocrats could wear splendid, large rings, well-off townspeople could afford simple rings made of plainer materials. Common rings were made of pewter, copper, brass, bronze, or even gunmetal. Fine rings, of course, were made of gold or silver or carved from ivory. Metal rings often had gems set in them, as modern rings do. Tiny Roman cameos were favorite ring gemstones. A royal ring made of gold had emeralds, garnets, or sapphires, while a common brass or pewter ring used colored glass to imitate the appearance of real gems.

Brides wore **wedding** rings, and lovers gave rings as gifts. The traditions of courtly love provided the late Middle Ages with ideas for sentimental jewelry. Some 14th- and 15th-century rings had engraved mottoes in Latin or French, such as "Love conquers all," "With all my heart," and "Think of me."

Rings could be the mounts for small **seals,** known as signet rings. They were uncommon before the 15th century. The matrix of the seal could be carved into a gem like onyx, or it could be engraved directly on the gold. It was carved with the intaglio technique so that when it was pressed onto wax, the design stood up from the surface. These rings could be less showy than gemstone rings, but a signet ring implied importance and wealth, so a signet by itself was an impressive piece of jewelry.

Ecclesiastical Jewelry

The Middle Ages had a special class of jewels worn, carried, and used by the rulers of the **church.** Some were adornments of the church itself, such as altarpieces and jeweled crosses. Reliquaries were among the largest, most expensive medieval jewels; they could be as small as a ring box or as large as a closet. Most were about the size of a breadbox. They were usually made as miniature churches or arks.

Abbots, bishops, and archbishops wore a pointed hat called a miter, and it was not only heavily jeweled but also could have brooches pinned to it. Each century, miters grew taller and wider. They were made of silk and were decorated with pearls and gems and embroidered in gold thread. The church's princes also wore copes, small decorative cloaks that required spectacular brooches as clasps. The clasp was called a morse, and it was invariably gold or silver, with gems. The cope itself had gems stitched onto its silk.

Even more importantly, bishops and archbishops wore rings that signified their office. There were episcopal rings, put onto the priest's finger when he was installed in office, and pontifical rings, used only when celebrating High Mass. Pontifical rings fitted over gloves and were only worn on these important ceremonial occasions. They were very large and expensive. Ordinary episcopal rings were hardly modest. The simplest were heavy gold with a gemstone such as an emerald or sapphire. Some had tiny reliquaries built in, with enamel and engraved religious symbols, in addition to gemstones. Bishops were usually buried with an episcopal ring.

Rosary beads were a devout, sedate kind of jewelry. Originally, rosary beads had been made from pressed rose petals grown in a garden dedicated to Mary—a rosary. Over time, rosary beads were made of other materials: bone, coral, pearls, gold, or gems. A rosary had 50 beads on a braided silk string and was worn about the neck. The beads made it easier to count long repetitions of prayers. The person praying would hold a rosary bead while repeating the prayer and then move to the next bead. As long as his or her fingers didn't slip, there was assurance of counting correctly. They were also called paternoster beads, and some had different-shaped beads to remind the one praying to recite the Paternoster between the common-bead Ave prayer, a salutation to the Virgin Mary.

Reliquaries could be built into rings or necklaces, like modern lockets. Relics could be as tiny as a coiled hair or shard of bone. A really grand rosary set for a bishop would have a small reliquary as its central pendant. Reliquaries like this could be good excuses for nuns and priests to wear jewelry, which otherwise would be considered too worldly.

Most priests and nuns were both permitted and expected to wear crosses. Crosses, of course, could be made of simple wood, but, with time and increasing donations, most clerics wore elaborate crosses. They could be reliquaries, of course, especially if the relic was a supposed shard of the True Cross itself, but crosses needed no excuse to be large and gem encrusted. Medieval crosses, whether carried on a staff or hung about the neck, are among the most stunning, elaborate, and showy pieces ever made.

Saints inspired devotional jewelry. Goldsmiths and other metalworkers made tiny images of saints like Saint Christopher for travelers and Saint George for soldiers. Saints' images could hang on a chain. There were also diptych pendants, similar to modern lockets. Two hinged panels clipped shut for wear on a chain but opened to show an engraved or enameled scene of a saint's life. Even simpler, pewter or lead **pilgrim** badges were religious souvenirs sold at saints' shrines. They were mass-produced with a mold, and pilgrims collected them as they traveled. They could fasten them to their hats or cloaks.

See also: Clothing, Gold and Silver, Hair, Hats, Magic, Relics, Weddings.

Further Reading

Campbell, Margaret. *Medieval Jewelry in Europe, 1100–1500*. London: V&A Publishing, 2009.

Cherry, John. *Goldsmiths*. Toronto: University of Toronto Press, 1992.

Egan, Geoff, and Frances Pritchard. *Dress Accessories, 1150–1450*. Woodbridge, UK: Boydell Press, 2002.

Evans, Joan. *A History of Jewelry, 1100–1870*. Mineola, NY: Dover Publications, 1989.

Norris, Herbert. *Ancient European Costume and Fashion*. Mineola, NY: Dover Publications, 1999.

Norris, Herbert. *Medieval Costume and Fashion*. Mineola, NY: Dover Publications, 1999.

Reeves, Compton. *Pleasures and Pastimes in Medieval England*. New York: Oxford University Press, 1998.

Jews

Jews were the largest minority ethnic group in medieval Europe. For the most part, Jews led normal lives in Europe. Their lives were more similar to their **Muslim** or Christian neighbors than to each other to the extent that climate and work shape a family's life. Still, there were ways in which they differed, not only in religion and **holidays.** Their traditions of education, government, and family law were not the same as their neighbors'. The Hebrew language was a powerful bond tying Jews in all parts of Europe into a common identity.

The earliest Jewish communities in Europe were in Italy, Spain, and Germany under Roman rule. Cologne, established as a Roman colony, had a Jewish population, living as farmers and wine producers, from the 3rd and 4th centuries. Spain's Jews, before the Muslim conquest, also lived as poor farmers. Muslim Spain honored Jews as physicians, scholars, and administrators. In Germany, most **cities** had significant Jewish populations by the 11th century. Jews migrated to England and France and also became established as small farmers, craftsmen, and merchants. Spain became known in Hebrew as *Sefarad,* and Germany was *Ashkenaz,* two words still used to distinguish Spanish or Arabic Jews from Northern European Jews.

Two medieval Jews in Germany had unusual careers. A Jew named Isaac, who lived in Aachen, went to Baghdad on a mission from Charlemagne. His fellow ambassadors died on the journey, and he became both survivor and leader. His most famous task was finding a way to escort a white elephant over the Alps, along with the many other rich gifts from Caliph Harun al-Rashid. Later, in the 14th century, Süsskind von Trimberg was one of the Minnesingers, the German **troubadours.** He traveled like a Christian **minstrel** until he was forced to wear a distinctive Jewish badge.

Many European cities had a Jewish Quarter, a voluntary neighborhood cluster of Jewish artisans and merchants. The location became less voluntary and more restrictive as Europeans became more prejudiced against Jews. Then Jews lived in the Jewish Quarter because they were legally required to live there.

Jewish men wore full, untrimmed beards that made them look different from their Christian neighbors. In 1215, the Fourth Lateran Council declared that Jews and Muslims must also wear distinctive **clothing** or a badge. The distinctive badge varied from place to place. The most common was a flat, funnel-shaped **hat** with a tall point. Some medieval illustrations of Bible scenes with Abraham or Moses show the patriarchs wearing these Jewish hats. In other places, they wore a yellow stripe or a square yellow hat. During the 14th century, at the height of anti-Jewish prejudice, some places required Jews to wear a red and white circle on their chest. After the

Jews were officially viewed as foreigners, even if their families had lived in the town for many generations. Unless they converted to Christianity, they were in a special class of people with foreign loyalties who needed to be watched. After the Fourth Lateran Council of 1215, Jews in Europe were required to wear badges to prevent them from blending in. Pointed hats and yellow badges, shown here in a 14th-century Bible illustration, were the typical French requirement. (Isadore Singer, ed., *The Jewish Encyclopedia*, 1901)

close of the Middle Ages, the most common badge became a yellow ring stitched to their cloaks.

Houses

Jewish **houses** were similar to Christian European houses, but there were some distinct differences. The home was the center of Jewish religious observance, even more than the synagogue. To some extent, Jews fit into the culture they were in: in Muslim Spain, their houses had beds on the floor, while they had wooden platform beds in Germany. In Spain, the most important function of the **garden** was to have a cooling fountain; in France, it was to have an adequate well and privy. In Spain, they often had separate sleeping and dining rooms, but in the small houses of France and Germany, they slept in one room and ate in the kitchen. Jewish homes in Spain often had small water **clocks** by the 13th century, and there were prominent Jewish clock makers in the Arabic water-clock tradition. There was a greater tendency for Jews to build houses of **stone** in cities where Christian houses were still typically wooden.

There were a few key differences that crossed all regions. Every Jewish house had a miniature Torah scroll called a *mezuzah* mounted in a special case on the right-hand doorpost. It contained some lines from the law and was specially made by a professional scribe. Women lit oil lamps or candles just before sunset on the Sabbath. Every Jewish home also had a decorative cup for the ritual blessing of wine on the Sabbath.

Jews had to pay attention to religious rules for washing and food preparation. Next to the bed, there was always a pitcher and basin so they could wash their hands immediately on waking. Jews were required to do much more washing and were more likely than Christians to own wooden bathtubs.

Jewish cooks had to follow the dietary rules known as *kashrut,* or kosher. This meant keeping meat and milk separate in all parts of the **kitchen** and in all dishes. They did not eat pork, the most common meat of Christian Europe. They also had to cook an extra meal on Friday and keep it hot in the coals until noon on Saturday, the Sabbath, since no new fires could be lit that day. In Spain, this meal was a vegetable and chickpea dish called *adafina,* while in Northern Europe it was a meat stew called *cholent,* perhaps from the medieval French word for "hot."

Jewish Communities

The first priority of a Jewish community in a European town was to maintain a public bath for their ritual washing needs. This bath was called a *mikveh.* Ritual washing required the whole body to be wet and used running **water** if possible. Minority communities did their best to provide this, from a reserved bit of lake shore to a public bath in town. The second priority was to organize a **school,** since prayers, the function of a synagogue, could be offered at home. Many Jewish communities also put a lot of effort into maintaining a **library.** The next priority was a rabbinical court to settle disputes of family law, such as marriage and inheritance.

Other community functions in the Jewish Quarter could include a communal kitchen, for making the large amount of food needed for a **wedding** or holiday, or a hall to meet in. Especially in Germany, many Jewish communities owned a hall for dances and weddings. There were **inns** for Jewish visitors in the larger communities. In Muslim Spain, Jews had **hospitals,** in addition to hospice care for the poor. Many Jews had been trained as surgeons and physicians. Finally, a Jewish community tried to provide its own cemetery.

Synagogues in Europe were similar to Christian buildings in their basic aspects, such as a meeting room and high windows, often with **glass,** for light. But they were not richly decorated, as Christian churches always were. In Muslim Spain, synagogues were fairly secure, but in Northern Europe, there was always a chance that a later medieval Christian mob could decide to vandalize a synagogue. For this reason, they were kept simple and dark and were not filled with overt signs of the building's purpose. Christian regulations did not permit them to be built as tall as the local church. Even large, elaborate medieval synagogues were small and simple in comparison with churches.

The chief possession of a synagogue was its copy of the law, the Torah scroll. In Europe, this was kept in a built-in structure called an ark, but in Muslim Spain, it was usually kept in a movable case. Both kinds were elaborately and expensively decorated. The scroll itself was also expensively decorated with **gold** and **silver** ornaments on the wooden rods that held the scrolls. The next most important mark of a medieval synagogue was an oil lamp kept burning at all times, in memory of the eternal flame of the old temple in Jerusalem. Wealthy European synagogues also kept a large candelabra, the *menorah,* next to the Torah ark.

Synagogues had a central reading desk and lectern, with styles varying regionally. In Spain, the lectern was elevated with a canopy over it, as in a mosque. Seating options varied; in Muslim regions, there was often no seating, and women stood with men. In Italy, some synagogues provided individual desks for the congregation, and most European synagogues at least had benches. In these synagogues, women had an upper gallery or a separate annex.

The Old-New Synagogue of Prague was completed in 1270. There is a Hebrew inscription with a Star of David over the main door. (Jim Milles)

Jews

The Middle Ages were a very active period in the intellectual life of Judaism. At a time when most Jews were anonymous in the larger Christian culture, rabbis like Gershom ben Judah of Mainz (10th century) and Solomon ben Isaac (known as "Rashi") of Troyes (11th century) wrote very influential interpretations of Jewish law. Medieval Jewish writings were concerned with how to interpret Jewish law for people living in non-Jewish societies outside Israel.

The rabbinical structure also provided for Jews to be self-governing to a high degree. They followed not only the laws of the outside community, but also their own restrictive laws concerning diet and daily life. They had their own court system to deal with disputes over Jewish regulations and family matters such as marriages and adoption. They could impose fines as well as banishment from their community. In Spain, Muslim rule gave them further power to impose corporal and even capital punishment.

During the Middle Ages, the rabbinical courts developed a system of ruling by probability. Probability was not yet a field of mathematics and was not applied even loosely to the secular use of **games** of chance. Rabbis were often faced with dilemmas concerning cases with inadequate witnesses or facts that could not be established. They created a method of estimating the probability of the facts being one way or another way and calculated which scenario was most likely. They ruled that the most likely situation was the truth. Although their study of probability did not extend into a modern level of complexity, they wrote rules for discovering the probability of a case that had several factors, each with its own probability.

Women

Jews had their own distinctive marriage customs. Like medieval Christians, they celebrated weddings in public so that everyone knew the wedding had taken place, but the ceremony was not considered a religious rite. Jewish weddings traditionally had a great deal of **music** and dancing, more than Christian wedding feasts at the same time. Their children were married younger than Christian children, since Jewish law considered girls adults at 12 and boys at 13. A typical medieval Jewish bride and groom were not much older than 12 and 14, although they were not expected to begin living as an independent married couple at that time. Jewish law also permitted a husband to marry a second wife, but the practice continued only in Muslim Spain.

The Sabbath prior to the ceremony, the bride was carried on a throne into the synagogue, as a public announcement of the intended wedding. On the wedding day, the bride and groom were conducted separately to a public location, usually outdoors but sometimes in a hall, where they stood under a canopy made of a prayer shawl (*tallit*). The groom placed a ring on the bride's finger, and the rabbi blessed them. The groom gave the bride a sip of wine from a special cup. Jewish brides in medieval Germany were the first to wear white, which was the color of mourning, in memory of the destruction of Jerusalem. Jews in Germany sometimes threw grains of wheat on the couple with wishes for fertility.

Wives had rights under Jewish law that they did not have under Christian law. It was against the law for a Jewish wife to become poorer or in any way worse off by marrying. A husband could not compel her to move into a worse house or town, unless it was in Israel itself. The wife herself had the right to compel her husband to move to Israel, which was considered a blessing even if they were poor there. Some marriage contracts stipulated that husbands must buy wives a certain quota of new clothes or **jewelry.** If she owned property before marriage, it remained hers, unlike in Christian law.

Medieval European rabbis like Gershom ben Judah also increased the wife's rights in divorce. At a time when the Catholic Church was making it virtually impossible for married couples to divorce, Jews were permitted to divorce if the husband gave the wife a certificate, called a *get.* Divorce was still rare in the Jewish community, but a Jewish wife could both refuse and demand a divorce. She could choose to divorce a man for making her life materially worse or for wanting to move to a place she didn't like. If she had been married before the age of 12 to a man she didn't like, she could refuse to remain his wife once she was considered an adult by Jewish law.

In Muslim Spain, Jewish **women** had equal rights with men and could own property or engage in commerce on their own initiative. In Christian Europe, Jewish women often worked in their husbands' businesses but did not usually trade on their own. In some cases, they carried out most of the business so their husbands could complete rabbinical studies. They also worked in the same home crafts that Christian women did; they spun, wove, and sewed and could sell these products.

Most girls did not learn Hebrew or study the Jewish law, but some did. There are medieval letters in Hebrew written by women, and many learned the prayers. Many more were familiar with the Hebrew **alphabet.** Yiddish first developed during the Middle Ages as a way for uneducated Jews, such as women, to write. It used Hebrew letters to write medieval German, with some borrowed Hebrew words. Early Yiddish **books** explained to women how to keep the holidays correctly. They also told popular medieval stories, such as the legends of **King Arthur.**

School

In Christian Europe, Jewish families taught their children at home or organized synagogue schools. Their children did not attend Christian Latin schools and often did not learn Latin at all. In Muslim Spain, Jewish children attended Islamic schools. They were educated in Arabic and in the Koran and studied Hebrew and rabbinical matters on the side. Since they were part of a system of schooling within the culture, they tended to stay in school longer, until age 18. Children in Jewish families were less likely to work than in Christian families, where learning a trade and helping in the family's trade were assumed. A boy's first responsibility was education, not work.

A Jewish boy began school around the age of six, with a new student ceremony. He was dressed up and carried into the synagogue by his father or a teacher. They gave him a wooden slate with the first and last letters of the Hebrew alphabet and an inscription that Moses had commanded to learn the Torah (the Jewish law). They put drops of honey on the tablet and let the child lick it off to teach him that learning was sweet. After this, the boys had to go to school for the same long school days that their slightly older Christian peers endured—from dawn to about six in the evening.

Jewish boys in both Christian Europe and Muslim Spain studied the Hebrew language and Jewish law. They were considered responsible for carrying out the law themselves, so the knowledge was not left to certain scholars among them. The most promising students went away from home to a *yeshiva,* a Hebrew studies school, to complete rabbinical training. Even then, they did not become rabbis. The title of rabbi was reserved for those who spent a lifetime learning not only the law and its commentaries, but also all of the rabbinical commentaries up through the present, a body of work that grew continually. In Spain, a Jewish boy who continued his studies past the basic level became an expert in Arabic composition, and many of these writers and poets tried to improve the state of composition in Hebrew, a closely related language. Medieval Muslim Spain and its network of communities in North Africa and Egypt became a powerhouse of Hebrew poetry.

Practical education was whatever training was needed for the family's line of business. Jewish boys could not enter Christian **guilds,** but in some cases they served apprenticeships for a trade. They learned arithmetic and accounting and whatever languages were additionally needed, such as Arabic or Latin. Among Jews, business contracts and letters were written in Hebrew.

Work

Normal education for Jewish boys included the basics of medieval **medicine,** which pushed a high percentage of Jewish men into the medical profession. This was especially true in Spain, and books by these learned Jewish doctors became standard texts. In Christian Spain, most kings had a Jewish physician, but in northern countries like France and England, Jews were not permitted to practice medicine, nor were they admitted to medical schools. Christian medical students, on the other hand, were not permitted to study surgery, while the medical tradition in Spain emphasized surgery. Jewish surgeons taught at Spanish medical schools, and there may have been some Jewish medical schools in Spain and Provence.

When Jews first came into Europe, they were farmers, like most peasants. Many continued to farm throughout the Middle Ages, even if only on a small scale to supply the Jewish community with kosher food. Many in Italy and France also owned vineyards and produced kosher wine. When Jews farmed, they most often owned their land, instead of holding it in fief from a Christian overlord. As prejudice against them increased in the 12th century, in some places they were barred from owning land, which pushed them more into commerce and banking.

Many Jews were involved in international trade; among other advantages, they used a common trade language, Hebrew, and often knew several other languages. Frankish kings, including Charlemagne, granted trade privileges to Jews to induce them to come and bring their import business. In Sicily, they were granted a monopoly on silk dyeing, and they were silk weavers in many places. In Spain, they had a monopoly on red kermes dye. The Jews of Barcelona and Majorca, two major Spanish trading hubs, were almost entirely employed in commerce, much of it for silk or fine ceramics. Jewish merchants became such an integral part of some international **fairs** that the organizers shifted the schedule to avoid the Jewish Sabbath.

Jewish law did not permit Jews to lend money at interest to their Jewish relatives, but they were permitted to lend to foreigners. Since Catholic law also outlawed charging interest on loans, one important role of Jews in medieval Europe was to lend money at interest. Being creditors to powerful Christian princes and merchants was dangerous for Jews, and it increased prejudice against them. Jewish traders further developed some of the methods of modern finance, such as letters of credit and checks, written in Arabic or Hebrew.

Jews were excluded from Christian guilds, but they still learned trades. Especially under Muslim rule, they were permitted to work in any trade. Around the Mediterranean, they worked in **glass, copper,** leather tanning, shoe making, and weaving silk. They made fine instruments such as **clocks, astrolabes,** and **jewelry.** In some places, Jews minted **coins.**

Persecution

The medieval Catholic **Church** made official proclamations that Jews needed to convert, but Popes routinely issued orders that Jews must be safe from harassment. Although folk belief came to blame killing Christ on

Jews, official doctrine in the Roman Catholic Church did not make these proclamations. During the early Middle Ages, there were no significant persecutions or legal discrimination. Even during the period of European anti-Jewish prejudice, many local Jews and Christians lived and worked together. There are records of Jews and Christians in joint partnerships, apprenticeships, and gift exchanges. Jews and Muslims in Spain, and then Jews and Spanish Christians, were also normally on very good terms. Most Jews lived peacefully, if overtaxed. However, they were also the group most singled out for mob violence, especially after the 12th century.

Anti-Jewish feeling in Europe may have begun in the 12th century by associating the Jews with the Saracens, who were rumored to have destroyed the Church of the Holy Sepulcher in Jerusalem. The First **Crusade** sent an army overland through Germany and Hungary in 1096, and it included a number of criminals who had been pardoned if they would fight for the Holy Land. Part of this army attacked Jews around Mainz and Cologne, although local rulers attempted to protect the Jewish community. Again, in 1236, Crusaders in France massacred as many as 2,000 Jews. The Jews may have seemed like foreigners or unbelievers to these mobs.

Jews were subject to discriminatory taxes in all parts of Europe. Under the Muslims, they paid the *jizya* tax as non-Muslims. In some Muslim cities, they shouldered a large part of the tax burden, in addition to supporting their own communities. Christian rulers not only taxed them, but also borrowed from them and then defaulted on the loans. To fund the Crusades, several kings forced Jews to lend large sums to them, never to be repaid. The usual way to default on such loans was to expel all Jews, requiring them to leave all property behind, forfeit to the Crown.

When Jews traveled, they were special targets for robbery and kidnapping. If they dressed as Christians, they were safer. If they were known as Jews, even Christians who were not robbers as a full-time profession would consider stealing their merchandise.

Spain was a refuge for most of the Middle Ages, but not always. The Umayyad emirs and caliphs had been relatively secular and easygoing; under them, the "Sefara"—the Jewish community—had its Golden Age. By the 12th century, civil war had permitted a large influx of North African Berber rulers. The Almohad dynasty was puritanical and tried to reform the lax ways of previous Muslim rulers. Jews were not protected or treated well, and many left Spain. The most famous medieval Jew, Moses Maimonides (in Arabic, Musa ibn Maymun), was born into a prominent Jewish family in Cordoba in 1135. The Maimon family left Andalusia and went to Egypt. They were treated with discrimination in Egypt, too, which pushed Moses to look harder at his neglected Jewish heritage. Like many well-educated Arabic Jews, he worked as a doctor in Alexandria. He became one of the best-known commentators and philosophers, both within Judaism and across Europe. His philosophical writings, in Arabic, influenced European study of Aristotle and Plato.

Conditions in Northern Europe also became less hospitable. England and France went through times of expelling and then recalling the Jews. Jews were chronically put under heavy, discriminatory taxes, and their estates could be confiscated at death on the grounds that they had obtained their wealth sinfully. According to popular rumor, they were accused of killing Christian children. The first documented rumor began in 1144 when a boy was found murdered in Norwich, England, and the people accused the Jews. The boy became Saint William of Norwich. After this, Jews were often accused when a child's body was found dead; just as often, a mob murdered some Jews in retaliation.

In England, the Plantagenet kings had declared that Jews were the king's property and must serve him. The Jews of York were massacred on the day of Richard I's coronation because a small number of them were traveling to London to present gifts, and a rumor spread that they were dangerous. The Jewish community was then forced to come up with much of the ransom money when Richard I was held captive in France. King Henry III forbade Jews from accepting land as security for loans in 1269; Edward I prohibited them from charging interest in 1275. In 1290, Edward I forced the Jews to leave England. They left behind all their money and property and went penniless to France.

In France, King Philip II had confiscated a great deal of Jewish money in 1180 and then expelled the Jews. He invited them back a few years later, in 1198. King Louis IX, the Crusader, publicly burned a copy of the Talmud and repeatedly confiscated Jewish property. In 1246, he had the Jews of Carcassone imprisoned until they could come up with a large enough ransom. The Shepherds' Crusade of 1320, led by out-of-work and starving shepherds, led to widespread massacres of Jews all over France.

There had been an active, relatively free Jewish community in the county of Champagne. They were involved as bankers and merchants in the successful Champagne fairs. When Countess Joan of Navarre married King Philip the Fair of France in 1284, the county of Champagne was no longer independent. The fairs began to fail as the French king imposed high taxes on all transactions. In 1306, he expelled all Jews. Jews were still in southern France, in the county of Toulouse, and in Germany. Germany had been a relatively safe place for Jews.

The last blow to Northern Europe's Jewish communities was the Black Death **plague.** The first outbreak in 1347, beginning in Italy and southern France, was fast and severe. As much as half the population died in many regions. It spread by an unknown means, and it killed people very quickly. Nobody knew why it was happening, and many blamed the Jews, among other scapegoats.

Even without a solid reason for blaming the Jews, a mob in a village near Marseille attacked the Jewish population on Palm Sunday. They smashed property, burned houses, and left 40 Jews dead in the street. The nearby villages began to follow, and many Jews were burned to death. In some villages, no Jews were left alive. The city of Marseille itself did not join in these mob activities, and Marseille's Jews survived.

As 1347 passed, there were increasing accusations that Jews had poisoned the water supply. In September 1348, a Jewish doctor living near Lake Geneva confessed, probably under torture, that he had imported **poison,** passed it around the Jewish community, and used it to poison wells. He led his interrogators to the spring he had supposedly poisoned and named conspirators. Many other Jews were interrogated and tortured. The actual poison was never found, but people believed it was made of reptiles or Christian hearts. The rumors passed quickly through Europe. Mobs took over and, in fear and anger, began killing Jews. The Jews of Narbonne and Carcassone, in southern France, were executed by mobs. The Jews of Basel, Switzerland, were herded into a wooden building and burned. All over Germany, Jews were attacked and often burned.

The Pope, the king of Aragon, the king of Germany, the duke of Austria, and the town elders of Cologne, Germany, all tried to stop the massacres. Although they could protect some Jews in their localities, they were not able to stop a mass of people who were terrified of the horrible plague around them. After the plague waned, the attacks stopped, but many people still thought Jews had poisoned the wells. Most of Northern Europe's surviving Jews went to the kingdom of Poland, where they were safe until modern times.

As the Christian Reconquest of Spain pushed south, Spain became even less of a refuge for Jews. More of them left and went to North Africa, Palestine, Italy, and even Northern Europe. A significant Jewish community remained in Spain until the final victory of King Ferdinand and Queen Isabella over the last Sultan at Granada. They expelled all remaining Jews.

See also: Alphabet, Banks, Crusades, Medicine, Muslims, Plague.

Further Reading

Baumgarten, Elisheva. *Mothers and Children: Jewish Family Life in Medieval Europe.* Trenton, NJ: Princeton University Press, 2007.

Chazan, Robert. *The Jews of Medieval Western Christendom, 1000–1500.* Cambridge: Cambridge University Press, 2007.

Cohen, Mark. *Under Crescent and Cross: The Jews in the Middle Ages.* Trenton: Princeton University Press, 2008.

Gay, Ruth. *The Jews of Germany: A Historical Portrait.* New Haven, CT: Yale University Press, 1994.

Lewis, David Levering. *God's Crucible: Islam and the Making of Europe, 570–1215*. New York: Norton: 2008.

Marcus, Jacob Rader. *The Jew in the Medieval World: A Source Book, 315–1791*. Los Angeles: Hebrew Union College Press, 2000.

Roth, Norman. *Daily Life of the Jews in the Middle Ages*. Westport, CT: Greenwood Press, 2005.

Stow, Kenneth. *Alienated Minority: The Jews of Medieval Latin Europe*. Cambridge, MA: Harvard University Press, 1998.

Taitz, Emily. *The Jews of Medieval France: The Community of Champagne*. Westport, CT: Praeger, 1994.

Trachtenberg, Joshua. *The Devil and the Jews: The Medieval Conception of the Jew and Its Relation to Modern Anti-Semitism*. New York: Jewish Publications Society, 2002.

K

Keys. See Locks and Keys

Kitchen Utensils

Medieval cooks fell into two categories, like modern cooks. There were amateur cooks for a family, usually the wife or mother, and there were professional cooks. Professional cooks for large-scale households, such as **castles,** were usually men, but there must have been many smaller **houses** that hired female cooks who had started not as apprenticed professionals but as amateur cooks in a home. The amateur cook's equipment varied tremendously from cottage to city house. Professional cooks had a reasonably standard set of equipment, and large kitchens in the late Middle Ages were well equipped, even with running water and floor drains.

The cooks' **guilds** had high standards and tried to enforce them. Professional cooks, in their treatises on the craft, emphasized the absolute necessity of keeping all surfaces and utensils spotlessly clean. Cooks, too, were supposed to be clean, with short, clean fingernails and clean hands and clothes. Cooks in illustrations sometimes wear linen aprons or towels to cover their clothes. Unfortunately, it required stern management to enforce these rules in a real kitchen. The kitchen of a large household was a hot place, with fires blazing even in summer. The cook and his helpers grew sweaty and dirty from soot, dirt on vegetables, and blood from the meat they were cutting. Their clothes and hands were often dirty. In the *Canterbury Tales,* Chaucer's Cook has an open sore on his leg. Cooks were also viewed by the general public as tricksters who would pass off dirty or spoiled food if they could.

A cottage kitchen had only the most minimal utensils. Every cook needed a metal pot, either brass or iron, with a lid. The basic cauldron had three legs and two handles, and it could be hung by hooks and chains from a beam. Until smiths could make cast **iron** pots, these cauldrons were probably usually **copper** alloys, brass or bronze. They were a major investment for a poor household, and when they finally cracked, they were often mended by itinerant tinkers or coppersmiths in town. Another basic pot was an open, wide pan for frying. A turning spit was needed if the family ever had a piece of meat to roast. The simplest cottage bread, a flat lump, could be baked on a flat stone with coals heaped over an overturned pan or lid above it. Every cook needed stirring and ladling utensils, and the simplest were home carved out of wood. Knives were the most important handheld utensils.

Even simple kitchens that supported a milk-giving goat, sheep, or cow had to deal with making products out of the milk before it spoiled. Butter churns were made like **barrels,** by coopers, as were cheese tubs and buckets. Dairy equipment included cloth bags or rush baskets to drain the cheese curds. Cheese rounds were wrapped and stored on shelves to cure. Small wooden bowls and tubs of butter could be stored on the same shelves, in a cool place.

Cottagers did not have many eating utensils. Their bowls were carved from wood or, in more prosperous times, turned on a lathe. Both cups and bowls could be fired pottery, either glazed or unglazed. Spoons were carved from wood or cast in pewter. Most eating was done with hands or with bread crusts to scrape out stew or pottage.

Bakers were usually a separate profession, since ovens that provided steady heat to surround a pan were not easy to make or maintain. Bakers' ovens were shaped like beehives, and bakers used long-handled trays to set round breads (and even pretzels) in and out of the oven's shelf. When baking was part of a large permanent kitchen, such as in a castle or royal household, the ovens were housed in a separate building.

Professional cooks in the late Middle Ages could be hired as caterers for an event, such as a wedding feast for a family whose daily facilities were not large enough or for a guildhall's annual feast. The professional cook and his staff (which included not only sous chefs but water boys) also needed rented kitchen utensils. They needed iron pans, wooden mixing bowls and spoons, and large ceramic pots for making pottage or mixing wine. The rented or borrowed utensils also included wooden buckets, brooms, and washing tubs to clean the place before and after. These lists probably assumed that the kitchen, as it was, came with several cauldrons, saucepans, and griddles and at least one turning spit.

A well-provisioned, permanent kitchen in the late Middle Ages, such as in a castle, manor, or abbey, had far more tools and amenities than a cottage kitchen. It had water pipes with taps, a basin to catch the runoff, and drains to carry it away. It had a floor drain to catch liquid slops and keep the floor from becoming slick. There were rags, towels, and cloth sacks, as well as soap and brushes. Kitchens also needed stockpiles of wood or charcoal and a supply of candles.

The fireplace, invented in the 13th century, revolutionized the room's layout. Tables could fill the main floor space, since there was no central fire pit. There was always at least one dormant table—that is, a permanent table with fixed legs, sturdy enough for all work. For unusually large cooking events, trestle tables could be set up in other parts of the room so that extra hands could be chopping and stirring. Large kitchens also had stools, since many tasks required someone to stand or sit, stirring a pot, for a long time. A stool was often near one of the fireplaces, since a kitchen boy had to stand nearby and stir or turn the food as it boiled or roasted. By the fireplace, there was always at least one bellows for blowing the fire hotter, and large kitchens had more than one. The fireplace came with andirons—the rack that held the wood and could support a spit. It also required fire irons (rakes, pokers, shovels, and tongs), turning spits, hooks and chains to hang cauldrons over the fire, and trivets or spiders to set pots on in the coals. Most cooks also had fire pans or fire baskets to carry burning coals.

The cauldrons used in the large fireplace could be very tall. Illustrations of medieval cauldrons in use show tall, narrow vessels shaped more like urns or vases clustered together with fire built up between them. Cauldrons could also be wide and often had feet. They were made of iron or brass. Large kitchens had 6 to 10 cauldrons of different sizes. Additionally, they had saucepans, frying pans, griddles, and chafing dishes made of iron or brass.

Cauldrons and pots required attending utensils. Skimmers were usually made of iron; they had wide, shallow bowls pierced with holes, and they skimmed foam from stews. Flesh hooks were very important utensils for a medieval cook, since so many meat dishes were made with pieces of meat boiled in pots. They had long handles and sharp tines, like a rake's, that turned. Cooks often needed to drain or strain their foods, so they had colanders made of copper or brass. There were also graters, sieves, slotted spoons, ladles, rolling pins, long forks, and tongs. In Italy, cooks needed drying racks for freshly made pasta. The best cooks also used pastry tubes, brushes, needles, and many other fine or unusual tools to achieve the results of appearance and shape needed to astonish the guests.

There were ceramic pots with lids that could be set in the fire's ashes with coals heaped over the lid. Many bean dishes were baked this way.

Early kitchens, whether simple or sophisticated, were necessarily centered on the fire. By the late Middle Ages, the fire was more often located in a hearth with a chimney built into the wall, allowing more open space in the room. A well-equipped fire had racks, hooks, and spits. Here, a boy turns a roasting spit so that the meat will not burn, while an older man tends some covered ceramic pots that have been set very close to the fire. Spoons in various sizes hang against the wall, a pitcher and a grater sit on a nearby table, and a fellow servant enters carrying a lantern, another basic kitchen need. (Paul Lacroix, *Moeurs, Usage et Costumes au Moyen Age et a l'Epoque de la Renaissance*, 1878)

Cooks needed pie dishes made of pottery, tin, or brass. To mix spices and grind herbs, every kitchen needed a stone mortar and pestle, and sometimes a slab of marble, as well, for finer grinding. They also used wooden spoons and spatulas and wooden mixing bowls, either carved and lathed from a single block of wood or in the form of a coopered tub, basin, or trough. Every kitchen also had barrels and casks to store raw materials, from flour to apples. They also needed wicker baskets for carrying just about anything from barn or pantry to kitchen.

Cooks used specialty knives including cleavers and paring knives. There was an array of serving dishes made of pewter, brass, bronze, and ceramic. Many flagons, pitchers, and ewers were made of pewter or latten (a name for various cheap metal alloys). Cooks used pewter vinegar pots and pewter saltcellars. Salt boxes for table use were decorative and functioned as centerpieces. Flagons brought ale and wine to the table, while ewers carried washing water to diners. Ewers had feet, as well as a handle and a pouring spout. Kitchens needed pewter, bronze, or latten basins to catch the wastewater, and these were kept in pairs with the ewers. Every diner needed a pewter spoon; the spoons were carefully collected and counted following a feast.

See also: Barrels and Buckets, Food, Guilds, Houses, Lead and Copper.

Further Reading

Cosman, Madeleine Pelner. *Fabulous Feasts: Medieval Cookery and Ceremony.* New York: George Braziller, 1995.

Egan, Geoff. *The Medieval Household: Daily Living c. 1150–c. 1450.* Woodbridge, UK: Boydell Press, 2010.

Henisch, Bridget. *The Medieval Cook.* Woodbridge, UK: Boydell Press, 2009.

Scully, Terence. *The Art of Cookery in the Middle Ages.* Woodbridge, UK: Boydell Press, 1997.

Wheaton, Barbara Ketcham. *Savoring the Past: The French Kitchen and Table from 1300 to 1789.* New York: Touchstone Books, 1983.

Knights

The concept of the knight in armor is central to our modern idea of medieval Europe. The French word for a knight, *chevalier,* meant horseman, and a knight was first and foremost a mounted warrior. The life of a knight, from boy to squire to knight to lord, was a long training schedule to create a specialist warrior. Knights were the special forces of the Middle Ages. Kings supported them by granting them rights to land, castles, and fairs; they lived on rent and other profits. In return for their freedom from milling or farming like other men, they spent their time training and keeping up their equipment. They were committed to assemble for any war that their lord demanded and to give their lives without hesitation.

Charlemagne was probably the first European king to use mounted warriors. His warriors were noblemen who owned enough land to support horses, but they did not yet live in fortified houses. Since poorer men did not have horses and could only be foot soldiers, riding a horse in battle quickly became a mark of distinction. Poorer men who had to work in the fields were not as likely to learn to ride well, so the ability to ride a horse also implied wealth and leisure. Mounted warfare became a mark of the privileged class, and it remained so for many centuries.

Horses were relatively new in Europe in Charlemagne's time. During the eighth and ninth centuries, the development of iron horseshoes allowed horses to travel over rough ground with less hoof damage. Saddles began to use stirrups, allowing the rider more control over his movement and the horse's. In the same period, changes in farming permitted fields to raise an extra crop of oats, which helped support horses for work and war. Horses also required acres of grazing land.

The real development of the knight began after 1000. In the heart of Europe—modern France and Germany—the central power of Charlemagne's kingdom had broken down. Although there was a French king, he controlled only a relatively small territory. Regional counts and dukes ruled most of the territory as vassals of either France or England. The counts and dukes built castles and needed warriors to create very mobile, flexible standing armies. They needed fighters mounted on horses, highly trained and both free and willing to fight for any cause. These fighters were loyal only to the local authority structure—to the count of Anjou or Toulouse or to the duke of Burgundy. They owed their income and prestige to their lord and were often rewarded with land and houses. Over the course of the 11th and 12th centuries, these fighters evolved into the familiar figure of the medieval knight. The knight had his own weapons, customs, rank, and code of conduct, set apart from other parts of society.

A change in inheritance laws made possible the golden age of the knight. Until around 1000, a landowner could subdivide his land among his children or give part of it to the church at his death. So much land was given to the church that families in France and Germany became too impoverished to fulfill their duty of military service. The new law of primogeniture gave the land to the oldest son to carry on the family dynasty and gave little or nothing to younger sons because the land was no longer partible. The older sons became the ruling barons who trained and supported knights. The younger sons, who trained for knighthood but owned no more than their horses and equipment, fought with little to lose and much to gain. They attached themselves to ruling knights as little more than mercenaries. Many of them received manors and castles from kings as rewards or were able to marry rich heiresses. Many more died in battle.

In northern Italy, where society followed different patterns of settlement and government, knights never became central; the military backbone was always the citizen militia. Southern Italy was dominated by Normans and was therefore more feudal. Norman knights also fought in Spain and brought their ideals to the Christian kingdoms.

During the 11th and 12th centuries, the church promoted pacifist ideas to protect the common people of Europe. Knights too often pillaged the countryside, attacked unarmed bystanders, or took part in wars against neighbors. The Peace of God, a doctrine that unarmed people must not be attacked, evolved into the Truce of God, a doctrine in which fighting was not permitted during certain holy seasons or on certain feast or fast days. Knights took oaths to protect, not harm, the helpless and to obey the church's rules for war. These oaths, and the code of conduct they promised, became an integral part of the concept of a knight.

Edward, son of King Edward III of England, was one of the leading knights of the Middle Ages. He died before he could inherit his father's crown, but during his lifetime he led a number of famous military campaigns. He was the commander at the decisive English victories of Crécy and Poitiers in the Hundred Years' War. When he captured the king of France and his son at Poitiers, he treated them with great respect, according to the rules of chivalry. He became known to history as the "Black Prince," perhaps for a black suit of armor, and his effigy remains one of the best-known symbols of knighthood. (Steve Vidler/StockphotoPro)

The fact that a knight's job was to kill posed a problem for the church. Knights were honored in society, and they were patrons of churches. Germanic society had always been comfortable with warrior values, but, as the Christian religion became a deeper part of that society, the church had to address the sinfulness of the knight's primary activity. One means was to recruit knights for the Crusades, which began in 1095. It seemed less sinful to kill those who threatened the access of Christian pilgrims to Jerusalem. Another means was the creation of tournaments, war games in which deaths were only accidental. However, the church did not approve of tournaments, since they still promoted worldly pride and often caused deaths. The third means was the investiture of the knight's life with religious symbolism and meaning through the creation of the code of chivalry.

Chivalry based its rules first on the knight's duty to defend the people he had promised to defend. To run away or give up was unacceptable; knights fought to the death or until they were captured and disarmed. The Peace of God duty not to kill the unarmed was another side of this rule, since the knight was supposed to protect the unarmed inhabitants of his lord's territory. The church hoped to keep society civil by expecting knights to extend this duty to all unarmed people, especially those who were unable to fight. Monks, women, children, and the very old or sick were unable to fight, and a knight was to consider it his duty to protect them if they needed it.

Chivalry also required a knight to be loyal to his lord and to his fellow knights. Loyalty was not always simple, since the same man could be a vassal of different kings for different estates he held. A knight was not supposed to seek individual glory at the expense of his fellow band of knights. A knight without ties of loyalty was called a knight errant—a wandering knight.

The rules of chivalry did not require kind or generous conduct on the battlefield. Knights still killed as mercilessly as they were able to. However, if they took a prisoner, they were not to kill him without need. Prisoners were to be treated well and ransomed. This put a limit on the barbarity of behavior in war, and it assured noblemen that they did not have to fear capture in war, even if they feared the dishonor that capture brought. The code of conduct did not prevent knights from killing ordinary bowmen or foot soldiers they captured.

By the 14th and 15th centuries, the chivalric ideal of the knight was more popular than ever, but wars were no longer dominated by knights. Wealthy knights focused on expensive plate armor and performance at tournaments. While some still took part in war, the lesser nobility increasingly paid a cash equivalent to personal service. The king used this money to hire foreign mercenaries of low birth who came equipped with crossbows and pikes. War continued to be as lawless and gory as ever, while the ideals of chivalry rose higher and higher.

The development of arms that did not need as much specialized training but were very effective against mounted knights made knighthood obsolete as a practical military force. Gunpowder first created cannons capable of breaking sieges, but soon after, gun makers created small arms that required minimal training and had none of the art and beauty of the knight's weapons. Gunpowder was dirty and loud; it was the weapon of craftsmen. By the middle of the 15th century, knights were unimportant to the outcome of a battle. By the close of the century, knighthood was an expensive aristocratic hobby.

Becoming a Knight

Knighthood training could only be given to boys from noble families. They had to own land (or hold it in fief from the king), and they must have the right to a coat of arms. Only the king could grant the right to a heraldic coat of arms. The coat of arms indicated that the family owed feudal service to the king and must provide a certain number of knights in time of war. A landless but noble family, perhaps a family that had recently lost its land, could still train a son as a knight. He would be known as a knight errant, a knight without a manor to support him.

The training for knighthood often meant living away from home for much of a boy's childhood. The most common placements were an uncle, most likely his mother's brother, or a powerful lord who had an informal school for knights at his court. The boys trained by the count were often the sons of his knights and vassals, and their presence and good treatment ensured their fathers' unbroken loyalty.

The first task for a future knight was to learn to ride a horse very well. Boys learned to ride ponies from the youngest possible ages. They learned basic riding (mounting, dismounting, jumping, and maneuvering) until it was second nature. A squire or full knight was expected to ride effortlessly. There was also weapons training with wooden swords and lances. Boys trained several hours a day in sword use, wrestling, and boxing. On their ponies, they aimed wooden lances at targets to practice handling a lance and a horse at the same time. The practice target was called a quintain. The quintain had a central pole with an arm that had a target and, on the other side, an arm with a large hanging sandbag. The rider had to hit the target and avoid the sandbag.

In some cases, boys training to be knights learned to read and write. They learned their prayers like other schoolboys, and they were taught the Latin military classics, such as the wars of Julius Caesar. At the height of the fashion for courtly love, young men were expected to read epics and romances.

An older boy took a turn as a page, serving at table. He was being trained in matters of social hierarchy and manners. Pages also helped knights dress and carried messages. Although they were being groomed to take a leading role in society, they were trained to serve and not to consider any kind of service beneath them. An ideal page was perfectly unobtrusive and polite, even if he was violent in combat training.

As teenagers, knights in training practiced wearing armor for many hours so the weight did not tire them. They learned to climb ropes or ladders in full armor and to jump on and off a horse easily. They continued advanced weapons practice and studied tactics through chess. They learned skills for hunting deer and boar.

In the last stage, they became squires for particular knights and began to accompany them to tournaments or war. This stage could last for an indefinite amount of time. For aristocrats, knighthood would come soon. Less wealthy young men could be squires for several years. One advantage of their service as squires was the travel; squires came to know knights from many countries, and, if they stood out as good future knights, they were themselves known by the time they became full knights.

The ceremony of creating a noble knight was called dubbing. Warriors who were merely trained soldiers could not be dubbed; they had to be from noble families. The dubbing ceremony was originally a matter of giving good weapons to a new fighter, commissioning his sword in the lord's service. In the original, simple ceremony, an established knight or lord gave a young man a sword and a pair of spurs, with a kiss and a declaration that he was now a knight. The ceremony was this simple on the battlefield if a squire had shown bravery and was made a knight on the spot.

During the 12th century, the ceremony grew more complicated. By the late 13th century, the ceremony was a complicated ritual with religious symbolism, and it remained elaborate until the end of the period. It was no longer a practical matter of being designated a fighter for the king; it was a rite of passage for the sons of noblemen. When a boy had trained with a group of young men, they were often knighted in the same ceremony, with the lord who had supervised them doing the knighting. If one young man was royal, he would be knighted first and might in turn knight his friends. There was significance in who dubbed a young man a knight, where, and when. Tournaments were common times to be knighted; the young man's father might sponsor the event in his honor. Some candidates made a pilgrimage to Jerusalem, where it was a special blessing to be dubbed a knight.

Geoffroi de Charny, one of most honored knights of 14th-century France, wrote a treatise on knighthood a few years before his death in battle. The ceremony he described was by then traditional, and each step had a rich

One of the greatest honors was to be knighted on the field of battle. A man given this honor was nearly always of noble birth and had completed basic knight training; usually, he was a squire who fought as well as the knights he served. (The British Library/StockphotoPro)

symbolic meaning. In Charny's description, the ceremony began the previous day, with confession of sin to a priest, Mass, and a long bath in which the young man pondered his sins. When he climbed out of the bath, he was to leave those sins behind. He went to rest in a bed dressed with new sheets until some knights came to dress him for the ceremony.

The knights dressed him in a symbolic set of clothing. First, they put on him a new white shirt that symbolized purity from sin and, next, a red tunic that symbolized a willingness to lose blood in defense of the weak. Black hose meant that death could come at any time but that this fear must be trampled underfoot. A white girdle symbolized purity and chastity. Finally, a red cloak symbolized humility.

The knights led the candidate to church in this dress and stayed with him all night to pray against sin. Some candidates may have held a sword hilt as a cross while praying. In the morning, they all went to Mass, and then to the dubbing ceremony. There, the presiding knight gave the candidate a pair of golden spurs to symbolize that the riches of the world must be trampled underfoot. The knights who were assisting buckled them onto his feet. The presiding knight then kissed the candidate and gave him a light tap on the shoulder with the sword. In other versions, the presiding knight sometimes slapped the candidate's cheek. He declared publicly that the young man was a knight, and the ceremony was over.

A large feast followed. In the Magna Carta, the king was restricted from collecting occasional, extra taxes except on the occasion of his first daughter's marriage or the knighting of his oldest son. A royal knighting meant an extremely sumptuous feast, but any knighting required a large feast. The feast could be costly enough that some men would remain squires most of their lives if their families could not afford the ceremony.

Courtly Manners

The code of chivalry stipulated a set of manners when the knight was not in battle. He was to make his manners pleasing to women. He had to know polite replies and comments for conversation with ladies, and often a knight was expected to know how to dance. A knight was not required to know how to read, but he should be able to speak well and give witty replies in company. He should keep himself clean and dress in fine clothing that would please ladies when he was in the hall. Young knights in the 14th and 15th centuries wore their hair long to the shoulder and may have curled it with a hot iron. They were clean shaven. Silk clothing in fine patterns and bright colors was popular even for men, and shoes had long points at the front.

By the 13th and 14th centuries, knights had to speak and act in very pious ways. They were not to fight during Lent or on Sunday, and they had to pray and go to confession. Knights were not supposed to chase after wealth, especially at the expense of brave deeds. They were supposed to help the weak, and some knights who took the code seriously rode off to help catch thieves or outlaws who had molested women.

The knight was expected to fall in love with a lady, either married or single, and to devote himself to winning her favor by doing great deeds and behaving well. Stories and songs at court told about brave kings and knights who fell in love with ladies—often ladies who were married either to their vassals or their lords. The stories were written to amuse and please ladies, so they portrayed beauty and virtue as more important than rank at a time when rank meant everything. Many of these stories portrayed the knights of King Arthur's Round Table in contemporary France; Lancelot's love for married Queen Guinevere was a model for how knights ought to behave.

Courtly manners were not only about politeness and love. A knight had to show outstanding courage; he had to take extra risks. Sometimes, in order to demonstrate his love for a lady, he told her that he would undertake an adventure to bring her honor and win her favor. One simple adventure was the *pas d'armes* in which a knight, usually a knight errant, took up a position by a bridge and challenged all who passed to fight. Only other knights were permitted to fight with the knight; merchants and farmers passed in peace because they were not noble. If he unhorsed an opponent, tournament rules of ransom applied.

Monastic Knights

The Knights Templars and the Knights of the Hospital began a tradition of religious orders of knights. These monastic knights embodied all the ideals of the Middle Ages. The ideals of monastic spiritual peace and warrior strength came together in the notion that the monastic knights fought a spiritual war with earthly weapons. Bernard of Clairvaux, one of the most extreme voices for the monastic ideal, praised the idea of the Knights of the Temple, calling them something new, unknown to past ages.

Monastic knights had to take the vows of both monks and knights. They promised to be unmarried and chaste, to live in poverty and own nothing but what the order gave them, and to follow the rigorous hours of prayer. When they were in the chapter houses of the order, they lived in cells like monks. Theoretically, their weapons and horses were not their own, but belonged to the order. They also took the vows of knighthood with an additional twist: they vowed to uphold the war mission of the order and to obey the head of the order. They did not owe fealty to any prince, but only to the order, and the order answered to the Pope.

There were three orders of knights during the time of the Crusades: the Order of the Hospital, founded in 1113; the Order of the Temple, founded in 1118; and the Teutonic Knights, founded in 1190. Each had a different mission and a history that played out very differently.

The Order of the Hospital began as the custodians of a hospital, a resting place, for pilgrims to Jerusalem. They were primarily monks, but their vows included a vow to take up arms to defend the hospital or the city of Jerusalem. They took in sick and wounded knights. Although the Hospitallers began in robes like monks, they began to wear chainmail. Some knights who felt themselves in need of penitence for violence joined the Hospitallers order. When Jerusalem was retaken by the Saracens, the Hospitallers moved to Acre as the Knights of Saint John, and some became the Knights of Malta and the Knights of Rhodes.

The Order of the Temple began as a group of knights who took vows as monks with a mandate to protect pilgrims and defend Jerusalem. At first, they lived in the Al-Aqsa Mosque, which was mistakenly called "Solomon's Temple," so they became known as the Knights of the Temple, or Templars. Many of those recruited to the Templars were knights who had been excommunicated by the church and wished to do penance. To take the vows of a Knight Templar was to get an automatic pardon for past sin and an automatic assurance of heaven if the vows were upheld. The knights lived by a strict monastic rule of poverty, obedience, and discipline.

The master of the Templars was not responsible to the governments of Palestine or Europe, but only to the Pope. In Europe, many wealthy people willed tracts of land to the Templars in order to obtain Papal indulgences. The order became conspicuously wealthy, managing farms all over Europe and maintaining several international headquarters. They began to develop international banking methods in order to transfer funds from one branch of the Templars to another. The Templars became one of the greatest financial powerhouses in Europe by the 14th century, in spite of the vow of poverty that individuals took.

The Templar knights were drawn into fighting in Spain against the Muslim government, helping the Christian kingdoms of the north take back territory. Templars built castles in Spain and brought back some of the Arabic culture to Europe. Gradually, many in Europe shifted from viewing the order as the pinnacle of Europe's ideal of spirituality to viewing them as unaccountable, too powerful, and possibly corrupt. The downfall of the order came when King Philip of France persuaded Pope Clement, the first Pope to live at Avignon in French territory, to convict the Templars of corruption and sorcery. The order was disbanded, the king seized their property, and the knights who headed the order were executed.

Last, the order of the Teutonic Knights was founded by a group of German knights who had come to the Holy Land with King Frederick II. Like the Hospitallers, its original purpose was the care of the sick and wounded in Palestine, but, as the order grew, it also worked to defend against the heathen on Germany's borders. The Teutonic Knights built castles and established border states in lands formerly held by Slavs, Wends, and Letts. The order became a secular power, a guard of Christendom's eastern border.

See also: Armor, Crusades, Monasteries, Tournaments, Weapons.

Further Reading

Bouchard, Constance Brittain, ed. *Knights in History and Legend.* Buffalo, NY: Firefly Books, 2009.

Bouchard, Constance Brittain. *Strong of Body, Brave, and Noble: Chivalry and Society in Medieval France.* Ithaca, NY: Cornell University Press, 1998.

Charny, Geoffroi de. *A Knight's Own Book of Chivalry.* Philadelphia: University of Pennsylvania Press, 2005.

Edge, David, and John Miles Paddock. *Arms and Armor of the Medieval Knight: An Illustrated History of Medieval Weaponry.* New York: Crescent Books, 1993.

Gest, Kevin. *Chivalry: The Origins and History of the Orders of Knighthood.* Hersham, UK: Ian Allen, 2009.

Gies, Frances. *The Knight in History.* New York: Harper and Row, 1984.

Kaeuper, Richard W. *Chivalry and Violence in Medieval Europe.* New York: Oxford University Press, 1999.

Keen, Maurice. *Chivalry.* New Haven, CT: Yale University Press, 2005.

Oakeshott, Ewart. *A Knight and His Horse.* Chester Springs, PA: Dufour Editions, 1998.

Oakeshott, Ewart. *A Knight and His Weapons.* Chester Springs, PA: Dufour Editions, 1997.

Read, Piers Paul. *Templars: The Dramatic History of the Knights Templar, the Most Powerful Military Order of the Crusades.* New York: St. Martin's Griffin, 2009

Wollock, Jennifer G. *Chivalry and Courtly Love in the Middle Ages.* Westport, CT: Praeger, 2011.

L

Lamps. See Lights

Latrines and Garbage

Waste disposal was a constant problem during the Middle Ages. There were three parts to the problem. The waste, whether human or **animal,** had to be removed from the immediate place where it was deposited, then it had to be transported to a place where it could be considered gone and forgotten, and then the people had to be able to live with its effect on the environment. Country **houses, castles, monasteries,** and **cities** had different ways of handling these problems.

Latrines

In less crowded places, waste disposal is a less pressing problem because there is enough space to allow the earth to process the waste. Rural peasant houses had latrine outhouses, as poor rural places all over the world still do. The platform, seat, and enclosure were called a privy. Country manor houses improved on this system only slightly. In addition to outhouses, they used chamber pots in the house and emptied them into a latrine pit.

A castle was usually placed in the country and was at first a stand-alone community until a town grew up around it. Although they had no immediate neighbors, castles were crowded places within their walls. Sanitation was a pressing issue. Castles called their latrines "garderobes," a euphemism chosen perhaps because they were designed to keep the user's robes clean. Garderobe wings or towers could be several stories high, with each layer built to have separate shafts for waste to fall into. In some castles, they took the form of lone latrine closets built into a tower or cantilevered out over a wall with a clear drop below. In larger castles, and more commonly, they were designed to use a few shafts, and each provided a few seats. They might be all in one room, placed with dividers for privacy. At least one garderobe was built near the main hall for the use of guests at a feast. In some cases, the shafts for the garderobes were situated next to chimneys, perhaps to warm the air in the shaft and make the latrine less chilly.

Castles that were sited next to a river tried to build their garderobes into the outer walls above the running water. Waste fell through long shafts directly into the water and was carried away from the castle without further annoyance. Castles that did not overlook running water had to use a latrine pit. Latrines could still be built into the walls so that waste fell out of the castle, but it fell into a pit that had to be dug out from time to time. A real drawback of this system was that, occasionally, an enemy became so determined to take a castle that they would send men to climb up the latrine

This castle garderobe has survived better than many since not only the closet and chute but also the seat were made of stone. Daylight shines up through the hole, which leads straight to the sea. (iStockphoto)

chute at night to get into the castle. Waste could also fall into the moat, adding to the moat's unattractiveness. If so, then the castle's residents periodically moved to another house while the moat was dredged.

The bigger, richer monasteries developed systems of simple plumbing. They channeled rain or spring **water** through pipes into the buildings and then used the wastewater to flush the latrines out. A typical "reredorter," the wing of a monastery devoted to latrines, was planned so many monks could use the facility within a short time, since they lived on a schedule. There was a row of wooden seats, separated by wooden walls for privacy, each with a shuttered window that could be opened for light and air. Some monasteries could have used rags from old robes as toilet tissue, while most others used hay.

Monasteries often had a source of running water, either piped in or by means of a creek or diverted river channel. Monasteries with water systems used the waste from all other washing and cooking to flush out the latrines, and a final waste ditch carried all the wastewater off the property. Sometimes, the wastewater went into the fishpond, where algae fed on the excrement; this was the first simple sewage treatment system. More commonly, the sewage flowed into the nearest river. Occasionally, it fed onto someone's property.

Town buildings with space to include a cesspit in the backyard did so. By the late Middle Ages, city ordinances usually required that cesspits be lined with **stone** to try to keep them from leaking into the surrounding soil and contaminating wells. Some cesspits used **barrels** to line the shaft. About every two years, they had to be dug out and the muck carted away. Digging out cesspits was a regular trade for some laborers. The manure from each pit was hauled out of the city in **carts.** It was a valuable resource for **agriculture** and was often sold as fertilizer after minimal processing.

A cesspit usually had a privy built over it. Frequently these were shared among several families and could have more than one seat. When a large city house had room for a cesspit, the owners sometimes placed a latrine at the back of an upper room (a solar), with a pipe carrying the waste to the pit outside. This was the closest thing to indoor plumbing. Anyone who did not want to climb down the stairs or ladder to go outside to the privy (or who did not have a privy) used a chamber pot and needed to empty it into a cesspit.

Some cities had public latrines to keep the streets from being filled with filth. London, in the 14th century, had a row of public toilets along the river where the tide in the Thames Estuary would flush the cesspits out twice a day. The privies were divided into men's and women's. River latrines gradually turned the city's streams into open sewers.

In 1357, King Edward III set out to inspect the Thames and Fleet rivers. These rivers stank badly even by medieval standards. Only 10 years earlier, the Black Death **plague** had swept through London, and nobody knew what had caused it, but "bad air" was considered a great risk factor for a repeat of the plague. He closed some latrines along the Fleet and Thames rivers and forbade the building of new ones. The rivers were dredged, and owners of the latrines that remained had to contribute to the cost.

Garbage

Cities had the most difficulty with sanitation. In cities, people, animals, and businesses were packed into a small space, with no room for each family or business to develop its own outhouse or latrine pit. Waste often went into the streets. This included not only human waste and animal waste, but also butchering waste (blood, entrails, and skin). Dogs, pigs, and rats roamed the streets eating what they could. Large city streets, especially in the 14th and 15th centuries, were sometimes paved and had gutters and drains. A wide street with two gutters could count on rain washing the streets at times. Cities like London also employed rakers to sweep the streets and carts and **boats** to carry the refuse away. Cities also tried to exterminate rats, although they were not aware of the rat's role in spreading disease.

Medieval people maintained a certain amount of recycling for pragmatic and economic reasons. Some food waste could be turned into materials for industry, like the bones and skin from butchering that went to make glue, leather, and parchment. Butchers may have dumped blood and entrails, but much of what could have been dumped was sold to pie makers or given to charity, since the poor were always happy to eat any animal products. Worn-out **clothing** could always be made into something else, and eventually it became either high-quality toilet tissue or rags sold to the **paper** industry. **Parchment** and paper were rarely thrown away; they were re-purposed by having something else written on the reverse or by being scraped or erased for a second use. Broken **glass** was called cullet; it was collected to be melted again by glassmakers. Candle ends, which could be melted down, were treasured to the point that they were part of some **servants'** wages and benefits.

Still, garbage disposal, particularly of industrial waste such as the scrapings and used chemicals from tanning, was a huge problem in cities. In Paris, there were civil trials in which neighbors sued butchers, arguably the messiest of the trades, for fouling the streets and stinking up the air. Butchers were supposed to haul their waste outside the city, but many put it into the street instead. The city finally forced many butchers to move outside the walls and locate along the Bièvre River, where tanners and dyers were also locating. The river soon became nearly clogged with sewage, which then flowed into the Seine and eventually out to the sea.

Italian towns passed stringent regulations for keeping the streets clean. Dumping water from upper windows was against the law; backyard privies had to be walled up and lined with stone so as to keep from leaking. Streets had to be kept clean; even grape skins were to be swept up. Neighbors were responsible for periodically washing the streets with river water. Dead animals had to be hauled outside the city, as did all other bone waste. All violators who were caught were immediately fined.

Toward the end of the Middle Ages, some cities had built drains and sewers into their main streets. Citizens who lived along these roads sometimes piped their waste into the city's main drain system. The hygiene-conscious Italian cities encouraged and at times required this, since it kept the alleys from becoming smelly marshes.

Ultimately, the waste all emptied into the nearest running water. Cities situated on rivers were easier to flush, but the resulting river pollution could be extreme. Smaller channels could become hard to navigate due to the volumes of floating waste, and even large rivers smelled bad. The water was no longer safe to use, which was a problem since many people had traditionally used river water. The fish were polluted as well and could not safely be eaten. Improperly treated waste could also contaminate wells, especially within a city. Cities tried to keep public water supplies clean, but it was not possible to keep anything entirely clean.

See also: Cities, Monasteries, Water.

Further Reading

Dean, Trevor. *The Towns of Italy in the Later Middle Ages.* Manchester, UK: Manchester University Press, 2000.

Gies, Joseph, and Frances Gies. *Life in a Medieval Castle.* New York: Harper and Row, 1974.

Gies, Joseph, and Frances Gies. *Life in a Medieval City.* New York: Harper and Row, 1969.

Hanawalt, Barbara A. *Growing Up in Medieval London: The Experience of Childhood in History.* New York: Oxford University Press, 1993.

Magnusson, Roberta J. *Water Technology in the Middle Ages.* Baltimore: Johns Hopkins University Press, 2001.

Wright, Lawrence. *Clean and Decent: The Fascinating History of the Bathroom and the WC.* Toronto: University of Toronto Press, 1967.

Lead and Copper

Medieval Europe used **gold** and **silver** for coins, **iron** for weapons and some tools, and only a few other metals for all other purposes. Copper was mined on Cyprus, in Germany, and in a few other places. Trace elements of metals like arsenic and antimony were found in the impure copper ore, and, for cheaper products, they were often left in to add bulk; the best copper, used for casting fine bronze and brass, had to be refined. Tin and lead were often found with silver and had long been mined in England, France, and Germany. Metal was also recycled. The Romans had used lead for many purposes, and the pipes, gutters, and tools they left around Europe were melted and recast.

Copper alloys commonly were used to make many household objects, especially for the **kitchen.** Bronze was an alloy of copper and tin, with very little zinc. Brass, on the other hand, was made of copper and zinc, with little to no tin. Gunmetal, also called latten, used copper, tin, and zinc together. Lead could be mixed into any of these, especially latten. Since medieval craftsmen had no sense that lead was poisonous, they did not hesitate to use lead in metal alloys for pitchers and other table utensils. Latten was the cheapest metal and could be used for many small cast objects, especially candlesticks. Pewter was an alloy of tin developed in the later Middle Ages. A poorer sort of pewter, used for pots and candlesticks, was made with lead and tin. Fine pewter was made of copper and tin, and it was considered nearly as good as silver. It had a higher proportion of tin, as compared to bronze, which was higher in copper.

Bronze items were cast using the lost-wax method. The desired shape was carved in wax, which was then packed into clay. When molten bronze was poured into the clay, the wax melted and poured out drainage holes. The bronze filled the spaces and, when cooled, took on the original shape of the wax. Bronze casters were sometimes called potters in English; casting molten metal is also called foundering, and the place that does it is a foundry.

Bronze casters made many kinds of kitchen pots, and they also made chamber pots. Households used as many bronze pots as iron ones, although later times used only iron skillets and cauldrons. Bronze casters also made church **bells,** which was an art in itself. Those who specialized in the craft were bell founders. The bronze for bells was approximately four-fifths copper and one-fifth tin.

Bronze and brass were used to make **funeral** effigies and memorials. Only royalty could afford three-dimensional cast bronze effigies. For one set of effigies of King Henry III and his daughter-in-law, Queen Eleanor of Castile, a goldsmith carved the wax originals. A bronze founder used these wax figures to mold and cast in bronze. Brass was a new material in the Middle Ages. It was cast in sheets and made into flat, etched funeral memorials.

Thousands of pilgrims came to holy places like Canterbury, the site of the martyrdom of Saint Thomas. They wanted to carry away a holy souvenir, but many of them were humble people who could not afford much. Lead badges were the cheap solution. A lead badge could be affixed to the pilgrim's hat or pack, and it would not easily break or rust. Lead pilgrim badges in many shapes were turned out by the thousands all over Europe. (Museum of London/StockphotoPro)

Lead was a very useful metal because it was soft and because its melting point was so low. It did not require specialized furnaces, but it kept its shape in air temperatures. Plumbers melted new and old lead into sheets and then cut it into roof tiles; lead roof tiles were the most popular kind. Lead was also used to hold together panes of glass, both clear and stained. Lead was easy to cast and bend, and it could be soldered in place with a mixture of tin and lead, using salt or tallow as the flux.

Lead pipes formed the **water** systems of many monasteries and cities. Rome had used lead for pipes, and no physicians had yet noticed lead poisoning, perhaps because it was widespread. First, the metal was melted and cast in sheets. Long strips of sheet lead were bent around a wooden pole, and then the pole was removed. The pipe needed a firm seam to make it watertight. Lead was easy to melt, but it always needed a mold, even for a seam. The new pipe was filled with sand and wrapped in clay, leaving only the crack where the seam needed to be. Now the craftsman could pour very hot lead into the crack, where it melted the edges of the pipe and then cooled, forming a welded seam.

Both pewter and pure lead were molded to make decorative shapes and pins, such as badges **pilgrims** pinned to their hats. Although lead was not a precious metal, lead pilgrims' badges could be mounted with small, inexpensive jewels. Lead could also form a white crusty oxide when exposed to ammonia, and this white lead was the main source of white pigment in paint. Roasted, it turned yellow and orange.

See also: Bells, Iron, Kitchen Utensils, Painting, Water.

Further Reading

Badham, Sally. *Monumental Brasses*. Botley, UK: Shire Publications, 2009.

Buckley, Allen. *The Story of Mining in Cornwall*. Fowey, UK: Cornwall Editions, 2007.

Egan, Geoff. *The Medieval Household: Daily Living c. 1150–c. 1450*. Woodbridge, UK: Boydell Press, 2010.

Harvey, John. *Mediaeval Craftsmen*. New York: Drake Publishers, 1975.

Magnusson, Roberta J. *Water Technology in the Middle Ages*. Baltimore: Johns Hopkins University Press, 2001.

Spencer, Brian. *Pilgrim Souvenirs and Secular Badges*. Woodbridge, UK: Boydell Press, 2010.

Libraries

In ancient times, there had been libraries of clay tablets and scrolls, and the Romans had both public and private libraries in many cities. Some public libraries in Rome were like modern reading rooms, and some were placed in the building that held the public baths. Each book, in the form of a **parchment** roll, had a little tag on the end of it bearing the author's name. Rolls were stacked on shelves or set upright into buckets. Some of these ancient Latin scrolls were still housed in the oldest medieval libraries, such as in Rome itself. Another form of **book,** the codex, was developed in the first century A.D. A codex was a stack of thin boards that were covered with parchment; little holes were drilled in the edge so the boards could be bound together with cord.

Christian writers in the early Middle Ages preferred the codex over the scroll for their copies of the gospels. In many cities, bishops amassed private libraries, usually consisting of either books of the Bible or commentaries on the Bible and religious issues. However, some bishops also had secular works in their libraries. In the seventh century, the famous scholar Isidore, bishop of Seville, owned a notable library. He had not only religious and biblical books but also copies of books by famous Latin writers of earlier centuries, along with medical books and legal writings.

In the early 800s, Charlemagne made great efforts to broaden Frankish book production. He set monks and scholars to copying books, and he organized schools to encourage literacy; he and his sons attended, to set the example. Under Charlemagne's encouragement, **monasteries'** book holdings expanded. Libraries that contained only 30 or 40 books before Charlemagne's reign had as many as 300 books by the middle of the ninth century. The largest monastic libraries had more than 600 books, an astounding achievement in the relatively primitive Frankish kingdom.

The greatest libraries of medieval Europe were located in Cordoba, the capital of **Muslim** Spain. Arab scholars were enthusiastic translators and writers, and the city kept hundreds of copyists employed. The caliph's library was reputed to have 400,000 volumes, and it was one of perhaps as many as 70 other city libraries. Other Andalusian cities like Barcelona had great libraries and became centers of learning that drew scholars from the Christian countries. The Muslim passion for translation preserved, at least in Arabic, many Greek classics that were otherwise lost. Aristotle's reentry into the scholasticism of Christian Europe began with the Arabic translations of his works, which then were translated into Latin for use in European universities.

As the monastic movement spread across Europe, monasteries developed libraries in conjunction with their scriptoria, especially in Italy, Germany, Switzerland, and England. The scriptorium was a well-lighted room where monks worked as scribes, making new copies of books and, like the rest of the monks, working six days a week. Sunday was not a workday, and in many monasteries the monks were to get a book from the monastery library and spend the day reading the Bible or other Christian literature.

Bologna's university was the first established in medieval Europe. Its library has one of the greatest antiquarian book collections in the world. (Kelly Borsheim)

Most monastery libraries had only a few hundred books, but they were required to have at least one book per monk. Books from the library also were used in the schools that many monasteries started, where the monks taught the village boys to read.

A few monastery libraries loaned books to the public, but with a strong emphasis on making sure the books were brought back. In some cases, the borrower had to leave something of value with the librarian as a deposit to assure return of the borrowed book. Some libraries coped with the problem by chaining the most valuable books to desks. The problem of borrowers' failure to return books, whether in public, private, or monastery libraries, brought about the creation of many forms of the "book curse." These curses threatened the careless reader with dire consequences if he failed to return the book, including eternal damnation, disease, agony, and the judgment of God himself.

By the end of the 14th century, there were more than 75 **universities** in Europe. Each one had its own library, often with a "great library"—a reading room where people could study. The university's "small library" was a storeroom for books loaned to members of the university. University libraries developed specific book collections for the study of theology, both church and civil law, medicine, and sciences such as geography and astronomy; these books were loaned to students. Residential colleges within the universities, acting as dormitories, also collected libraries for their students. Other sources of books for students were stationers' shops—the publishers of the day—where books were copied and bound and loaned to students for a fee.

See also: Books, Monasteries, Parchment and Paper, Printing, Universities.

Further Reading

Butt, John J. *Daily Life in the Age of Charlemagne.* Westport CT: Greenwood Press, 2002.

Casson, Lionel. *Libraries in the Ancient World.* New Haven, CT: Yale University, 2001.

Murray, Stuart A. P. *The Library: An Illustrated History.* New York: Skyhorse Publishing, 2009.

Lights

The primary source of light in the Middle Ages was the sun; nearly all work was done during daylight hours. Workers began with the sun and stopped work at sunset. Many **guilds** specified that craftsmen could not work at night, since the available light sources were so poor. It would be too easy to miss flaws in the work. Certain kinds of work required many windows, and workrooms had as many windows as could be managed without losing sufficient heat. Many crafts worked in the open air.

The secondary source of light, indoors, was the fire. Most houses had open fire pits or hearths in the center of the room. Since windows provided light but also allowed heat to escape, houses in the northern regions had few windows, and they were typically shuttered in the winter. **House** interiors were dark, and the fire provided the light for most inside activity. It was enough for spinning, basic sewing, animal care, and basic cooking. When fireplaces were invented for castles and began to be incorporated into some newer **city** houses, fires could be brighter without filling the room with smoke, and they probably provided more light.

Fires could be started with a spark from fire irons. The friction of the irons being rubbed together cast sparks onto kindling materials. Lightweight, dry materials like straw, tow, dried toadstools, and dried weeds caught the spark. Dry twigs and good kindling wood made the fire grow, and finally solid wood could be piled onto it. Oak, ash, and beech were the best woods for household fires. Starting a fire was such a production that most households tried to keep their fire from completely dying out.

Banking large coals of burning wood with ashes slowed the combustion and meant that in the early morning, the servant or housewife who raked through the ashes could find coals that soon glowed red again. If the coals did not light, neighbors were often willing to send a few good coals over in a fire pan. Another simple tool, the pottery *couvre-feu,* or curfew, was a ventilated lid that could help bank the fire for the night. With good kindling, the fire was soon hot again. Fires could be made hotter with a bellows. Men also blew on fires to make them hotter.

Fire could be a portable light when carried in an **iron** or **pottery** basket called a cresset. Lighthouse beacons were controlled fires in cressets. Watchmen in cities kept cressets with burning wood all night; they could carry them to the scene of a disturbance.

The liturgical year included several festivals when candles and other lights were featured. A medieval Latin hymn for Easter describes the lighting of a new fire with fire irons and the variety of lights brought from home to be kindled at the new fire. Pottery oil lamps with wicks flickering into light, pine torches spitting sparks into the air, and beeswax candles, still smelling of honey and dripping wax onto the floor, are described vividly.

Torches were the most ancient kind of light and were used less as the Middle Ages passed. Their natural pitch content made the wood burn well for a long time. They were used in outdoor processions at night and in

Cressets were small baskets to carry coals and fire. The cressets pictured here could be carried like torches. They were the only kind of light that could be picked up easily and carried outdoors to the scene of an emergency, so night watchmen always had cressets and a central fire source. (Francis Douce, *Illustrations of Shakespeare, and of Ancient Manners,* 1807)

public meetings at night where steady light was needed. Some **castle** halls had wall brackets for pitch torches; pine torches could burn at an upright angle and sometimes burned fully upright.

A small, personal type of torch was the splint. Some kinds of wood burn very well, such as birch and the heartwood of a pine. Thin sticks were dried well and then used as wooden candles. They could be put into brackets or carried between someone's teeth while doing farm chores or housework after dusk. Some had to be carried pointing downward in order for them to burn.

Rushlights were another very ancient form of indoor lighting. The rushlight is like a very thin, primitive candle. A rush is a marsh grass that was cut in the fall at about 18 inches long. Dried, it was dipped once or twice into melted fat so that the hollow tube would fill with the fat, and then it was dried again. To burn it, the peasant rested it against an **iron** bracket that held it at an angle. It burned quickly; a full-length rushlight lasted no more than 20 minutes.

When beeswax came into use for making candles, rushes were the obvious choice for a wick. The earliest wax candles were probably made by pouring wax onto the rush with a ladle and then rolling the candle on a table as the wax cooled. By the 14th century, candle makers were using pewter molds and were also dipping candles by tying the wick material to a rod and dipping it repeatedly into liquid wax. Wax candles came in all sizes during the Middle Ages. Some thick candles were called torches; they may have had more than one wick. Candles for lighting a home, and candles for dripping wax onto envelopes, were proportionately smaller.

Beeswax candles were a luxury, and most people saw them only at church. Candles were part of the worship service, and many **monasteries** and churches kept bees to supply their candle needs. **Funerals** required candles, as did some baptism rituals; candles burned before **saints**' shrines. Gifts to churches were often made in the form of beeswax. Manor houses and castles could also obtain wax candles, but they were too expensive for common people. In wealthy houses, though, candles could even be grouped together in a chandelier, a holder with room for more than one candle. The word *chandelier* now refers to a hanging light, but a medieval chandelier could be moved from room to room. The evening meal was generally eaten in the dark during the winter, and aristocratic households used candles on the dining tables so the food could be seen.

Tallow candles were cheaper and could be used in practical situations. In great houses, the cooks began to work before it was light and needed to use candles in the kitchen. Some of these candles had lanterns to hold them. Candles were always a fire hazard; many inquest records mention that a

Medieval lanterns sheltered a candle from the wind. (Museum of London/The Bridgeman Art Library)

candle had been left burning in a room and had fallen and caught the room on fire. It was not normal practice to leave a light burning at night. Candles were not allowed in some stables, where they were a fire risk. Hospitals and monastic infirmaries kept a candle burning at night.

Candles were held by candlesticks when they were not held simply in the hand. Some candlesticks had a spike to set the candle on, which may be the oldest kind. They could be used with any size candle. Newer candlesticks had a socket that had to fit the candle, so they may have been in use only after candle makers began using molds. There were also candle lanterns, made of tin or **copper,** with large holes punched to allow the light to shine out. They had hinged or sliding doors to place or remove the candle and a pierced top to allow heat and smoke to escape.

One of the documented uses of candles was the candle **clock** invented by King Alfred to time his hours of work and study. He ordered his craftsmen to make six candles that would each burn for four hours and had them marked off at regular intervals. He burned the candles before saints' **relics** in his possession, so they did double duty of timekeeping and devotion. To keep the candles from burning at different rates due to drafts, he ordered a lantern made with panes of thin, translucent horn. A clock lantern like this was too expensive for any but the wealthiest to use.

Oil lamps gave a steady light and were used in many places, especially in regions with access to good oil, such as olive oil. These lamps, like oil lamps from antiquity, had a bowl to hold the oil and a spout to hold the wick. The wick soaked up oil and allowed it to burn off at the spout. Lamp design did not change for many centuries, so it is difficult to date the few lamps that have been recovered. In Northern Europe, some were made of cast iron and had an arm standing up as a bracket to hang on a wall peg. There were also simple carved **stone** and **pottery** lamps. In the Mediterranean countries, they were usually ceramic, shaped as a bowl with a spout, and were often decorated beautifully. The wick usually floated in the oil, held by a piece of cork. By the late Middle Ages, some oil lamps with floating wicks were made of clear glass. Ceramic and glass lamps were often hung from the ceiling by chains or held on the wall by a bracket. Another late medieval improvement was a bracket that held the wick in place, neither floating nor leaning out a spout.

See also: Beekeeping, Houses.

Further Reading

Egan, Geoff. *The Medieval Household: Daily Living c. 1150–c. 1450.* Woodbridge, UK: Boydell Press, 2010.

Eveleigh, David J. *Candle Lighting.* Princes Risborough, UK: Shire Publications, 2003.

Thwing, Leroy. *Flickering Flames: A History of Domestic Lighting.* Rutland, VT: Charles E. Tuttle, 1962.

Woolgar, C. M. *The Senses in Late Medieval England.* New Haven, CT: Yale University Press, 2006.

Linen. See Cloth

Locks and Keys

The technology for locks and keys had existed since ancient times. The Romans took Egyptian and Greek lock traditions and developed them into primitive forms of the tumbler-locks we use today. Roman locks were installed in doors and caskets, and they also came in the form of padlocks—stand-alone locks with a locking loop of metal. They also developed the use of wards, obstacles that block the entrance of a wrong key. Most Roman locks were made of **iron** and have corroded over time, but their keys were usually bronze, and many have been found.

Medieval European lock and key technology followed the same principles. There were built-in locks in doors and in the lids of caskets, as well as padlocks. Late medieval caskets that were intended as strongboxes for valuables had hollow lids that held many locking mechanisms to make the strongbox as difficult as possible to open. Several keys were needed to open the box if it resisted brute force such as an ax. The most skilled blacksmiths made locks, and the profession grew into its own locksmiths' guild. Locks and keys were made of both iron and **copper** alloys such as brass and bronze.

A generic lock has a barrel that encloses a mechanism and a plate that is riveted or welded to the door, chest, or casket that holds the lock. Inside, there is a mechanism to hold the clasp fast unless an object of the correct size and shape is slid in to release it. The key is a shank with a ring to hold it (called the bow) and a bit on the end. The bit has to be made with precision to fit into the mechanism. The end of the shank, where the bit is attached, is part of the precision shape and is often thinner; it is called the pin. Wards are placed in the lock mechanism to stop most keys from entering, but the proper key has grooves or clefts to evade the wards.

Many medieval locks were slide locks. A slide lock's key does not turn as a modern rotary key does; it fits into a hole to release flat metal strip springs. These metal pieces are shaped like the point of an arrow and are somewhat flexible. The lock is snapped closed by pushing them into a tight-fitting hole; they spring open so the hole cannot fit them out again. The key is a lever (the shank) with a turned-up bit at the end, fitted and shaped to slide into a hole in the spring strips. It can pull them tight again so they will fit back out the same hole. This was a common type of lock and key all over medieval Europe and has continued to be used in less developed places into modern times. The bits of slide lock keys could be turned at an angle to the shank. They were shaped differently, with a variety of holes, lines, and wedges cut out of the bit.

Medieval locks also included rotary mechanisms. In this mechanism, a spring holds a bolt in place, hidden inside a metal casing (the barrel). The key needs to fit into a precision space so that it acts as a lever to move the bolt back. A rotary key had a pin that extended beyond the bit; it fitted into a hole that allowed the key to turn on an axle if its bit fit the mechanism. It could also be hollow (a pipe key), so that it fit onto a pin inside the mechanism, for the same reason. Rotary keys were shorter than slide lock keys.

In some mechanisms, the key had to turn a full circle; this is called a dead bolt, and the key is actually sliding the bolt. In other locks, the key presses against a spring as it turns only a quarter turn, and this releases the bolt. Dead bolt locks were widely used in the 11th and 12th centuries. In England, Norman-era keys have been found with very elaborate, precision-crafted bits.

Pipe keys were most often used for casket locks. Solid keys with an extended pin could be used to open a door from inside or outside, but a pipe key only worked in one direction. Extra security was possible by making the pipe key's hollow not quite round and precisely fitting the mechanism inside to this shape.

After the 13th century, locksmiths made more complicated locks with better wards. Keys were more decorative. The bow, instead of a simple

The face plate of a door lock protected and hid the mechanism behind. It was easier to make an elaborate plate than to design a lock that could not be picked. By the late Middle Ages, locks had become reasonably sophisticated. (Dreamstime.com)

loop, was often a lozenge, trefoil, or kidney shape. Doors and caskets could still be unlocked by a thief with patience and skill with a bent wire, so some high-security doors and lids had more than one lock. Some complex locks required more than one key, but it was easier to place multiple locks on something. Sometimes there was a skeleton key that could open all the locks, so the owner did not need to fiddle with so many keys. Of course, this meant that a clever thief could imitate the skeleton key.

The final achievement of locksmiths in the 15th century was a very expensive lock, usually custom-made for royalty, in which there was no visible keyhole. The owner knew of a place to press that made a spring pop open a slide to reveal the hole, and sometimes there were more layers of similar security. By the close of the Middle Ages, locks and keys at their best were stronger than the wooden chests they guarded. Brute force, such as splitting the wood and smashing the lock with an ax, could still open strongboxes.

See also: Furniture, Iron, Lead and Copper.

Further Reading

Egan, Geoff. *The Medieval Household: Daily Living c. 1150–c. 1450.* Woodbridge, UK: Boydell Press, 2010.

Monk, Eric. *Keys: Their History and Collection.* Princes Risborough, UK: Shire Books, 2009.

Machines

The people of medieval Europe were fascinated with machinery. The technology of the time seems basic to us: the lever, the gear, the crank, and the wheel. But the concept of making machines at all was new and exciting. Machines could make a man's work ability faster, stronger, and taller. Machines did not grow tired, and a man could tend or guide a machine instead of proving the force himself.

The two great users of machine technology were war and industry. War machines of the time included crossbows, catapults, and drills. Industrial machinery, however, was the greatest source of innovation. Using water, wind, gravity, and human muscle, machines were applied to lifting, grinding, smelting, cutting, and pounding. Roman treatises on engineering and military machinery were available to medieval students of engineering. After about the 10th century, the most inventive minds rapidly built on this foundation.

The first mechanical principle harnessed was the use of gears, which could turn vertical motion into horizontal motion and transfer power from the source to machines. The earliest gears were entirely wooden, with wooden pegs as teeth. **Mills** continued to use wooden gears all through the Middle Ages. As the iron-making skills of the time developed, later machines incorporated metal gears that had less friction and did not wear out as quickly. In **clocks** and other small precision instruments, **iron** and brass gears were a necessity.

In the 11th and 12th centuries, the gear systems of mills became more and more complex as more industrial functions were mechanized. Belts worked with gears to transfer power from the source to a machine in a mill. Medieval engineers learned to use different sizes of wheels and belts to create more speed. When spinning wheels were invented in the 13th century, they used a large wheel with a belt to create a much faster spin on a smaller wheel. Many other machines and mills used this principle. By the end of the Middle Ages, proficiency with belts had progressed to where spinning wheels used two belts to drive both the spindle and a thread winder at different speeds.

By the 11th century, mills were using flywheels to keep the spinning motion smooth. A flywheel uses inertia by concentrating weight at the circumference of a circle so that it tends to keep spinning once started. Flywheels added speed to any spinning engine or axle.

The foot treadle was another important discovery of the 13th century. Instead of changing power from vertical to horizontal, it began the even more important transition from reciprocating motion to circular. A foot can move up and down, and a treadle can turn this into spinning motion to power a lathe. Foot treadles also operated large horizontal looms.

Another advance was the bowspring, which was first used in its simplest form—an overhead branch that wanted to spring back up when pulled down. If a saw was attached to this simple spring, the job of lifting the saw back up was much easier for the human operating it. Combined with a foot treadle, the spring made sawing go much faster. A lathe operated at high speeds if its spindle had a cord wrapped around it, attached to a foot treadle below and a branch overhead. The operator had his hands free to cut and shape and needed only his foot for power.

The last simple machine to be developed was the crank, which evolved from the windlass. It seems simple and obvious in modern times, but the crank was not invented until the 14th century, when it begins to show up in pictures as part of a grindstone. The first cranked grindstones had a crank on both ends of their axles so that two people could make them spin as fast as possible. A crank also helped wind a crossbow's bolt back; turning the crank many times required less strength than pulling the bolt back by main force. The crank went on to become the simple machine for cranes and wells.

In the 15th century, inventions began to use complicated cranks and started to integrate them with other machine principles. The carpenter's brace, which uses a compound crank to power a hand drill, first shows up in records in Flanders around 1420. An Italian drawing of the 1450s shows a waterwheel with two cranks and connecting rods operating a pump, and we have the first records of a paddle-wheel **boat** in the same period in Italy. Connecting rods permitted one power source to turn five paddle wheels or three separate mechanisms. With this invention, machinery was poised to move into the modern age.

When a flywheel was added to a crank, it smoothed and multiplied the crank's motion. Any dead spots in the process of turning the crank were smoothed out by the inertia of the wheel. A grindstone with a flywheel kept spinning if the operator's arm got tired. During the 15th century, mills began using a flyball governor to regulate the speed of their waterwheels. The governor was a small device with a ball on a chain; once put in motion, it used inertia to keep spinning. The faster it spun, the higher the ball rose in its orbit. A mechanism connected to the governor raised and lowered a gate on the mill as the flyball rose or lowered; when the millrace became too strong and the milling equipment could be driven too fast, the flyball governor whirled its ball higher and triggered the mechanism to lower the gate and cut the amount of water.

Theorists and inventors explored the means of powering movement. They were fascinated with the idea of creating a machine that would power its own perpetual motion. Villard de Honnecourt, an outstanding engineer of the 13th century, left behind notebooks that included his concept for perpetual motion: a wheel with an odd number of free-swinging mallets, each filled with mercury, fastened to its outer rim. As the mercury moved inside the hollow mallet heads and the wheel turned, there would always be enough force at the top of the wheel to make it turn and raise the mallets at the bottom. The mercury-filled mallets would become their own waterfall, powering the wheel. Other inventors suggested using magnets. The modern generator that creates an electrical flow by spinning magnets around a coil of wire seems a direct descendant of these medieval brainstorms.

Another popular and fanciful use for machines came with the invention of clockworks. Not content to ring a chime on the hour, a medieval clock maker created a mechanical show of crowing roosters, spinning dancers, or hammering workmen that came out and performed. Even before **clocks** were invented, the gears and weights that drove them were being used in other gadgets. There were "automata," toys for the rich, such as a bird that appeared to drink from a cup. Villard de Honnecourt explained how to use a gyroscope to suspend coals inside a ball, thus keeping one's hands warm without allowing the coals to touch the sides of the ball and burn the holder.

One toy was an early experiment with the power of steam. The experimenter had a **pottery** jar with only a small hole near the top, corked. Heating water to boiling, he allowed pressure to build up until the cork popped out and steam came out in a stream. The jug could be made in an amusing shape—such as a man appearing to spit the steam—to entertain guests. Another more useful gadget experimented with the power of rising hot air by operating a fan inside a chimney, powering a meat-roasting spit or vents to regulate the fire's heat. This rare gadget appeared only at the close of the

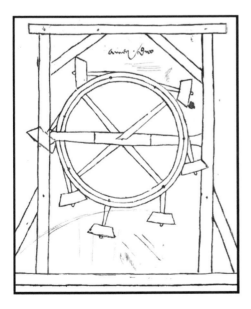

Villard de Honnecourt hoped that moving mercury inside each hammer's hollow head would provide enough force to keep the wheel turning indefinitely. As far as we know, he never built a model to try the idea. (Jean-Antoine-Baptiste Lassus, *Album de Villard de Honnecourt*, 1858)

period, and only in **cities,** but it was a step forward that was utilized by the next industrial revolution.

See also: Clocks, Mills, Tools, Weapons.

Further Reading

Bowie, Theodore, ed. *The Medieval Sketchbook of Villard de Honnecourt.* Mineola, NY: Dover Publications, 2001.
Gies, Frances, and Joseph Gies. *Cathedral, Forge, and Waterwheel: Technology and Invention in the Middle Ages.* New York: Harper Collins, 1994.
Gimpel, Jean. *The Medieval Machine: The Industrial Revolution of the Middle Ages.* New York: Penguin Books, 1977.
White, Lynn, Jr. *Medieval Technology and Social Change.* Oxford: Clarendon Press, 1962.

Magic

The word *magic* means "of the Magi." The Magi were the wise men of Persia, the Zoroastrians. In the Bible story of Jesus's birth, some Magi came to see the baby, having read in the stars that a great birth had just taken place. In medieval times, this ability to read the stars and know charms and spells was originally associated with the Zoroastrians and wise men of the East, so it was called magic.

Although the popular idea of the Middle Ages is that witches and witch hunts were common, the heyday of interest in witches came in the 16th and 17th centuries, not during the medieval period. The **church** and the civil authorities outlawed and prosecuted the practice of magic, but there were few trials, and they were confined mostly to the period of the Cathar Inquisition. Most common superstition and magic went on as part of daily life.

Sleight of hand, the form of magic the modern world enjoys as entertainment, also was practiced as entertainment in the 14th and 15th centuries. Some were so simple that a modern watcher would quickly suspect the trick, such as using a very fine hair to pull on an object to make it move or suspend it in midair. Some entertainers played shell games—making a ball vanish under a set of cups—or could get free from a rope with a concealed knife. Entertainment magic at royal courts could also involve mechanical toys. If the creator would not explain or show the mechanism, then the court could be astonished at the action of the automaton. Any self-propelled vehicle was a cause for wonder. One engineering trick made a toy bird appear to drink wine.

Real magic in the Middle Ages came in two forms, although it was not always easy to tell them apart. Natural magic was just a part of nature; most natural magic has been defined by modern science as natural processes, while other beliefs were harmless superstitions. The other kind of magic was occult, demonic magic that called on spirits. It was not accepted by most of society, and certainly not by the church.

Natural Magic

Natural magic was difficult to understand and define. Since all healing was miraculous in some sense, then all **medicines** had magical properties. The antibacterial properties of garlic have now been verified and measured, but to a medieval healer, garlic simply had a natural power of magic over some hurts and illnesses. The lodestone (**compass**) had a magical property of always pointing north, and magnetized stones magically drew together. Some natural magic was imaginary but was considered real at the time. For example, astrology explained that the stars gave certain plants or minerals powers to cure or protect. No less an authority than Thomas Aquinas believed that the stars worked influences on things on earth, causing magnetism, the medicinal properties of herbs, and the growth and death of all life forms. When so many things were unexplored and unknown, the world was full of magic. The real and the imaginary were not well distinguished.

Normal medical practice involved natural magic: a medicinal herb could have more strength if it was picked at dawn or at midnight. Its magic was increased by using it in combination with other herbs or substances or by preparing it with certain rituals. If a plant looked like a snake, its sap would help with snakebite—that was natural magic. The principles of natural magic were sympathy and antipathy. Sympathy meant that things worked on or cured what they resembled or had some affinity for. Antipathy was the opposite; if two animals were antagonists in the natural world, then a remedy from one could help cure wounds caused by the other.

Similar to natural magic was the magic of faith. It was ordinary medical practice to appeal to the proper **saints** to help with a problem. Saying certain prayers a number of times could also help the sick, since Jesus had promised to answer prayers requested in his name. If a saint or God himself accomplished a miraculous healing, rescue, or divine punishment, it was not considered magic.

Traditional medicine, as reflected in the Anglo-Saxon works "Lacnunga" and the "Leechbook of Bald," combined the natural magic of herbal lore with more explicit magic. The use of a salve based on goosefat and herbs accompanied other rituals. The user might have to act out a ritual at dawn or at midnight, at a crossroads or under a full moon. The magic ritual usually included an incantation in which the disease was commanded to leave. Bible terms were invoked, but not as ordinary prayers: for example, a medicine was to be stirred with a stick on which "Matthew, Mark, Luke, and John" had been carved.

Natural magic blurred quickly into a more explicit magic that was in a gray area between what the church encouraged and what it condemned. Some felt that superstitious rituals and taboos merely drew on the principles of the stars and the world, while others felt that they amounted to calling on spirits and invoking supernatural power in unorthodox ways.

There are four basic principles of magic in these traditional medical rituals. While any doctor of the time could prepare an herbal medicine or salve, the magical method would require him or her to observe certain taboos in the preparation: speak these words, remain silent, go barefoot, don't use **iron,** or don't have sex for a day in advance. To a nonmagical mind, these taboos and rituals have no connection to the effectiveness of the ingredients. Another principle was to select ingredients not on the basis of their components, but on the basis of some physical trait, such as resemblance to the disease. Jaundice, which made the skin yellow, was treated with something yellow. Male **animals** were considered stronger, so the hair, bone, or flesh of a male animal was supposed to make a stronger medicine.

Astrology and incantations were the two other markers of magic. A remedy's strength was thought to depend on qualities the stars projected into it; certain remedies needed to be tried under certain astrological signs. The rays of the sun would add or subtract power from the herbs or other ingredients of a medicine.

In the old Germanic tribes, written letters were considered magical; cutting runes into a rock or a piece of wood not only conveyed information, but it also worked magic. Runes could cure or kill, depending on the skill of the one using them. Medieval occult magic continued to put emphasis on the written word. Incantations had to be spoken over the preparation or use of medicine; they could also be the medicine: for example, write the names of the saints on a paper, and tie it to the sick person, or speak a word like *abracadabra* over the remedy while preparing it. There were many variants on Latin and other languages that created magical phrases to add power to a medicine or salve.

Charms were special incantations to speak over ailments, usually phrases with reference to the Christian religion. They were often very short stories about angels or Christ healing a person of a particular problem, such as toothache or headache. Repeating the story in its exact words was supposed to cure the problem. While most charms called on the powers of Jesus and the saints, some charms called on spirits to control the weather or give supernatural power in some other way.

Amulets were objects carried to give magical protection against certain problems. A hare's foot was a common amulet that protected its wearer from danger. Rosemary could keep away venomous snakes and evil spirits. Mistletoe could ward away conviction in a court of law. Some amulets had to be created with charms and other magical powers, such as herbs collected under a certain astrological sign while reciting a prayer.

In aristocratic circles, some believed gems had magical powers of protection. A sapphire could cure eye disease; Saint Edward the Confessor's ring could cure epilepsy. Gem dealers encouraged these legends as a way to sell gems. **Books** called lapidaries explained the magical power of gemstones. The bishop of Rennes' popular lapidary claimed that the magic of gemstones was merely the natural magic God had created in gems. Sapphires could dispel envy, and magnets could detect marital unfaithfulness.

Relics could operate as amulets; dust from a saint's tomb, or the host itself (surreptitiously taken home from Mass), could be carried as a protector. Relics differed from true amulets in that the owner believed the power was not in the relic, but in the prayers of the saint in heaven, but the dividing line between a relic and a hare's foot was not always clear to the common people. The church viewed the misuse of relics as superstition, not as true magic, and tried to teach the people not to use them this way.

Talismans were similar to amulets, but they had written words. A talisman's words might be a prayer or the names of a saint, but often it was a set of nonsense words or a pattern. One common pattern was to form the opening words of the Lord's Prayer, *Paternoster,* into vertical and horizontal lines that crossed at the central *N.* Another was to form a magic square

This amulet from pre-Christian Iceland is in the shape of Thor's hammer. At the top, a dragon's head provides extra magic for the amulet's owner. Amulets like this one were used well into Christian times, but Christians also made their own charms based on the saints. (Werner Forman Archive/ StockphotoPro)

465

in which the same words read at the top and bottom and vertically: *sator, arepo, tenet, opera,* and *rotas* formed a square like this. *Tenet* is a Latin word, as is *opera,* but they had no meaning in the square. The power of the letters was not in their meaning or in invoking any saint.

Exorcisms were rituals to drive out demons that were causing illness. They could be carried out by priests under rituals prescribed by the church, but they were done more often as folk remedies. The ritual typically consisted of a text for the exorcist to read while making the sign of the cross at many points and "abjuring" demons and elves to leave the person alone. Names of saints were invoked, but mysterious foreign names were also invoked, with incantations of Latin and other foreign words.

Astrology and Alchemy

Astrology and alchemy were magical sciences. They were connected to astronomy and chemistry, but they sought to use the power of the stars and minerals to gain power. They were not illegal, and some monarchs made use of both magical sciences.

Astrology, the magical science of the stars, came to Europe through Arabic books of lore. It appeared to be very scientific, and medical schools began to incorporate its teachings. Astrology was a part of natural magic, rather than occult magic; the stars had certain powers, and these powers were morally neutral. It was a matter of scientific study to learn what the stars were influencing or predicting. Many European kings, including the scientific emperor Frederick II, had astrologers to tell them when they should do various things.

Arabic texts on astrology also suggested ways to incorporate the stars into magic rituals. These rituals incorporated many of the common traditions (written names, herbs, and charms) but included references to the constellations and used astrology to recommend when to use the rituals. Some charms went farther and instructed the user how to pray to the stars or planets.

Alchemy was a form of natural magic that evolved into the true science of chemistry. In early forms, alchemy invoked stars and spirits or used charms and amulets. While the goal of the alchemist was to produce **gold,** the actual practice of alchemy involved many practical techniques still used in chemistry. Alchemists distilled, melted, classified, and observed. Their laboratory equipment began as the apparatus of natural magic but became the tools of science.

The magical side of alchemy often depended on the supposed secret writings of the ancients. Aristotle had written a secret treatise and had taken it into the grave; the priests of Egypt had preserved ancient knowledge. One book, supposedly by Aristotle, was widely read, but the text frequently

Medieval alchemists were unscientific scientists, but some of their discoveries led to the development of chemistry. They combined elements and other minerals, but with only magical theories of why materials reacted with each other. The alchemist's tools resembled those of a modern laboratory. (Paul Lacroix, *Moeurs, Usage et Costumes au Moyen Age et a l'Epoque de la Renaissance*, 1878)

mentioned how it must be kept secret. Legends grew up around other figures, such as Pope Sylvester, who had begun life as a humble scholar in **Muslim** Spain, the scientist-cleric Roger Bacon, and the monastic author Albertus Magnus. The stories told about how they had obtained secret knowledge with magic. In some stories, they discovered hidden treasure, and in others, they made heads that could talk. There were stories that these men had written secret books about their lore—the original wizards' books.

Occult Magic

Occult magic was an appeal to the spirits to achieve what Christians considered it was only proper for God's power to do. It often had its roots in pre-Christian pagan religion. Just as Christians had prayer rituals to invoke the help of the saints, pagans had used rituals to invoke the help of their gods and spirits. However, some medieval occult magical practices are not directly connected to pagan religion as we know it.

The chief aims of occult magical practices were usually love charms, charms to become pregnant, or charms to inflict death on an adult or unborn baby. While there are records of both men and women using charms and potions, women had a greater reputation for this knowledge. Younger women tended to go to old midwives to ask for a love potion or a charm for or against becoming pregnant. Many midwives were practical physicians who delivered babies and did not dabble in charms, but some did.

Since the early Middle Ages, European rulers had tried to outlaw occult magic. Since they themselves believed in natural magic, they did not try to outlaw the simple use of folk remedies and charms. They did try to regulate charlatans who traveled about performing exorcisms or curses. Charlemagne decreed that those found guilty of sorcery should become **slaves** on church estates and that those who sacrificed to the devil should be executed. Other kings extended these prohibitions to charms and potions, probably because they believed in their power and considered them to be no different from hurting someone with a weapon.

The church listed sins of magic in its manuals for penance, and both theologians and preachers spoke strongly against magic. Franciscan and Dominican friars, who preached to the common people in the 13th century, spoke against magic frequently. Bernardino of Siena, in the early 15th century, collected objects from magical rites and burned them publicly. Theologians tried to define the line between natural magic and occult magic. A magnet was considered natural magic, so the church acknowledged some forms of magic; Thomas Aquinas attributed the magnet's powers to the stars. But other forms of magic could not be natural and must be occult, and therefore illegal. The church also condemned magical use of herbs or even holy relics in ways that seemed superstitious rather than properly faithful.

During the Inquisition in Toulouse, which sought to end the Cathar religion, the inquisitors also asked about magic. Some people accused others of witchcraft. The accused confessed, often under torture, that they had used wax images to inflict pain and death, had carried out rituals to dedicate themselves to the devil, and had made charms and potions to harm others. The inquisitors recorded their testimony and permitted them to repent of these things as sins, but the civil authorities tried them as witches, and most were executed.

Most other trials of witches during the Middle Ages involved high-profile cases. When the Frankish emperor Arnulf died suddenly in 899, probably of a stroke, some people were accused of bewitching him. King Lothar II claimed that his lack of children was caused by witchcraft and sought to divorce and remarry on those grounds. The Knights Templars were accused of practicing magic against the king of France and the Pope, and Joan of Arc was convicted of witchcraft by the English. When people were officially condemned for witchcraft, they were burned alive.

However, for much of the period, there was a legal deterrent against bringing accusations of sorcery and witchcraft. The accuser was expected to prove his allegations, and if he could not, he could suffer the penalty the defendant would have faced. This made trials for sorcery rare, but in towns and villages, when someone was suspected of casting hostile spells and charms on others, the people often took informal action and killed the witch by drowning, burning, or other means.

True occult magic took the principles of common magic and went further. Magicians used rituals and taboos, resemblances, and incantations but with more elaborate, secret, and usually violent alterations. Spirits other than saints and angels were invoked, and the purpose was often to do harm: to kill, to curse, or to make someone do something against their will. Charms were curses when they were intended to bring trouble on someone. The natural magic of similarity, or sympathy, was often invoked. An object that resembled someone, either naturally or perhaps by being shaped to resemble him, could be used to gain power over him. A knife stuck in a dairy barn wall resembled a cow's teat and could be used to steal milk or curse the cow. A wax figure of a person could serve as a proxy for inflicting pain on the person.

Divination was the practice of telling the future, usually from signs in nature but sometimes from man-made objects like dice. Diviners claimed to interpret thunder or bird calls. Thunder had different meanings in each month, particularly in months when thunder was rare, and it could prophesy anything from good harvest and peace to death for certain people and war. Diviners could look for portents in a reflecting basin or even in holy oil put onto a fingernail. There were also many superstitions about lucky and unlucky days or events. "Egyptian days" were always unlucky, and nobody should get married or undertake anything important on them. Divination could uncover unknown information, such as the identity of a thief or the location of lost property.

The darkest side of medieval magic was the necromancy that took place among some priests, monks, and others who were ordained for a church role, including many **university** students. They could read, and they had access to many books others did not know. They knew the rituals, and they were able to concoct corrupt versions. Most priests and monks remained wholly orthodox, but a small minority began to dabble in black magic. Necromancy was different from superstitious common magic in that it intentionally called on the devil and demons.

The most common kind of necromancy was a perversion of the rites of exorcism so that instead of chasing away demons, the ritual invoked their power. Much of what we know of these unusual medieval rites comes from inquisitors of the 14th and 15th centuries. The inquisitors burned the books they found, but they wrote an account of the contents, and they also heard confessions of repentant necromancers. While some of the rites they wrote about invoked demons' names or used magical actions similar to medical magic, other rites explicitly worshiped demons by making images and praying to them. Some magic rites used circles or triangles, and some sacrificed animals or other substances.

The goals of necromancy were similar to the goals of simpler kinds of magic. The magician wanted to know secret information about the present or the future or wanted to have skills and powers without study or practice. The magician wanted powers beyond those of other human beings. Some wanted to conjure illusions to fool other people.

See also: Jewelry, Medicine, Relics.

Further Reading

Bartlett, Robert Allen. *Real Alchemy: A Primer of Practical Alchemy.* Charlottesville, VA: Ibis, 2009.

Davies, Owen. *Popular Magic: Cunning-Folk in English History.* London: Hambledon and London, 2007.

Griffiths, Bill. *Aspects of Anglo-Saxon Magic.* Swaffham, UK: Anglo-Saxon Books, 2003.

Kieckhefer, Richard. *Magic in the Middle Ages.* Cambridge: Cambridge University Press, 2000.

Kors, Alan Charles, and Edward Peters, eds. *Witchcraft in Europe, 400–1700: A Documentary History.* Philadelphia: University of Pennsylvania Press, 2001.

Pollington, Stephen. *Leechcraft: Early English Charms, Plant-Lore, and Healing.* Swaffham, UK: Anglo-Saxon Books, 2008.

Skemer, Don C. *Binding Words: Textual Amulets in the Middle Ages.* University Park: Pennsylvania State University Press, 2006.

Maps

Medieval maps began without a tradition of geographical mapping. The first maps portrayed a theological idea and leaned on Roman knowledge. Pushed by the pragmatic necessities of sea voyages, Mediterranean sailors in Genoa and Venice developed more accurate maps for finding ports. The two types of maps did not influence each other at first. By the late 14th century, new geographical information coming from travelers like Marco Polo forced mapmakers to revise their methods. By the middle of the 15th century, world maps were influenced by sea charts and began to show more accurate shapes and sizes for land and water. **Road** maps developed even more slowly, since only a few people traveled and generally depended on local guides. Regional maps did not appear until late in the Middle Ages, and most people did not use maps in their daily lives.

The Classical Tradition

The Greek tradition began with an earth that was round, rather than flat. Pythagoras, a sixth-century B.C. mathematician, taught that spheres were perfect shapes and that since the moon was clearly a sphere, the earth must be also. Aristotle observed that travelers and astronomers experience the earth as a sphere. **Ships** going out to sea disappear, hull first, at the horizon, and a southbound traveler sees new stars appear over the horizon in front of him while familiar stars disappear behind him. During a lunar eclipse, the shadow of the earth falls across the moon's surface, and the shadow is curved. For these reasons, the ancients taught that the earth was a sphere.

Eratosthenes, the third-century B.C. librarian at Alexandria, estimated the size of the earth with relative accuracy. He also devised a system of latitude and longitude and made a map of the known world. Ptolemy, in the second century, devised maps using projections of a round world onto a flat surface. His book on geography included a world map and 26 regional maps. Some astronomers in the last years of the Roman Empire believed that the earth revolved around the sun, although Ptolemy rejected this idea.

Medieval Europe inherited little of the classical knowledge of the globe and its size. Their access to Aristotle was limited to translations into Arabic, and then into Latin, in the late Middle Ages. They were avid students of astronomy, but the possibility that the solar system was organized around the sun, not the earth, did not come to their attention; they had only Ptolemy's astronomy, and his insistence on a geocentric universe persisted in all medieval calculations and models. Ptolemy's geography book was not in circulation in Europe until the 15th century.

However, through Roman writers like Pliny the Elder, medieval scholars had ample descriptions of the world the Romans knew. Far-off places had traditional names, like "Taprobana" for Sri Lanka or "Sithia" for Russia. Travelers all reported that there were places where dog-headed people and other **monsters** lived, and they were placed in traditional mythical places, duly marked on maps. Everything around the Mediterranean had supreme importance, most especially the Holy Land. Africa and Asia were less important because less was known about them. Ptolemy's geography was always considered the height of correct science.

Medieval Mappae Mundi

The medieval world map was based more on theology than on geography. The language of the Old and New Testaments of the Bible was taken quite literally, including such expressions as the "four corners of the earth." Jerusalem was considered to be the center of the world, and a true medieval *mappa mundi* showed the Garden of Eden and a place where tribes called Gog and Magog were shut up until the end of the world. Some maps made during this time included images of monstrous animals both real and imagined. There also was widespread disbelief that there could be another side of the earth to the south ("the Antipodes") because obviously men would have to walk upside down.

The largest, grandest maps that took up an entire oxhide or more have mostly been lost. After their use had run out, some were cut up to make book covers or other documents. One that still exists hung on the wall at Hereford Cathedral. If this map is typical, the grand *mappa mundi* also included commentary about the world and its history. Sri Lanka, here called Taphana, has a legend stating that it has two winters and two summers, dragons, and 10 cities. Some places have notes explaining the strange customs of the residents, such as placing newborn **babies** in a snake pit or willingly committing suicide off a cliff. The places have no bearing on realistic size, shape, or even relative placement, but they were brought alive with pictures and notes.

There are more than a thousand known smaller *mappae mundi* of the type commonly known as T-O maps. They were abstract and theological in form and intention and often were drawn by a bishop, a monk, or some other churchman. In these maps, the three known continents of that time (Asia, Africa, and Europe) were drawn within a circle surrounded by a ring of ocean (the *O*). Within the circle, two bands of water formed a *T*. The top of the map pointed east, toward the Orient; from this practice we get the word *orientation*.

In the typical T-O map, the top land represented Asia, with a horizontal band of water below to show the Don and Nile rivers, which were seen as Asia's border. The triangle of land in the lower left was Europe, and in the lower right, Africa; the water between them was the Mediterranean

One of the best-preserved mappaemundi is in Hereford Cathedral. The map was a highly inaccurate representation of the world's geography, but it accurately summarized the way Europeans viewed the world as a concept. (Hereford Cathedral, Herefordshire, UK/The Bridgeman Art Library)

Sea. The waters make a Greek *tau,* a form of the cross that early Christians used in times of persecution because it was less conspicuous than a Latin cross. There was no attempt to make the land's shape anything more than abstract.

The maps were often decorated, sometimes with little heads with puffed-out cheeks symbolizing the winds, sometimes with a picture of Jerusalem in the middle. On some maps the continents were named for Noah's three sons, Shem, Ham, and Japheth. Others were heavily decorated with symbols or pictures.

Road Maps

The earliest known forerunner of any kind of road map was a **pilgrim** guide written by an unknown traveler around A.D. 330, the *Itinerary from Bordeaux to Jerusalem.* A sort of map in prose, it gave the pilgrim necessary information about places and distances along the way, with detailed descriptions of hostels and places to change horses or donkeys. It had no real map, only a travel guide. Later pilgrims' guides included maps, but they came in the form of a strip of road to be unrolled along the journey.

The most famous road map still extant, the Peutinger Table, is a 12th-century copy of a late Roman map. It is 22 feet long but only a foot wide; it was made by sewing many pieces of parchment together. It showed all the public roads, Roman settlements and **cities,** and parts of Asia, including India, Sri Lanka, and possibly China. Roman roads were still in use in medieval times; for the most part, they were well built. The strip map shows distances, along with places the traveler will be coming to. Roads are shown in strips of countryside illustrated with towns and other landmarks like mountains and forests; long green strips represent rivers and other bodies of water. Both the countryside and the bodies of water are flattened to show roads as continuous.

Maps of specific countries were not much needed, since people knew their own locales or depended on written descriptions of property lines and so on. One exception is a landmark map of England, made around 1245. The mapmaker was Matthew Paris, an English Benedictine monk and a skillful historian and artist. His best-known work is *Chronica Majora* ("Major Chronicles"), an account of European events from 1235 until his death in 1259. His chronicles included illustrations of people and places, architectural drawings, scientific diagrams—and maps.

Among the maps of Matthew Paris is an itinerary strip map of the same type as the Peutinger Table. It showed roads, distances, and towns between London and Apulia, a region of southeastern Italy on the Adriatic Sea. He also drew a map of the Holy Land, oriented with east at the top, reflecting the era of the Crusades. His map shows Acre, a city held by the **Crusaders,** as

Matthew Paris's map of England, Wales, and Scotland was Europe's first modern geographical map. Although portions of it are inaccurate, the well-traveled places near London are accurate enough to help guide a traveler. (The British Library/ StockphotoPro)

larger than Jerusalem or Bethlehem; pictures of buildings, **animals,** and ships are scattered around the map, along with inscriptions in French and Latin.

Paris's landmark national map of England and Scotland was a type of map not yet really in use. Part of the last of Paris's chronicles, *Historia Anglorum* ("History of England"), this illuminated manuscript map has many features we look for today. It had a detailed coastline, islands and rivers, and names of regions; it named all the cities and towns, symbolizing them by **castles** and churches. It even showed Hadrian's Wall, the old Roman fortification, along the Scottish border. Paris's map of England may have been the first to place north at the top. That the map is not to scale (England is too wide and not long enough north to south) is due to the page size available at that time.

Late Medieval Sea and Land Maps

Portolan sea charts were not true maps, but they were perhaps the most practical and heavily used of all medieval maps. They were sea charts made by ship captains to give information about the point-to-point or port-to-port direction to sail. Portolans also usually showed very detailed information about coastlines; they indicated dangerous places such as reefs and shallow water and noted places where supplies and fresh water were available. They were especially useful in the Mediterranean Sea.

Sea charts influenced land maps during the 14th century, especially in Mediterranean seagoing places. Maps made in Portugal, Spain, and Italy could not ignore the accurate shapes of the land and water as shown on portolans. During the 14th century, some maps were produced that were a compromise between the traditional Roman-Christian world map and the observation-based sea charts. The 14th century was also digesting the revelations of Marco Polo, the first European traveler to spend ample time in China and then return. Polo's geography provided names and descriptions that were based on both his own observations and Asian, not Roman or Biblical, tradition. He estimated distances and described the relative placement of these new cities and islands. Asia was clearly larger than the old maps had shown, and it began to appear possible that the old maps were wrong about other places. There was renewed interest in observational geography.

The Catalan Atlas of 1375 was commissioned by the king of Aragon as a gift for King Charles V of France. It was the most complete summary of medieval geography in its time, and it represents the blend between traditional world map and accurate sea chart. The atlas was produced by Abraham Cresques and his family of renowned chart makers, Catalonian Jews who worked in Majorca. The atlas was painted on a series of vellum-covered wooden panels. The first part of the atlas gave information about the **calendar;** the sun, moon, and planets; the signs of the zodiac; tides; and how to tell time at night. The rest of the atlas was devoted to world maps painted in brilliant colors. South, not north (or even east), was placed at the top, so China was on the left and the Atlantic Ocean was on the right. Marco Polo's reports influenced the mapmaker to include more accurate Asian places, but there were still colorful figures showing traditional characters like Alexander the Great and Prester John (a legendary Christian king in a remote place). The Catalan Atlas does not, however, include the Garden of Eden.

In 1397, a copy of Ptolemy's *Geography* arrived in Florence from Constantinople. For a time, these maps influenced European world maps. Ptolemy's work explained the concept of projecting a spherical world onto a flat map using lines of latitude and longitude. There had been a few grid maps in the 14th century, but the concept of using measured latitude and longitude to create an accurate flat map was new. Maps in the 15th century blended Ptolemy's accurate method with Ptolemy's outdated information. Maps began to shrink the Holy Land to a small area and have closer estimates of distance. Europeans had firsthand knowledge of places such as Norway that Ptolemy could only estimate. They could criticize the old maps and began to recognize that their own maps could be inaccurate. From this time, world maps began to be recognizable to modern eyes.

See also: Compass and Navigation, Pilgrims, Roads.

Further Reading

Edson, Evelyn. *Mapping Time and Space: How Medieval Mapmakers Viewed Their World*. London: British Library, 1999.

Edson, Evelyn. *The World Map 1300–1492: The Persistence of Tradition and Transformation*. Baltimore: Johns Hopkins University Press, 2007.

Ehrenberg, Ralph E. *Mapping the World: An Illustrated History of Cartography*. Washington, DC: National Geographic Society, 2006.

Moreland, Carl, and David Bannister. *Antique Maps*. London: Phaidon Press, 1994.

Thrower, Norman J.W. *Maps and Civilization: Cartography in Culture and Society*. Chicago: University of Chicago Press, 2008.

Whitfield, Peter. *New Found Lands: Maps in the History of Exploration*. London: Routledge, 1998.

Wilford, John Noble. *The Mapmakers*. New York: Random House, 1981.

Masons. *See* Stone and Masons

Measurement. *See* Weights and Measures

Medicine

Medieval medicine was a blend of old beliefs and traditions from classical times, the herbal traditions of the Franks, Saxons, and other Germanic tribes, faith-healing superstition within the Catholic **Church**, and a slowly growing body of practical surgical and medical knowledge. Roman medical knowledge was best captured in the works of Galen, the leading physician in second-century Rome. During the Middle Ages, no medical schools departed from the framework of Galen and of Aristotle.

The fall of the Roman Empire to the invading Germanic tribes was a setback to the development of medical observation. Among the Visigoths of Spain, for example, physicians were considered low-ranking tradesmen. They were poorly paid, and they were fined if a patient died. To the East, the Byzantine Empire continued to practice Roman-style medicine but did not add any advances to medical literature, in spite of great wealth and civilization. The first official establishment of physicians in Europe came with the Rule of Saint Benedict, which required Benedictine **monasteries** to grow medicinal herbs and to admit sick lay people as well as treating sick monks. These monasteries were the first **hospitals** and began a long European tradition of religious oversight of medicine.

In the later Middle Ages, the Pope forbade monasteries to treat the sick outside their communities. Some secular hospitals had been established by then, often originally for the housing and care of **pilgrims.** Secular physicians, sometimes trained at **universities,** operated in large towns and **cities.** Sick people were still most likely to remain at home.

Faith in Medicine

Medieval beliefs emphasized the role of the supernatural in healing. Every healing was a miracle, in a way, since any sickness or injury could bring death. If someone prayed to a **saint** and got better in the course of nature, the saint received the credit. This makes no sense to postmedieval minds, but they lived with a constant awareness that death could come at any time.

Saints' special standing in heaven permitted them to ask favors of God, and they were thought to have a keen interest in ailments or problems related to their own lives or deaths. Saint Apollonia's teeth had been knocked out during her torture and martyrdom, so people with toothache called on Saint Apollonia. Saint Agatha's breast was cut off, so all issues having to do with breasts, from breast-feeding to infection to cancer, were under her care. Throat disease and choking came under the care of Saint Blasius, who had saved a boy from being suffocated. Many diseases were named for the saints who looked after them. Hookworm was Saint Gothard's Disease, gout was Saint Maur's Disease, and rabies was Saint Herbert's Disease. Measles was Saint Lazarus's Disease, and cancer was Saint Giles's Disease. Remedies, too, were named for saints, such as Saint Jacob's oil and Saint Bartholomew's tea. There was nothing systematic about these names; some diseases were called by the name of more than one saint, just as some saints took care of more than one disease.

Sometimes, the sick were brought to the shrines of either local saints or the saint thought most likely to help. **Relics** from the shrines could also be brought to the sick. The original relics were fragments of bone from the saint in question; the skeleton of Saint Margaret was held by the queens of France and was brought into the room in its reliquary when a queen was due to give birth to a baby. Relics could also be derivative, such as dust from around a tomb or **cloth** that had been held in the presence of the relics. There were also saints' medals. A medal of Saint Benedict, founder of the monasteries, had great healing power in the eyes of medieval people, since he was the patron saint of all disease.

Prayers to the saints, or special charms invoking saints' names, were part of other remedies. A physician might prescribe a remedy like theriac or ginger, but it had to be taken with certain blessings or prayers. Saints could work through herbal or **spice** medicines, but it was dangerous to proceed without any prayer to the saints at all.

Medical Theory

Medieval medicine was based on Aristotle's idea, also endorsed by Galen, that there were four humors, or temperaments, in a body. These humors were expressed in both mind and body, in both personality and health. An imbalance in humor resulted in disease. Aristotle also divided the world into four elements: air, fire, earth, and water. There were also four qualities of things: hot, cold, dry, and wet. Air was considered hot and wet, while fire was hot and dry, earth was cold and dry, and water was cold and wet. The four humors of the body were based on the same system.

The four humors were liquids thought to exist in the body: blood, phlegm, yellow bile, and black bile. A temperament majoring in blood was called sanguine and was hot and wet like air. A body producing more phlegm was phlegmatic, and it was cold and wet like water. Yellow bile was warm and dry like fire, and its temperament was choleric. Black bile was cold and dry, like earth, and its temperament was melancholic. If the body produced too much black bile, the result would be a gloomy personality, along with a physical tendency to coolness and dryness.

Imbalance led to disease. The imbalance might come from diet or bad air. It might come from bad habits of living. The physician's job was to examine the patient, determine the patient's basic body temperament, and decide what had gone out of balance. Measles, for example, was a hot, dry disorder because it involved a high fever. Other illnesses might be hot and wet or cool and dry. Diet, medicine, and other practical remedies were prescribed to regain the proper balance. The system was not factually correct, but it was very consistent and logical, and it was not until the discovery of microbes that it was displaced.

Medieval doctors had to make a careful examination of the patient in order to diagnose the imbalance. Feeling a patient's pulse showed the doctor the state of the heart, and examining urine provided discoveries about the liver. Every good medieval doctor carried a urinal to take a sample from a patient; they were attentive to color and smell. One of the leading medical textbooks of the time was *De Urina* ("Of Urine"), a careful catalog of the many observations and diagnoses based on urine.

Aristotle was known to medieval medicine only through the work of Avicenna, who translated the works of Aristotle into Arabic. It had become difficult to find Greek manuscripts or people who could read Greek, but since Arabs and **Crusaders** mingled at the edges of Europe, such as on Sicily, it was not as difficult to find monks who knew both Arabic and Latin. Avicenna and other works brought Aristotle back into Latin. With the Arabs came astrology, the science of the stars. A patient's horoscope could determine diagnosis, since the positions of the stars and planets showed the disturbances in the earth's atmosphere. Astrology seemed very scientific at the time because science was more closely connected to philosophy than to observation. Only a university-trained physician could diagnose with astrology.

A certain amount of medieval medical care came from an accumulation of practical experience. Infected wounds could be improved with a hot poultice; spiderwebs stopped bleeding. Medieval medicine also recommended bleeding to remove excess or infected blood or to restore balance. Physicians debated how much bleeding was effective, such as whether it was better to bleed a patient until he became unconscious. Different schools of thought taught variations, but everyone believed bleeding gave a patient relief. Physicians managed bleeding until the 11th century, when barbers began to do it. Physicians also cauterized wounds or diseased tissue by burning them with a hot iron.

Balanced Diet

The medical science of **food** was based on the idea that foods were either hot or cold and either wet or dry. The cook or diner was to strive for balance to maintain the body's natural state of moderate warmth and wetness. Medieval understanding of the stomach was that it cooked the food. The stomach, therefore, must be kept warm. Its fires should not be drenched with too much water or cold food.

Different foods were considered to take part in one of the four elements of the earth (fire, air, water, and earth). Most spices were considered hot and dry. Fruits were both wet and cooling, and medical practice saw fruit as wholesome only when cooked and served with spices to balance these qualities with heat and dryness. Many medieval recipes were created from medical assessments that a certain meat or fish was cooling or dry and needed balance from particular spices. Too much heat would bring on fever, while too much cold would bring depression and cold illnesses.

Pork was cool and moist; beef was cool and dry. Pork must be spiced heavily, while beef also needed moisture. Because birds flew in the air, they were considered warm and dry; they were not spiced, but rather were served with a cooling, moist dish. Lamb was warm and moist, which could imbalance the body, and its consumption was discouraged. (The traditional British accompaniment of mint jelly with lamb could be a last holdover from a medieval cooling recipe.) **Fish** was cold and wet, like the water it swam in, and so fish was served with a great deal of pepper and other hot spices. Lampreys, a type of eel, were considered very cold and wet; they were soaked in wine, roasted, and spiced so that they were as hot and dry as possible.

Foods were often labeled unwholesome without regard to modern ideas of bacteria or poison. A food might be unwholesome for a particular individual but not for others. Physicians ordered patients to follow restrictive diets that would not make sense to modern dieticians. A man with a naturally melancholy temperament was told to avoid cool, dry beef, which would exaggerate his cool, dry humor. Instead, he would be advised to eat birds and take spices. A man with a hot temper would be advised away from spices, which might lead to overheating diseases such as fever. A cowardly man of cool blood should drink warming alcohols to put a hotter spirit into him. Old men needed warming and should take spices; young men needed a cooling, moist diet. Seasons also needed to be balanced. The cold of winter required pepper and cloves, and meats had to be hot and dry (such as chicken) or spiced.

Aristocratic households included a spicer who oversaw the preparation of balancing sauces. In consultation with a physician, the spicer prepared a meal balanced between hot and cold and between wet and dry for the lord's constitution. Some paintings of royal **feasts** show the king's physician standing behind his chair, supervising what the king could eat. After a meal, whole spices or spiced wines prepared for digestion, since the stomach had to be kept warm. Candied ginger was a favorite dessert for the aristocracy.

Diseases

Medieval medical books were filled with accurate descriptions of diseases. Most went by different names from today's diseases, but some, like leprosy and malaria, bore names that continue into the present. Diseases were named for saints, by description, or, at times, by what was thought to cause them. Cancer, especially breast cancer, was known. Physicians believed cancer was caused by demonic crabs inhabiting the flesh, and they tried exorcism but could not cure it. The word *cancer* comes from the Latin word for crab.

There were many common ailments such as toothache, headache, stomachache, and wound infection. Irritable bowels, vomiting, diarrhea, and lung disease were known. There were also many common wounds that had to be treated surgically, especially on the battlefield. The most common ailment was childbirth, which is not a disease, but it had a very high rate of mortality for both mother and child. Medical books discussed the proper way to deliver a baby when its head was not positioned correctly downward.

There were also many infectious diseases that came in epidemics. The most famous is the Black Death **plague** of 1347. This disease broke out of Asia for the first time and became a returning epidemic all through the Renaissance. Many less famous epidemics came and went before it.

Saint Anthony's Fire was an infectious disease characterized by red skin, high fever, and sores. Sometimes the name may have described shingles, a painful but not fatal sickness, but its more serious form involved infected sores that quickly became gangrenous. Some victims lost limbs, and many died quickly. The epidemic returned at least six times.

Smallpox and measles both caused fever and scarring blisters called pocks (or pox), and both were treated by bleeding and careful administration of diet. Smallpox came to Europe when Crusaders returned home from Asia, and it spread during the 13th century. Diphtheria, an infection of the throat, caused death by suffocation or dehydration. Cholera and dysentery, infections of the intestines, also came in epidemics. Malaria was known as well, and although medieval physicians did not know it was caused by a parasite transmitted by mosquitoes, they were sure swamps transmitted it. They attributed it to bad air, leading to its name, *malaria*. Syphilis was another serious infectious disease that was often fatal. It was misdiagnosed as leprosy, but medieval physicians recognized that it was sexually transmitted, while true leprosy is not.

Tuberculosis had been well described by the Greek physician Hippocrates in classical times, and it was one of the most pervasive infectious diseases. Sometimes it was called the wasting disease (or later, consumption), because patients wasted away to skeletons while coughing up sputum and blood. The only known treatment was to go to a warm, dry **climate,** but most patients could not afford this, and most died. Tuberculosis could also attack the spine or settle in the lymph nodes of the neck. The medieval name for the lymph disease was scrofula, or King's Evil, and many came to believe the touch of a king could cure it. Most medieval kings had special days when they touched people who had King's Evil.

Leprosy was another common infectious disease. It was an incurable skin condition in which white or red blotches broke out over the skin, leading to rotting and either a distorted appearance or a loss of limbs. At times it was overdiagnosed, since it was a disease people particularly feared. Some diagnosed lepers may have suffered from other skin diseases, and reports of lepers getting well may indicate these cases. There was no treatment for leprosy. Lepers were isolated and were legally considered dead. In some places, there was a ritual **funeral** for a leper, in which a priest said the prayers for the dying and the family accompanied the leper to a grave, where the priest threw some dirt on him. Even without this ritual, lepers could not form legal contracts or inherit property. They lived in separate leper houses or colonies until they died. Strict quarantine may have helped stop the spread of leprosy; the peak may have been around 1400, when France had as many as 10,000 leper houses. It became a less serious problem in the Renaissance.

Although medieval doctors had no theory that could account for infectious diseases, they began to know by experience that some illnesses could be transmitted by air or touch. Recurring epidemics of the plague, throughout the 14th and 15th centuries, made this observation even more important. Some physicians wore protective goggles and facemasks when visiting plague victims. They recognized that rooms with an open window were safer than closed, stuffy rooms, and they recognized that gloves should be worn when touching an object such as a patient's urinal. They also did useless things like keeping rose perfume near their noses. By the time the plague had returned several times, 15th-century cities began passing quarantine ordinances. If a traveler came from a plague region, he had to stay 40 days in an isolated place like an island.

Remedies

Medical works from the ancients had included ingredients such as ground earthworms, dog excrement, and dried cicadas. However, most medieval prescriptions seem to incorporate less exotic ingredients, like wine, vinegar, and other herbs. Opium had been known since Roman times, but it was not widely available. Some medieval medical books recommend it, particularly those from the Byzantine East or the Arabic lands, where it was more likely to be available.

Physicians took seriously their duty to prepare medicines for the sick. They used a mortar and pestle to grind herbs and spices very finely. An eye-cup was a mixer for creating salves for treating eye infections. Physicians may have had their own stock of spices and other ingredients or at times may have drawn on the resources of the household.

Prescriptions made by physicians were not available to the poor. The poor used garlic and wild herbs as medicine. Earache was cured by dripping warm goose fat into the ear. Vinegar stopped bleeding, helped toothache, and treated burns and infection. As pepper slowly came down in price, it too was used as medicine by common folk. Honey, a widely farmed substance, was used in salves for eye and skin problems. Although it was available in every region, it was too expensive for the poor.

The most important medicine in the Middle Ages was theriac, an antidote to poison. Theriac could cure not only poisonous bites, but also other diseases where **poison** could be involved; considering the mysterious nature of disease, poison could be involved in infection, plague, epidemic, or migraine. Theriac came to be a cure-all. There were many recipes for theriac. The name did not indicate the ingredients, but rather the purpose. Its most common ingredient was the flesh of a poisonous serpent, on the grounds that it would counteract the serpent's venom. It could include herbs, honey, yeast, nut oils, spices, and the dried flesh of other poisonous creatures such as scorpions. Theriac was supposed to be mixed carefully and then aged for at least a year. Adults could ingest theriac, but it was considered too strong for children, who could only have it rubbed on their skin.

Medicines for the wealthy were based on spices. Spices were part of rebalancing the body's humors, and they had the added benefit of being very costly and therefore presumed to be very effective. All spices had been rated by physicians on a scale of one to four for how hot or dry they were. Pepper and cinnamon were the hottest; they were emergency medicine for cold and wet illnesses. Ginger and galangal were considered hot and wet and were used for illnesses that appeared cold and dry. While a fever itself might be hot, at times the physician decided that its true cause was coolness in another part of the body, such as the stomach. So fever could indicate a cooling illness. Overall, pepper and cinnamon were the most common medicinal spices.

Nutmeg was a popular remedy for stomachaches or gas. It was not considered hot, but it was very drying. Roger Bacon, writing in the 13th century, recommended cloves, nutmeg, and mace for the dangerous cooling of old age. Because poison was considered a cooling process, spices were also viewed as antitoxins for poisoning and were key ingredients in many theriacs. Pepper and ginger had both been used this way since ancient times.

The fact that these medicines were generally ineffective did not make people stop believing in them. Sometimes they appeared to work, and for common ailments, especially of the stomach, spices can help. Ginger helps with nausea, but it cannot help with poisoning or cancer of the stomach. Because spices helped sometimes, and because they were exotic, expensive, and endorsed by the sages, medieval patients who could afford them continued to believe in their powers.

Pepper was a central ingredient in medieval medicine. It grew in the Far East, where it was harvested and dried. The pungent black berries seemed a perfect agent for warming the body. Classified as hot and dry, pepper had to be mixed with some wet foods, and it was the best medicine for any illness considered to cool the body. Migraines were caused by a cold brain, so pepper was sometimes administered through the nose. (Antonio De Azevedo Negrão/Dreamstime.com)

Spiced medicines were not always taken by mouth. The cooling brain disorders of epilepsy, mental illness, and vertigo had to be addressed by putting medicine as close to the brain as possible, which meant into the nose. Disorders of the eyes, which were considered cool and wet, were treated by salves put directly into the eyes, and their remedies had to be hot and dry, which often meant pepper. Pepper was also packed into the anus to cure intestinal diseases. Gout could be treated by applying spices to the skin of the afflicted area.

Because spices were so costly, spicers were tempted to mix in cheaper substances or say that domestic herbs were imported in order to drive up the price. Spices were medicinal, so this practice was considered criminal. There were harsh penalties against falsifying or adulterating a stock of spices. Physicians worked with certain trusted spicers—or apothecaries, as they came to be known. In some cases, they worked together to keep prices high, especially for wealthy patients.

From ancient times to modern times, and including the Middle Ages, the chief culprit for the spread of infection was thought to be bad air. Bad air was night air, which was cool and wet, as well as the air of certain places where disease lurked. Bad air usually smelled bad, just as disease and death smelled bad. Good air was dry, warm, and good smelling. People sought to live in places of good air and avoid places with bad air.

Spices were a popular way of warding off infection caused by bad air. When the plague broke out, the rich used mixes of spices, such as cinnamon, cloves, saffron, myrrh, and mace. These were carried around in pomanders, burned in the house to fumigate it, or just strewn about the house. Poor people carried sweet-smelling flowers or burned herbs and fragrant wood in their homes to rid them of bad air. Onions had a potent smell and were obviously healthful, so planting onions could also draw bad airs away from a house.

The word *pomander* came from French—*pomme d'embre,* an "amber apple." It was originally a lump of ambergris, a substance found in the digestive tract of sperm whales. Ambergris has a pleasant, musky odor and is solid, waxy, and flammable. It has historically been used as incense, perfume, spice, and medicine. A lump of ambergris could be worn on a chain; people believed that its healthful odor would ward off the bad airs of a plague. During the Middle Ages, many pomanders were lumps of wax with aromatic spices embedded in them; the wax was enclosed in a metal or **pottery** container hung on a chain. Physicians often carried pomanders as they made rounds to the sick.

For sexual dysfunction, physicians also recommended spices. A high libido was hot and dry, while fertility was hot and wet. For increasing sexual desire, physicians prescribed pepper, cinnamon, and nutmeg. Medieval newlyweds could be served a drink much like eggnog, seasoned with cinnamon and nutmeg. For fertility, ginger was best, since it was rated as both hot and wet. Cloves were second best. Physicians warned against taking too many spices because they might dry and heat the constitution and produce both excessive desire and other types of disease, such as fever. The coldest and driest herb was agnus castus, native to the Mediterranean. Some monks, who wanted to dampen sexual desire, used this as seasoning.

Surgery

Surgery was not considered on par with real medicine, although some physicians and surgeons argued that the two could not be separated. While most people who were seriously injured simply died, battlefield surgeons began to form useful practices for saving lives where possible. The basic surgeon's kit began with his bag to carry the instruments. He carried a sharp knife for cutting veins or doing other surgery, a probe to examine wounds, and a cup for drawing out infections. Some medical **books** discussed surgical methods, so we know how some surgeries were performed, but they were not routine procedures. Wounds often became infected, and it was difficult to control for a good outcome.

Military surgeons dealt with many head wounds at **tournaments.** They became adept at identifying which skull wounds could be bandaged and healed and which were fatal. They learned to bore a trephine hole into the skull to relieve inner pressure from blood or other fluid. Sometimes they used a short piece of **silver** pipe to press into a wound containing a barbed arrow; this caused the arrow to be enclosed in metal, and the barbs would be released. They also dealt with serious wounds in which intestines spilled out; they learned how to clean them, replace them into the abdomen, and keep the wound open with a drain until it healed. They treated gangrenous wounds with amputation. The patient had no painkiller, and the wound was cauterized afterward.

In the case of women who died in childbirth, sometimes surgery was attempted to rescue a live **baby.** However, male doctors were not permitted to attend at births, and midwives only rarely attempted surgery. Stones in the bladder could be cut out by being pressed to the surface so that a small incision and scoop could remove them. A stone caught in the urinary tract of the penis could similarly be pushed closer to the surface and removed with a small cut that would heal. But surgery was rarely used to treat other diseases. Methods of stitching the patient and keeping the site from infection were primitive.

Cataracts, a common eye affliction, were treated by traveling cataract surgeons who popped the bubble in the eye with a needle. Vision returned immediately, but the long-term outcome was not good; the patients eventually went blind.

By 1300, there were advances. Some teachers from a school of surgery at the medical school of Bologna established a similar surgeon's college in Paris. One of its leading surgeons instructed doctors to use waxed thread to hold blood vessels together to stop bleeding in a serious wound. Surgical sites and wounds began to be sutured. Some began to instruct that a wound should be washed in wine, which was a simple disinfectant. They had no understanding that bacteria cause infections and die in alcohol, but they considered wine a healthful, clean liquid, and those who tried it found that infection was less common.

Guild-trained surgeons and the rare university surgeons were mostly in large towns and cities. University-trained surgeons, in fact, could refuse to actually do any surgery. In small towns, surgery was usually performed by a barber, because he had the tools. Barber surgeons removed teeth, opened abscesses, did bleedings, and eventually set bone fractures and did simple operations, such as for stones in the bladder. Barber surgeons in England began their own guild in 1302; it was chartered by the king during the 15th century, recognizing their right to practice and train in surgery. They conducted their own lectures and dissections.

Medical Training

The innovation of medical schools at universities began a transition from ancient into modern practices. One of the best-known works of the old medical tradition of Europe was the "Leechbook of Bald," written in

Anglo-Saxon around the year 900. Bald collected the classical knowledge available in his time but largely recorded many folk remedies. Some of these remedies are shockingly wrong, such as applying dried human feces to a cancerous wound. Bald recommended warding off a poisonous spider bite with a drink of ale, raw egg, and sheep's turd. Some remedies were charms to speak over the sick or rituals to enact using dirt from a grave or cow's milk, but without any real medicinal intent. Some were home remedies that may have helped, like pennyroyal tea for an upset stomach. Such traditional compilations preserved some useful herbal knowledge, but they were superstitious and unscientific.

Even at universities, medical training emphasized authority over innovation. The main task for a student at a medical school was to memorize the traditional and accepted works: Hippocrates, Galen, and Avicenna. Some schools featured dissections, but many did not expect students to observe real patients.

Some medical books of the Middle Ages discussed ideas such as the four humors and which foods to eat for certain diseases, and some mostly

Since medieval hospitals only cared for the poor, the heart of medical practice was the home visit. A physician visited his patient each day and made a care examination. He studied the patient's pulse rate, skin, and urine. After the exam, the physician held a consultation, often out of the patient's hearing. He gave instructions for diet, rest, and medicine. The sick person's family and friends were responsible for carrying out medical orders, while the physician himself rode to the next house. (National Library of Medicine)

rehashed Galen and Aristotle. Most included at least some eyewitness descriptions of diseases and injuries, and some had practical manuals for diagnosing diseases and treating wounds. Some provided surgical instructions or discussed the common problem of delivering babies safely for both mother and child.

The leading medical writer of the Middle Ages was a Persian doctor named Ibn Sina, better known in English as Avicenna. Combining Galen's teachings with Islamic medicine, he interpreted Aristotle's system of the four humors and added his own observations. Avicenna's work came to Europe as interpreted by a rhyming poem written in Salerno, Italy, the home of the first medical school in Europe, which was renowned for its work in healing injured or sick Crusaders.

The physicians of **Muslim** Andalusia wrote medical books that were eventually translated into Latin. The Koran prohibited dissection, so Arabic medical writing lacked direct observation of anatomy. Male physicians were prohibited from treating female patients and had to rely on the observations of midwives in writing about female diseases. Abulkasim, court physician for Caliph Abd al Rahman III, wrote a lengthy book on surgery that described his observations and experiments. He operated on the thyroid, removed kidney stones and tonsils, and extracted arrowheads. He described many case histories. Abulkasim's work became standard in European medieval medical schools.

The **Jewish** doctor Moses Maimonides was originally from Andalusia but was driven out when his family refused to convert to Islam. His medical books were written in Arabic while he was living in Egypt. He derided superstition such as astrology and was an active, practical doctor who saw thousands patients in the Sultan's palace and in his home. He included his own observations as he summarized the medical knowledge he had been taught.

Most medical books dealt only lightly with surgery. The only influential medical book that came out of the Byzantine Empire was by Paul of Aegina and was written around 600. Paul wrote extensively about surgery, and his work was used in many medical schools. Another influential surgery textbook was the *Practica Chirurgerie* by Roger of Salerno. This work, written around 1200, described diagnosis and treatment of head injuries, broken bones, bleeding, epilepsy, and goiter. Roger of Salerno recommended cauterization to stop bleeding and iodine-rich seaweed to cure goiter. He suggested treating a badly healed broken bone by breaking and resetting it. He described suturing wounds and even blood vessels and recommended allowing a wound to become infected and to heal with wet dressings. It was probably nearly impossible to avoid infection during the time. Other surgical experimenters and writers, though, recommended washing a wound with wine to avoid infection.

Medical schools at universities in Padua, Bologna, Salerno, and Paris were the top schools. Salerno was founded in the 10th century, near the famous monastery of Montecassino. It remained as a functioning medical school until 1811. Salerno blended the medical traditions of Arabs, Jews, Greeks, and Latins. It relied on the incorrect theories of Galen and Aristotle, but it rejected superstitious remedies and taught students anatomy with dissection. The school issued the first modern anatomy book, based on dissections of pigs, and stated that pigs are the animals most similar to humans, although they do not look as similar as apes do.

Physicians who spent the required time studying, and who passed their exams on the medical books, took the Hippocratic Oath. They became the top echelon of medical practitioners. Some went on to innovate and teach at medical schools, while others became court physicians who refused to get their hands dirty but preferred to give orders to others.

See also: Food, Gardens, Hospitals, Plague, Spices and Sugar, Universities.

Further Reading

Adamson, Melitta Weiss. *Food in Medieval Times.* Westport, CT: Greenwood Press, 2004.

Benedictow, Ole Jorgen. *The Black Death, 1346–1353: The Complete History.* Cambridge: D. S. Brewer, 2006.

Bowers, Barbara S. *The Medieval Hospital and Medical Practice.* Burlington, VT: Ashgate, 2007.

Dendle, Peter, and Alain Touwaide. *Health and Healing from the Medieval Garden.* Woodbridge, UK: Boydell Press, 2008.

Gordon, Benjamin L. *Medieval and Renaissance Medicine.* New York: Philosophical Library, 1959.

Horden, Peregrine. *Hospitals and Healing from Antiquity to the Later Middle Ages.* London: Ashgate, 2008.

Lindberg, David C. *The Beginnings of Western Science.* Chicago: University of Chicago Press, 2007.

Prioreschi, Plinio. *Medieval Medicine.* Omaha, NE: Horatius Press, 2003.

Rawcliffe, Carole. *Leprosy in Medieval England.* Woodbridge, UK: Boydell Press, 2009.

Turner, Jack. *Spices: The History of a Temptation.* New York: Knopf, 2004.

Menageries. See Zoos

Mills

Harnessing **water** and wind was one of the major achievements of medieval Europe. Water and wind technology had appeared in other parts of the world, chiefly in China, but there is little evidence that this power was used for things other than grinding grain until medieval Europeans began experimenting. In medieval Europe, wind and water powered an industrial revolution. By the end of this era, harnessed natural power had been applied to nearly every manufacturing process.

The mill was a central part of every community. Every grain-growing place (nearly all of Europe) required a mill nearby where farmers, usually peasants, could bring their grain. Millers rarely owned the land they built on; they paid rent to the landowner in flour, cash, or eels from their mill-ponds. Their income was taken straight from the grain brought to them. They kept a portion and sold it for profit. Since peasants could not watch or control the milling process, they were dependent on the miller's honesty. Many medieval stories, including Chaucer's *Canterbury Tales,* depict millers as cheats. It seems likely that most peasants believed the miller had kept more flour than he was due much as modern people often believe car salesmen have cheated them.

Water Mills

In Roman times, waterpower was limited to grinding grain. Romans had **slaves** for other work and did not look for mechanical substitutes. In early medieval Italy, mills at first remained tied only to grinding grain, though, in the later Middle Ages, northern Italy became heavily developed with other industries. In **Muslim** Spain, waterwheels did not develop beyond the primitive level. Water mills ground flour and lifted water into irrigation channels but were never exploited for other industrial uses. For water to become a real industrial force, rivers had to be plentiful and swift.

Northern Europe had much more favorable rivers for water mills. Mills were well established in Frankish lands by the time of Charlemagne, whose laws protected mills. They also were used in Anglo-Saxon England. These early mills could have been horizontal-wheel mills, copied from the Roman ones. Archeological evidence suggests that the horizontal wheels were closer in size to a large cartwheel than to a 19th-century waterwheel and that they were fed water directly by a wooden pipe leading from a millpond at a higher elevation.

Small horizontal-wheel mills operated at the margins of Europe throughout the Middle Ages. These primitive mills are usually built over a small stream, and a shaft sticks below the building into the water, where a small turbine is mounted. Primitive mills like this, found in Scotland, Norway, Romania, and parts of Bohemia, may have been maintained by the community. Each user ground his own flour; there was no professional miller.

In France and England, though, the mills were larger operations and required professional millers. These millers paid rent to the landowners, often

The Luttrell Psalter appears to show an overshot, vertical waterwheel on a small rural mill. A country mill like this was probably used for grinding flour, but mills in larger towns were built to serve many other crafts. (HIP/Art Resource, NY)

in the form of flour and eels. The standard arrangement for the miller was to grind a farmer's grain and keep a portion of the product. He could sell it or use it for his rent. Manors had their own mills, too, where the lord's own grain was processed. **Monasteries** often built mills.

During the 13th century, mills in Northern Europe changed to using vertical wheels. Vertical wheel development added much more power to waterwheels. The medieval water mill could grind far faster and more efficiently than the horizontal-wheel mill. They were then adapted into complex power trains that could run many other machines.

Vertical wheels had many slats, or buckets, for the stream to push against. The first wheels were designed as undershot wheels; the stream passed under them, pushing the slats forward and up. Later medieval mills used overshot wheels, but these required a natural waterfall or significant engineering to create a source of falling water. Only overshot vertical wheels could produce enough power for the many industrial uses that water mills were soon applied to.

The power train depended on wooden gears, chiefly to turn horizontal power into vertical power. Simple medieval gears were wheels with wooden or metal teeth; wooden gears made with wheels and pegs were the most common, although they broke easily. Using the heaviest gears to transfer power from the waterwheel to a drive shaft, power trains could add more gears along the way to drive additional **machines.**

Waterwheels drove hammers that beat on **cloth** for fulling or crushed metal ore, olives, paint pigments, linen rags for **paper** pulp, or grain mash for beer. **Armor** makers used waterwheels to run polishing wheels, and carpenters used them for wood saws. Blacksmiths built larger ironworks because waterpower could drive large bellows tirelessly, and this increased firepower heated the **iron** to the higher temperatures needed for steel and pig iron.

Cistercian monasteries always included a stream diverted through the main building, first to turn waterwheels to power the monastery's work, and then to flow through **latrines** on its way out. Some Cistercians used waterpower to crush olives or maintain iron forges. The main monastery at Clairvaux, in France, ground and sieved wheat flour, tanned leather, and fulled cloth.

By the late Middle Ages, there were so many water mills operating in France and England that they blocked travel on the rivers. Mill operators built dams and dug channels to alter the river's flow for their advantage, which often affected the conditions for mills downstream. There were bitter lawsuits over new mills when they cut waterpower for other mills. Kings tried to license mills to regulate them.

Towns dealt with the high need for mills by digging millrace channels at river bends. They diverted some of the water from its natural course, forcing it through narrow, straight channels with strategically placed waterfalls. A town with the right site could operate 10 or 12 mills within a short stretch, enabling the craftsmen to power a number of businesses.

Some water mills were located under town **bridges,** while others floated and were tethered mid-stream. There is 12th-century evidence for floating mills on the Seine near Paris and in Venice. There were a few mills that operated with the power of rising and falling tides, but they were not as successful. Waterwheels were not useful in coastal, flat regions where the streams were too slow. Tidal mills could not provide the same power as river-powered mills, but they occurred throughout the later Middle Ages along the coasts of Italy, France, England, and the Low Counties.

Windmills

Windmills appear to be a European invention. Although many medieval inventions originated in China or India, wind technology remained primitive in China. Coastal Europeans, who had strong sea breezes but few fast streams, developed windmills as an alternative source of harnessed power. Windmills show up in written records around 1180 in England and Normandy. The technology appears to have spread quickly; during the Third

Crusade (1190–1192), engineers in the Crusader army built the first wind-mill in Syria.

By 1200, windmills had spread to most parts of Europe. Flanders (modern Netherlands) invested heavily in windmills. Its steady sea breeze was put to work pumping water out of the low-lying land. Windmills powered wheels with buckets that scooped water up and poured it into canals or troughs. Other windmills ground flour and worked other kinds of machinery. The largest number ground wheat and other grains using a pair of heavy horizontal millstones.

Medieval windmills were post mills. The windmill was built around a post that supported the building and allowed it to turn so it could catch the wind from any direction. The mill's central post was supported by four or six cross-trees, large oak legs resting on stone blocks. The central post rose up into the building, and it held a large wheel with a bearing. This supported the mill's floor, which was raised above the ground. Sometimes the cross-trees and post were visible, but often the miller built a housing around them to protect them from the weather. Medieval illustrations show both kinds of design; without a housing, the mill seems to stand on chicken legs, while with it, it looks like a tower that stands on the ground.

Inside the mill, the main floor was supported by beams that turned around the central post, with an upper floor reached by a ladder. The gears and beams were all made of wood, though some edges and joints were reinforced with iron. Millers kept things running smoothly by oiling them with

The original windmill of the Middle Ages turned on a post so that it could catch the wind as its direction shifted. The four large sails were wooden frames covered with tightly stretched canvas, like ship's sails. In this picture from an illuminated manuscript, the miller has placed a weather vane on top of the building. As the wind shifted, he turned the heavy mill by hand, perhaps with the help of an ox or donkey, until the sails had full power. (Richard Bennet, *History of Corn Milling*, 1899)

tallow. The machinery was attached to the axle of the sails, which came into the upper floor. The standard post mill had four large sails. Each sail was made of a wooden frame with canvas stretched across it.

The mill had to be turned on the post so that its sails faced into the wind most efficiently. The mill had a long beam that was used as a tiller to turn it. The beam often had a wheel at the end so it could roll in a circle around the mill, and sometimes it could be hitched to an animal. By the late Middle Ages, some mills had a smaller set of sails mounted on the tiller beam. When the main sails were pointed into the wind, the tiller's fantail was protected from the wind and did not move. When the wind direction changed, the small sails drove the tiller forward, turning the mill into the wind again.

Although most medieval windmills were rotating post mills, later ones had a stationary building. By the 14th century, some mills were built of stone and could house heavier equipment. The sails still needed to be turned to face the wind, but the mill had been redesigned so that only a cap on top needed to turn. The cap was made of wood, and it carried the sails as it moved on a track.

See also: Iron, Machines, Water.

Further Reading

Gies, Frances, and Joseph Gies. *Cathedral, Forge, and Waterwheel: Technology and Invention in the Middle Ages.* New York: Harper Collins, 1994.

Hills, Richard Leslie. *Power from Wind: A History of Windmill Technology.* Cambridge: Cambridge University Press, 1996.

Holt, Richard. *The Mills of Medieval England.* Oxford: Blackwell Publishing, 1988.

Langdon, John. *Mills in the Medieval Economy.* Oxford: Oxford University Press, 2004.

Lucas, Adam. *Wind, Water, and Work: Ancient and Medieval Milling Technology.* Leiden, Netherlands: Brill Academic Publishers, 2005.

Squatriti, Paolo. *Water and Society in Early Medieval Italy, AD 400–1000.* Cambridge: Cambridge University Press, 2002.

Minstrels and Troubadours

The entertainers we know as minstrels went by many other names during the Middle Ages. They were *ioculatores* in Latin, players and entertainers, and *gleemen* in Anglo-Saxon England. Their most common name in medieval French was *jongleurs,* which became the modern word *jugglers.* Jongleurs could often juggle, but they did much more. They were the all-purpose professional musicians, actors, and players of the time and could be found at **fairs,** in **castles,** and in **city** squares.

Jongleurs and minstrels were never considered respectable, even in medieval times. They did not mind their own business, like most farmers or craftsmen, but traveled from town to town, performing in the squares. Most of them were relatively poor; they spent much of their time outdoors. The jongleurs in this French picture are standing in the city square. They may be acting out a drama, or they may be telling stories. (Paul Lacroix, *Moeurs, Usage et Costumes au Moyen Age et a l'Epoque de la Renaissance*, 1878)

Troubadours, the courtly poets who sang in 12th- and 13th-century Provence, were of a higher class. Most were nobility, and some were noble ladies. *Trobar* meant "poem" in the language of Provence. *Trobadors* considered themselves poets set to music; they created the first important poetry in vernacular speech, rather than Latin. By romanticizing the concept of love, they permanently changed Europe's view of women.

Minstrels and Jongleurs

A minstrel in *Beowulf* makes a stately appearance, singing heroic songs for the king and his men. He was a *scop* (pronounced "shop"), a composer of verse, not just a singer. He accompanied himself on a harp. Scops were honored and seem to have lived at royal halls, though some may have traveled. Traveling singers were known as gleemen and could have learned the songs and stories the scops wrote.

In Charlemagne's time, both in England and in the land of the Franks, there were not only court poets and wandering singers. There were also many other entertainers. They sang and danced, juggled and tumbled, put on plays, and traveled with trained **animals.** The *ioculatores*—players—were part of a tradition of singers, dancers, and clowns that stretched into Roman times.

There were essentially three categories of minstrels, although the dividing lines are fuzzy. Musicians sang and played many different instruments, and, although they were ranked below the noble troubadours, they were at the top of the general minstrelsy scale. Next were the jongleurs and mimes, who could do nearly anything else. They did literal tumbling, acrobatics such as headstands and handsprings. Some had puppet shows; others wore costumes and acted like animals. Some had trained animals; others had learned **magic** tricks while in the Middle East on **Crusade.** These performers could travel widely, since their acts did not depend on a common language. A third group, the smallest, was made up of dropout scholars. They traveled with minstrels and used their learning to entertain. They were satirists and may have performed essentially stand-up comedy. They may also have been the origin of court jesters.

There is not a large body of evidence for medieval jesters as a separate profession from minstrels. Some halls may have employed midgets or simpletons as fools, but, for the most part, minstrels did all the things that popular belief attributes to jesters. They sang and joked, and they traveled with their patrons. The official court jester with a floppy, belled hat belongs more to the Renaissance.

During Lent, all performances stopped. Some minstrels traveled to the minstrel schools in France, where they exchanged stories and songs. Royal minstrels received licenses to travel. Travel was very important for minstrels, since they had to provide not only the old favorite songs and acts but also new, fresh material. The minstrel school in Paris was the central place to learn new songs, but any foreign travel, even to another region of the same country, brought the minstrel into contact with different songs, stories, and tricks. Minstrels taught each other to play new musical instruments, and they traded the ideas for accompaniment and **dance** tunes.

Minstrels of all kinds used musical instruments to accompany themselves or others. We have some written records of their music, but music notation at that time did not record the rhythm, only the rising and falling pitches. It is hard to reconstruct what the **music** actually sounded like. The instruments were chiefly stringed: harp, lute, and various forerunners of the violin. The lute was plucked (often with a quill), while the vielle was usually played with a bow. The harp became the most common accompaniment instrument, and in the modern imagination it is virtually synonymous with minstrels.

Their music ranged from dance tunes, to bawdy **tavern** songs, to refined epics about the lives of the **saints.** They could also mock or parody important people to please the crowds; alternately, they could flatter great men to receive more pay. The music was not usually complex. It was restricted to refrains that could be more musical between sections that were recited as stories. The music also provided sound effects to go with the story.

Heroic stories, called *romans* or romances, were among the most popular. Some of the legends of Europe had their start in minstrels' songs; the singers developed new stories about well-known heroes, and in that way the legends grew. The three traditional topics were called "Matter of France," "Matter of Rome," and "Matter of Britain." Matter of France meant the deeds of Charlemagne and his knights, including the **"Song of Roland."** Matter of Rome meant stories about the ancient heroes, such as Aeneas. Matter of Britain meant the legends of **King Arthur** and his knights. It also included other early British legendary kings, such as King Lear of later Shakespearean fame.

A low form of romance was the popular ballad, a rhymed story in the common language. **Robin Hood**'s legends grew out of the ballads sung about him and other outlaws. Other stories, *contes*, told of lesser-known heroes, knights, kings, and saints. The typical 14th-century story of "Aucassin et Nicolete" told about two teenagers in love, and it alternated singing and telling. The heroes of these contes faced troubles, wandered into far-off lands, and found true love. Minstrels also sang *lais*, which were shorter lyrical songs. Fables, or *fabliaux*, told about human weaknesses and were often vulgar like some of the stories in the *Canterbury Tales*.

Their dress at first was not different from the **clothing** of those around them, but as their profession became more established, minstrels and troubadours developed fancier costumes that made them stand out. They wore brighter colors than other people, and typically they had short hair and no beards. The distinctive jester hat developed only at the close of the Middle Ages at first more as part of a **holiday** tradition than as part of everyday minstrelsy. This hat often had donkey ears, an exaggerated crest like a rooster's, or large droopy points. It was made in garish colors. During medieval times, though, minstrels wore hoods like anyone else, if perhaps louder and more attention grabbing.

Using stage names or chosen names descriptive of their skills, minstrels performed at **weddings** and many other feasts. At royal weddings, there were hundreds of them. They performed in castles and great halls, as well as at public marketplaces and fairs. Some minstrels were attached to the service of a lord, at least for a time, and traveled with him when he attended a feast. At the feast, they entertained in public and were paid by the host. Good minstrels were paid very well by the nobility, and some aristocrats who grew addicted to entertainment impoverished themselves.

The most skilled minstrels were permanent employees of great households. The records of Richard I of England show that he kept some favorite minstrels for many years. They accompanied him to war. Later medieval kings kept large groups of minstrels who could form a small orchestra and put on plays. By the time of England's Henry IV, the royal minstrels wore livery (a household uniform) and received a regular salary. They were required to play at five major feasts, and most were to be on standby at all other feasts. One reason for the growth of minstrel employment in great households is that the common minstrels gained a reputation for thieving and causing trouble. In the early Middle Ages, minstrels were always permitted to come into any castle or manor, which led to abuses by enemies posing as minstrels. Increasingly, minstrels needed licenses and letters of recommendation. At the close of the Middle Ages, the English king Edward IV set up a **guild** for minstrels to keep impostors out.

Although the best were paid well and could find stable homes in the service of lords, most minstrels walked long distances in all weather. Many were poorly paid for public performances, especially if they had low skills or a lack of connections. Some attached themselves to parties of **pilgrims** to provide entertainment in exchange for provisions and tips. Some performed at saints' festivals and fairs. Minstrels were vagrants by nature, and, by the close of the Middle Ages, cities had begun to license and regulate them. In some periods, minstrels needed written licenses to distinguish them from vagabonds. Most people worked in one place, but minstrels were always on the road. The disguise of a minstrel was popular for thieves and others who wished to be incognito.

The **church**'s attitude to minstrels was usually negative. Money given to minstrels could have been given to the poor, and minstrels encouraged mockery and levity. Individual bishops and abbots welcomed minstrels for their entertainment and news. A small minority of clergy studied the minstrels' ways, borrowing their tunes for the church. Saint Francis had trained as a minstrel and called his friars "*ioculatores Domini.*" The Franciscan tradition of writing Christmas carols for the common people recognized the power of cheerful popular music.

In Arras, a French-speaking city in Flanders, the jongleurs formed a confraternity to guard a special **relic** of the Virgin Mary. They said that Mary had appeared to two jongleurs and had given them a holy candle, the Sainte-Chandelle that could heal ergotism, a disease called Saint Anthony's fire in the Middle Ages. Ergotism is caused by a deadly fungus that grows on rye in wet weather, but they did not know this; to them, it was a mysterious affliction. The jongleurs called themselves the Carité de Notre Dame des Ardents, and they held three-day festivals like guilds and parishes to celebrate their saint's day. They put on an annual play to reenact the appearance of Mary to two jongleurs. In this town, although jongleurs everywhere still had reputations of loose morals, the jongleurs became a leading force in religion and even in some aspects of government. Every outbreak of ergotism pushed the Carité and its holy candle into prominence again.

Troubadours

The poetry of the troubadours grew in the distinctively different culture of southern France—the regions of Aquitaine and Provence. Their language, known as Occitan or Provençal, was a halfway point between French and Spanish. Among their cultural differences from the rest of Europe, women had always had more rights of inheritance and sometimes ruled as countesses or duchesses. This region had more contact with both **Muslim** and Christian Spain, and their poetry may have been influenced by Arabic poetry. Their nobles were knights in the full tradition of French chivalry, but they were not Norman or Frankish in descent and were less violent. In this culture, an alternative form of Christianity grew; it was based in the old Arian theology to which the Visigoths had first converted in Roman times. Known as Albigensian or Cathar doctrine, the religion was pacifist and vegetarian and gave **women** full rights while insisting on abstinence from sex.

During the 12th century, the poetry sung at the small courts of Provence, Toulouse, Aquitaine, and Poitou elevated women to a new, powerful status. The songs developed conventions that permitted them to express strong feelings and make sexual innuendos without explicitly targeting or shaming any particular women. Most songs were addressed to *midons*, "my lady," who might be the lord's wife or any other woman. The songs addressed her intimately and personally, as though she, listening, would know that the song was addressed to her, without her name being used. Some used plain language, but later troubadour poetry invented sophisticated conventions of allusion, euphemism, and metaphor.

Scholars know little about the troubadours and their musical customs, in spite of how widespread and influential they were. In 1209, the Pope proclaimed a Crusade against the heresy of the Albigensians (Cathars). There was a full war against the strongholds of Toulouse and Provence, led by England's Simon de Montfort. Many towns were burned and massacred, and a follow-up Inquisition led by Dominican monks questioned people about their beliefs. The kings of France used the opportunity of a weakened south to annex the territory. The culture of Occitania was destroyed, along with manuscript **records** of troubadours. Troubadours who survived the war fled to Spain and Italy. They helped spread their musical and poetical style, but, removed from its native culture, the original art form died out by around 1300.

Because of the Albigensian Crusade's destruction, scholars can only guess at how the troubadours composed and performed. Some written music and many poems still exist, along with some medieval-era short biographies of leading troubadours. There are some treatises that specify the rules of the poetic conventions, but none are about the music or its performance.

Nobody knows if the poets also composed their own music or how they sang the songs.

It seems likely that, in most cases, a nobleman wrote the poetry and worked with a trained musician to compose the music. It also seems likely that most of the music was performed by these trained musicians—the jongleurs. There were probably exceptions, and certainly there were jongleurs who also wrote poetry. But unlike in modern times, when a singer's lyricist is not considered the primary artist, the nobles who wrote the poetry were considered the true troubadours.

The first known troubadour was Duke William of Aquitaine, who died in 1126. He may have been imitating Arabic poetry, or he may have been exercising his own imagination. Beginning at his court, five more generations of Provençal troubadours spread out over the region. At least half were nobility, and as many as 15 were noble women. Other troubadours were trained jongleurs who wrote for their patrons and their ladies.

Bertran de Born and Arnaut Daniel were famous troubadours whose lives were typical of their time. Bertran de Born was a minor nobleman, the lord of Autafort (or, in French, Hautefort). He was a vassal of Eleanor, duchess of Aquitaine (granddaughter of the first troubadour) and queen of England, and her son Richard I of England. De Born's political fortunes went up and down as he sided against the king in a rebellion and then won back his favor (and his castle). He entered a Cistercian abbey in old age and died there around 1215. Arnaut Daniel, another prolific and famous troubadour, was probably a professional jongleur, and he seems to have been well educated. A *razo*, a troubadour's introductory legend, claims that Arnaut performed for Richard the Lionheart in a competition at his French castle.

Their songs were written down, though existing manuscripts do not date to the earliest times. Many songs were written long after they had been composed. Different versions of the same song can be found in different collections. The collections of the time were made for aristocrats and are hand lettered and painted. They gave the lyrics and melodies, but medieval methods for writing music did not include a good system for indicating rhythm, so modern musicians who want to sing these songs must guess at how they went.

Some troubadours wrote very sophisticated poetry in their songs. Arnaut Daniel's work was admired by Petrach, Dante, and, in modern times, Ezra Pound. He developed the form of the *trobar clus*, the poetry of allusion and symbol to cloak the direct meaning. Some of the forms of poetry he pioneered have survived into modern use, including the sestina (which uses the same six words to end lines in each stanza, but in a different order). Troubadours preferred complicated rhyme schemes, often repeating rhyming words and whole lines.

A lord and lady sit at ease in their hall and listen to a troubadour. The lady holds a lapdog and the hall interior appears refined and luxurious. The troubadour, as befits his higher standing among musicians, wears neat, fine clothing and good shoes. He plays a viol to accompany his song's poetic lyrics. This painting probably depicts the court of King Alfonso X of Castile, who cowrote a book of troubadour songs. (Gianni Dagli Orti/Corbis)

As the troubadour style spread north into French dialects, the word *troubadour* shifted to *trouvère*. The earliest identified trouvère is Chrétien de Troyes, who also wrote epic poems. King Richard I (the Lionheart) also wrote courtly trouvère songs. As suggested in the legend of Arnaut Daniel's royal performance, the trouvères had competitions with prizes in the 13th century in northern France. The composer could perform his song or ask someone else to sing for him.

By the 14th century, the style spread to Germany, where the composers and performers were known as minnesingers. The ideal of courtly love became a fixed part of Northern Europe's culture, and it continued to influence songs, poetry, and popular customs long past the close of the Middle Ages.

The classic troubadour song described an ideal of unfulfilled love. The poet has fallen in love with a noble lady whose beauty was perfect and ideal and whose mind was refined and wise. The poet is not able to tell the lady of his love, but it may be seen in sighs and tears. He suffers, and the truth of his love is in the depth of his sufferings. His rivals jealously criticize him to the lady, and he trusts in her noble judgment to disbelieve their lies. He hopes she will grant benevolence and mercy on his suffering and give her love to him.

In a culture of arranged marriages, these ideas were very new. The ideal of courtly love elevated emotion and denigrated marriage, which was often about property and family alliances. Although arranged marriages were often happy, they could also involve great disparity in age or temperament. Divorce was unknown, although some nobility successfully divorced by petitioning the Pope to dissolve the marriage on the grounds that their spouse was a cousin. (Eleanor of Aquitaine divorced the king of France this way and remarried the king of England.)

The noble ladies who talked about courtly love rejected love within a marriage because the relationship had been forced on them. It was not possible, they said, to love without free choice. Therefore the only valid love was love for someone other than one's spouse. Troubadour songs explicitly celebrated adulterous love, although many songs praised this love only as an ideal, rather than as a sexual relationship. The lady of the songs was usually a noble and powerful lady, and real adultery with her could be very dangerous. It is impossible to know how much the songs explored fantasies, rather than telling about actual Provençal social reality.

Troubadour music was very popular with ladies. It permitted them to discuss and express emotion that did not previously have a place in official culture. The poems of female troubadours tended to be more personal, less ideal, and more deeply emotional than the conventional male troubadour songs. They expressed hurt feelings, joy, longing, and doubt. After the troubadour songs opened up the world of emotional expression in literature, European poetry never went back to the early medieval fare of epics. Postmedieval stories and songs were more likely to celebrate personal lives and feelings long after the troubadour style had faded.

See also: Animals, Fairs, Feasts, Music, Women.

Further Reading

Akehurst, F.R.P., and Judith M. Davis. *A Handbook of the Troubadours.* Los Angeles: University of California Press, 1995.

Aubrey, Elizabeth. *The Music of the Troubadours.* Bloomington: Indiana University Press, 1996.

Bogin, Meg. *The Women Troubadours.* New York: W.W. Norton, 1980.

Chambers, E.K. *The Mediaeval Stage.* 2 vols. London: Oxford University Press, 1903.

Montagu, Jeremy. *The World of Medieval and Renaissance Musical Instruments.* Woodstock, NY: Overlook Press, 1980.

Norris, Herbert. *Medieval Costume and Fashion.* Mineola, NY: Dover Publications, 1999.

Seay, Albert. *Music in the Medieval World.* Englewood Cliffs, NJ: Prentice Hall, 1975.

Symes, Carol. *A Common Stage: Theater and Public Life in Medieval Arras.* Ithaca, NY: Cornell University Press, 2007.

Van der Werf, Hendrik. *The Chansons of the Troubadours and Trouvères.* Utrecht: Oosthoek, 1972.

Monasteries

The Middle Ages could be defined as the "Age of the Monastery." The presence and influence of monasteries shaped Europe tremendously. The medieval idea of holiness consisted of withdrawing from the world and living a life of self-denial. The difficulty was that monasteries had to make compromises when they began to own property and administer daily living for many people. Monasteries often became more similar to the secular world in their daily life and wealth. The Middle Ages saw a repeated pattern of reform and corruption. A new movement would arise, calling men or **women** to the monastic life, and then over time it would become part of the establishment, only to find itself the target of the next reform movement's criticism.

Monks all took a vow of poverty, but their institutions received many donations of land and other goods. By the close of the Middle Ages, about half of England's land was owned by some portion of the **church,** often by monasteries. Abbots and priors received rent from peasants and town citizens, in addition to the income the monastery derived from selling extra produce like wine or wool. Although the individuals owned none of it, the monks in well-established houses lived in luxury. The popular **Robin Hood** tales and other medieval stories poke fun at fat abbots and worldly priors. When the reputation of monasteries fell too low, a new reform movement would launch an order with a fresh dedication to poverty.

Monasteries operated outside the church hierarchy; monastic orders were under the direct oversight of the Pope, rather than the local bishop. The head of a monastery was an abbot, and his assistant was the prior. When a monastic order created "daughter houses," they were often called priories and were ruled only by a prior, rather than by another abbot. The priories remained under the oversight of the abbot at the original monastery. Each monastery had lower officials who oversaw supplies, the scriptorium, or some other aspect of monastic life. When a monk entered as a novice, he could move up through a regular chain of promotion to become a prior or an abbot.

Monastic Orders

The idea of monastic living came from the deserts of Egypt and Syria, where premedieval hermits lived ascetic lives. Benedict of Nursia, a sixth-century monk in Italy, wrote his guide for monastic living at Monte Cassino. The Rule of Saint Benedict became an absolute monastic law during Carolingian times, including the rigid application of diet and dress appropriate to the mild Italian climate. Further reforms made Benedictine monks recite such an elaborate liturgy every day that they no longer had time for the manual labor Saint Benedict had outlined.

The medieval monastic orders varied in how they solved the problems of rigorous asceticism versus good health and the need for self-supporting work versus the demands of the liturgy. Over time, the Benedictines became less ascetic and allowed more meat and other luxury **foods,** while the Carthusians followed the strictest interpretation of the rule. Carthusian monks lived in unheated cells even in cold climates, and they never ate meat at all. The Rule of Saint Augustine was even more relaxed; Augustinian canons ate a varied diet and enjoyed more comforts and freedom. The Cistercians, who were Benedictine monks under the reformed rules of the monastery at Citeaux, followed an austere diet but did not occupy themselves with prayers and singing all day. Cistercians focused on manual labor; their monasteries became centers of agricultural and industrial innovation.

Monastic orders generally solved the problem of balancing labor and prayer with two levels of monastic profession. Choir monks had their heads shaved in a tonsure, a circle of **hair** around a bald top. They wore the cowled robe of their order and went barefoot or in sandals. They did not work but either studied or sang the hours. Choir monks were educated; they could read and write Latin. In the strictest orders, like the Carthusians, the choir monks lived in isolation so that they could pray and contemplate. The same monastery had a larger group of lay brothers; they did not wear tonsures or cowled robes but had taken monastic vows. The lay brothers could be illiterate, but they had to be good workers. Lay brothers plowed, milked the sheep and cows, butchered pigs and smoked bacon for sale to the community, or even smelted **iron** or fulled **cloth.** Monasteries with large lay communities usually had more acreage and were self-supporting. They grew most of their own food and kept up a cash product like wine, wool, or cheese.

Each order had begun with a movement for reform when the previously dominant order's compromises began to seem too worldly. The Benedictine monasteries were the original movement in Europe, and they spread through the Christian world until there were Benedictine monasteries in every country, even in newly Christian Sweden. The abbey at Cluny, France, was the model for the best practices of the Benedictines; their closest imitators were often called Cluniacs. Benedictine monks wore black robes and plain **shoes.**

The Augustinian Canons were created in order to bring non-monastic clergy into line with Benedictine rules. The Rule of Augustine was less ascetic and strict, since those who lived by it had not chosen to become full monks. Canons were supposed to be serving in the world, not cloistered in a monastery. Although their rule was not as strict as Benedict's, the imposition of a uniform rule on clergy who were not monks was a reform in itself.

The Cistercian Order began in 1098 when a group of Benedictine monks set out to make a more primitive, more rigid life. A charismatic young monk named Bernard, later Saint Bernard, joined them. The primitive, fanatical character of their monastery attracted many who felt the religious life ought to be stringent in its devotion. By 1152, there were over 300 monasteries modeled after Bernard's abbey at Clairvaux. They fully developed the distinction between choir monks and lay brothers, since such stringent devotion could only be practiced by a few. The choir monks wore undyed wool, so they were sometimes called White Monks, although their everyday robes were natural gray. They wore sandals, as Benedict had originally directed, rather than shoes.

The Carthusian monks began as a small monastery in the foothills of the Alps in 1109. They lived as hermits, praying and contemplating in individual cells with food passed through a window. The choir monks only saw each other for church services; the work was done by lay brothers. The only work the choir monks did was copying and mending books. Although Carthusians officially wore white robes, in the Middle Ages they were known for wearing coarse, dirty clothes and hair shirts. This strenuous life of devotion attracted some, and the Carthusian Order also grew, though not as rapidly as the others. Their monasteries were called charter-houses in English.

Although the Benedictine Order had taken in women as nuns, the Cistercian monks resisted, considering women a sinful distraction. Some convents grew up individually, including the French Fontevrault, where Eleanor of Aquitaine died, or Sempringham in England, which became a model for other English convents. In the early 1200s, many well-to-do young women in France and Germany, and particularly in Flanders, were drawn to a life of poverty. They did not join existing convents, but they lived together, refusing to own anything. They were known as Beguines. In 1233, Pope Gregory IX took them under his direct protection.

The next wave of monastic reformers criticized the way other monks withdrew from the world, leaving the poor ignorant and helpless. The Mendicant Orders, the friars, began as wandering preachers, rather than as cloistered monks. Saint Francis of Assisi was the first; he was a wealthy young man who had a dream that compelled him to seek a religious life. He gave up his possessions and wandered, barefoot in a rough brown robe, preaching. By 1209, companions had joined him, dressing like him in natural brown or gray robes and sandals, and an order began. The Franciscan friars were the last official order commissioned by the Pope, who felt there were too many orders springing up. The rule of their order forbade them to own possessions, especially land, so they had to beg. By the time of Francis's death in 1226, Franciscans had carried his vision as far as Spain, Hungary, and England. But after his death, the order, now ruled from Paris, changed

In the foreground, Carthusian monks are fishing with lines and nets. Behind them, the monastery's chapel towers over the red roofs of the lesser buildings. Monasteries were often built in a square with a wall to contain the monks and keep out the world's distractions. In an age of great uncertainty, the monastic life offered more peace and security. (Ann Ronan Pictures/StockphotoPro)

its rule and permitted only educated men to join. In England, Franciscans were called Greyfriars.

Dominican friars began as an answer to the simple poverty of the Cathar preachers. Saint Dominic, a Spaniard, began to walk about the Cathar strongholds of southern France in 1206. His followers also spread throughout Europe; they adopted the Rule of Augustine, but with a lifestyle of wandering preaching. Like the Franciscan friars, as time passed, the Dominicans settled into priory houses and became establishment monks, often attached to **universities.** Their official robe style was white, with a black-cowled mantle, so that in England they were called Blackfriars. Thomas Aquinas, the most famous theologian of the Middle Ages, was a Dominican friar.

Carmelite friars were a small order of hermits on Mount Carmel, near Haifa, in Israel. When they were driven out by the **Muslims,** they spread across Europe, founding Carmelite houses. Between 1238 and 1300, they became urban friars, rather than hermits, scattered across Europe; the English called them Whitefriars. Another small order, the Augustinian friars, also began as hermits around 1223 and also became friars at universities. The life of a hermit seems to have been initially popular but hard to sustain over decades.

Life in the Cloister

The ideal of the monk was to withdraw from the world and use a simple communal life to master the temptations and passions of the flesh. The buildings in which the monks lived were designed to support this goal. They were self-contained towns that needed little from the outside world, but all buildings were connected. A typical monastic layout had two large communal areas, the chapel and the cloister, a square walk that opened onto a lawn. The word *cloister* came from Latin *claustrum,* "an enclosure." The cloister itself was an enclosure, but the word *cloister* also came to stand for the enclosed way of life and the entire monastic compound.

The chapel was the heart of the monastery. All the monks, both choir monks and lay brothers, had a rigorous schedule of Mass and prayers to attend. They had to wake up in the night and sing Matins; Benedictine monks and lay brothers went back to sleep until dawn, but Carthusian choir monks stayed awake until the next service. Choir monks spent most of their days and nights going into the chapel to sing the hours, while lay brothers had a less demanding schedule but still attended two or three times a day. In the Benedictine ideal, the monks were to offer up continual prayer for the secular world that was busy doing other things. The strictest Cistercians sang or recited the entire Psalms (150 songs) every day.

The cloister, the square walkway that led to other buildings, enclosed a grass lawn, the garth. Monks were supposed to contemplate nature and appreciate beauty, so the cloister lawns were carefully tended. Most had green grass and some trees and bushes. Monastic cloisters were especially fond of rose bushes. The monks were permitted to walk and sit in the open area when they were not at work.

The ideal of the monastic life was to work and live in silence. Monks were not permitted conversation in some parts of the compound, while in others it was only discouraged. In the refectory (the dining hall), conversation was forbidden. Monks developed hand signals for asking to have food brought by the lay brothers who served. They listened to the Bible being read while they ate and then left in silence. Elderly monks were permitted to talk in the infirmary, but they were discouraged from telling amusing stories.

There was always a lavatory room or stand next to the refectory. The monks had to wash their hands before eating, partly as a symbolic gesture. Monasteries were generally cleaner places than many other medieval communities. They had laundry facilities and planned for weekly baths. They were not only cleaner, but they were also more interested in health care. As a preventative measure, monks routinely had blood let. Several times a year, on a schedule, they went into the infirmary or lavatory and a barber or another monk cut a vein to drain their blood into a basin. Although this seems barbaric to modern eyes, it was considered excellent health care in its time. Monks who were weak from bloodletting could spend a night in the infirmary.

Depending on the plan of the order, monks slept in a communal dormitory or had individual cells. In either case, their bed furniture was restricted to a bed, a shelf, and a hook. They were expected to keep a certain few tools about them: a needle to mend their clothes and a knife to cut food or mend pens. Their clothes had to be embroidered with their names, since robes were laundered together, but they were expected to launder some small articles themselves (they could hang them to dry in the cloister). Although they were required to go barefoot on some occasions, they owned shoes and boots, and the order usually issued them a pair of new boots every year, which they greased to keep waterproof. They also kept combs, razors, soap, and towels. Monks in private cells sometimes had running **water** with a washing stand. There were few other possessions monks were allowed to have. However, establishments that were more lax turned a blind eye to some monks and nuns who kept pets. Convents seem to have been frequently filled with lap dogs and tame birds. Some visiting abbots had to impose rules against bringing **animals** into chapel.

Latrines were located near the dormitory; they were called the reredorter. They were planned for large-scale use; the monks did not have private toilets but used a room full of stalls with pit toilets. For the Middle Ages, the latrines were very up-to-date and sanitary. In many cases, water carried the waste out of the grounds; either a cistern flushed the latrine pit or a stream continually flowed through it.

According to the Benedictine Rule, all but a few of the buildings in the cloister compound were unheated. The chapel, the dormitories, the workrooms, and the refectory had no provisions for fire at all. The kitchen, of course, had its cooking fires. The infirmary was heated, and one other building was heated on purpose. It was called the calefactory, the warming house.

The chapter house was another communal building, and it was used for all meetings. Meetings began by reading out loud a chapter from the order's rule, which gave the room its name. The chapter house could be used for other meetings and even for conversation. The chapter house had a parlor for receiving outside visitors or indulging in conversations, and monks often received their daily work assignments and **tools** in the parlor. The monastic **library** was also connected to the chapter house. Each year, at the beginning of Lent, every monk received a **book** from the library that would be his to keep for a year, to read and meditate on. Monks read books like Augustine's *Confessions,* collections of letters by early church fathers, commentaries on the Bible, lives of the **saints,** and sermons by contemporary abbots and bishops.

Monks had visits from family several times a year. There were guest-houses in these outer zones, near the gate, so family members could stay

In the illumination within a large letter *O*, an abbot leads his monastic community in prayer. The tonsured choir monks sit on one side, but on the other side, novices or guests with full heads of hair appear to be included. One monk stands ready to read a Bible passage in Latin. (The British Library/ StockphotoPro)

a few nights after their journey. **Pilgrims,** too, stayed at monastic guest-houses. Monasteries on main **roads** found their resources taxed by too many guests, and they had to restrict their hospitality. Less stringent monasteries sometimes rented space to doctors and shops for pilgrims. Some outside tradesmen came and went, too; professional barbers and tailors made visits to monasteries on a regular schedule.

The cloister compound contained many practical work and farm buildings. Even in a monastery without a large staff of lay brothers, the monks had to do some manual work to keep their community fed and clothed. Most monasteries kept **bees** so they could make their own candles, and many had fishponds. Large monasteries that did full-scale farming had the complete set of barns, butchering sheds, smoking sheds, dairies, and poultry yards. Some had **mills,** and Cistercian lay brothers could even run iron foundries or weaving and fulling sheds.

Men and women who were joining the monastery or convent were novices. They lived apart from the rest of the monks, and they were under special care. Their lives were usually not as rigorous; they were permitted more food and **clothing.** Each person had to live for a year as a novice to be sure the life of the cloister was really his or her permanent choice. When the time came to make a full profession as a monk, there was a reception ceremony with the whole community present. The newly professing monk made a will giving away all his possessions, and his head was shaved in a tonsure. During a Mass, he took the vows of poverty, chastity, and obedience. In some orders, the new monk spent three days in seclusion before joining the community.

The youngest residents of a monastery were the oblates. Until the Fourth Lateran Council of 1215 outlawed the practice, parents could give a young child to a monastery as a sacrifice to God. The child was usually around the age of beginning school or work training—between 7 and 10. Oblates were raised and taught at the monastery, and when they were of age, they took full vows. Some of the most famous medieval saints were oblates given to the cloister when they were very young; the monastery was the only life they knew.

Convents often found themselves caring for elderly ladies who either joined as nuns in their last years or just came to stay at the convent as guests. Monasteries, too, ended up providing nursing care for more than just their own aging monks. They kept infirmaries, but individuals also could rent a room or come to stay at the guest quarters. Monasteries also became an early sort of boarding **school;** they took in younger children of both poor and wealthy families and educated them. Many of these children took vows, renewed them when they were older, and lived out their lives in the monastery or convent. Not all were oblates; some were only there for temporary education.

Both monasteries and convents dealt with their share of community problems. There were conflicts and fights, and even some cases of violent mental illness that caused a brother to be locked up. The requirement of chastity caused continual problems for brothers and sisters who fell into temptation. Nuns were kept under great restraint and isolation; even when a convent was built next to a monastery and was under its protection, the sisters were never allowed into the monastery for any reason. Monks were supposed to keep themselves underfed and engage in cold baths to suppress sexual stimulation; they were also to avoid watching animals mate. Hired **servants** who had wives were supposed to live outside the precincts so that even their wives could not come near the brothers. Monks who oversaw novices were supposed to be careful neither to leave them alone nor to be alone with them without a third person as witness. Even with all these rules and safeguards, there were always reports of nuns becoming pregnant and sub-priors having affairs with servants' wives.

One of the monastic vows was the vow of stability, a promise not to leave the cloister without permission. Monks and nuns who became unhappy did sometimes run away. Some orders did not accept them back; a runaway Carthusian monk was unfit to be a Carthusian. Other orders accepted them back if they showed remorse. The rigors of monastic life—waking up at night for Matins, avoiding speech, always obeying the prior, seeing women and children so seldom, eating the bare minimum—were not easy to keep up over a lifetime. But compared to the rigors of secular medieval life, the monastic life was not as difficult as it appears to modern eyes. Many people never had enough to eat and did repetitive, dull work. The monastery offered friendship, health care, and security for the present life with the sure promise of heaven in the next life.

See also: Books, Church, Hospitals, Latrines and Garbage, Music, Water.

Further Reading

Brooke, Christopher. *The Age of the Cloister: The Story of Monastic Life in the Middle Ages.* Mahwah, NJ: Hidden Spring Books, 2003.

Carmody, Maurice. *The Franciscan Story: St. Francis and His Influence since the Thirteenth Century.* London: Athena Press, 2008.

Kerr, Julie. *Life in the Medieval Cloister.* New York: Continuum Press, 2009.

Knowles, David. *The Monastic Order in England.* Cambridge: Cambridge University Press, 2004.

Lawrence, C.H. *Medieval Monasticism: Forms of Religious Life in Western Europe in the Middle Ages.* New York: Longman, 2000.

Milus, Ludo J.R. *Angelic Monks and Earthly Men.* Woodridge, UK: Boydell Press, 1999.

Venarde, Bruce L. *Women's Monasticism and Medieval Society: Nunneries in France and England, 890–1215.* Ithaca, NY: Cornell University Press, 1999.

Monsters

Medieval readers appear to have been highly naive and credible in their willingness to believe in both monsters and monstrous humans in other parts of the world. The standard Latin bestiary **books** included mythical animals with real **animals,** and there was no way for medieval Europeans to distinguish them. The Latin literature of the fantastic included a supposed letter Alexander the Great wrote to Aristotle to tell him about the amazing things he had seen in India and the *Liber Monstrorum,* a book about monsters. In Alexander's letter, real elephants and hippopotamuses were mixed in with fantastical poisonous snakes, men clothed in tiger skins, and talking trees.

The mythology of monsters combined the imaginative lore of the Greeks and Romans, which seemed unquestionably true to many in the Middle Ages, with the traditional monster lore of Northern Europe. Where the two overlapped, it seemed certain that the monsters truly existed. Dragons were known all over the world, as were elephants, and since few had seen elephants, the lack of actual dragon sightings meant nothing. Latin stories and Norse stories both talked about dragons, so they must be real.

Most monsters were considered evil. They were outside of God's household of faith, and some considered them to be the offspring of Cain, Adam's murderous son, or of Ham, Noah's mocking son. These men preserved the knowledge of sorcery, according to the legend, and the monsters were their offspring and were evil to the core. One notable exception was Saint Christopher, a dog-headed man who was martyred for his Christian faith. Some monsters were neutral, and some even symbolized tenets of the Christian faith. The phoenix symbolized resurrection.

Other monsters may not have been considered real even to medieval readers. Some—especially hybrids of known animals—were merely artistic creations. The field of **heraldry** created a wide range of creatures that may or may not have been considered real. Some were based on poorly reported distant animals, such as the transformation of the real jackal into the fictional "thos," a maned wolf with cloven hoofs. Some were purely artistic, such as winged stags. Most existed in between these clear categories, such that some people may have known they were fictitious, while others believed in their existence.

The dragon is the most outstanding case of a monster that nobody had ever seen but that everyone believed was real. The dragon, in every place and time, has been a large winged lizard, usually with the ability to breathe fire. There was no specific region assigned to dragons; they were thought of as migratory, seeking out treasure to hoard or victims to eat. Some dragons were drawn as small as a wolf, no more than predators of sheep, while others were drawn huge, with wide wings and long tails. Dragons were generally considered to be evil and destructive, but they were also noble, perhaps due to their association with **gold** or perhaps because a Roman legion used a dragon as its emblem. **King Arthur** also was believed to have used a dragon as his emblem after his father saw a vision of a starry dragon.

In medieval dragon stories, **saints** and bishops were often able to command dragons. The most famous was Saint George, who first appeared in a 13th-century Latin book of saints' lives; the story originated in the Byzantine Empire. Saint George was a Roman Christian who came to a town in Libya where a dragon was terrorizing the town. Having fed the dragon all their sheep, they were feeding him their children, and that day the king's daughter had been sent to die. Saint George wounded the dragon, and he used the princess's girdle to put it on a leash. They led it back to the town, where the townsfolk all became Christians in exchange for the dragon's public execution. There were other stories of dragons that flew into a region and terrorized everyone until a holy man commanded them to go away or submit to death.

There were two small but terrifying monster reptiles. The basilisk was eventually renamed the cockatrice. It was probably at first a true report of a large crowned lizard in Asia, but, in time, medieval artists and writers gave it a rooster's head. It was said to be exceptionally poisonous; it could kill not only with its bite, but also with its touch, the sound of its voice, its smell, and a glance of its eyes. Medieval bestiaries recommended reflecting its look back with a mirror so it would kill itself. It was also good to keep a weasel to fight with it or a rooster to frighten it by crowing. The

Medieval artists were never quite sure what some mythical beasts looked like. The dragon shown this French commentary on the apocalypse (the end of the world) does not have wings or legs. It appears to be more like a giant snake than like a lizard. The four-footed beast behind it is called the behemoth, an animal mentioned in the book of Job, but without any real description beyond its great size and strength. A world that could contain these amazing beasts could easily have giant frogs or any other kind of monster an artist could imagine. (Paul Lacroix, *Science and Literature in the Middle Ages*, 1878)

salamander, which we know today as a small, harmless lizard, was considered a large, poisonous lizard that lived inside volcanoes.

Any number of reptilian monsters were thought to live in the sea. The Norwegian sea monster was called the kraken; they believed it was large enough to be mistaken for an island. Reports circulated that other monsters had washed up on beaches or had been sighted in lakes. Sailors believed sea monsters lived in the distant oceans. Other sea monsters were less dangerous and had specific names. They were animals, but in fish form. The marine lion was, literally, a **fish** thought to be shaped like a lion. There was a marine sow, a sea dog, and even a monk fish, a fish with a monk's head and tonsure. The ocean was a mysterious, large place, and it was full of strange things; anything could be out there.

The phoenix was a large bird monster borrowed from classical mythology. It looked like an eagle, but it was purple, the most royal color. Classical mythology reported that the bird lived on a nest of spices (surely the most expensive kind of bed). Every 500 years, it set its bed on fire, died in the fire, and was reborn as a small maggot that grew into a new phoenix. Bestiaries explained that God created the phoenix as a symbol of the resurrection of Jesus.

Some monsters were hybrids of known creatures. Medieval books told about mermaids and mermen who were fish on the lower half and human-like on top. They were considered dangerous and deceptive, and humans were told to avoid them, although they were beautiful to see and hear. Mermaids were popular devices on shields. There was also the centaur, brought from Greek stories. It had a human head and arms and the body of a horse or bull. The satyr, believed to live in Ethiopia, had the upper half of a man and the lower half of a goat. The most elaborate hybrid was the griffin. Bestiaries stated that griffins lived in Bactria, between the Himalayan Mountains and the plateau of Central Asia. The griffin had the lower body of a lion and an eagle's upper body and head, with blue or white wings and red eyes. Griffins were considered evil, but they were also interesting and noble and appeared on many heraldic crests.

The unicorn was the king of monsters and appeared in the most coats of arms, paintings, and tapestries. There was no doubt as to the unicorn's existence in reality. The Latin Bible used a word like *unicorn* to translate a Hebrew word now interpreted as "wild ox." The medieval Bible, then, appeared to refer to unicorns. This made them seem more real because the Bible talked of other animals of the Near East that were not seen in Europe. If lions were real, why not unicorns? Bible manuscripts sometimes had illustrations with unicorns, and sometimes unicorns were present in scenes of Noah's ark. All travelers in India reported seeing unicorns, and if they did not, artists drew unicorns anyway, since everyone knew unicorns lived in India. When Marco Polo, traveling in Asia, saw a rhinoceros, he was certain he had finally seen a unicorn. Rather than doubting the unicorn's existence, he reported that the artists had surely gotten it all wrong; this was no beautiful beast, but rather a boar-like creature that lived in mire.

Some early unicorn pictures show an animal the size of a goat, with cloven hoofs. Some gave him a low-slung body more like a lion's. Some pictures showed unicorns with spots like a leopard or a fawn, and others with a curved horn. By the late Middle Ages, artists had settled into depicting the unicorn as a white **horse**, the size of a small horse, with a goat's beard and the long, straight spiraled horn of a narwhal. Its tail often was still more like a dog's than a horse's, with a brushy plume.

Some medieval writers described the unicorn as the fiercest beast in the world. Pictures showed it attacking elephants, lions, and armed hunters. During the unicorn's mating season, it was the fiercest of all and could attack anyone with success. In hunting pictures, the unicorn gored dogs and horses. The lore of *Physiologus,* an early bestiary, assured Europe that a unicorn could only be captured by a trick. It could not resist the purity of a young girl, and it would be entranced and come to her. It would lay its head in her lap or allow her to pet it. Then, said *Physiologus,* she could lead the unicorn to the king. But in depictions of unicorns in books, **tapestry,** and **sculpture,** hunters usually kill the unicorn with spears while it is distracted by the girl.

The bestiaries also stated that the unicorn had the ability to purify poisoned water by dipping its horn. Pictures showed animals coming to drink at a stream and waiting until the unicorn has done its work. Sometimes, poisonous animals are shown running away. For this reason, there was a

Early unicorns were much less horse-like than the modern depiction of a unicorn. Artists knew that they had one horn, but apart from that, some unicorns looked more like goats, lions, or donkeys.
The white horse of later unicorn mythology began to show up only at the end of the Middle Ages, usually on tapestries. (Richard Huber, *Treasury of Fantastic and Mythological Creatures,* 1981)

market in unicorn horns, which were most often narwhal horns but were sometimes carved from an elephant's tusk. They were used to purify food or drink that could have been poisoned.

The unicorn's meaning increased with pictures that interpreted it as symbolic of Christ or love. Christ was pierced on the cross as the unicorn was pierced by hunters. The analogy could not be extended any more than that, but another analogy with Christ presented itself: as the unicorn allowed itself to be tamed by a young woman, so Christ's divine nature allowed itself to become a baby in Mary's womb. In some 15th-century depictions, the unicorn could symbolize a man's love, which permits a young woman to tame it and slip a collar on it. When the unicorn is shown tamed, in a collar or within an enclosure, love is more likely the meaning than Christ. The unicorn could also symbolize the virtue of chastity, since it was tamed by young maidens and could purify **water.** In some illustrations, a chariot drawn by a unicorn suggests that the woman riding in the chariot is particularly chaste. In some pictures, a lion and a unicorn together symbolized a marriage: the union of the brave and the chaste.

See also: Animals, Books, Heraldry, Tapestry.

Further Reading

Dennys, Rodney. *The Heraldic Imagination.* New York: Clarkson N. Potter, 1975.

Freeman, Margaret B. *The Unicorn Tapestries.* New York: Metropolitan Museum of Art, 1983.

Lavers, Chris. *The Natural History of Unicorns.* New York: William Morrow, 2009.

Orchard, Andy. *Pride and Prodigies: Studies in the Monsters of the Beowulf-Manuscript.* Toronto: University of Toronto Press, 1995.

Resl, Brigitte, ed. *A Cultural History of Animals in the Medieval Age.* New York: Berg, 2007.

Rose, Carol. *Giants, Monsters, and Dragons: An Encyclopedia of Folkore, Legend, and Myth.* New York: Norton, 2000.

Music

Music, for most of the Middle Ages, was either a village folk song or part of the grand liturgy of a cathedral. Officially, music belonged to the **church** and the **university.** Music theory was a part of any serious university education and had been since classical times. It was a branch of mathematics, since the ratios between sounds could be expressed as **numbers.** It was also theology. God was defined as the purest and highest beauty, the highest possible perfection. When music is pure and perfect, it depicts God's perfection for man's ears. Medieval theorists favored harmonies with the most consonance, such as octaves or fifths. Pure unison singing sounded more perfect to them. Out of a religious and theoretical framework, choral and instrumental music moved to greater complexity and then out of the church.

Plainchant

The music of the Latin Mass began as a simple unison form known as plainchant. Some chants were sung with a lead singer, called a cantor, singing a line and the choir responding. Although the music as written shows no embellishment, it is possible that individual soloists provided their own grace notes and variations. There was no set rhythm or timing; these matters were up to individual singers. The choir and soloists sang the prayers and Bible passages required for the day and hour.

Because the Benedictine liturgy was prescriptive and unchanging, variety came in changing the music to which the words were set. A "Magnificat" had to use the same words, but it could alter the tune or arrangement; it could repeat a phrase with musical variations. With each century, the liturgical music became more elaborate, and it began to take over the service. Some liturgical music was composed for special occasions, such as Easter or the nativity. These pieces created musical **drama** out of the story, with different singers and the choir responding to each other to create a play. Sometimes it was acted, with choirboys or monks walking into the sanctuary as angels or shepherds.

The modern major scale was only one of the possibilities in medieval music. The modern pattern of whole steps and half steps had been developed mathematically, but a melody could be based on any of the eight modes. Each one was a different arrangement of the whole and half steps. The choir director knew, from his training, which mode was in use for a particular hymn. The need to train choirboys began the process toward standardization and a written form for music.

Guido d'Arezzo, an 11th-century Benedictine monk, is given traditional credit for standardizing the way the scale was named. He noticed that the mode we now call the scale formed the rising tones of a well-known hymn to Saint John. The first syllable of each phrase was the next note of the scale: "*Ut queant laxis / Resonare fibris / Mire gestorum / Famuli tuorum / Solve polluti / Labii reatum / Sancte Iohannes.*" Based on the rising phrases of this hymn, the tones of the scale were named: *ut, re, mi, fa, sol, la, si.* (*Si* was formed by the initials of Sanctus Iohannes.) Later, *do* substituted for *ut*, perhaps for ease of pronunciation. In English, the last note became *ti*, but on the European continent, it is still *si*.

Polyphony

By the 13th century, polyphony was the focus of professional musicians. Polyphony, the use of more than one tone at the same time, presented a number of challenges that required several centuries to work out experimentally. First, how could they use more than one tone without dissonance? Dissonance, which is acceptable in modern music, was not acceptable to medieval ears. With more tones and a more complicated movement of voices, the challenge became harder. Rules of harmony were developed, but they were always being pushed.

Another problem posed by polyphony was that performers had to know how long to sustain their notes in relation to each other. If the harmonies were to be sung with a strict one-to-one note movement, it was not difficult, but if one voice was to sing multiple notes while another sang fewer, then the rhythm and duration mattered greatly. Written music had not developed a good way of showing this.

Moving into the 13th century, musical treatises began to discuss harmonies for three and four voices. At first, harmonization was kept simple by restricting one of these new voices to a repeated note, purely as accompaniment, not as a competing tune. The development of the motet pushed harmony to the next level. As the form developed in medieval church music, it used three voices, with movement in at least two of them.

The new innovations were not welcomed by theorists, and polyphonic music began to seem a distraction to the Mass. The Cistercians and Dominicans forbade the use of polyphony in services around 1250. In 1324, Pope John XXII forbade motets and other complex polyphony, restricting liturgical music to an older, simpler technique.

Secular Music

For most of the Middle Ages, the secular music of **troubadours** and **minstrels** seems to have been melody alone, without harmony. Innovation occurred first in church music, where society's energies were focused. When a trend was no longer current in the church, it came more into secular use, so when the church banned complex polyphony, it came into secular music. Manuscripts from the late 13th century document motets—songs for two or three voices. The harmony techniques are clearly those of church music, but the songs are of love.

Secular music focused on forms for **dancing.** In France, there were the rondeau, the lai (or virelai), the ballade, and the chace. The types of songs were mostly determined by the poetic style of the lyrics, as they had begun with the troubadours of Provence. The chace was a canon, or what we call a round in English, in which the second voice sang the same melody as the first voice after waiting to come in. These songs had complex patterns of repeated melodies and rhythms to accompany formal dances. They could be witty; some imitated birdcalls.

The earliest Italian songs were the madrigal (simpler in harmony than the Renaissance madrigal), the caccia, and the ballata. The caccia was a canon, or round, using two voices plus a tenor acting as a bass line. The ballata was similar to the French virelai and may have begun as a dance. The best-developed examples of ballata come from the end of the 14th century; they are for two and three voices and use patterns of refrain and stanza.

Musical Notation

The earliest musical staff had four lines and used both lines and spaces. Some later staffs had six lines. Notes were squares, and some systems used color to show duration. Other systems used color to indicate half tones and had no notation of how long to sustain a note. Because notes covered a range greater than four, five, or six lines could show, the meaning of a line or space sometimes shifted.

Medieval clef signs were not fixed, as the modern soprano and bass clefs are fixed. A set of marks around a line defined the line's meaning, and all spaces and lines were read relative to it as steps up or down. This definition might change in the middle of a line of music if the composer needed the range to be lower or higher. The gradual evolution of conventions for standard clefs led first to the system of C clefs that moved up and down, showing where C was, and then to the G and F clefs that are still in modern use.

The problem of duration—of how to note the rhythm and timing of a tone—was the most vexing. The **cathedral** of Notre Dame developed a system of rhythm patterns so that the singer could be shown by marks called ligatures which rhythm pattern was indicated (short-short-long or long-long, etc.). The next innovation was mensural notation, which tried to indicate the duration of a note, rather than its place in a rhythmic mode. This became more important when parts were written separately but needed to be sung together. For a time, there were competing systems that used rectangles, squares, and diamonds, with and without tails. Over the century of experimentation, some tried pointing tails up or down to indicate duration, and others tried hollow or filled-in notes or notes with dots.

Philippe de Vitry's 1330's treatise *Ars Nova* suggested a system of time signatures, permitting a composer to better define the value he wished the basic note to have. By the close of the medieval period, music notation had not yet been standardized. In manuscripts, methods for notation could differ within the group. Color, solid or hollow notes, tails, and flags could all show duration. Simple time signatures, written as a proportion, were in primitive use.

Musical Instruments

Few medieval instruments survived. There are some late medieval pipe organs and a few violins and harps; there are bone whistles used by the common folk. Most musical instruments are known only from **sculpture** and **painting,** particularly from illustrations in manuscripts. In psalters, King David is usually shown with some kind of harp or lyre, and his musicians reflect the fashions of the time in which the picture was drawn. Stained **glass** windows often showed angels playing the instruments of the time.

Some instruments came to Europe from the Middle East, returning with **Crusaders.** The names of these instruments sound Arabic: rebec, nakers, añafil, and shawm. Some poetry manuscripts compiled by one of the Christian kings of Spain have many illustrations of Arabic-origin instruments used in **Muslim** Spain. The instruments were changed and improved in Europe. Native flutes and harps were combined with the new instruments to create hybrid forms.

The main way instruments were classified during the Middle Ages and the Renaissance had to do with their volume. Loud instruments (*instruments hauts*) should be played together in outdoor settings such as processions, while softer, quieter instruments (*instruments bas*) could play gently indoors. Shawms and trumpets were always loud, while stringed instruments and flutes were always soft.

During the early Middle Ages, skill with musical instruments was confined to traveling minstrels. They played solo or in groups, both to accompany songs and for dance music. During the troubadour period—the 12th and 13th centuries—more amateurs learned to play. In the late Middle

The theme of King David playing his harp was a favorite of medieval artists. In some pictures, David's harp is more lute-like, and in others, it is a primitive lyre. Here, his harp resembles the Irish harp, with a fully developed frame and sounding board. The four musicians surrounding him represent the other main genres of musical instruments: viol, horn, bagpipe, and drum. (Paul Lacroix, *Moeurs, Usage et Costumes au Moyen Age et a l'Epoque de la Renaissance*, 1878)

Ages, amateurs played a larger role. Town watchmen were often musicians who could play a trumpet or some other loud instrument to sound alarms. By the late Middle Ages, town bands had formed, with the watchmen as leaders. They played loud instruments for festivals, and some formed **guilds.**

Standards for tuning instruments to universal pitches were unknown until the Renaissance. Every instrument was tuned by the player's ear. An organ in one church might have its pitches tuned very differently from another. Every minstrel's harp was tuned individually. Town bands were the beginning of group instrumental music, and they began to find ways to tune instruments together.

Keyboard

As early as the 10th century, Winchester Cathedral had a pipe organ built in. It had 400 pipes, and it required a team to work its bellows. The bellows blew air across the pipes, which were worked with slides. There were no stops to keep air from going to some sets of pipes. The music was always multitone and sonorous.

The first primitive keyboards were in place during the 12th century, but the keyboard needed to improve for the organ to be useful for more than sustained notes and chords. The most important improvement was to rediscover the use of springs to make the keys come back up after being pressed. Roman organs had used springs, but early medieval keyboards had not. In the 14th century, the organ was the primary church instrument. By the turn of the 15th century, the stop had been invented; by moving levers, the organist could block air from some ranks of pipes. The organist could now choose which pipes to play at the same time. The church organ had many rows of pipes and two keyboards. Its sound was mellow compared to later pipe organs. Every organ had a different tone—some were louder, some more nasal, others sweeter.

There was also a portable organ called the portative, which could be worked by one musician. It was not used in church. It is probably the forerunner of the accordion, but in medieval illustrations it looks like a small pipe organ. It could be set on a table or held on a lap. One hand worked the keyboard, while the other pumped a small bellows at the back.

During the 14th century, keyboard stringed instruments were invented. The clavichord came first, in the early part of the century. Its strings were hammered by small metal blades called tangents. The clavichord was quiet, and the player could use the keys to produce a vibrato sound on the strings. A similar instrument was perhaps even closer to the construction of the modern piano. It was called a dulce melos or a chekker, but the references to it are obscure.

The harpsichord was invented in the later 14th century, but it only became popular during the Renaissance period. Its strings were plucked by quills, producing the sound of a harp but controlled by a keyboard. The harpsichord was a large instrument from the start; it stood on legs and was shaped like a modern baby grand piano. The strings were covered by a top, but sound holes were cut it in. In one early drawing, they are filled with tracery roses like a lute's.

By the 15th century, the modern chromatic keyboard had been developed, with its distinctive pattern of white and black keys. Two octaves required 26 keys that included the half steps of sharps and flats. With spring-loaded keys and a real chromatic scale, the clavichord and harpsichord crossed into modern musical instruments.

Strings

Stringed instruments were used only for secular music, to accompany singing or dancing. The instruments that evolved into the modern guitar and violin are not easy for modern readers to differentiate. They varied in how many strings they had, even if the instruments appeared similar in shape or use. There must have been several systems for tuning the strings. Instruments with three or four strings probably tuned them to fourths or fifths, to the individual player's preference. When there were more strings, they were often drones and could be tuned to the tone the minstrel preferred. Stringed instruments could have a sounding box to magnify the volume and tone and fewer strings that were shortened by pressing fingers to a fingerboard. The same instrument was sometimes plucked or bowed, and, over time, its size and shape varied. Only in the postmedieval period did stringed instruments begin to be somewhat standardized.

In the early Middle Ages, some minstrels used a lyre called the rotta. An example of this instrument was found in the Sutton Hoo **ship** burial, although it was in fragments and had to be reconstructed. It was long and flat and had an oblong hole cut by its strings, leaving a portion of the sounding board or box for fingering. By the 10th century, bows had been invented, and sometimes the rotta was bowed. There are medieval illustrations showing this lyre played both ways. The rotta fell out of use during the 12th and 13th centuries but had a revival of popularity in the 15th century. These revived rotta lyres were bowed and became another stage in the development of the modern violin.

Another medieval harp was the triangle-shaped harp shown in an Irish coat of arms, and its form came from Ireland. Minstrels used these harps extensively. In pictures, they have eight strings and are tuned with a specialized wrench, often shown in the illustration. By the 13th century, the harp was larger than its earlier form, and, although it could still be held in the lap, its frame had a larger sounding board built in. The pillar closest to the player's body grew thicker with each new design, and it also began to have brays, *L*-shaped pegs that held the strings while increasing the volume. By the 15th century, harps were based on a hollow sound box with sound holes. These late harps were strung with brass wire and produced a very sweet sound, like **bells.**

The psaltery was an instrument similar to a modern zither; its sound box was the length of the strings. It was also called the canon. In the 15th century, a hammered psaltery called the dulcimer came into use. The dulcimer's strings were strung double, and they were separated more so that hammers could strike individual strings more easily. Some had an individual bridge, and others had a higher, more arched bridge.

The rebec was shaped like a lute but had only two strings. It was plucked, rather than bowed. Its use was most during the 12th century, when it was a new instrument brought back with the Crusaders, but it had a revival in the 15th century. It was usually tuned in a higher range of notes, so it could be used for dance music.

A lady, probably a nun, plays the psaltery in this ink drawing. She holds the sounding box of the instrument close to her body and plucks the strings. The man is dressed as a friar; he plays a gittern, an early form of guitar. (The British Library/ StockphotoPro)

The 13th-century fiddle was large, and it had three, four, or five strings. Its hollow body was usually oval, though in some forms it was waisted like a modern violin. The body may have been carved from a single piece of wood. Its strings stretched across a bridge to tuning pegs that stuck into the back, rather than out at the sides like a modern violin.

It is not clear whether the fiddle's bridges were always flat, but they may not have been curved until the 14th century. Bows used with these fiddles were not straight like modern bows; they were semicircles, more like archery bows, and had long handles. A bow used with a flat bridge could not sound the middle strings individually; it could play the top and bottom strings and chords of all the strings. The invention of the curved bridge made musical possibilities for more than two strings and for bowing rather than plucking.

The fiddle is most often shown played vertically, like a cello, but it is also shown resting on the shoulder like a violin. It may have been played vertically more often in Spain and other southern countries and on the shoulder more often in the north. In the 15th century, the fiddle grew more like a modern cello, large and with tones in the bottom range. In Italy, a smaller fiddle had evolved—the violeta. It had four strings, a curved bridge, and a bow. It was played only on the shoulder, and it was smaller than the modern violin.

The organistrum, which developed into the Renaissance hurdy-gurdy, began as a large stringed instrument that required two players. Its melody strings and drone strings were played with a rosined wheel that produced a continuous sound. Melodies were not played by directing pressing fingers to the strings, but instead by means of a keyboard that controlled tangents, small wooden wedges, that pressed the strings. At first, one player worked a crank to turn the bow wheel and the other played the keys. It was first used as a church instrument until churches adopted the pneumatic organ.

The organistrum developed into a one-person instrument sometimes called the symphony. A crank worked the bow wheel, but the instrument had been restyled so that it was like a box, and the keys that worked the tangents faced away and down from the player. Around the 13th century, the organistrum was not used in church any more, and as the "symphony," it became an instrument of secular entertainment. Its Renaissance form, the hurdy-gurdy, looked more like a violin. It is still used as a folk instrument in some parts of Europe, with a crank to turn its bow wheel and keys to play the melodic strings.

The medieval guitar of the 12th and 13th centuries, called in Northern Europe a gittern, could also be called a citole or mandore. It was held and played like the modern guitar, but it had a wide range of variation. The modern guitar has a flat back, a flat bridge, and frets along the fingerboard. The medieval guitar or gittern could have a flat back or a rounded back and either a curved or flat bridge. Frets on the fingerboard could have been made by tying gut around the neck at the correct intervals, and they were optional. The number of strings varied from five to six. Strings could be made of gut or metal. If they were metal, they were tied to a peg at the bottom, but if they were made of gut, they could be tied to the bridge itself.

The lute had a separate development; it was originally an Arabic instrument called *al-ud*. It had a rounded back, built of wooden ribs, and a flat front with sound holes. These sound holes were not simply holes; they were filled with wooden tracery shaped like roses. The strings were gut and were strung double, attached to a flat bridge. They were played singly, plucked with a quill.

Wind

Horns were first associated with war and the aristocracy. The earliest horns seem to have been made from animal horns; the **hunting** bugle's name came from the Latin *bucullus*, an ox. These early horns could be large; when carved from elephant tusks, they were called oliphaunts. Roland's famous horn in the **"Song of Roland"** was an oliphaunt. They played a single note, which could be varied in its harmonics by tightening the player's lips.

A musical adaptation of the horn had finger holes. These holes were cut into the horn so the length could be changed for different tones. The player could also put his hand into the open end to change the tone. There is still a Swedish folk instrument that is a cow's horn with finger holes.

Real trumpets first came from Asia, via the Middle East, and came back to Europe with returning Crusaders. The trumpet's name in Arabic was *al-nafir*, and in Spanish, *añafil*. They were made of brass, and they were straight and very long. The trumpet seems to have been made in pieces and fitted together; medieval pictures always show it with round joints along its considerable length. We know them best from pictures of heralds with their trumpeters; the trumpets were often hung with banners.

In the 15th century, very long trumpets were adapted to be less cumbersome. Metalworking advances had allowed instrument makers to create tubes that gradually widened in mathematically precise harmonic form, and then to bend these tubes without distortion of the sound. A long trumpet could be curved into an *S*, or it could be looped around itself. Some mid-15th-century trumpets had slides, in both straight and looped shapes, as the precursor of the trombone.

The shawm also came into Europe from Arabia during the Crusader period. There are pictures that appear to be primitive shawms in ancient pre-Roman Etruscan culture, but its use had died out in Europe. Its sound came from a vibrating reed, like a modern oboe's, but it was designed differently.

A modern oboe's reed is held between the player's lips, but a shawm's reed was not. The player rested his lips against a mouthpiece that held the reed, but the reed itself was held freely inside his mouth. Its sound was louder than a modern oboe's; it tended to squawk. The end of the wooden shawm was shaped like a ball. During the Middle Ages, the exact size and shape of this reed horn could vary. Its modern descendants include not only the oboe, but also the bassoon, the clarinet, and the bagpipe.

Bagpipes may have come from the Middle East as well. They come into the pictorial record during the 12th and 13th centuries, at a time when many other Arabic imports came to Europe after the Crusades. The player has a mouthpiece to keep a large leather bag filled with air, and one arm squeezes the air out through a pipe with finger holes. This way, the pipe music does not have to stop for the player to take a breath. Medieval illustrations show variations on these instruments, including small air bladders at the top of the instrument, near the player's mouth. The pipe used in a bagpipe seems to have been a type of shawm.

Early medieval musicians also used panpipes made of different-length reeds tied together. They are shown in psalter illustrations of King David. They also had simple flutes with finger holes that were played like recorders. By the 12th and 13th centuries, illustrations show musicians playing flutes in both the transverse position—horizontal like a modern flute—and vertical like a modern recorder. They did not have a lot of finger holes, usually about six. Panpipes were not as commonly played, but a variation on the recorder-like flute was to add a drone pipe so that the pipes appear double. Only one of the pipes was fingered. The true recorder had been developed by around 1400. Its mouthpiece was carved and it had a small bell at the end. There were finger holes to make an octave, including a thumbhole; the last hole, played by a pinky finger, was moved to the side, as it is on a modern recorder.

There was also a very simple flute with only three holes; it was designed to be held and played in one hand. There were two holes in the front and one for the thumb. With only these holes, the pipe was able to play a full octave. The other hand beat a drum, called a tabor, that was held by a strap. The music played in a flute and tabor ensemble was simple, but since one person could produce both tune and beat, it was a popular mode for folk dancing.

Percussion

The tabor, used in a pipe and tabor set, was a round, flat drum with a string of gut stretched across as a snare. It was held upright by a strap around the player's body, so the player's hand was free to keep time on it with a drumstick with a knob. The tabor's stretched leather drumheads were double, on front and back. They were held tight by being laced together with cord around the rim of the drum's frame, like later military drums.

There was also a timbre, the forerunner of the tambourine. It had a round, open frame covered with a taut leather drumhead on one side. The frame held pairs of small cymbals. People also played pairs of the wide, shallow bells that, in modern times, are called cymbals, but in medieval times, were just bells. There are also images of people playing triangles.

The large kettledrums now called tympani (Latin for drums) also came to Europe after the Crusades. An early form was small enough to carry as a pair suspended from a belt. They were called nakers, *naqara* in Arabic. They were played with heavy drumsticks. Pictures suggest that these drums, too, often had a tight gut string that acted as a snare. They were a very common form of drum and are shown in many pictures.

Church services also used bell music. Bells were suspended on a frame and struck by a hammer. These are most often called cymbala in medieval writing. The bell sets used in churches were handbells hung on a frame; it is possible there were ways to use a keyboard or levers to ring these bells, like a modern carillon. In the 15th century, some illustrations show a table full of bowls that acted as bells. They were played by small mallets.

There is no evidence of polyphonic instrumental music until very late in the Middle Ages. Some sheet music exists from the 14th century. Most instrumental music appears to have been played as a single melody on an instrument. By the 14th and 15th centuries, some instrument makers had created larger instruments that played in harmony with smaller ones of the same type. Instrumental music was imitating the complex vocal harmonies of the cathedral choir. A 15th-century painting shows three musicians playing recorder, and one recorder is smaller than the other two. It may have been pitched one-fifth higher so that it would be a natural descant harmony to the others. Smaller and larger shawms, trumpets, and violins also came into use. As instrumental polyphony increased, musical instruments that could be adapted to playing more than one note at the same time were honed to higher quality. Keyboard technology for organs and harpsichords improved.

See also: Cathedrals, Dance, Minstrels and Troubadours.

Further Reading
Berger, Anna Maria Busse. *Medieval Music and the Art of Memory.* Berkeley: University of California Press, 2005.
Caldwell, John. *Medieval Music.* Bloomington: Indiana University Press, 1978.
Cattin, Giulio. *Music of the Middle Ages.* New York: Cambridge University Press, 1984.

Goldon, Romain. *Byzantine and Medieval Music.* New York: H.S. Stuttman, 1968.

Hoppin, Richard H. *Medieval Music.* New York: Norton, 1978.

Knighton, Tess, and David Fallows, eds. *Companion to Medieval and Renaissance Music.* New York: Schirmer Books, 1992.

Montagu, Jeremy. *The World of Medieval and Renaissance Musical Instruments.* Woodstock, NY: Overlook Press, 1980.

Santosuosso, Alma. *Letter Notations in the Middle Ages.* Ottawa, Canada: Institute of Mediaeval Music, 1989.

Seay, Albert. *Music in the Medieval World.* Englewood Cliffs, NJ: Prentice-Hall, 1975.

Stevens, John. *Words and Music in the Middle Ages: Song, Narrative, Dance, and Drama, 1050–1350.* Cambridge: Cambridge University Press, 1986.

Wilson, David Fenwick. *Music of the Middle Ages.* New York: Schirmer Books, 1990.

𝔐𝔲𝔰𝔩𝔦𝔪𝔰

Muslims were a powerful cultural force during the Middle Ages, the height of their Caliphate. Their writings were in all the **universities,** and their traders could be found at the largest **fairs.** The exports of the Muslim countries were medieval Europe's finest luxury goods.

Origins of Islam

Mohammed, an Arabian merchant in Mecca, reported having visions in 610. In these visions, the angel Jibril (Gabriel) commanded Mohammed to learn, recite, and believe new revelations about the nature of a monotheistic God called Allah. Mohammed previously worshiped the local pagan deities of Mecca, whose central place of worship was the Kaabah. He told his visions to his scribe, who wrote them on various materials that came to hand; these revelations and sayings were not collected until after Mohammed's death. The first believers were Mohammed's first wife, Khadija, and his scribe, and then his wife's relatives and friends.

Because Mohammed's anti-idolatry message disrupted the idol commerce of Mecca, the tribal leaders drove them out in 622. The city of Medina was looking for an outside arbiter for their tribal quarrels and invited Mohammed to be their judge. The Arab and **Jewish** tribes were at first welcoming and tolerant of the small core of Muslims, and Mohammed's early teachings reflected a pro-Jewish trend, such as forbidding the eating of pork. The Arab leaders of Medina all converted to Islam, but the Jewish tribes did not change their beliefs. Mohammed turned against the Jews, who were massacred and exiled. He continued to war against Mecca until he conquered it and rode into the city in full possession of its authority. Islam took over the cubical Kaabah as its central place of worship.

Mohammed died in 632 in Medina. He had been both spiritual leader and civil governor of his Muslim polity, and there was no appointed successor. His fathers-in-law and sons-in-law succeeded him, but then the Muslims became disunified. Infighting between factions characterized the Muslim empire for the rest of the Middle Ages. Shi'ites would only follow those who could claim descent from Mohammed's family, while the majority Sunnis were willing to follow any strong caliph.

During the same time, the Byzantine Empire and the Persian Empire had been frequently at war between 571 and 630. Both empires had lost many soldiers, destroyed much property, and drained their savings. The boundary zone was just north of Arabia. It included modern-day Egypt, Israel, Syria, Jordan, Lebanon, Turkey, and Iraq. The city of Jerusalem was particularly damaged by conquest and reconquest. With Jerusalem, the ancient cities of Damascus, Alexandria, Caesarea, Antioch, and Nineveh were ruined. Rural areas of Armenia, Asia Minor (Turkey), and Mesopotamia were depopulated and could barely feed themselves. The armies that defended these territories were mercenaries who were accustomed to guarding city walls.

Under the first caliphs after Mohammed's death, the Arab tribes and their allies set out to conquer their known world. They met little resistance. Relatively small, untrained armies of Arabs on camels and **horses** were able to conquer enormous swathes of territory and overcome armies that would once have rolled over them. They occupied Damascus in 636, and Ctesiphon, Persia's capital, in 637. In 638, they took Jerusalem, and then Caesarea and Alexandria in 640 and 641.

After conquest, conversions were only forced on pagans who worshiped idols. Jews and Christians were termed "People of the Book" because, like Muslims, they looked to a written revelation for moral and theological guidance, rather than to an idol. They were not forced to convert, although they lived under restrictions and blatantly discriminatory laws. Muslim rulers followed a principle of taxing non-Muslims with a special tax called a *jizya*. In fact, the tax income of the empire relied on non-Muslims not converting. As more of the conquered peoples became Muslims, tax income dropped, which pushed the armies of Islam to try for more conquest. Non-Muslims faced legal discrimination in addition to a special tax. Those who did not recognize Mohammed as Allah's only prophet were, in the eyes of Islamic law, already not able to tell the truth. Therefore, non-Muslims were not permitted to testify in court against a Muslim.

Muslim Europe

Early medieval Spain was ruled by the Visigoths, a Germanic tribe that had invaded the Roman province of Hispania in the seventh century. The Umayyad general Tariq ibn Ziyad, a North African Berber, rapidly conquered most of Visigoth Spain in 711. The Visigoth nobles pulled back into small kingdoms along the Pyrenees mountains and preserved Christian Spain until their Reconquest drive began in the 11th century. The Visigoths had been extremely repressive against Jews, so Spain's Jews welcomed and helped the Muslim invasion. They became full collaborators, helping govern the cities for the Arab conquerors.

Muslim armies pushed north. They captured the Spanish coastline and the southern coast of modern France, which was then the independent duchy of Aquitaine. They held the cities of Barcelona, Narbonne, and Marseille. The northern kingdom of the Franks was ruled in name by ineffective Merovingian kings and ruled in reality by their stewards, the major-domos. In 732, the majordomo Charles, later nicknamed "Martel"—the hammer—met Muslim troops at the northern border of Aquitaine, near Tours. Tours was only 150 miles from Paris, and it was the farthest north the Muslims went into Europe. Charles Martel defeated a much larger army very decisively. His successor, Pepin, began to push the Arabs out of Provence and Aquitaine.

Most of southern and central Spain, now known as al-Andalus, or Andalusia, remained Muslim for most of the Middle Ages. Further political infighting in the Middle East moved Andalusia into greater prominence. In 750, the Umayyads of Damascus were all killed by the rival Abbasids, who claimed descent from Mohammed's uncle Abbas. This violent change of dynasty drove the only surviving Umayyad prince, Abd al-Rahman, into exile. He traveled far from Damascus and ended up in Andalusia. Abd al-Rahman seized control of Cordoba and began expanding and unifying the Muslim kingdom. In 959, his descendant Abd al-Rahman III proclaimed himself the true caliph. The family had married many Christian princesses from the north, and Caliph Abd al-Rahman III had blue eyes.

Abd al-Rahman I and his successors built Cordoba into a great city with paved streets, a magnificent mosque made of red and white horseshoe arches, and a palace, Madinat al-Zahra. Cordoba at its peak may have been one of the largest **cities** in Europe. The palace was filled with **gardens,** high fountains, pools, fine buildings, statues, and a **zoo.** One of the legendary marvels of the palace was a pool of quicksilver (mercury) that made the room dance and spin with reflected beams of sunlight. The al-Rahman rulers imported palm trees and other native plants from the Middle East and spread Syrian agricultural methods through Spain. Both Jews and Christians served as advisers and viziers to the Cordoban caliphs.

North African Berber troops of a more fundamentalist Islamic faction destroyed the palace in 1009 and Cordoba in 1013. Many well-educated and skilled people moved from the ruined city to other cities such as Seville and Granada, and the Muslim Andalusian culture became decentralized. Granada and Seville built gardens and palaces similar to Cordoba's. The

The style of Arab warfare shocked Christian Europe, which had been accustomed to fighting on foot. The early Muslim armies used both horses and camels to move very swiftly. (Jupiterimages)

smaller Muslim kingdoms, called *taifas,* did not equal the wealth of the earlier capital of Cordoba, but the Alhambra palace in Granada became the most famous palace. It was built during the 14th century as Muslim power waned.

The island of Sicily was governed by the Muslim Caliphate from 965 to 1072, when it was captured by invading Normans. Its capital was Palermo, and it was ruled by a sultan. Under Muslim rule, Middle Eastern plants such as oranges, lemons, pistachio nuts, and **sugar** cane were planted. Middle Eastern irrigation methods modernized farms. Although Sicily was a Norman kingdom by 1130, Arabic continued to be spoken in many parts of

The dynasty founded by Abd al-Rahman built their capital, Cordoba, into one of the greatest cities in the world. The grandest building was the mosque, modeled after the medieval mosque in Damascus. Its striped horseshoe arches on onyx pillars were constructed partially using stones and pillars from ruined Roman buildings. The conquering Christian kings preserved the beautiful building, although they remodeled it into a cathedral. (Corel)

Sicily for a long time. The Norman rulers learned Arabic and adopted many Muslim customs. In nearby Malta, the native language of Maltese evolved from Arabic. The German emperor Frederick II was born to the queen of Sicily in 1194 and was educated there. He spoke and wrote fluent Arabic and corresponded with sultans and Arabic scholars. When he became king of Jerusalem in 1229, he reinstituted the Muslim call to prayer.

The Muslim culture of Spain permitted polygamy as a normal family institution; the caliphs and emirs had harems of Muslim and Christian slave girls, in addition to several wives. Muslim girls were kept secluded and rarely attended **school.** Many were raised in harems, and they usually married into polygamous families. They had few legal rights. However, there were some educated **women,** and several hundred women were paid **book** copyists at the height of Cordoba's wealth.

Muslim Influence on Europe

Trade and scholarship were Islam's biggest influences on medieval Europe. As the power of the Byzantine Empire lessened, Arab trading cities were the source of exotic luxury goods. Spanish Andalusia, in particular, spread Middle Eastern technology. Arabic culture was viewed as more complex, refined and fashionable than Latin culture. Arabic science and poetry were admired and copied; both Jews and Christians in Arab regions spoke fluent Arabic and wrote poetry. Poetry and science both had longer traditions and higher social esteem in Muslim culture.

Damascus was a major center for raising silkworms and weaving silk, and the art came to Spain by the ninth century. Spanish silk brocade was a major export to Northern Europe. Baghdad, the new Abbasid capital of the Islamic Caliphate, became the most innovative center for **pottery.** Its tin-glazed white wares were exported until the method of glazing with tin caught on in Europe, first in Andalusia and in Italy and then in Northern Europe. White pottery with colored decorations became known as maiolica, named first for the Spanish island of Majorca, which served as a large trading port. Arab traders, often from Andalusia but sometimes from Sicily or the Middle East, attended the fairs of Champagne and other large fairs. They traded fine leather from Cordoba, kermes red dye, silk, and pistachio nuts for northern furs and wool.

Middle Eastern foods also came into Northern Europe through Andalusia. Oranges, dates, figs, and sugar came from Majorca and Barcelona. The word *candy* came from the Arabic word *qandi,* for crystallized sugar. There was a large sugar-processing plant on the island of Crete. Caramel and nougat were sweets invented in Andalusia and other Muslim places. Other Middle Eastern dishes came into Spain's customary diet and then into medieval recipe books.

Islamic scholarship was a great boost to European learning. Every region the Muslims conquered had its greatest works translated into Arabic, and Arabic became the language of the global library. Christian scholars studied Arabic texts in Cordoba and Barcelona, and they partnered with Arab scholars to translate many of these works into Latin. The medical texts of Avicenna and Averroes became standard works in medieval European medical schools. Arab-trained physicians, some of them Jews, were employed by European royalty. One, known as Petrus Alfonsi ("Piers Alphonse" in Chaucer), became a physician to William the Conqueror and wrote Latin works on Arabic concepts of astronomy.

The first translation of the Koran into Latin began around 1142, when Peter the Venerable, an abbot from Cluny, came to Toledo, then the capital of Christian Spain. He hired an Englishman who lived in Toledo to set aside his translation of al-Khwarismi's work on algebra and create a Latin Koran for him.

Arabic **numbers,** borrowed from Hindu mathematics treatises, came into use in medieval Europe very gradually and were established by 1500.

The **astrolabe** was introduced to European sailors and astronomers from Andalusia in the 11th century. It was made of brass, and it usually had Arabic letters and numbers on its face. Astrology and astronomy both came into Europe through Arabic, most often through the Spanish centers of learning.

See also: Astrolabe, Cloth, Food, Horses, Jews, Medicine, Numbers, Pottery.

Further Reading

Fletcher, R. A. *Moorish Spain.* Berkeley: University of California Press, 2006.

Lewis, David Levering. *God's Crucible: Islam and the Making of Europe, 570–1215.* New York: W. W. Norton, 2008.

Lindsay, James E. *Daily Life in the Medieval Islamic World.* Westport, CT: Greenwood Press, 2008.

Matthew, Donald. *The Norman Kingdom of Sicily.* Cambridge: Cambridge University Press, 1992.

Menocal, Maria Rosa. *The Ornament of the World: How Muslims, Jews, and Christians Created a Culture of Tolerance in Medieval Spain.* New York: Little, Brown, 2002.

O'Shea, Stephen. *The Sea of Faith: Islam and Christianity in the Medieval Mediterranean World.* New York: Walker and Co., 2006.

N

Navigation. *See* Compass and Navigation

Numbers

During Europe's Middle Ages, the reigning numeric system was the Roman one. Although Greece had used **alphabetic** letters for counting, the Romans pioneered a system of tally marks and letter symbols. I, II, and III were just tally marks, and V was a symbol for 5. By putting a tally mark before or after V, the counter could make 4 or 6. VII and VIII were 7 and 8. X was a symbol for 10, and tally marks before or after added and subtracted. IX was 9, while XII was 12. XV was 15, and IXX was one short of 20—that is, 19. With the addition of the symbols L for 50, C for 100, and M for 1,000, the Romans could designate any number with accuracy.

There was no convenient way to do arithmetic, since every number was a sum of its parts and symbols. The only way to calculate "C minus XXIV" was to work it in one's head or on an abacus and then write down the symbol for the answer. However, the Roman system was a good way to register numbers in a marketplace; it was a very concrete number system.

By 500, the scholars of India had developed a decimal number system in which place value determined the real value of the digit. They used only nine symbols that resemble modern numbers. Some scholars of the Jain sect pioneered early algebra equations and solutions methods. They called solving an equation "pulverizing" it, as though grinding it down to see what number was left.

One of the intellectual projects of the **Muslim** empire was to translate the classics of other languages into Arabic. This was the first ambitious effort to bring all human knowledge into one **library.** Arabic-speakers translated works from Chinese, Hindi, Egyptian, Babylonian, Latin, and Greek. Among the other scientific concepts Muslims brought into the Mediterranean world, the Indian number system made its entrance. A significant part of India was under Muslim rule, so it was an easy transfer of knowledge within the empire.

Al-Khwarizmi was probably a Persian living under Muslim rule in the eighth century. He wrote **books** on arithmetic and algebra that explained the methods developed in India. His name in Latin was written *Algorithmus,* which is where we got the word for a mathematical method. He explained many algorithms for using the new Indian number system to add, subtract, multiply, and divide. He showed how to find square roots and do operations with fractions. The word *algebra* comes from a Latin form of Al-Khwarizmi's Arabic word *al-Jabr,* which meant "transformations." In this work, the basics of balancing equations and dividing by coefficients are explained. He also explained how to solve quadratic equations, but he did not make use of negative numbers.

Omar Khayyam, an 11th-century Persian, is best known for his poetry, but he was a professional astronomer and mathematician to the sultan. He wrote a book about algebra that expanded on Al-Khwarizmi's older work. He defined algebra—separate from arithmetic—as the use of equations to find unknown numbers with polynomials. He recognized the validity of irrational numbers and further developed the mathematics of conic sections.

The monastic scholar Gerbert of Aurillac, who later became Pope Sylvester II in 999, was educated in or near Barcelona. He learned the Indian-Arabic system of numbers and then became the tutor to the future German emperors Otto II and Otto III. As he rose in the hierarchy of the church, he wrote about and applied the mathematics and science he had learned in Spain. As bishop of Reims, he designed a hydraulic organ and wrote treatises on astronomy. He reintroduced the use of the abacus for calculations, but in the Arabic form, which was more sophisticated than the Roman. He explained the abacus with Arabic numerals, not Roman ones. He introduced a counting board with square counters to explain the method. The counting board became a standard part of commercial banking. As they began to use the new numerals, the counters got turned around, and some Indian-Arabic number symbols came into European use turned to the side or upside down from the way they were originally oriented.

Gerbert's counting board dealt only in the simplest arithmetic with whole numbers, but it was Europe's first introduction to place value. Gerbert called the first column of numbers 1 through 9 "digits," a comparison to the numbers we can count on our fingers. The word *digits*, of course, later came into general usage and has remained current. He was not as successful in explaining the larger place-value columns. They were not fingers; they were joints—"articuli"—but the idea of elbow or shoulder numbers did not resonate with Europeans. The concept of place value did not catch on except with a few scholars who continued to explore it.

One of the simplest concepts invented in India and developed in the Arab empire was the idea of zero. In a system dependent on place value, noting a zero is very important. The Arabic word for "nothing," *tsifr,* came into Latin as both *zephirum* and *cifra*. The forms *zero* and *cipher,* as well as French *chiffre,* meaning "a figure," all stem from these words. The English use of *cipher* to mean a code also recalls the mysterious nature of the new system. Gerbert of Aurillac may have understood the use of zero, but he did not attempt to explain it in 1000.

Europe's conversion to the Arabic system took several centuries. During the 12th century, there were increased efforts to translate Arabic mathematical treatises into Latin. Adelard of Bath translated an Arabic copy of

Euclid's Greek treatise on geometry and then an Arabic work on trigonometry. Plato of Tivoli translated more works and demonstrated how to solve a quadratic equation in Latin. Robert of Chester translated Al-Khwarizmi's algebra treatises. These works were not widely available but could be studied at some **universities.**

Leonardo of Pisa, usually known by the surname Fibonacci (son of Bonacci), grew up in the commercial and university city of Pisa. As a teenager, he joined his father in the city of Bugia, North Africa, to help with a commercial warehouse. He learned the Indian-Arabic system thoroughly for bookkeeping, and he may have studied with Arabic scholars in his travels around the Mediterranean. Back in Pisa around 1200, he wrote a book, *Liber Abaci,* that carefully explained the Arabic system and its advantages to a European audience. He introduced the words *multiplication, factor, numerator,* and *denominator.*

The German emperor Frederick II, a famous scholar himself, read the book and drew Fibonacci into an algebra competition. His court mathematician wrote three algebra problems and sent them to Fibonacci and two scholars of the Latin numeral system. In a public demonstration before Frederick in Pisa, Fibonacci solved all three problems, while the Latin numeral scholars could not. He went on to write *Practica Geometriae* and *Liber Quadratorum,* which explained trigonometry and quadratic equations in Latin with Arabic numerals.

Fibonacci's book, *Liber Abacus,* provided the first major introduction of Arabic numbers to medieval Europe. Although he was not at first a scholar, his private studies with Arabic mathematicians in North Africa and around the Mediterranean rim brought him to the attention of Emperor Frederick II. (iStockPhoto)

Liber Abaci is now most famous for presenting a medieval word problem. If a pair of rabbits produces one pair of offspring after one month, and a month later both pairs each have produced another pair, and a month later the rabbit pairs all have produced another pair, how many rabbits will there be after one year? Fibonacci demonstrated a table of Arabic numbers that neatly predicted the rabbit numbers after one year, two years, or any amount of time. The table's pattern of numbers is still taught as Fibonacci numbers, and the pattern also predicts patterns in nature, such as the rate at which the swirls of a snail's shell will enlarge as they travel outward.

Around 1230, an English scholar, John of Holywood, wrote a Latin book that explained the basics of Arabic arithmetic. *Algorismus Vulgaris* became a standard textbook at universities. Arabic numerals were still not in popular use, but thousands of students could learn the system.

Most Europeans had some objections to the new number system. The concept of zero was difficult, since Roman numerals were primarily for counting and there was no symbol for "nothing." It was not easy at first for them to see why 50 was 10 times larger than 5 when it only had "nothing" added to it. Italian bankers had been among the early acceptors of the system, since it simplified accounting. However, Arabic numerals were easier to falsify, so, in 1299, the city of Florence banned their use. Many other **cities** followed Florence's lead and refused to use the new numbers in commerce or government.

During the 14th century, European scholars produced not only translations but also original works on theoretical mathematics. Around 1325, Thomas Bradwardine wrote treatises in Latin, using Arabic mathematics, that established the beginning of mathematical physics. A French scholar, Johannes de Lineriis, invented the modern fraction, written as two numbers stacked vertically with a line between, around 1340. By the later 14th century, theoreticians in European universities were working on concepts of infinity, exponents, and coordinate geometry.

The 15th century saw popular acceptance of the new numbers. Theoretical scholarly achievements advanced more. A Persian, Al-Kashi, computed pi to 16 places around 1430. Even in the heart of Europe, the close of the Middle Ages saw major advances as mathematics was applied to architecture, art, and astronomy. By the end of the 15th century, some arithmetic textbooks were intended for use outside the universities. They demonstrated long division and multiplication, and some taught how to use the new numbers in accounting. By 1500, Arabic numbers were fully in use in commerce and in schools.

See also: Banks, Muslims, Universities.

Further Reading

Berggren, J. L. *Episodes in the Mathematics of Medieval Islam*. New York: Springer, 2003.

Flusche, Anna Marie. *The Life and Legend of Gerbert of Aurillac: The Organ-Builder Who Became Pope Sylvester II*. Lewiston, NY: Edwin Mellen Press, 2006.

McLeish, John. *The Story of Numbers: How Mathematics Has Shaped Civilization*. New York: Fawcett Columbine, 1991.

Posamentier, Alfred S., and Ingmar Lehmann. *The Fabulous Fibonacci Numbers*. Amherst, NY: Prometheus Books, 2007.

Sigler, Laurence. *Fibonacci's Liber Abaci*. New York: Springer, 2003.

Young, Robyn V., ed. *Notable Mathematicians: From Ancient Times to the Present*. Detroit: Gale Research, 1998.

Painting

Art in the Middle Ages was part of religious expression. Where we view art itself as an end product, they viewed it only as a means to an end. For most of the period, the goal of art was spiritual devotion. They believed that love came from seeing and that people needed to see depictions of Jesus, Mary, and other **saints** in order to love them.

Art could also be purely decorative, but it focused mainly on making churches beautiful. **Churches** had as much art as they could find in their local culture, whether it was carved wood, carved **stone** or ivory, wall paintings, **gold** or **silver,** sculpted figures, or embroidered hangings. Decorative art reached a high level of sophistication by the end of the Middle Ages.

Byzantine art was primarily religious. Continuing a tradition from Christian Rome, art in Constantinople focused on mosaics and the stylized devotional paintings called icons. Icons were wood panel paintings that showed Jesus and the saints, typically in somber colors, and often utilized gold leaf. The gold leaf served as a shining halo around the head of a saint and sometimes as decoration on **clothing.** Faces and figures tended to be slender and tall, eyes were large and dark, and mouths were rarely smiling. Western Europe under the Franks borrowed its earliest ideas about art from visits to Constantinople. Charlemagne's chapel at Aachen had paintings, wood carvings, and gold decoration in direct imitation of what his ambassadors had seen in the East, and early medieval art copied from Charlemagne.

During the 11th, 12th, and 13th centuries—the period we call the Romanesque—the object of the painter or sculptor was to create an image that evoked emotion in the viewer. Often, the goal was religious devotion, but some art was made to beautify a room or building. Realistic detail was important, but only as it conveyed the meaning of the image accurately. Figures could be out of scale to each other as long as the viewer could tell what they were. Buildings could be shown unrealistically small for the people who were walking into them as long as the picture made the story clear. Colors had to be clear and bright, and certain colors were symbolic of purity or royalty. Gold, applied to the image to make it shine, was very important, and expensive materials made the picture better. There were artistic conventions for portraying clothing or body position, and, as long as these conventions told the viewer what was happening, it was acceptable if they did not look exactly like reality. Idea symbols, such as halos to show holiness, were part of the images.

Medieval artists showed no awareness of different clothing or building customs in different places or times. A medieval painting of Moses showed him in a contemporary robe and hat, and depictions of Bible towns like Jerusalem or Jericho were identical to medieval European walled **cities** and **castles.** Although they did not give their viewers any understanding of the real world of the Bible, they created **records** for us of their contemporary buildings, clothing, tools, and food.

Even during the Romanesque period, some artists achieved good proportion or realistic detail. However, the value of art did not depend on artistic realism. The value of art was dependent on its content, its materials, and its success in using artistic convention to convey the message.

In the 13th century, the goal of artistic work began to shift. Painting technique improved after several centuries of stable apprenticeship training in the arts. Apprenticed painters began to practice figure drawing, and individual artists emerged as more talented and skilled than others. More materials were available: more painting tints, more kinds of stone or **pottery,** and more possibilities in stained **glass.** Great realistic detail was possible, and it was more often sought and achieved during the Gothic period.

Gothic stained glass art, wall paintings, **book** illustrations, and sculptures all improved dramatically. They still used bright colors and conventional symbolism, but they began to use more individual detail. A row of ladies could be posed in slightly differing natural poses, and their hairstyles would not be identical. Figures were not as symmetrical. Faces had more individual detail, and the drapery of robes, whether painted or carved, looked more like the pull of gravity on real fabric.

In 14th-century paintings, scenery was more in proportion to the figures; in a group of figures, some were layered behind the others to create a realistic sense of depth. The chief artist of the 14th century was the Florentine painter Giotto di Bondone, usually known as simply Giotto. He painted panels and frescoes; he documented the legendary life of Saint Francis of Assisi and painted many Bible scenes on the walls of the famous Arena Chapel in Padua. He painted the fresco murals of Florence's Peruzzi and Bardi chapels. When Giotto died in 1337, Florence gave him a state **funeral,** the first time any artist had been honored this way.

Giotto's ability with realism was strikingly better than the painters before him. He painted buildings with three dimensions and a vanishing point, instead of flat like the 13th-century painters. Squares turned to trapezoids, growing smaller with distance. Porches and eaves cast realistic shadows on the walls. Faces are depicted at many different angles, from full face to full profile, and proper perspective and shadow were always maintained. Contemporary viewers wrote that Giotto's figures were so close to life that they seemed to breathe and move. Gold leaf, halos, and religious symbols were still very important in the works of Giotto and his Gothic contemporaries.

After the Black Death **plague** of 1347–1350, art in Europe changed. Many artists and their patrons had died, and all craft training, including art, was disrupted. Society became preoccupied with death and, to some extent, disillusioned with the official church, which had not been able to keep up with the people's needs. Patrons began to commission portraits

Giotto, the most prominent painter of the Middle Ages, commemorated the life of Saint Francis in a series of wall frescoes in the church in Assisi, Italy. His use of natural poses and visual perspective stunned his contemporaries and influenced all painting after him. (Giraudon/The Bridgeman Art Library)

as secular remembrances of themselves, instead of only commissioning religious works. It was more important to the late Gothic painter to portray real life than to evoke devotion.

Technically, painting leaped far ahead in the 15th century. Perspective came fully into its own. Giotto's use of perspective had been correct but shallow; late Gothic painters created halls that receded and **roads** that wandered to a true vanishing point. Flanders was the center of a new realistic style of art, and artists like Jan van Eyck were leading innovators. Figures were turned asymmetrically, and they leaned, slept, stooped, crossed their arms or legs, looked bored or angry, or gazed at some unseen object. Rowers strained at oars, and Jesus on the cross slumped like a real dead body. Plants and flowers were not generic or symbolic; they were recognizable European plants.

In popular art, the figure of Death, as a skeleton or a Grim Reaper, became popular. Death was often dancing, pulling unwilling people into his **dance** with other skeletons and corpses. In the Dance of Death pictures, some people were rotting; ugliness was acceptable because death and life could be ugly. Nudity was more acceptable in art, perhaps because so many dying people had been seen or buried naked and the sight of the human body was more commonplace. Sometimes religious art depicted the resurrection of the dead, with the rising dead as nudes. Artists began to sign their works, from stained glass panels to frescos to portraits.

The Mechanics of Painting

Medieval paintings were not typically done on stretched canvas, as later became standard. Wall paintings were the standard decoration not only in churches, but also in many **castle** interiors. In Italy in the late Middle Ages, wall paintings were often frescoes: tints painted directly onto wet plaster to bond with the drying wall itself. Paintings were also created on wood panels. These could be hung on a wall, or they could be altarpieces that stood at the front of a church. Wood, not canvas, was the usual platform for paint.

Paintings were also book illustrations. If medieval artistic artifacts were counted as items, the paintings in books would far outnumber wall paintings and altarpieces. By far the greatest number of artists in the Middle Ages were worked in monasteries and cities, patiently creating detailed pictures of daily life to illustrate a book of hours or a psalter. Much of what we know about the period comes from observing the many scenes these artists painted: building, spinning, farming, cooking, caring for children, jousting, and scenes with **animals** of all kinds. Medieval book painters recorded daily life in such detail that we can trace the development of some **tools** and clothing styles, and we can see when **eyeglasses** first came into use.

Painters used different materials for walls or for books. Paint was a chemical bond between the tints and the material, and some kinds of paint and painting techniques worked only on **parchment** or only on plaster. Half the art of painting was knowing the secrets of mixing and using paint, while the other half was, of course, drawing images that were realistic and beautiful.

Paintbrushes were made from animal hair, usually a squirrel's. The hair was bound on the end of a stick, much the same as today's brushes. When a painter worked, he did not usually use a flat palette like a modern painter. Paints were often mixed in oyster shells or wooden dishes. Archeologists have discovered oyster shells with very old paint pigments still visible. Artists worked on upright easels if they were painting a book page or a wood panel. Many illustrations show artists working this way.

Paint is a binding agent mixed with pigments. To modern readers, who think of paint as made by chemical companies, the natural ingredients used by medieval painters can be startling or humorous. Toward the end of the Middle Ages, painters and apothecaries had developed some artificial tints, sometimes with fairly complicated chemical processes. Some binding agents were more suitable for books or for walls, and some pigments worked only for one or the other. Some paints could not be used next to others, since they would create a chemical reaction that changed the color. A large part of a painter's education was in managing the chemicals and knowing which ones to use and how.

Paint for books began with egg whites turned into glair, a liquid that mixes well with pigments and pours and brushes well. Egg whites do not mix well with anything until they have been beaten or strained. The finest method required the artist to hand whip the egg whites with a wooden whisk until they were very stiff and then allow them to turn back into liquid, which was called glair. When pigments were mixed into glair they sometimes formed bubbles, and the best way to stop this was to add a bit of earwax to the mix.

The other binding agent for book painting was gum arabic, the sap of an acacia tree. Other tree gums also were used. When the gummy substance was soaked in water, it provided a solution that would carry paint well. When parchment scraps were soaked and then boiled, they dissolved into the **water** and formed a jelly called size. Size was a good binding agent for some blue pigments. Other odd ingredients for book paints included spinach juice, apple vinegar, **sugar,** and stale beer.

The binding agent for wall or wooden panel painting was usually egg yolk. This was the main paint used in Italy, and it was called tempera paint. Egg yolk dried quickly and was glossy and long lasting. Its yellow color did not alter the paint's color much. Oil as a medium for tints came into use only in the late Middle Ages. Especially in northern regions like Germany, paint for murals was based on linseed oil.

Medieval paint pigments were bright and clear, not shadowed or nuanced as later Renaissance painters preferred. Most pigments needed to be crushed finely before being mixed into the binding agent. The painter first used a mortar and pestle, but the finest grinding required a small slab of marble with a block of marble rubbed across it. The crushed pigments were mixed into a thick paste with water and stored either wet or dry. The painter used a small amount of the pigment mixed into the medium (such as egg yolk or glair) to make the amount of paint he would need for the day's work.

The most common white pigment came from white **lead,** which was produced in a chemical reaction between lead, acidic fumes from vinegar, and carbon dioxide from fermenting tanning bark or dung. The process grew a white crust on the lead, which could be crushed into a stable, thick white pigment. It was also poisonous.

Black pigments were natural. They could be from **iron,** as in most black ink, or from soot rubbed off a lamp. Black pigments could also be made from the carbon charcoal of grape vines or peach pits. Other charcoals would do, but artists preferred these plant charcoals.

There are natural clays that make good paint pigments, as well as a few red clays. They are high in iron and are called ochres. They were the original prehistoric red paints of cave walls. Several red pigments were made from crushed insects, and another common red was extracted from the wood of the brazil tree. The most successful red tint, though, was both artificial and **poisonous.** Vermillion red was made from a chemical reaction between mercury and sulfur. Cinnabar is a red sulphide of mercury and occurs naturally in Spain. In Roman times, chemists learned how to extract mercury from cinnabar. Vermillion was the result of adding sulfur back to the mercury; it was artificial cinnabar.

The best blue pigment came from a mineral, azurite. It produced a paler blue paint if it was crushed more finely. When coarsely ground azurite was mixed with size to produce blue paint, it required several coats, but the finished dried product had a sparkling quality like the original mineral. An even better blue called ultramarine came from crushed lapis lazuli, a mineral found in Persia, but ultramarine paint was rarely used, and only for the most expensive items, where the goal was to show off conspicuous wealth.

Most blue tints came from plants. The best came from indigo, a plant imported from India, but Europe had a similar dye plant called woad. Both plants produced a blue dye as sap. Woad had also soaked up potassium, and if craftsmen burned woad roots, they could get very high-quality potassium ash to use for making lye. Woad also ruined the soil it grew in by drawing the potassium out, and medieval farmers did not have good methods for replacing it. Woad leaves and indigo leaves were processed similarly for their pigment. Dried and crushed, they were fermented in water until foam collected on top; this was skimmed and dried to make the concentrated pigment. The water itself could be used to dye cloth. Another common plant called the turnsole had seeds that produced a strong juice. It could dye pieces of **cloth** red, purple, or blue, depending on what else was mixed with it, and the pieces of cloth served as storage for the pigment. The pieces of cloth were called clothlets, and they could quickly stain water or glair into an active, bright paint.

The advent of artificial dyes brought copper blue. Although **copper** is naturally green, with the addition of ammonia (easily obtained from urine), it turns blue. The color became chemically stable if lime was added, and this chemistry process produced a cheap, bright blue that became an all-purpose paint for walls, wood, and books.

Yellow could be made in many different ways. Some clays produced yellow ochres, particularly if they contained limonite. Yellow ochre paints were used mostly for wall murals. Bile from the livers of **fish** or turtles also produced yellow pigment. Saffron, the powdered stigma of the crocus flower, was an important **spice** in cooking as well as a yellow pigment. Unripe buckthorn berries gave yellow pigment, as did an herb called weld, which was often used in dyeing.

Some chemical processes also made yellow pigments. White lead, when roasted slowly, turned yellow and then orange. A kind of false-gold mineral called orpiment created a good yellow pigment, but it was not compatible with other pigments like verdigris and white lead. They could not be used where they would overlap or touch because the chemicals reacted and destroyed the colors. Manuscript painters used a chemical pigment known as mosaic gold; it was a tin sulphide that was difficult to make and involved tin, mercury, sulphur, and sal ammoniac.

Some clays produce a dull green pigment useful for scenery on large wall paintings. A mineral called malachite is often found with azurite, and, when it was crushed, it produced a green pigment that was used in the same way as azurite blue.

A chemical process created the most common green pigment. Copper oxide was made by exposing a sheet of copper to the acidic fumes of vinegar, and the chemical reaction created a green crust on the copper. This green pigment was called verdigris. Verdigris was not a stable chemical, and, unless the perfect binding agent was used, it would turn dark with time. Medieval painters were aware of this, but the green lasted reasonably well for several centuries, so they did not know how severe the darkening would eventually be. Verdigris green appears on many wall paintings, where it is now brown or black. In book illustration, it lasted better. It was usually dissolved in wine and made reasonably good paint.

Saffron yellow was often mixed with verdigris, but white lead paint was chemically incompatible with it. Several plants provided good greens that were compatible for mixing with white lead. Sap green and iris green were made from the juice of the ripe buckthorn seed and the iris flower. The iris flower gives a purple juice when it is squeezed, but this juice turns green when alum is added. Some other flowers and leaves, such as nightshade, also made green pigment. Finally, blue pigments with saffron added made green.

Purple in Roman times came from the whelk, a shellfish that produces purple dye. Medieval purples probably did not come directly from shellfish because the whelk dyes were so expensive. They were made from a plant called turnsole or from a type of lichen. Or, simplest of all, they were blended from red and blue, as long as the chemicals in the red and blue were compatible.

Gold and **silver** were used directly in painting. Gold was powdered and mixed with a medium like glair, but gold does not grind to powder easily. It first has to be turned into an alloy, using another metal like copper or mercury, in order to overcome gold's natural property of holding together. Gold can be beaten into a very fine sheet or wire and will not become brittle, so it did not grind, either. Silver was easier to grind, and it could be mixed into the binding agent like another pigment. Painters sometimes tried to mix powdered silver with yellow saffron powder so it would look like gold.

While gold was difficult to crush for paint, it could be beaten into very thin sheets of gold, called gold leaf, and glued to parchment or wood. Gold leaf had to be burnished so that it would shine, and the most likely burnishing tool was a tooth mounted on a wooden handle. Sometimes colored paint was put onto the gold leaf so that the dry paint could be scraped away in places to allow the gold to shine through. This technique is called sgraffito.

When an artist prepared wood as a surface to paint, he began by sanding it carefully. In Germany and France, hardwoods like oak were available, and they required only a surface layer of chalk to be prepared for painting. In Italy, only softer woods were available, so the artist covered them with a layer of plaster called gesso. Gesso was made of chalk or gypsum mixed with glue. When it dried, it could be polished into a perfectly hard, smooth surface that took paint well. Areas requiring gold leaf first received a layer of red clay, and then the gold was painted onto the clay and burnished. Paint might go over the gold leaf for a sgraffito technique. This was especially used on wooden altarpieces because it allowed gold stars or golden rays to shine out from a dark surface.

For general work with wood panels and frames, artists used glue, rather than nails. One common artists' glue was made from cheese and lime. The cheese was soaked and crushed in water, and powered lime was mixed in. The glue was very strong and has lasted many centuries. Another kind of glue was made from soaking and boiling animal skin and cartilage until they dissolved. Stockfish, too, could be made into fish glue this way.

If a wall was to be painted, it was first carefully plastered to make the surface very fine and smooth, rather than painting directly on stone or brick. Sometimes a coat of tar went first, to waterproof the wall. Wall painting in Northern Europe was generally done on a dry surface. It was nearly always indoors. Many walls of **castles** and chapels had murals showing scenes from the Bible, the lives of saints, or daily life. The scenes were large, often nearly life-size. **Hunting** in a **forest** was a common motif.

Medieval wall painters also decorated some portions of walls with drapery, as though the wall were curtained. After 1300, there was a fashion to cover walls with "diaper," an allover pattern of diamonds similar to modern wallpaper patterns. To keep the designs even, painters used stencils, often cut from thin sheets of lead.

Fresco painting developed in Italy during the 14th and 15th centuries and was used into the Renaissance. It was a cheap substitute for Byzantine-like **glass** tile mosaics and woven **tapestry** wall hangings. A fresco painter started at the top of a wall. He put a layer of fresh rough plaster on the wall and sketched the lines of what he was going to paint. Over this, he put a thin coat of fine plaster so that the lines still showed through. He only plastered as much as he could paint in one day before the plaster dried. Fresco painting depended on the weather, which had to be just right so that the plaster dried on time—not too quickly or too slowly.

Fresco painting is the best-known wall technique, but it was mostly used in Italy at the end of the Middle Ages. The artist tinted fresh plaster, working quickly and only applying as much plaster as he could paint before it dried. Fresco colors have proven very durable over the centuries, especially when the work was not exposed to the weather. Most other wall painting techniques have suffered chemical changes in their colors, but fresco tints may be as bright as when they were first applied. (Claudio Giovanni Colombo/iStockphoto)

The fresco artist painted with tints that bound directly with the gypsum in the plaster; they were not mixed with the binding agents used in other painting techniques, such as egg or gum arabic. Some tints, such as lapis lazuli blue, had to be put onto dry plaster. Fresco painting did not take details well, so early frescos were touched up with egg tempera paint. Some frescos had only the backgrounds put onto the wet plaster, while the rest was painted in tempera. Experiments with oil painting on plaster showed that it disintegrated over time, and traditional fresco was better. The tempera details held up better but were also prone to flaking off over the centuries.

See also: Books, Gold and Silver, Records, Sculpture.

Further Reading

Binski, Paul. *Painters.* Toronto: University of Toronto Press, 1991.

Holcomb, Melanie. *Pen and Parchment: Drawing in the Middle Ages.* New York: Metropolitan Museum of Art, 2009.

Nees, Lawrence. *Early Medieval Art.* New York: Oxford University Press, 2002.

Petzold, Andreas. *Romanesque Art.* Upper Saddle River, NJ: Prentice Hall, 1995.

Rosewell, Roger. *Medieval Wall Paintings in English and Welsh Churches.* Woodbridge, UK: Boydell Press, 2008.

Stoksad, Marilyn. *Medieval Art.* New York: Westview Press, 2004.

Thompson, Daniel V. *The Materials and Techniques of Medieval Painting.* New York: Dover Publications, 1956.

Toman, Rolf, ed. *Gothic: Architecture, Sculpture, Painting.* Cologne, Germany: Ullmann and Konemann, 2007.

Toman, Rolf, ed. *Romanesque: Architecture, Sculpture, Painting.* Cologne, Germany: Ullmann and Konemann, 2004.

Wolf, Norbert. *Giotto di Bondone, 1267–1337.* Cologne, Germany: Taschen, 2006.

Parchment and Paper

Parchment was the standard writing material for most of the Middle Ages. It was simply leather, treated specially to make it into a smooth, white surface. Paper was a new invention brought from Asia during the 13th century. Paper was made by mixing plant fibers with water and spreading the mixture over a screen or a mold. The fibers dried, resulting in a sheet of paper. The results were similar, but the technologies were very different and required radically different manufacturing processes.

Parchment could be made from the skins of goats, sheep, cows, or other **animals.** Vellum was a very fine, expensive parchment made from the skins of young animals (calves, lambs, or kids). Because of their larger size, cows provided the materials for larger sheets of vellum used for large **books** such as large Bibles or choir books. Fatty animals provided poorer quality parchment. Apart from questions of size, different regions used primarily the animals they naturally raised. Parchment making kept pace with butchering, recycling some portion of the skins.

Fresh skins had to go straight to the parchment maker, where they were soaked in **water** so that blood and fat could be scraped off. Then the clean skins were soaked for a few days in a solution of lime (calcium oxide) and water. This loosened the hair so it could be rubbed off easily, and it drew out some of the fat in the skin. The wet skin was stretched on a large hoop. Workers used curved blades to scrap the hides smooth. They also rubbed them with substances to treat the surface: ashes and lime to draw out fat and alum to harden it. Additionally, the surface of the drying parchment was sanded smooth with a pumice stone. Where pumice was not available, some parchment makers baked ground **glass** into bread and used that to rub the skins.

When the skins were fully scraped, sanded, and dried, they could be removed from the hoops. They were cut to size, usually for books. Most parchment required a last treatment of chalk or pumice dust. For some purposes, it was painted with a thin coating of glue or with coats of white

Parchment took several days to prepare, from a fresh animal hide to smooth, white, polished vellum. It had to be stretched and scraped while wet. (Musee Conde, Chantilly, France/Giraudon/The Bridgeman Art Library)

paint. Parchment could also be dyed blue, purple, green, or other colors. Gold paint stood out well against dark colors.

The technology for making paper was developed in China. The use of paper moved westward to Europe by two routes: through North Africa and into Spain and through Central Asia along the Silk Road. Samarkand, which is located along the Silk Road, became a center of papermaking because of its good crops of flax.

The increased paper production of the late Middle Ages was dependent not only on gaining paper technology from China, but also on the availability of linen rags. Chinese paper had used mulberry tree bark, which was unavailable in Europe. Until technological and agricultural advances made linen towels, shirts, and sheets common, there were not enough materials to make paper in Europe. Worn-out linen could be bought and shredded for paper; the linen rags were first torn up, soaked, shredded, and beaten. Then the linen pulp was spread into a mold, pressed, and dried. Dry sheets were sanded with a stone and then dipped into sizing made of gelatin and alum.

The first water-powered paper mills were in **Muslim** Spain because the technology came from Baghdad during the 11th and 12th centuries. The first paper mill in Europe was established in 1270 in Fabriano, Italy, and the first watermarks were used in Italy in 1282. Water-powered paper **mill** technology reached Northern Europe during the remaining medieval centuries, arriving in England in the 15th century.

Europe's acceptance of paper was slow. Parchment was easily available, and there was little demand for paper because few people could read. Also, the **church** disapproved of paper because of its Muslim origin, and laws forbade the use of paper for public documents. In 1221, Emperor Frederick II declared that documents written on paper had no validity in law.

But as paper became less expensive than parchment, handmade books were easier to create and depended only on the number of scribes who could be employed. Commercial stationers contracted with scribes to make copies of books for **universities.** The availability of paper books was a step toward the invention of a mass-printing technology, and the role of paper changed dramatically with the invention of **printing.**

In the first step in manufacturing paper, the fibrous material was prepared in a vat using linen rags soaked in water that was kept warm and stirred with a pole. For higher-quality paper, silk rags were used, and the rags were cut by hand, rather than by machine. The paper mold was a wire screen in a wooden frame, topped with a second, removable screen that determined the size of the sheet of paper. This screen was called a deckle, from the German word for "cover."

The vatman dipped the mold vertically into to the fibrous liquid and then laid it horizontally. A worker shook the pulp on the screen, forward and backward and then side to side, to mat the fibers together to make stronger paper. Then the deckle was removed.

After adequate draining, the mold was turned face down on a piece of wool felt. The mold was lifted off, the paper clung to the wool, another felt was laid on top, another sheet of pulp was added, and so on. The whole pile, which might be as tall as two feet high, was put into a screw press to squeeze out as much water as possible, lowering the height of the stack to about six inches. For finer paper, the sheets were pressed a second time. The felts were then reused for the next stack.

The paper then was dried over horsehair cords in groups of four or five sheets; grouping the sheets helped the paper dry fairly flat. Paper that was to be used for writing was dipped in a starchy liquid (a sizing made of animal- or vegetable-based glue) and again pressed and dried.

The forms used for drying left a pattern in the paper. The mill at Fabriano developed the watermark, a design that identified a specific mill. This watermark design was made of fine wires so the design was pressed into the finished paper. Sometimes the paper mill also used a heavier cord that would leave a slight indentation along the margin of the paper to show where the writing should stop.

See also: Books, Cloth, Pens and Ink, Printing.

Further Reading

De Hamel, Christopher. *Scribes and Illuminators.* Toronto: University of Toronto Press, 1992.

McMurtrie, Douglas C. *The Book: The Story of Printing and Bookmaking.* Oxford: Oxford University Press 1967

Thompson, Daniel V. *The Materials and Techniques of Medieval Painting.* New York: Dover Publications, 1956.

Pens and Ink

In a time when all **books** were handwritten, pens and ink were the signature tools of the scholar or student. Pens were handmade by each individual scholar, and, at times, ink must have been a homemade concoction as well.

Medieval pens were usually made from quills or reeds. Feather quills were the most common, but hollow stems of marsh reeds could be cut the same way. The outer wing feathers of a large bird such as a goose or swan have large, translucent tubes as center ribs. Scribes cut away the feather's soft part with a penknife and dried the quill. They carved the tip to have a single fine point and then split the point vertically. Dipped in an inkpot, the quill would hold and distribute a drop of ink. The split point would spread to make a wider line as the scribe pressed harder.

Perhaps because writing and illustration usually took place in the same monastic scriptorium, the act of writing is one of the most frequent themes of painted book illustrations. Medieval painters were not careful about relative size of objects, but they provide accurate detail about pens and inkpots, the writer's tools. Here, the quill pen has been stripped of the soft feathering, and the writer's left hand rests on the penknife to hold the page steady. (Bibliotheque Municipale, Valenciennes, France/Giraudon/The Bridgeman Art Library)

The penknife was an important secondary tool. It had a long wooden handle and a short, sharp blade. The scribe used it to sharpen his quill frequently, quickly carving in strokes toward himself. He also used it for scratching out mistakes, for holding the parchment or paper flat and steady, and as a hand rest. As the quill was in his right hand, the penknife was always in his left.

A small number of pens were made of brass. A brass pen was a stick, roughly round or hexagonal, with a point on the end. The long point had grooves that held a certain amount of ink after being dipped.

Inkwells in a scriptorium were often made from hollowed horn. Each horn fitted into a hole drilled in the slanted writing table. Portable inkpots were made of **pottery** or brass and had lids. Many medieval illustrations show scribes working with both kinds of inkwell; if the writer is shown sitting outdoors, his inkpot is always the portable, lidded kind.

The word *ink* is short for Latin *incaustic*, which means "burned in." Since burning is a chemical reaction with oxygen, other forms of oxidation were also called "caustic," and the black color was "burned" onto the page by means of drying in the air (a form of oxidation). Medieval ink was usually made from iron, tannic acid, and gum arabic. Other recipes existed, and some ink contained charcoal or the soot from a lamp. Some ink stayed black over time, and some turned to lighter colors.

Iron gall ink began with the acid produced in an oak tree when it hosts a gall wasp. The wasp lays an egg in the bud of an oak tree, and the larva produces a marble-sized ball as its early home. It drills its way out as a mature insect, leaving behind the gall. These galls were filled with tannic and gallic acid. Tannic acid is a mordant used in dyeing; a mordant binds the dye color to the cloth chemically. The acids were obtained by crushing the galls and soaking or boiling them in water or vinegar. Ferrous sulfate, called copperas, was a naturally occurring iron-rich mineral. When it was mixed with gall acid, it turned brown and then black. Gum arabic added to the mix made it dense enough to be picked up by quill pens.

Iron gall ink turned darker with time as it bound with oxygen in the air. If it was used fresh, it could be too light for the scribe to see his letters easily. But after it blackened, it remained dark and clear. Some iron gall ink found in early medieval manuscripts remained clear black for a thousand years.

Other colors of ink were used for special purposes, not counting the paints used to create pictures on a page. While blue or green ink could be used, red was the second color choice. On a **calendar,** red marked special days, and a red letter marked a special place on a book's page. Red ink began with the egg white base called glair. Vermillion, an artificial form of cinnabar, mixed into the glair with gum arabic. Brazilwood chips were the other common red tint for book ink.

Not all writing was done with pens and ink. People who needed to take quick notes at work needed a way to write things down for a short time without using expensive parchment or paper. For this, they used wax tablets. The best writing tablets were made of carved ivory, but lesser tablets were wooden with a layer of wax. People used a bone or metal stylus to scratch lightly into the wax.

See also: Books, Painting, Paper and Parchment.

Further Reading

De Hamel, Christopher. *Scribes and Illuminators.* Toronto: University of Toronto, 1992.

Thompson, Daniel V. *The Materials and Techniques of Medieval Painting.* New York: Dover Publications, 1956.

Pilgrims

Since the earliest days of Christianity, believers had felt closer to their deceased friends and leaders when they were near their burial places. They came to believe that these bones and burial sites had a special holiness. When Emperor Constantine converted to Christianity, his mother Helena traveled to Israel and the Sinai Peninsula to find Mount Sinai, Calvary, Bethlehem, and other sites from Bible stories. She believed she had found these places, and Constantine ordered a church to be built over the site where Jesus had been buried. From that time on, Christian believers began traveling to Jerusalem and Rome to experience the special holiness. During the Middle Ages, pilgrimages became big business. By the close of the medieval period, pilgrimages had travel guidebooks, souvenirs, cruise packages, and a host of official and illicit businesses based on pilgrim travel.

Pilgrim journeys could be long and dangerous or relatively short and easy. Any trip to a **saint**'s shrine was a pilgrimage, and every region had its own saints' shrines. French pilgrims could travel to Saint Denis in Paris to venerate the tunic of the Virgin Mary, and English pilgrims could go to Walsingham to venerate Mary in a shrine built as a replica of her early home where an angel had appeared. Englishmen could go to Canterbury and visit the relics of Saint Thomas the Martyr, a medieval celebrity in his own right. Italians could take a ferry to Venice to pray before the bones of Saint Mark. But pilgrims felt that their journeys had more merit if they were more difficult and expensive. The most important pilgrimage sites were Constantine's Church of the Holy Sepulcher in Jerusalem, Spain's Cathedral of Saint James at Compostela, and Rome, the burial place of Saint Peter and Saint Paul and the home of the Pope.

Until the 11th century, the constant trickle of European pilgrims to Jerusalem met no real obstacles from the new **Muslim** regime. Each Muslim dynasty had a different attitude and approach to outsiders and their religions. In 1095, the Pope heard reports that pilgrims were being harassed and turned away, and these reports led to the call for the first **Crusade.** The Crusaders established Latin-speaking kingdoms between Jerusalem and Antioch (in modern Turkey). Pilgrims took advantage of their newly favored status and began coming to Jerusalem in greater numbers. Two monastic orders of **knights** were established to help and protect them. The Knights of the Hospital managed hospices for pilgrims (and, in some cases, **hospitals** for the sick and wounded), while the Knights of the Temple were supposed to guard the roads to keep them safe. The Crusades ended up changing the political balance and international trade, but they were always closely intertwined with the ideals and needs of pilgrims.

Pilgrimages were undertaken out of a variety of motives. Some noblemen made pilgrimages to Jerusalem in order to be knighted at the Church of the Holy Sepulcher at midnight. Many pilgrims were expressing religious devotion, pure and simple. These included monks, priests, and lay people who felt their religious belief deeply. The most famous late medieval pilgrim was Margery Kempe, who published a detailed account of her pilgrimage to the Holy Land. Her motive was fanatical, emotional piety, and she believed God had called her to be a pilgrim. Like Margery Kempe, many people, both lay and cleric, had a lifelong romantic vision of finding true meaning in life by sacrificing comfort and safety to go to the Holy Land.

Other pilgrims had made a vow in a time of trouble—if a saint helped them, they would make a pilgrimage to that saint's shrine. When they fulfilled this vow, they always gave a gift of money at the church. Often, they left a small memorial image of the way their prayer had been answered. These were frequently made of wax and sometimes of ceramic; least often, they were made of **silver** or **gold.** A tiny ship represented being saved from shipwreck. A wax leg meant a leg had been healed. Wax images left at these shrines range from babies to houses to ships to mysterious objects understood only by the donors.

Pilgrimages were very often undertaken as penance, seeking forgiveness of sin before life on earth ended. The **church** promised forgiveness of sin could be won by meritorious pilgrimages. Penance could be voluntary, as when a knight felt he needed to find forgiveness for the violence of his way of life. It was also often involuntary, imposed as a penalty by a judge. The promise of a pilgrimage could be part of a plea bargain. It could also be part of a treaty—the defeated city or baron had to promise to go on pilgrimage to repent of rebellion or war.

When a pilgrimage was taken for penance, the pilgrim had to arrive at the place and present himself to the abbot, bishop, or priest. There was a set of

In medieval art, pilgrims are indicated by simple dress, staffs, and brimmed hats. Here, the artist documents stages of the pilgrim's journey to the Holy Land. A group of pilgrims could only travel so far by foot or horse, and then they had to contract with a ship to ferry them across part or all of the Mediterranean Sea. Many discomforts and dangers lay ahead. (Bettmann/Corbis)

rituals to undertake for a set amount of time. Some pilgrims began to crawl or bow from when they first saw the destination and remained in that posture until they arrived. Some penances imposed further penalties and hardships. A repentant knight or an aristocratic lady often vowed to make the trip on foot, or even barefoot, so his or her feet became cut and bruised to show repentance. One arrogant count was sentenced to wearing shackles as he made his court-ordered pilgrimages.

Pilgrims wore certain badges and kinds of **clothing.** Crosses, red or white, were the particular mark of a pilgrim. The cross would be sewn onto their cloaks and **hats;** their hats often had a practical brim since the pilgrims would be out in all weather. Men allowed their beards to grow, and all carried staffs. They carried only small bags, for theirs was not a trip of luxury. Pilgrims were expected to be unkempt and not have many changes of clothes.

Both the bag and the staff were blessed with holy water before the pilgrim set out. The bishop or priest gave the pilgrim a letter certifying his or her status as a real pilgrim, since there were thieves who posed as pilgrims. The pilgrim had another task before setting out; he or she had to settle all debts and make a will. There were many dangers, and some pilgrims did not return home.

After a pilgrim had reached his destination, he often displayed some memento of the place on his hat. A palm stood for the Holy Land and a scallop shell for the beach at Compostela. Many shrines sold badges made

Even in the Middle Ages, tourists wanted to leave their mark on places they visited. Medieval pilgrims to the Church of the Holy Sepulcher scratched crosses and their names onto the building's stone walls. (Alfred J. Andrea)

of **lead** or pewter. Each one depicted the saint holding some symbols of his life or death or of the miracles done at his shrine. Pilgrims collected badges and pinned them onto their clothing. On a typical pilgrimage, they stopped at all shrines along the way, visiting the **relics** and collecting badges.

Pilgrims wanted to come home with more than just badges. Many carried mementos for friends who could not come and brought these rosaries or crosses into each shrine to take in some of the holiness the relics could impart. Some had been commissioned with bringing home holy relics for friends and family or for someone who was very sick. They might chip off a piece of the tomb; Saint Martin's at Tours had to put up a railing to stop people from taking pieces of the stone shrine. Some souvenir relics could be as simple as a strip of linen held as close as possible in the presence of the saint's shrine to soak in the holiness. Pilgrims also mixed oil with dust from the tomb or burned a little oil on a cloth by the tomb. There were often peddlers in the area, trying to sell bits of bone or hair that they claimed were from that saint or some other. In Jerusalem, there were many bits of wood passed off as shards of the true cross, thorns purportedly from the crown of thorns, or bottles of saints' tears or blood.

A typical pilgrimage from England to Rome took 50 days each way. **Monasteries** that released monks to go on pilgrimage to the Holy Land allowed a year. Pilgrimages to Compostela from France or England took only a few months, while a pilgrimage to the nearest shrine (Canterbury or Walsingham for Englishmen, Saint Denis or Tours for Frenchmen) took only a few weeks. No journey went as quickly as possible; everything was subject to delays due to sickness, weather, and storm.

A pilgrim's journey usually took him over mountains such as the Alps or Pyrenees or over the sea. Mountain travel was dangerous due to snowstorms. Storms also came at sea, as did pirates. Pilgrims walked into war zones and sometimes found themselves stuck in a besieged city. Some pilgrims had allied themselves with bishops or rulers whose enemies arrested and robbed them. They were often attacked by ordinary robbers at **inns** and in **forests.** They caught infectious diseases or food poisoning. A silent danger was polluted or toxic rivers in some localities, and pilgrims or their horses could become sick from drinking there. The locals could not always be trusted, since they might reassure the traveler that the **water** was perfectly safe only to skin the dead horse or make off with the dead pilgrim's money.

Pilgrims had to avoid carrying **coins.** Many pilgrims funded their journeys through begging. Wealthier pilgrims paid a deposit with a merchant's banking service so that, at a certain destination, they could receive the sum in another currency to fund the next stage. Some who began with sufficient funds ended up begging in order to make it home after misfortune and robbery.

Certain orders of knights formed to protect pilgrims. The Knights of Saint James were supposed to guard the region of Compostela. The Knights of Malta began as an order that ran a hospice for sick pilgrims in Jerusalem. Some of these orders ran hostels for pilgrims along the road. The Templars, especially, also acted as bankers for travelers.

There were also simple travel services for pilgrims. Literate pilgrims wrote **books** about their travels, and, if they had been along a route more than once, some wrote guides and **maps.** These maps showed strips of **road,** not as the road really lay on the true geography but as a string of places the traveler encountered. They marked unsafe water, good inns, and robbers' haunts. Guides could be hired, but it was always a risk. Was the guide honest, or was he planning to lead the pilgrims' group into an ambush? Pilgrims had to hire **horses** and mules along the way, as well as **boats** and **ships.** Guidebooks told them which rentals and junkets to avoid.

The city of Venice was not only a pilgrim destination itself, it was also a chief travel hub to the Holy Land. Ship owners organized hostels and travel junkets for pilgrims who arrived in Venice. The doge, realizing how important a hub Venice had become, extended protection to all pilgrims. The city offered advice and shelter, and there were offices where returning pilgrims could report complaints about Venetian ships. The galleys were owned by the city of Venice, and all captains were supposed to follow protocol for how they charged and treated their passengers.

Monasteries took in pilgrims as they traveled. In some places, there were no inns, and only monasteries and convents would take in pilgrims. Inns, when they existed, varied in comfort and security. In some places, travelers slept in the same bed together. Frequently, they stayed together in a main room, even if they slept on the floor or on separate cots. Robberies were frequent. Pilgrims could also rent a house for a few days, if they were able.

In 1300, the Pope declared a Jubilee year for pilgrimages to Rome; pilgrims could expect a plenary indulgence—the forgiveness of not just a few sins, but of all. Rome was packed to capacity as pilgrims poured in from all over Europe. In 1350, the Pope declared another Jubilee year. Europe was barely recovering from the plague and had lost as much as one-third of its population. Still, with a keen awareness of death, European pilgrims came in the same numbers as before. After that, pilgrimages gradually lost some of their pious fervor, and by the 15th century, they were drifting toward secular tourism. During the Protestant Reformation, nations that cast off the Catholic Church suppressed shrines and burned relics. The Catholic Church, too, did not encourage pilgrimages as much as before. Skeptics doubted the power of relics, and the pilgrims on the roads to Rome and Compostela reverted to their scanty premedieval numbers.

See also: Church, Maps, Relics, Saints, Taverns and Inns.

Further Reading

Harpur, James. *Sacred Tracks: Two Thousand Years of Christian Pilgrimage.* Los Angeles: University of California Press, 2002.

Kendall, Alan. *Medieval Pilgrims.* New York: G. P. Putnam's Sons, 1970.

Sumption, Jonathan. *The Age of Pilgrimage: The Medieval Journey to God.* Mahwah, NJ: Hidden Spring, 2003.

Ure, John. *Pilgrimages: The Great Adventures of the Middle Ages.* New York: Carroll and Graf, 2006.

Webb, Diana. *Medieval European Pilgrimage, c. 700–c.1500.* New York: Palgrave, 2002.

Webb, Diana. *Pilgrims and Pilgrimage in the Medieval West.* New York: St. Martin's Press, 1999.

Plague

Medieval people knew many epidemic diseases, although they did not know what caused them. Outbreaks of ergotism, typhus, influenza, and other sicknesses often struck towns. What made the plague stand out was that its symptoms seemed to include every possible malfunction of the human body. It spread fast and killed quickly, and its victims experienced symptoms of many illnesses at once.

There were two widespread, devastating plague periods during the Middle Ages. The first was during the reign of the Byzantine emperor Justinian, in the sixth century. The second, which is more famous, came to Europe in 1347. At the time, it was called the Great Mortality, but we now call it the Black Death. Between these plague periods, we have no records of mass epidemics. Infectious disease on a large scale seems to have been unknown for nearly 800 years. The two pandemics that bookended the Middle Ages shaped its political and social history. Both epidemics cut Europe's population in half, disrupting empires and traditions.

The Plague of Justinian: 541

Records from this early medieval plague are limited. The outbreak was first recorded in Constantinople in 541, and it is commonly called the Plague of Justinian. It may have begun in Egypt and moved north to Constantinople with imported grain. The plague eventually spread all around the Mediterranean Sea and into Europe, Asia, and North Africa. The death rate may have been as high as 50 percent in many places. The plague subsided, but it returned in waves for another two centuries.

The plague's effect on the fading Roman Empire was severe. During the sixth century, barbarians were attacking Italy. The plague weakened Italy's defenses and permitted the Goths to invade freely. Justinian was not able to defend Italy due to his army's losses to plague. The Byzantine Empire was weakened in the East, as well. When **Muslim** Arabs invaded Palestine and Syria in the seventh century, the depopulated Byzantines, also weakened by wars with Persia, could not defend their territory.

The Black Death: 1347–1350

In the prelude to the greatest worldwide pandemic in history, there was a series of catastrophes. Seismic activity in Asia sent clouds of volcanic ash into the atmosphere, which accelerated a general cooling trend in the **climate.** At several points in the early 14th century, winters were harsher than usual, summers were cool, and it rained so much that crops were ruined. In each famine period, as much as 10 percent of Europe's population died of starvation. The Hundred Years' War between England and France began in 1337 and left the French countryside traumatized, often with burned land and ruined houses. In Italy, civil wars between rival families and **cities** were so frequent that the Popes chose to live in Avignon, France, rather than in Rome.

The Black Death, as the plague of 1347–1350 is now called, attacked a weakened worldwide population. It is difficult to estimate how many people died during the Black Death. Some **records** seem accurate, and some

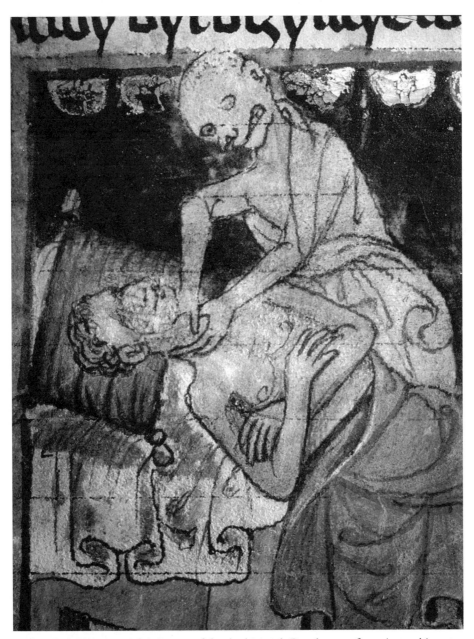

After the plague, people's image of death changed. Death was often pictured in art, and the character of Death was always gruesome and corpse-like. Sometimes Death drew people into a dance, but other times, as in this image painted about 25 years later, Death relentlessly chose unwilling victims to murder. (Werner Forman Archive/ StockphotoPro)

do not. Estimates based on records of estates, churches, and families calculate death rates that range from 25 percent to 60 percent. Mortality varied, as well. Some villages were completely wiped out, while others survived and kept their work going the whole time. In Ireland, one of the last regions visited by plague, native Irish who lived in the hills were struck lightly, while the English living in coastal towns died at rates similar to England's. It is difficult to determine the death rate for any one place, let alone for a larger region. The most common mortality rate used for Europe as a whole is 30 percent. At least one in three people died; in some towns it was closer to two in three. Some cities had a death rate of close to 50 percent.

Symptoms

The hallmark of the plague was an egg-shaped swollen lymph node on the groin, in the armpit, or on the neck. The modern name for this swelling is bubo, from the Greek word *buboin,* meaning "groin." From this term comes the name "bubonic plague." As the patient grew sicker, more lymph nodes swelled. A bubo could grow large, to the size of an egg or apple, or it could remain small. They were usually acutely painful, and sometimes they burst open, oozing black blood. As the illness progressed, many patients also developed bruise-like markings on their arms or legs.

The violent symptoms of the plague often began with coughing. The illness attacked the lungs early, and the patient coughed blood or, having swallowed some, vomited blood. As the patient grew sicker, blood was discharged from the anus, as well. Patients developed high fevers in most cases. Another symptom that all contemporary observers recorded was that sick people smelled very bad. There was a particularly offensive, rotting odor on the breath and bodies of the sick.

The plague of 1347 was extremely contagious. Contemporaries reported that people became sick from touching something a sick person had touched or from merely looking at a sick person. **Animals** also caught it. The plague altered its form during the epidemic. Those who caught it first were most likely to fall sick quickly and violently, and not always with buboes. They died within two days. Those who fell sick during the later stages of the epidemic always developed buboes, but their lungs were not as affected. Some of these recovered; those who died were sick for closer to a week.

There may have been three forms of the infection, depending on where it settled. The form that is most common now, the bubonic form, is also the least contagious and least fatal. The infection is mostly in the lymph system; it is not spread through casual contact, but only by fleabites. The infection can also be pneumonic, in the lungs. Pneumonic plague produced the bloody coughs and rapid, airborne contagion. In the rarest cases, plague can go straight to the bloodstream in septicemic form. Septicemic infection results in rapid death, within hours, because the massive amounts of bacteria overwhelm the body before the victim has time to develop other symptoms, such as buboes. The outbreak of 1347 may have been predominantly pneumonic, with some cases of septicemia, based on the descriptions of observers.

Spread through Europe

The European outbreak of 1347 was heavily documented by many writers, since literacy was widespread by then. We have records from towns and cities, parishes, bishops, private individuals who kept journals, and at least two well-known writers, Petrarch and Boccacio. Boccacio was in Florence when the plague struck, while Petrarch was in Avignon, where his beloved Laura died from the plague. We know a great deal about the plague in Italy and England, where meticulous record keeping went with large-scale commerce, but we know relatively less about Spain and Germany.

All sources from around the Mediterranean agree that **ships** from Genoa spread the infection first. Genoa had established a colony, called Caffa, on the Black Sea. It was on the Crimean Peninsula, where modern Feodosia is located. Inland, the Tartars had conquered Russia, and war broke out between Caffa and the Tartars. The besieging Tartars caught the plague, and, as they became too sick to fight, they flung dead bodies into Caffa. The plague spread in Caffa, and some escaped in ships and headed back to Genoa. It is less clear what happened after that because there were reports of Genoese death ships in Constantinople, Sicily, Sardinia, Italian ports such as Genoa and Naples, and Marseille. It seems unlikely that the same ships from Caffa called at all these ports, since their crews were dying rapidly. What is clear is that the trade network, extremely active in the Mediterranean by the 14th century, rapidly spread the highly contagious infection.

Constantinople, at the mouth of the Black Sea, was the first region to fall sick in great numbers. Genoese ships passed through the Aegean Sea and reached Messina, Sicily. Sicilians rapidly caught the plague, and it passed all through the island. The Italian peninsula followed, and, at the same time, the plague entered France through the port of Marseille. It spread rapidly through these regions. As the rumor of the Genoese death ships spread, ports became unwilling to allow ships to stay, and some cities drove them away violently. The city of Genoa itself drove off its ships with burning arrows.

The plague was so highly contagious, though, that nothing could hold back its march through Europe. By the end of 1347, Messina, Marseille, and Genoa were infected, and a month later, Avignon, Venice, and Ragusa were sick. In March and April of 1348, the plague entered Spain and infected the inland Italian city of Florence. In June it entered Paris, and around August 1348, the plague came to Rome and to the coast of England. As the plague spread throughout France, London was struck in the fall of 1348. Around April 1349, an English ship brought the plague to Norway, where it spread into Sweden. Coming from a different direction, the plague was in Germany around June 1349, beginning with Bavaria and Vienna. It entered Poland in the summer of 1349, and by the winter of 1350, it had reached Scotland. Ireland had a lighter case of plague, and the disease did not reach Iceland at that time. In 1352, the plague reached distant Moscow. During the same years, the plague also spread through the Middle East, ravaging Egypt, Palestine, Arabia, and North Africa.

In each place, the plague lasted for about a year and then died out. New cases became weekly, rather than daily, then every few weeks, then monthly, and finally there were no new cases. In 1349, Italy's plague ended, and relief from plague followed in other countries at the same pace the plague had entered.

The plague continued to return in waves until the 17th century. Although the disease was not native to Europe, it was established in the local rat population for two centuries until it finally died out even among the rats. Europe continued to lose up to 10 percent of its population with each wave of plague; the wave that followed the Black Death, in 1361, struck down many of the children born since the first plague.

Treatment and Prevention

Medieval medical ideas were based on the late Roman works of Galen, who lived through a similar plague but did not absorb its lessons. There was no workable theory of contagion, and physicians debated whether diseases were passed from one person to another, rather than through bad air or a pernicious astrological combination in the skies. The medical faculty of Paris determined that the plague's severity was due to a bad conjunction of three planets in 1345. This created a disturbance on the planet, causing bad air; poisons from the earth had been drawn out into the atmosphere. The physicians of Paris recommended that south-facing windows should be blocked off to guard against warm, damp air. In Spain, Arab doctors held the same views but were not permitted to recommend preventative measures. According to Islam, people lived or died by God's will alone, and a belief in contagion was irreligious and dangerous.

The prevailing idea that bad air caused the plague pushed many people to use pleasant-smelling flowers or **spices** to avoid infection. They carried small bouquets under their noses when they went into the streets, and those who could afford cinnamon or cloves used lockets or pressed the spices into oranges and carried them. The other prevailing idea in **medicine** was that the proper balance of the body maintained health, so especially at this time, people needed to keep a temperate diet that was properly balanced.

Medieval writers recorded extremes of behavior among their fellow citizens. Some became terrified of the bad air and contagion around them and isolated themselves. The Pope survived the plague by remaining indoors with roaring fires going at all times. Others took in supplies for a few months and shut themselves inside with their families, boarding up windows and bolting doors, hoping the plague would pass them by (it worked in some cases). Some responded to the overwhelming death rate by living carelessly. They believed that an excess of **food,** drink, and dancing would drive off the humors of the bad air and keep them balanced. They went to **taverns** and entered private homes, looking for alcohol and fun. Still others fled the city and went as far into the country as they could, hoping to escape the contagion. In most cases, it was futile.

Cities did have rudimentary ideas about waste disposal and proper burial of corpses to try to control infection. The cities that retained basic services throughout the plague organized a daily collection of bodies on biers or, in the case of Venice, by **boat.** When the cemeteries filled, they dug trenches or pits, layered the bodies in with some charcoal ash or dirt, and covered the top as well as they could. In many cases, the sheer number of the dead made it difficult for cities to bury them well enough to keep dogs from digging them up and spreading more infection.

Although the people of that time had no concept of microscopic organisms that could pass from one person to another, they also knew that being close to a sick person was dangerous. Care for the sick and dying, which was normally orderly and thorough, fell apart in most cities. In Florence, where the public order nearly broke down, relatives abandoned the dying, even their own children. Although many or perhaps most families continued normal care for their sick, the terror of the plague was too much for some.

Across southern France and Germany, a rumor spread that **Jews** were causing the plague by poisoning the water supply. The town of Chillon, in the county of Savoy, sent letters to other German towns to warn them that a Jew had confessed to the plot. Although the Pope, the king of Aragon, the duke of Austria, and some city governments tried to protect the local Jews, people in Germany, Flanders, France, and Spain massacred their Jewish populations. Strasbourg recorded the death of 16,000 Jews; in Mainz, where Jews struck back and killed 200 Christians, 12,000 Jews were recorded as dead. The Jewish population of Germany, from the Swiss border to the northern towns on the Baltic, became extinct. Some Jews fled to Poland and Lithuania, where the king of Poland offered them protection.

Effect on Society

During the Black Death, many people believed the epidemic was God's punishment for their sins. A town's first response to the approaching plague was often to organize a ceremonial procession through the streets with a **saint**'s **relics** carried at the front, and they offered many prayers for mercy for the people's sins. But as the plague grew worse, a less moderate religious response began. Centered in Germany, the movement is known as the Flagellants.

The Flagellants were monks and laymen who believed that only a dramatic demonstration of repentance would suffice. They went on **pilgrimages** of 33 days each during which they whipped themselves three times a day. On these pilgrimages, they arrived in a town and led a procession to the church, where they whipped their own backs and each other's with whips that were barbed so as to wound deeply. The townspeople looked on with awe or were pulled into the frenzied emotion. Some joined the Flagellants for month-long pilgrimages, while others went on rampages against the remaining Jews. The Flagellant movement was very popular in Germany and as far away as Flanders, but when it came to England, it met with less enthusiasm. As the plague ended in Europe, the Flagellants went home.

Across Europe, two contradictory social changes took place immediately following the plague. Contemporary writers stated that survivors had lost their moral standards; at the same time, there was a rise in personal piety that began to develop European religion away from the medieval model.

The attitude of "eat, drink, and be merry" stemmed from the immense grief, too great to be fully comprehended, combined with the loss of some social institutions and conventions. Survivors felt very relieved. They pursued fun to drive away the memories and to enjoy life before the next catastrophe. Italian writers observed this trend the most strongly. They reported that women were dressing immodestly and acting immorally and that feasting and drinking were at irresponsible levels.

At the same time, the breakdown of social connections during the crisis had frightened many survivors. They recalled the improper, hasty burials, and they knew cases in which no family members had survived to bury or mourn the dead. Priests were not able to keep up with the demand for visits to the dying or burial rites. Survivors of the plague knew that if another plague struck, they might find themselves with no burial rites or prayers. In many Italian cities, they began to form societies that promised to see to each other's **funerals.** These societies began to do charitable acts, such as caring for the poor, and meet for prayer. Piety became a personal matter, rather than just for monks and priests. There was also a surge of interest in occult **magic** and ways to contact the dead. Witchcraft became a bigger concern than before the plague.

As the Black Death plague hit its peak in continental Europe, the common people of Germany, France, and the Netherlands appealed to God. Men vowed to complete 33-day pilgrimages as Flagellants, walking from town to town and publicly whipping their backs to show repentance for society's sins. These Flagellants are arriving in the cloth-manufacturing town of Tournai, bearing a crucifix and banners. (Ann Ronan Pictures/StockphotoPro)

Europe's pre-plague economy had been based on feudal **agriculture.** When the population of Europe was cut by an average of 40 percent, many estates could not get in their harvests. There were not enough peasants to work the lord's land, and peasants resisted some other feudal provisions. In many places, when a peasant died, the lord's estate took his best animal as a death tax. In a time of extreme mortality, the peasants resisted this tax, which impoverished them when they were already struggling. Feudalism, with its restrictions on where a peasant could live and what he could do, no longer made sense.

Land values dropped. There were not enough people to farm the land, and some acres began to revert to **forest** or swamp. Food production dropped, but, with fewer people to feed, prices for food also went down. The only value that rose was the value of labor. With so few laborers, and so many places to fill, poor men demanded high wages.

Landowners found themselves in a weak position because they had to expend cash in order to get work done that used to be done for free. Their farm produce was worth less, but they paid more to produce it. **Servants** were hard to find, and more skilled labor positions were now available for them to move into. Landowners in many places petitioned for laws that would keep the old order. With wages frozen and peasants not permitted to leave, their estates could keep running. In England, after at least four more outbreaks of plague, the peasants finally exploded in a revolt in 1381.

When land prices fell and many farms were left vacant, estates, **schools,** and individuals were able to purchase or lease land at good prices. Most historians believe much of Europe had been relatively overpopulated, leaving many peasants without land. Survivors found themselves farming more prosperously, with more to eat.

So many priests died in the plague that bishops had to rush uneducated men into vacancies. The **universities** of Oxford and Cambridge both expanded in the years immediately following the Black Death, so as to train more priests. The educational standard of priests in England rose, as a result.

The plague may also have influenced both architecture and education. Medieval **masons** were highly trained and took years to learn their craft. Some historians believe the deaths of many master masons during the Black Death disrupted the training process. Later masons did not have the skills to create the elaborate stone features of earlier **cathedrals.** Teachers, another educated group, also suffered losses. In England, this may have hastened the shift from French to English as the national language. Until that time, children who went to school (a minority) learned French, but after the plague, schools did not require mastery of French in a teacher, and most children were educated only in English.

Ideas about Causes of the Plague

In the late 19th century, Europeans in India and China witnessed an outbreak of plague that became known as the Third Pandemic. It began in China in 1855, and, over the next 70 years, it spread through Asia and beyond. During this epidemic, researchers could observe and study the plague. The Swiss biologist Alexandre Yersin isolated the destructive bacillus in 1894, and it was named for him: *Yersinia pestis.* By 1900, researchers were certain the plague was being spread mostly by fleas on rats. Fleas are specific to host species. Rat fleas are called *Xenopsylla cheopis,* while fleas that prefer humans (and pigs) are called *Pulex irritans. Y. pestis* is particularly suited to *X. cheopis,* the rat flea. During the Third Pandemic, observers saw many dead rats just before an outbreak among humans; as the rats died of plague, the fleas moved to a less preferred host—humans.

The mechanism of transmission in the flea is dependent on how severely the flea is infected by the bacteria. If the *Y. pestis* bacteria remain in its digestive tract, the flea is unlikely to transmit it to the rats or other animals it bites. However, if the bacteria begin to multiply rapidly, the flea's stomach becomes blocked. The only way it can restore its own ability to digest blood is to vomit bacteria into the animal it is biting.

Researchers used this knowledge to understand what had happened during the Middle Ages. Rats infested ships, **houses,** and fields. As merchants traveled, their rats and fleas traveled with them. As in the Third Pandemic, the infection was passed through blood contact with the fleas, which discharged *Y. pestis* bacteria into each bite.

However, the Black Death was not entirely like the Third Pandemic. Its contagion moved much faster, and its mortality was much higher. There were outbreaks of plague that did not appear to be connected to the movement of rats, and medieval observers did not comment on the number of dead rats in the streets. On the other hand, excavations where medieval plague victims are buried have turned up traces of *Y. pestis*.

The medieval plague may have been worse due to differences in the population and its ability to handle an epidemic. In the years before the plague, medieval Europe and Asia had suffered several major famines. These famines probably weakened immune systems, especially for **babies** born during the famines; these babies were adults during the Black Death. During the modern outbreak, doctors used public health measures such as quarantine, while medieval towns did not. When modern public health measures broke down, the death rate increased rapidly.

The infection itself may have been a more virulent strain of *Y. pestis*. Some evidence points to an origin not in the rat population, but in a group of Asian marmots called tarabagans. These large rodents live in burrow communities on the steppes of southern Russian and northern Kyrgyzstan, and the Silk Road, a major trade route during the later Middle Ages, ran through their territory. The earliest records of the medieval outbreak, around 1339, come from Lake Issyk Kul, in tarabagan country. From there, the plague spread east to India and China and then west to Europe. It is possible that the strain of *Y. pestis* active among tarabagans was deadlier than the later-studied rat strain. It may have been more likely to develop into pneumonic disease.

A fourth difference may be that the infection spread not only through the rat flea, *X. cheopis,* but also through the human flea, *P. irritans.* Europeans in the 14th century rarely changed their clothes, and they all had fleas and lice. If the infection went from an infected human to *P. irritans* and was then spread by both types of fleas, some of the contagion stories make more sense, especially cases in which it was unlikely that rats moved from place to place.

See also: Climate, Funerals, Jews, Medicine.

Further Reading

Benedictow, Ole Jorgen. *The Black Death, 1346–1353: The Complete History.* Cambridge: D. S. Brewer, 2006.

Cantor, Norman. *In the Wake of the Plague: The Black Death and the World It Made.* New York: Simon and Schuster, 2001.

Gottfried, Robert S. *The Black Death: Natural and Human Disaster in Medieval Europe.* New York: Free Press, 1985.

Herlihy, David. *The Black Death and the Transformation of Europe.* Cambridge, MA: Harvard University Press, 1997.

Horrox, Rosemary, ed. *The Black Death.* Manchester, UK: Manchester University Press, 1994

Karlen, Arno. *Man and Microbe: Disease and Plague in History and Modern Times.* New York: Simon and Schuster, 1996.

Kelly, John. *The Great Mortality.* New York: Harper Collins, 2005.

Rosen, William. *Justinian's Flea: Plague, Empire, and the Birth of Europe.* New York: Viking Press, 2007.

Ziegler, Philip. *The Black Death.* Dover, NH: Alan Sutton Publishing, 1991.

Plays. *See* Drama

Plow. *See* Agriculture

Poison

Many of those who were poisoned by **food** suffered only from natural bacteria in a time when there was no refrigeration. But many herbal poisons were well-known, and in Constantinople, deliberate food poisoning happened often enough to be one of the most common royal deaths. Kings had to protect against poisoning, and their households did so methodically. Poison could be on a tablecloth, a cup, a trencher, a spoon, or in any dish of food.

Hemlock, a common leafy green plant, grew in several forms. Water hemlock, which grew in damp meadows and by ponds, contains a toxin that causes seizures. Another kind of hemlock, called *conium* in Latin, was the source of the poison Athens used to execute Socrates. One of its alkaloids, coniine, causes muscle paralysis that eventually stops the victim from breathing. Aconite, also called wolfsbane or monk's hood, was a common flowering plant with a natural anesthetic. In concentrated form, it is a lethal poison. The thorn-apple, in Latin *datura,* also has toxins that cause confusion and death. Henbane and deadly nightshade also caused hallucinations and confusion with tachycardia and, if strong enough, death.

Herbal poisons were used to control unwanted **animal** populations. Wolves and foxes could be poisoned with black hellebore, if it was mixed

After King John of England died of dysentery in 1216, rumors flew that he had been poisoned. His death by poison came to be accepted as fact; this painting shows the king accepting the deadly cup. Since medieval monarchs traveled a great deal and were expected to drink ceremonial cups in public, it was hard for them to avoid a cup offered by an apparently friendly hand, like this monk's. (The British Library/ StockphotoPro)

with animal fat and honey. Aconite poisoned rats when it was mixed with cheese. Head lice could be killed with larkspur seeds and vinegar.

Some minerals, too, were known poisons. Mercury, separated from the cinnabar in which it naturally occurred, was used in some technology. Arsenic was used as a chemical in mixing paint and could easily be purchased from an apothecary.

One test for poison was to have a **servant** eat some of the suspect food. The assumption was that the effect of the poison would show up fairly quickly. The other important poison test involved the horn of a unicorn. Travelers to the East claimed they had seen unicorns disinfect water by dipping a horn into it, and some classical writers had claimed it was impossible to be poisoned by drink in a cup made from a unicorn's horn. People also believed the horn would shake or sweat in the presence of poison. Royal households kept the largest possible piece of horn on hand for testing food for poison. Since the unicorn is a mythical beast, the horns were really ivory from an elephant or a narwhal.

Poison on a tablecloth could be counteracted by rolling the unicorn's horn across it. The horn tested the hand-washing water and the hand-drying towel, which was kept on a servant's shoulder, draped openly so everyone could see it did not contain any kind of poison. Everything the king would come into contact with could be tested or made safe by the horn.

Salt was tested by tasting it, and then it was placed at the king's place. Each dish was tested by the horn and by tasting it while it was still in the kitchen. The dishes were brought to the table, covered with clean cloths, under many watchful eyes to make sure nobody tampered with them between the kitchen and the table. The unicorn horn remained at the king's place and was used to test or disinfect every food or drink brought to him.

See also: Food, Monsters.

Further Reading

Collard, Franck. *The Crime of Poison in the Middle Ages.* Westport, CT: Praeger, 2008.

Scully, Terence. *The Art of Cookery in the Middle Ages.* Woodbridge, UK: Boydell Press, 1995.

Pope. *See* Church

Pottery

During Roman times, potters used wheels and kilns and produced vases, urns, cups, and bowls. In parts of Northern Europe ruled by the Romans, as far north as Britain, potters produced wheel-turned pots in imitation of Roman technique but of poorer quality. The invasion of Germanic tribes disrupted the pottery traditions. During the Middle Ages, skill with ceramics was slowly rebuilt, especially around the Mediterranean, where the Roman crafts were never entirely lost.

Potter's wheels were used in most of Europe through most of the Middle Ages, although some more primitive places used hand-shaped pots. Wheels were usually made with a small shaping wheel on top and a large, heavy flywheel by the potter's feet; once the flywheel was kicked into motion, its weight kept it turning so that it did not need to be kicked continuously.

Unglazed pottery was cheapest; it was molded and fired and had a surface like an unglazed **brick**. Unglazed wares made common cooking and baking dishes and the most common storage or water jugs. The three glazing options were **lead**, tin, and **salt**. Lead glazes had been used all through the Roman Empire. Lead's poisonous nature was not known, so people did not hesitate to add it to drinking and eating vessels. Lead glazes were clear and hard after firing. Tin-glazing techniques were imported to Europe from the Islamic empire, chiefly around Baghdad. Ground tin oxide in clear glaze turned white after firing. Salt glazing was invented in the late Middle Ages in Germany.

After glazing, pottery had to be fired in a kiln. Clay changes its molecular structure when it is exposed to very high heat; it becomes unable to absorb

water. Most of medieval Europe used a kiln of some kind, although in the more primitive Germanic areas during the Dark Ages, pottery firing may have been achieved by burying the wares in bonfire ashes. European kilns used chimneys so that the updraft made the fire hotter. There were usually two chambers, one above the other, and a brick structure that encased the chambers and created the chimney; German kilns were often bottle shaped. Medieval kilns could reach 1,000°C. In 14th-century Germany, the invention of stoneware required hotter kilns with new technology that could reach 1,200°C.

Islamic Pottery Techniques

Ceramics were most highly developed in China, and, during the medieval period, traders imported Chinese ceramics first to the Islamic empire and then into Europe. Chinese porcelain was characterized by its white color, made from kaolin clay, and by its clear glazes and very hard firing. Potters in the Middle East and around the Mediterranean began to copy this as they could. The search for a way to recreate Chinese porcelain pushed Islamic potters to innovate, and their pottery developed quickly and eventually created wares that the Chinese, in turn, tried to imitate.

Several factors unique to medieval Islam shaped the ceramics traditions. Islamic rulers discouraged the use of **gold** and **silver** vessels at table, which meant that ceramics were more in use by wealthy **Muslims** than by wealthy Byzantine Christians. Religious tradition forbade drawing the figures of people or **animals**—it was as if the artist were trying to take on the role of Allah in creation. Although this was not often enforced, there was a general trend to exotic geometric or floral motifs, especially in making **tile** for mosque walls. Bowls and vases sometimes depicted animals or people. As pottery techniques permitted more detailed designs, many dishes had verses from the Koran painted in decorative Kufic script, and this, in turn, influenced other designs.

Chinese kaolin was not available, but potters in ninth-century Iraq created a white glaze that had tin oxide added to it, and it could imitate Chinese white porcelain. Over the next three centuries, they learned a range of techniques of tinting and firing. They tinted unfired tin-glazed wares with cobalt for blue, and **copper** for green, so that when fired, the white dishes had elaborate blue or green designs. Painting the glaze before firing is called inglazing. Then potters learned to paint a white dish that had already been fired, using paint made of silver and copper oxides, before firing it a second time. This is called luster painting; lusterware became the dominant pottery style as it spread into the Mediterranean region. Slip painting was another decorative option. They painted a design onto unglazed pottery using slip, a mix of water and mineral-tinted clay and then fired it with a clear glaze. Minerals for slip painting produced the colors red, brown, and black. Islamic ceramics with slip painting often have elaborate Koranic inscriptions. Sometimes vessels first decorated with slip painting had a colored glaze, such as blue.

The last medieval ceramics techniques developed in the Islamic countries were fritware and enamel painting. Fritware had large amounts of crushed quartz mixed into the clay to make it both stronger and colored white. Because of its strong composition, it could be decorated with relief carvings, rather than enamel or other colors. Enamel painting was developed in Iran; enamels were mineral glazes that could be painted onto glazed, fired dishes to add new colors and designs. They provided strong colors and were painted with brushes, so potters could achieve good detail. The vessels were then fired again, at a low temperature. Persian enameled dishes had a range of colors: blue, black, green, brown, red, white, and gold or silver leaf. Islamic tile mosaics on buildings favor white, blue, and black because of these techniques. Cobalt for blue was a commonly available mineral in the Middle East.

European Pottery

The Islamic techniques came to the Mediterranean region first, through North Africa into Spain and through trade with Venice. At the same time, the North Europeans had simple pottery methods they continued to use. As with other crafts, northern and southern gradually blended by the 15th century.

In Spain, two traditions competed and finally blended. The Christian kingdoms in the north, based in Visigothic culture, used more primitive pottery techniques, while Muslim Andalusia in the south imported pottery and skills from Egypt. While northern potters were making simple gray pots and pitchers, the Muslim potters of the south learned the Egyptian method of making lusterware. Their twice-fired pottery used crushed silver, copper, or even gold in the second glaze. The metal adhered to the pottery and made it shine. They also imported cobalt for blue glaze. The famous blue and white wall tiles of the Alhambra palace were lusterware with cobalt blue designs. The height of their art was showcased in the Alhambra's collection of large decorative vases covered with intricate designs based on Arabic script.

When the Reconquest made most of the peninsula Christian again in 1248, Muslim potters altered their style to blend Christian and even Gothic elements. They learned to paint heraldic designs. Many moved to the Valencia region, and they exported ceramics all over Europe. The Valencia style, by the close of the Middle Ages, used not just cobalt blue but also other bright colors and had perfected the luster techniques. The Spanish techniques and art were the dominant model for Italy.

In early medieval Italy, the Roman techniques continued to be used, although there was no further development under Gothic rule. Contact with the Byzantine Empire renewed interest in glazes and decorating plain wares. Most lead glazes turned yellow or green. The most common decoration on a vase or jug was to draw a decoration in white slip on the red clay, then scratch through the white slip to allow the red clay to show in lines, and then coat it with a clear lead glaze, which turned yellow.

After 1250, pottery in northern Italy was often covered with white tin glaze that allowed for much more decorative painting. By the end of the Middle Ages, this decorated white pottery was called maiolica. The term *maiolica* came from the Spanish island of Majorca, which served as a shipping point for many tin-glazed wares that originated in Spanish Andalusia and imported the tin-glazing technique from Baghdad. The clay vessels were fired in a kiln and then dipped in tin oxide glaze. After they dried, the potter could paint designs using copper paint that would turn green when refired. When the vessel came out of the kiln, it was pure white with green leaves or geometric designs. Maiolica pottery was very appealing and became a major industry for Florence, Faenza, Orvieto, and other towns. Although the term *faenza* came to stand for the style in Northern Europe, each town tended to have a style of decoration that was distinctive: green leaves in Florence, vines and grapes in Orvieto. As the 15th century passed and Italy moved into the Renaissance period, potters developed more tinted glazes and could paint in a variety of colors.

In Northern Europe, pottery was not as widely used. In the southern regions that produced wine and olive oil, storage jars and pottery lamps were much more important. Wood was the chief building material of the north. In Southern Europe, pottery vessels all through the medieval period included jars, pitchers, bowls, lamps, cooking pots, portable stoves, urinals, trays, and funnels. Northern Europe used metal or wood for many of these vessels and only maintained simple pottery techniques for pitchers, cups, and some cooking pots until the pottery of the Mediterranean began to make its way north through trade.

French pottery in the Middle Ages did not develop much until the 13th century. Before that, they made basic jugs and jars glazed with green, yellow, and brown lead glazes. Norman pottery around Rouen used some white slip decorations and relief designs. Tin glazing came first to Avignon, along the Mediterranean coast, from Italy. The potters began making white tiles that they called faience, after the Italian city of Faenza.

In Flanders and the Netherlands, pottery was plain gray until they found a deposit of red clay in the 13th century. With the red clay, they could make white slip decorations similar to the Normans' designs, and they discovered colored glazes. Flemish pottery was soon in demand; they made jugs and jars, cooking pots, and curfews (fire covers to bank the ashes). Tin

Beautiful maiolica pottery began with Eastern tin glazing. After tin glazing technology came to Spain, Italy, and France, each region developed a style unique to its tradition and aesthetic sense. The style of Valencia, Spain, was modeled on Islamic styles in Egypt and Baghdad, and featured geometric patterns. (Hermitage, St. Petersburg, Russia/The Bridgeman Art Library)

glazing came at the end of the medieval period, in the 15th century. The Low Countries adopted the technology quickly; they began to produce decorated white dishes to compete with imports from China. During the postmedieval period, this industry became famous for its fine dishes, such as delftware.

Most medieval English households used pottery only for pitchers, storage jars in the kitchen, and drinking cups. Pottery cups were most favored by the poor who could not afford drinking horns, silver cups, or even wooden tankards. Potters did not have **guilds** until the late Middle Ages because making pottery was a part-time seasonal activity. After the 13th century, pottery had more status in England, and there were guilds. By the 14th century, potters were making a wider variety of goods, from bowls to cisterns.

The clay of England was typically red-brown; it was sometimes decorated with white slip, as in Normandy. Most early pottery was not glazed. The first glazes used in medieval England were based on naturally occurring lead powder, or galena, which was dusted onto the damp pot. The pots turned yellow when fired, or, if blended with copper, they turned green. The few pitchers and mugs that survived into modern times are typically bright, dark green and very shiny.

After shaping a pitcher on the wheel and adding spout and handle, the potter could use a different kind of clay as slip to make simple designs. Firing lead glaze over the whole finished piece made it glossy and yellow. All of the pottery in a region looked roughly the same, but the slightly different yellow, green, or brown decorations and glazes made each ewer and vase unique. (English Heritage Images)

English medieval pitchers were sometimes decorated with the figures of animals or people pressed onto the upper shoulders of the pitcher. Pitchers still extant today include decorations of dragons, birds, lions, **ships, and fish.** Other pitchers were decorated with faces, often bearded, looking outward. Water pitchers for table were sometimes made in the shape of animals or people so that the servants could pour water for guests from sheep or horses. The jugs were carefully made in naturalistic animal shapes with added handles, with the animal's mouth as the spout.

Germany, like the rest of Northern Europe, at first produced simple utility vessels, either unglazed or fired with lead. However, southern Germany had a strong tradition of making highly decorated tiles that were used in walls, floors, and stoves. This led Germany's potters to innovate, and they developed the only new ceramics inventions in Northern Europe.

The Rhine Valley potters invented stoneware, pottery that had been fired in unusually hot kilns until it had fused harder than most pottery and became as hard as stone. The local clay was gray, with much sand in it, and it was well suited to such high firing. It was generally not glazed in the medieval period because the known glazes did not work at such high temperatures. Stoneware was a popular export, and the Rhine River was a good export waterway, so the industry developed in many river towns. Stoneware did not make good cooking vessels, but it was good for storage jars and bottles. It was particularly good for drinking cups. The new beer industry was rapidly growing, and stoneware provided its pitchers and tankards.

In the 15th century, the Rhine potters developed salt glazing. They threw salt into the kiln, and its vapors adhered to the pottery to produce a thin glaze. Because the vapor produced such a thin glaze, the best way to decorate the pottery was by pressing relief molds onto the surface, instead of painting it. Early German salt-glazed vessels are usually covered with very fine, beautiful molded decorations. The natural color of a salt-glazed vessel depended on how much iron was in the clay as it reacted with the salt. The clay around Aachen, in modern Belgium, fired a rich reddish-brown with salt. In Siegburg, the local clay fired white.

See also: Bricks and Tile, Kitchen Utensils, Lead and Copper, Muslims.

Further Reading
Cooper, Emanuel. *Ten Thousand Years of Pottery.* Philadelphia: University of Pennsylvania Press, 2000.

Gaimster, David. *German Stoneware, 1200–1900.* London: British Museum Press, 1997.

Houkjaer, Ulla. *Tin-Glazed Earthenware, 1300–1750.* Copenhagen: Danish Museum of Art and Design, 2005.

Lewis, Griselda. *A Collector's History of English Pottery.* Woodbridge, UK: Antique Collectors' Club, 1999.

Pancaroglu, Oya. *Perpetual Glory: Medieval Islamic Ceramics from the Harvey B. Plotnick Collection.* Chicago: Art Institute of Chicago, 2007.
Poole, Julia E. *English Pottery.* Cambridge: Cambridge University Press, 1995.
Poole, Julia E. *Italian Maiolica.* Cambridge: Cambridge University Press, 1997.
Staubach, Suzanne. *Clay: The History and Evolution of Humankind's Relationship with Earth's Most Primal Element.* New York: Berkley Books, 2005.

Printing

Books were handmade manuscripts until printing made mass production possible. During the early 14th century, the first printed books appeared. Movable type had not yet been invented, but these books used woodcuts, also called block prints. Flanders and the Netherlands region were the most active areas in printing block books. The production of block books continued for many years even after the development of the printing press and its key element, movable type.

Making a block print involved using a piece of wood and cutting away the white space, leaving the surface of the block as the picture or letters. The block was cut with the image reversed, left to right. When the artist applied **ink** and pressed the block firmly down on **paper,** the image would be correct. These block prints were probably originally designed to be hand colored, but most remained as black-and-white images. Printers were able to make use of color by applying red, blue, or even **gold** ink to an opening initial or other decoration. Block printing was much faster than handwriting a manuscript, and the block could be used again and again, until the pressure on the ink-wet wood finally caused it to wear out.

The earliest woodblock prints that we know of were used for religious instruction; they have woodcut pictures and hand-lettered text. **Saints'** lives and Bible stories dominated all medieval literature. *Apocalypse* was an important series of block books, with pictures telling the story from the last book in the Bible, the "Revelation to Saint John." *Apocalypse* was published in at least six different editions. Another very influential block book was *Ars moriendi,* "The Art of Dying." It showed devils tempting the dying man to lose his faith, and then angels helping him remain steadfast to the end, in several scenarios of various temptations. Another widely known block book was *Incipit biblia pauperum,* the Poor Man's Bible. Each picture shows a central scene from the life of Jesus, flanked on the left and right by pictures showing (respectively) Old and New Testament scenes or stories that teach the same lesson.

Woodcuts allowed printers to manufacture playing cards. Cards became popular, especially in Northern Europe, and card playing inevitably led to gambling; German records from several **cities** indicate that gambling became a huge problem and that cards were banned in the late 1300s. There were also other kinds of cards that people gave to one another, an early form of greeting cards.

By 1450, all of the needed materials and most of the necessary technology were in place for the invention of printing. There were mills that could supply paper in quantity. Artists had begun using oil-based **paint,** and an ink that would work on metal type could be produced the same way. The screw press, which produced the kind of firm and even pressure needed for printing, was already in use for block printing on **cloth** and paper, among its many uses. Goldsmiths knew how to do metal casting; they had stamping tools with small metal letters to imprint book covers and make coins.

The one requirement for printing that was not yet in place was the ability to make large quantities of metal type that was both moveable and reusable. The type needed to be small and must be cast so that each little letter (a "sort") would be on a perfectly square base to fit tightly against other letters. The type had to be reusable, and the sorts needed to be easily and quickly made in the quantities necessary for a printed page. Two related inventions also were needed: a tool that would hold the type while the printer was assembling a line (a "compositor's stick"), and a frame where the whole page could be tightly assembled to go onto the press (a "chase").

Johann Gutenberg of Mainz, Germany, was probably the first printer to solve all these problems. The primary work for which Gutenberg is known is the Gutenberg Bible, commonly called the 42-line Bible. It was created during the 1450s; from examining the details of the type, experts conclude that six compositors worked on the Bible, probably for at least two years. The Gutenberg Bible was the first major book produced with true movable-type printing.

Trained as a goldsmith and metallurgist, Gutenberg set up a shop to mass-produce souvenir mirrors for **pilgrims** going to a shrine at Aachen. He also had a press on which he printed woodblock playing cards, among other things, but he was working on developing movable type. In 1448, he used a form of moveable type to produce a highly successful Latin grammar textbook known as "the Donatus"—the name of its author, a monk and scholar who lived in late Roman times. Using the same type, Gutenberg printed one-page papal indulgences—in press runs of 200,000—for Pope Nicholas V, who was trying to raise money for a **Crusade** to Cyprus. A few copies of the indulgence are extant, as are some other very early printed objects—a scrap of paper with a portion of a poem printed on it, a 1448 calendar that was printed with freshly cast metal type, and a Bible known as the 36-line Bible.

During this time, Gutenberg also experimented with making a more efficient press by combining elements from several kinds of industrial presses. He probably had a fair-sized staff working for him on these projects,

The first printing press used recently developed screw-press technology. To print one page, the printer had to ink the sheet of type, load a paper into the press, and turn the press's screw. The unique innovation of the process was in casting lead letter dies that could be melted down when they grew dull and quickly recast. (Francis Rolt-Wheeler, *The Boy with the U.S. Inventors*, 1920)

including calligraphers, designers, pressmen, and metal workers. His major contribution, however, was developing a handheld adjustable mold that could make the thousands of small metal pieces of type—the sorts—that were necessary for efficient and flexible printing.

To make a sort, the craftsman first carved a letter in relief, in left-to-right reverse, in the end of a steel punch. This process required several tools, including files, a counter-punch, a graver (a small cutting tool), and a specialized graver (a scauper) to cut out the center of round letters. With a hammer, the craftsman punched the letter into a soft **copper** blank to make an impression called the matrix and filed it smooth. He then inserted the matrix into the handheld mold and used a small funnel to pour a mixture of **lead,** antimony, and bismuth into the mold. This alloy was used because it melted at a low temperature and also cooled rapidly. The finished letter, on its square lead base, was dropped onto a tray to cool. The mold was adjustable so that thin letters like the small *i* or *l* had a thin base and larger letters like *M* or *W* had a wide base. The mold also made special characters like numbers, the dots used as punctuation, decorative capital letters, abbreviations, and ligatures.

An experienced worker could make four to six sorts a minute; this efficiency made it possible for the shop to produce thousands of characters in a day. In Gutenberg's shop, the number of different characters was very high; experts studying his printing have counted 290 alternate characters. Gutenberg greatly admired handwritten manuscripts and wanted his books to have that look. Therefore, he had his men make several versions of some of the letters (for example, eight versions of lowercase *e*) in a Gothic script, with slight differences between them so the finished book would look handwritten.

The first step in printing a book was to set the type. The compositor had to be an educated man, with a good grasp of grammar, spelling, Latin, and even Greek. He sat in front of two cases where the sorts were kept in compartments, capital letters in the upper case and little letters in the lower case. (We still speak of letters as uppercase or lowercase.) As he read from the manuscript, he placed the type line by line in a composing stick; each finished line went into a galley (a shallow tray, open at one end), and the finished page was locked into a chase.

The chase was then placed on the press stone (a large piece of marble) and inked. The water-based ink that was used in manuscripts or for wood-block printing was not suitable for printing with metal type because it would not adhere to the metal. Printers developed a linseed oil varnish similar to what artists had begun to use as oil paint. The ink used for the Gutenberg Bible had a high metallic content of copper, lead, and titanium, which made the ink somewhat reflective, a quality it still has in extant copies. To apply the ink to the type, the inker used two "hemispheres" made of leather and equipped with handles. A hemisphere in each hand, he dipped the leather into the ink and pressed it against the type, trying not to splatter.

The night before printing, paper enough for the next day's printing was wet down and stacked to partially dry overnight. At printing time, the moisture still in the fibers made the paper absorbent enough to take the

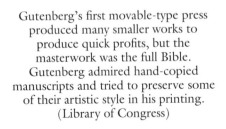

Gutenberg's first movable-type press produced many smaller works to produce quick profits, but the masterwork was the full Bible. Gutenberg admired hand-copied manuscripts and tried to preserve some of their artistic style in his printing. (Library of Congress)

ink. The press itself was like a vise with a screw mechanism that pressed a plate (the platen) firmly down. It was an adaptation of the winepress, enhanced by some features from textile and paper presses. After a page was printed, it was set aside to dry, and another sheet of paper was placed on the press. The sheets had more than one page printed on them, and they had to be printed on both sides. Extremely careful planning was needed for the pages to be correct when they were cut and folded into quires (sections of the book). Decoration (colored initial letters and so on) was done by rubricators. The finished cut and folded pages were gathered into groups of pages and sent to be bound between leather-covered boards.

Gutenberg's invention revolutionized printing, and printers' shops all over Europe were soon using the new methods to meet the demand for books. German printers particularly set up print shops in several other countries, including England. It is estimated that between the invention of printing and the end of the century, a period of only 45 years, more than 10,000,000 books were printed.

The first printer in England was William Caxton, who published over 100 books during the late 15th century. Many of them were his own translations. Originally a wool merchant, he learned the printing trade in Cologne and set up a press in Bruges, where he printed the first books in English. When he returned to England, he brought eight fonts of Gothic type and set up a printing shop of his own. His early published books included Chaucer's *Canterbury Tales, Troilus and Criseyde,* Malory's *Morte d'Arthur,* and many others. Caxton is equally well-known for editing some of the books he published and for helping standardize the English language through his publishing. He sought to follow what is known as the Chancery Standard, a written form of English developed during the reign of Henry V in the early 15th century.

See also: Alphabet, Books, Games, Parchment and Paper.

Further Reading

Hellinga, Lotte. *William Caxton and Early Printing in England.* London: British Library, 2010.

Howard, Nicole. *The Book: The Life Story of a Technology.* Westport, CT: Greenwood Press, 2005

Man, John. *Gutenberg: How One Man Remade the World with Words.* New York: Wiley, 2002.

McMurtrie, Douglas C. *The Book: The Story of Printing and Bookmaking.* New York: Oxford University Press, 1967.

Olmert, Michael. *The Smithsonian Book of Books.* Washington, DC: Smithsonian Institution, 1992.

Prisons

City prisons were a new development after the 12th century. They housed debtors, prostitutes, and thieves. At first, they were not intended as punishment in themselves; they housed those who were awaiting sentences or debtors who could be freed if their debts were paid. Before that, crimes had been handled at the most local level; the landowner locked up a suspect and had a trial quickly, if at all. By the 15th century, prison time itself was used as civil punishment.

Punitive sentences began as a means to limit the suffering of poor debtors who could never buy their release because they would never be able to pay their debts. Around 1300, cities like Venice began to translate the amount of debt into time spent in prison. Since many of these debts were really fines imposed by the city, the city could make a formula for what length of time in prison was equal to a fine.

Into the 14th and 15th centuries, citizens could receive sentences of varying lengths for failing to pay fines, breaking curfew, gambling, failing to defend a ship against pirates, bigamy, assault, or breaking the city regulations of a craft. While some sentences were as short as three days, some were as long as five years. The average medieval prison stay could have been around two years. Prisons could become overcrowded and release those who had been in the longest. Officials also released prisoners on some church **holidays.**

As cities grew, they had defensive structures they no longer needed. Some cities used old forts and towers as prisons, while others had outgrown their original gates and had massive gatehouses within the new city walls. The city of Paris kept prisoners in the Châtelet, while the city of London used some of its wall gatehouses, including the later-famous Newgate Prison. **Women** were housed in convents at first, in some places, but the nuns complained because many of the inmates were prostitutes and their former customers came to the convents. Cities began to build women's prisons as separate facilities. Because women inmates were vulnerable to abuse, their quarters were made increasingly secure.

Supervisors, from city officials to priests to committees, and including the doge of Venice, visited prisons regularly to make sure prisoners were cared for. Friars often served the inmates, taking care of them as a service and holding prayers and Masses with them. Prisons began to distinguish wards for separating inmates not only according to wealth and rank, but also for violence and disease. Most prisons also developed a lockdown ward for the insane. Inmates could be subjected to corporal punishment within the prison—as a penalty for fighting, for example. They could be flogged or even dismembered; some were executed, if they were violent enough. Most prisoners served their time without incident.

The old Chatelet fortress became a prison as medieval Paris outgrew its early walls and defenses. Its design for keeping attackers out proved successful at keeping criminals in. (Paul Lacroix, *Moeurs, Usage et Costumes au Moyen Age et a l'Epoque de la Renaissance,* 1878)

Prisoners usually had to pay fees for their upkeep, as well as other fees and taxes. This payment was part of working toward release. Poor prisoners were cared for at only a basic level; wealthier prisoners could pay extra for more amenities. Since the poorest prisoners could not afford to pay the fees to remain in prison, they ended up staying there indefinitely because the mounting fees were recorded as debt.

Daily life in a medieval prison was above all boring; there was no work, and there were no activities beyond prayers and the charitable distribution of food. Inmates talked, gambled, and fought. They could have visitors, and, in fact, visitors were expected to come frequently and help pay their fees or give them **food.**

See also: Cities, Monasteries.

Further Reading

Geltner, G. *The Medieval Prison: A Social History.* Princeton, NJ: Princeton University Press, 2008.

Pugh, Ralph B. *Imprisonment in Medieval England.* Cambridge: Cambridge University Press, 1968.

R

Records

Most of what we know about medieval Europe is based on some kind of written record created at the time; the only other record is the archeological one. Examining standing **castles,** excavating buried walls and **houses,** digging in trash pits, and looking at collected artifacts in museums, historians can see some of the setting and props of medieval life. The archeological record is the bedrock of understanding the medieval material culture. But many things have been lost; medieval people and those who came after them were tremendous recyclers who melted, cut, shredded, and burned much of the past. Few clothes have come into the present; over time, they were passed down to younger and poorer folks, cut into children's smocks, made into rags, stuffed into pillows, and sold for **paper** pulp. Whatever could rot or rust often has done so, and only the **stone,** bronze, and **gold** remains.

The written record created at the time does not always tell us what we want to know. The Middle Ages was not a time when the past was valued, except in terms of the wisdom of the ancients, such as Pliny or Aristotle. Italian sculptors carved Roman pillars into **saints,** and Roman plumbing was melted down to make new pipes or lead **pilgrims'** badges. There was little effort to preserve the details of their own time until the 14th and 15th centuries, when some people used the new paper technology to start keeping journals. When they did create records, they were writing about what interested them, from the price of hay that season to the miracles worked at the local saints' shrine. We have to look at what interested them to piece together what interests us.

Moreover, the loss of records has been immense. There were ordinary problems like floods and fires. The Great Fire of London, in 1666, burned more than half the city, and many medieval guild records were lost. In certain periods, people recycled their records as materials for rags or wrappings, to make a list or to mend another book. In other periods, they destroyed them on purpose. When the English closed all the **monasteries** in the 16th century, many books were lost or destroyed. During the French Revolution, peasants deliberately destroyed anything that had belonged to royalty. The 15th-century household account books of Duke Philip the Good of Burgundy were used to make cannon cartridges in 1793; only one volume escaped destruction. Historians would be able to glean many facts about the economy of the time if more volumes had survived into the present.

Written records are both written texts and visual depictions. There are stylized, decorative texts and images, and there are detailed, accurate ones. There are personal accounts and public writings, propaganda and legends. By carefully examining these records, historians can find clues about daily life that the record makers did not intentionally explain.

Visual Images

The only records of medieval clothing are in **paintings** and **sculpture.** By comparing different artists' **book** illustrations and tomb effigies of the same period, we can generalize and understand what people wore. What we cannot know easily is whether the picture is showing something typical or unusual. Book illustrators often showed scenes that were not connected to the text, which was usually religious. There was no narrative to explain the picture. Are these people dressed for a party or wearing their everyday garb? Was this detail, such as **bells** hung from their belts, a fad that year, or did they put bells on for Christmas games?

Most of what we know about **tools** comes from pictures. Medieval illustrators drew many scenes of building, so we have hundreds of images of scaffolding, cranes, hammers, and saws. Some crafts were depicted more often than others; we have few images of tanners or butchers compared to **masons** and plowmen. Still, the great variety of imagination that painters could exercise in creating psalters and books of hours means that many activities are shown at least once: sharpening **pens,** pruning vines, cutting leather for **shoes,** polishing **armor,** and many more.

In the 14th and 15th centuries, many more people commissioned memorial brass plaques. Instead of having only a few expensive tomb effigies of queens, for these centuries we have figures of thousands of men and women etched on brass in awkward but detailed formal poses. The names permit us to trace the histories and dates of the people, so we can see with more accuracy what people wore and considered important in different decades and social classes.

Government Records

Literacy came to the Franks with Christianity, and although most nobles could not read until after the time of Charlemagne, they employed clerks to keep records. Frankish estates kept surveys now called polyptychs because the parchment was folded many times. They kept lists of their tenants and how much rent they paid each year. These simple books are among the first records of Europe's economy.

The Franks and Anglo-Saxons kept tax rolls listing all tax-paying adults and how much they were assessed for. In 1085, William I of England, better known as William the Conqueror, authorized a detailed taxation census of his new realm. In the 20 years since his conquest in 1066, he had rewarded his followers with many manors and **castles.** The survey set out to learn how much land was held by the **church** and how many people, plows, and **animals** were on each manor. The book was known at the time simply as "the King's great book," but by the 12th century it was known as the *Domesday Book,* a nicknamed based on the Bible's account

The *Domesday Book* was a tax roll compiled for King William I. Its rigorous detail was unmatched in its time and remained the highest standard for centuries after. Most economic histories use the *Domesday Book*'s database, although it leaves unanswered many questions that modern scholars ask. (The British Library/ StockphotoPro) of a great book used on Judgment Day, in which every man's deeds are recorded.

The *Domesday Book* preserved a snapshot of the economy in one year. Each county's entry began with a list of the men who held manors in it, beginning with the king himself and including bishops and abbots. Each lord's land was then subdivided into hundreds and half-hundreds. Within each parcel, every manor was listed, with the names of the men who farmed it and how many villeins (workers obligated to stay on the estate) and slaves. The census stated its assessment for taxes and military duty and told how many plows worked the manor. For some counties, the book lists livestock: horses, cattle, sheep, and pigs.

There are official records of legal codes produced under the kings. While we cannot tell how well these laws were enforced, we can get a sense of what prompted the law and what the circumstances were. A particularly detailed legal document is England's Magna Carta, the document that rebellious barons forced King John to sign in 1215. The Magna Carta listed all the ways the king's power had to be limited, and from this we can see what was considered normal. Also in 1215, the Pope issued the results of the Fourth Lateran Councils; the five medieval all-church councils produced detailed rulings on vexing problems of church government. These documents are among the official, intentionally created records of the Middle Ages.

Town and county governments kept coroners' records, and these are among the richest records of medieval life, although they recorded only deaths. In medieval England, inquests asked why the death occurred and took statements from witnesses. A typical entry is short, but it tells the name and age of the deceased and the way the death happened. This tells us what that person was doing at the moment of death and what others were doing. A child falls into a river on the way to **school;** a **baby** is mauled by a pig wandered in from the street; a child is burned to death when a servant's careless candle catches the **house** on fire. Historians can study where accidental deaths occurred and get a good sense of where people were on a typical medieval day.

Manorial and town courts kept records of infractions reported and fines imposed. In many cases, the records are so laconic that we learn little of the lives they speak of. An ale brewer is fined, but the court does not say why, because fining ale brewers was too common for interest. Peasants are fined for taking wood, hay, and animals from the lord's land, but we know nothing more about their lives. Peasants paid fees at events like a **marriage** or a death, but we do not know how harsh the fees were economically or whether they were always exacted.

However, we learn about normal life by reading about what disrupted it. There are records of lawsuits and contract disputes. A modern reader of an apprenticeship contract finds it all so foreign that it seems hard to understand what could go wrong. Reading a body of court records of apprenticeship disputes, the assumptions and offenses of medieval life become clearer. A medieval father objected more when his son was not properly taught skills and less if he was not treated kindly, unless the unkindness was dangerous. Masters complained most often of apprentices who ran away. **Guilds** were reluctant to break contracts without a period of time for either party to amend his ways.

Dowry, betrothal, and marriage contracts appear frequently in the court rolls, as families argued over whether the terms had been fulfilled. The medieval practices of family law, such as wardship of orphans, would be virtually unknown apart from court records of disputes. We know from court records that orphans' wardships were sold, sometimes repeatedly. We know that both men and women tried to hold each other accountable for promises of marriage, even marriages made orally without a written contract. The evidence of witnesses tells us where people were and what they considered normal in daily life; the incidents they testify about took place in homes, **taverns,** and workplaces. We get a sense of how friendships were formed in the testimonies about how long each witness had known the parties to the lawsuit.

In English village court records, we can observe their method of community policing. If anyone was attacked, he or she had to "raise the hue and cry." In calling for help loudly, that person placed everyone in earshot under the obligation to drop his or her work and run to help. When a village did not respond to the call, the victim could bring a complaint to the magistrate and have not only the attacker but also the village fined.

Personal Wills and Notarial Accounts

Wills, especially in the late Middle Ages, often had detailed inventories of a person's possessions, including clothing, books, dishes, and tools. Much of our knowledge of people's lives comes from close scholarly reading of many old wills. By studying a person's profession, and his or her comparative wealth, scholars can determine how well a profession was flourishing in a time or how much social respect it commanded in society.

Notaries kept records of wills and other contracts in large towns. In the progressive Italian towns, notary service was a well-developed profession. Italy's towns could have had some ongoing notarial services since Roman times, but they at least revived the Roman practice of public notaries when the University of Bologna began to teach Roman law in the 11th century. Italian notarial records go back to about 1150. Charlemagne copied Roman practice by instituting the role of a notary among the Franks, but these notaries were mostly private secretaries for a long time. As private secretaries to princes and courts, the notaries recorded many decrees and court records, but they did not at first record the family matters of private individuals. During the 13th century, increased trade with Italian merchants brought the institution of public notary services to the north. At the **fairs** of Champagne, notaries recorded sales and contracts. In England, notaries existed but did not become as central, and guild clerks kept many contractual records.

Notaries made a living writing legal documents through dictation for people who may not have been literate. They wrote the wills and contracts into notebooks, so they served also as the record-keeping service. Most wills were not recopied. Notaries served as practical lawyers for everyday affairs; they knew what a document needed to include to make it complete and legally enforceable. After 1200, Italian notaries wrote down the place where the document was created (at the dying person's home, for example) and the approximate time of day. When **clocks** proliferated in the 14th and 15th centuries, notaries could write the hour.

Medieval people could expect to die at any time, since death in the form of infectious disease or accident came suddenly. However, most made wills when death could be imminent. This happened when they became sick or were going on a journey. Anyone who went on **pilgrimage** had to make a will first. Wills are a major source of our knowledge about the lives and possessions of people at the time. We can learn a great deal about their family structures and what they owned, since most wills disposed of all the things by name. At the same time, when someone died, the executor of his will often made an inventory of all of his (or her) possessions. These inventory lists are very complete and provide intimate details of the household's goods.

During the **plague** of 1347, notarial records in some Italian towns lapsed. At first, people attempted to call in notaries to make wills, and survivors attempted to have the normal procedure for executing the will enforced. However, so many people died so quickly that, at first, the notaries were overwhelmed with work, and then the process became chaotic. When a family member went to find a notary, the notary had died. When an executor tried to enforce a will, he found that the survivors and witnesses had died. Some people died so quickly that they had no time to attend to legalities, and often whole families died. Burial wishes meant nothing, since the towns were swamped with corpses to bury and resorted to mass graves with minimal rites. The notarial notebooks in towns that tried to keep their legal systems functioning paint a vivid picture of the rapid spread of the plague's chaos.

Notaries recorded other documents, after their primary business of certifying wills. They also recorded dowry and marriage contracts and apprenticeship contracts. Sales and rental of land and houses, and sales and purchases of other commodities like wine, cloth, and wool, were recorded with notaries. They witnessed the purchase of future crops and rights to use the produce of land (usufruct). They also oversaw the appointment of legal representatives for various reasons, such as guardianship, and witnessed debt and its contracts for interest and repayment. Servants who contracted with a master, merchants who agreed to transport goods, and even singers who agreed to sing in a chapel needed legal agreements. Because so many people needed a notary's services, and because they came in random order to the notary's office, a notary's notebook is a wide-ranging record of the types of people in a town.

Business and Church Records

Even before literacy and **paper** made written records easy, most businesses kept accounts. Italian corporations of the 13th century kept extensive accounting books; their clerks developed the system of double-entry accounting. They had shareholders, currency exchanges, loans, and international sales. When these records have been kept safe, they provide very detailed information about travel and manufacture and can tell some about family life.

Castles and courts kept household records of which craftsmen, merchants, and entertainers they had paid. Although some records have been lost, there were so many castles keeping records of salaries that a great deal of our information about work and the economy has been derived from these account books. The steward in charge of a major **feast** often recorded all the **food** purchased, how many servants and cooks were employed for the event, and how much each **minstrel** was tipped. A lady or queen's household accounts kept track of how much linen and silk thread had been purchased and how many seamstresses had been hired to make a certain winter gown.

The church kept its own records, especially in the late Middle Ages. Early church records are more institutional than personal, such as treatises on divorce or other legal cases. One of the richest veins are penitential guides, books written for local priests to help them give appropriate penances for confessed sin. The books list possible sins in great detail. If a man had sex with an unmarried or a married woman, his penance was a certain amount—but if the woman was his sister or mother, it was greater. The penitential books do not tell how common these sins were, but it rounds out our picture of medieval society to know that someone felt certain sins needed to be listed at all.

Saints' exploits created many records of daily life. Every parish church or **monastery** wanted to record the reported miracles worked by their saint's **relics.** When a visitor, monk, or workman (or even an animal) had an illness or an accident and was cured at the saint's shrine, the event went into a record book. Taken together, these incidents explain what all these people, **horses,** and dogs were doing during the day and what illness or accidents were most common.

The Cathar Inquisition created volumes of interviews. The inquisitors asked peasants, townsmen, and aristocrats detailed questions about their lives and beliefs. We have a great deal of knowledge of the kinship structures, work, and values of Provençal peasants thanks to the Inquisition.

In the late Middle Ages, parishes began to record baptisms. We do not have this information for the early Middle Ages. Baptismal records gave the parents' names, the godparents' names, the infant's christened name, and the date. By comparing baptismal records with other local records, such as court and tax rolls, historians can understand family structure and relationships, as well as infant mortality.

Finally, the church provided an informal record by keeping texts of some sermons. Even in the Middle Ages, a good preacher knew how to tie his message to the listeners' lives. Sermons could include analogies to the lives of animals, stories of people's lives, and warnings against the temptations of the time. When a preacher warns against playing cards, we know that playing cards have been imported and are gaining popularity.

Biographies and Literature

Medieval people sometimes wrote about their lives or others' lives. They wrote family genealogies, which were sometimes accurate and sometimes legendary and amplified by hearsay. A rare early memoir was written by a Frankish lady named Dhuoda, who wrote advice and thoughts for her son around 840. Some of her story is hard to comprehend because she did not write for people of the future, but there is still much to glean about Frankish lives, especially of **women.** The people most likely to write memoirs were abbots and bishops. They were literate, and they sometimes felt they had wisdom to share. The French abbot of Nogent, Guibert, wrote a biography in the 12th century. Guibert was an intelligent man who loved to write; he wrote a history of the First **Crusade,** but his best-known work was his autobiography. He wrote about his early family life, his parents' characters, and the childhood events that shaped him. Margery Kempe, a 15th-century pilgrim, wrote the first real autobiography in English, recording her thoughts and feelings as she pursued her fanatical devotion to the Holy Land and back.

The Middle Ages were a time when great men were admired and imitated. There are contemporary biographies of saints, written by their disciples. Saint Hugh of Lincoln and Saint Peter Damian were among the churchmen who inspired such respect and love that their lives were quickly written. Most, if not all, of the monastic founders became the subjects

The most famous of Bede's eighth-century books is his *History of the English Church and People*. He included the history that he knew firsthand as well as legendary history from a few centuries before. Only four manuscripts of the original Latin text survive into modern times. This page is the cover of the eighth century book preserved in the British Library. (HIP/Art Resource, NY)

of contemporary biographers: Saint Bruno, Saint Francis, Saint Bernard, and Saint Dominic. Church clerks also studied secular great men; a monk named Asser wrote the biography of King Alfred shortly after the king's death. One of the most detailed records of the life and court of King Louis IX (Saint Louis) was written by one of his **knights,** Jean de Joinville. He knew the royal family and recorded private conversations with both king and queen; he kept a journal on the king's two Crusades. Biographies covered not just the saints and kings, but also famous knights and generals like England's William the Marshal. Some monks and priests wrote detailed histories, too, like the Frankish Gregory of Tours and the English Venerable Bede.

Paper mills brought down the price of keeping records. By the 14th and 15th centuries, people below the ranks of bishops and dukes were writing letters. Italian merchants wrote letters to each other, and to those at home, as they traveled. A rich vein of information about medieval England is preserved in the letters of several generations of the Paston family of Norfolk. They wrote to each other as they traveled and as family members settled at a distance. They explained marriage negotiations and child-raising problems, and they expressed personal feelings and opinions. Personal letters are some of the few places where we get the direct voices of medieval women.

Le Menagier de Paris is a work that crosses between personal memoir, letter, and literature. In this large work, sure to be cited in any historical study of medieval life, an aging husband instructed his teenage bride in household arts and behavior. No detail was too trivial for him. He told her how to keep away ants and fleas, how to care for potted plants, how to create a good public reputation, how to roast chicken, and how to buy beef. He wrote directly for her but seems to have considered it a gift to extend beyond his death, so he wrote in a wide scope that would take in all the needs of her lifetime. The book stands as one of the greatest monuments of medieval record keeping.

Other writers created treatises and encyclopedias for publication. By the end of the Middle Ages, there were books on farming, cooking, medicine, animal care, and many crafts. There were advice books for women: how to choose a spouse, how to take care of yourself as a widow, how to raise babies. Knights wrote books on chivalry and how to win at **tournaments;** hunters wrote about the customs of **hunting.** Much more is known about the 14th and 15th centuries from these treatises.

See also: Books, Painting, Parchment and Paper, Weddings.

Further Reading

Andrea, Alfred J. *The Medieval Record: Sources of Medieval History.* Boston: Houghton Mifflin, 1997.

DeWindt, Edwin Brezette. *A Slice of Life: Selected Documents of Medieval English Peasant Experience*. Kalamazoo, MI: Medieval Institute Publications, 1996.

Epstein, Steven. *Wills and Wealth in Medieval Genoa, 1150–1250*. Cambridge, MA: Harvard University Press, 1984.

Gies, Joseph, and Frances Gies. *Marriage and Family in the Middle Ages*. New York: Harper and Row, 1987.

Greco, Gina L., and Christine M. Rose. *The Good Wife's Guide (Le Menagier de Paris): A Medieval Household Book*. Ithaca, NY: Cornell University Press, 2009.

Hanawalt, Barbara A. *Growing Up in Medieval London: The Experience of Childhood in History*. New York: Oxford University Press, 1993.

Martin, G., and Ann Williams, eds. *Domesday Book: A Complete Translation*. New York: Penguin, 2003.

Reyerson, Kathryn L., and Debra A. Salata, eds. *Medieval Notaries and Their Acts: The 1327–1328 Register of Jean Holanie*. Kalamazoo, MI: Medieval Institute Publications, 2004.

Thorley, John. *Documents in Medieval Latin*. Ann Arbor, MI: University of Michigan Press, 1998.

Relics

A relic was a physical memorial of a **saint,** a very holy deceased person with special influence in heaven. Relics were most often bones, but they could also be **hair,** teeth, **clothing,** objects the saint had used, or objects the saint touched. They could even be objects that had come into contact with the saint's tomb, near the original relics.

The medieval **church** believed holiness was an ethereal but real substance. This sanctity originated from the saint's soul, but it also remained in the saint's bones, hair, teeth, clothing, and other possessions. Sanctity could be transferred from one relic to another, like magnetism.

The church believed each saint in heaven knew where his or her relics were and wanted to make sure living people were honoring him or her adequately. Since the saint had the power to grant prayer and work miracles, it was wise to honor the saint and gain his or her favor. At least once a year, on the saint's day, the relics were taken out in a procession so everyone could honor them. The relics also came out in times of national distress, such as during an epidemic or a war. In a solemn procession around the church, the bishop or priest walked with banners and reliquaries, while the people walked behind with uncovered heads.

Relics were kept in highly decorated containers called reliquaries. Most reliquaries were shaped like a box or a house. They were made of **gold** or **silver,** where possible, and were covered with decorations. Some were small, but many were very large. One unusual sort of reliquary from the late Middle Ages was shaped like a bust of the saint whose relics it held. Most were carved from wood and were hollow inside; some portion hinged to open. They were painted to look as lifelike as possible.

Seeing and venerating relics was the main object of medieval **pilgrimages.** Pilgrims wanted to show penance or thank the saint for a prayer granted. They often left images to represent their prayers at the saint's shrine, such as wax ships, wax crutches, wax animals, and wax bodies or individual crippled limbs. Wealthy pilgrims left silver images. Many pilgrims left either **coins** or gifts of other kinds, such as **animals** or other farm produce; these gifts made up much of the income of each shrine. Relics helped finance many **cathedrals.**

Although early Christians had revered the burial places of their patriarchs, such as the Apostle Peter (later Saint Peter of Rome), the fad for relics began with Emperor Constantine's mother, Helena. In 328, she led a pilgrimage of discovery to the Holy Land with the intention of finding all the artifacts and places of the Bible. Helena was willing to believe in anything the locals told her, and she was not at all surprised when she found "the True Cross," still complete and bearing the sign Pontius Pilate had tacked onto it. She also found the Crown of Thorns that Jesus had worn, and she went into the Sinai Peninsula and "found" the mountain where Moses supposedly had received the Ten Commandments. Emperor Constantine built the Church of the Holy Sepulcher over the supposed place of Jesus's tomb in Jerusalem, and Helena placed the True Cross and the Crown of Thorns into it. These relics had to be rescued when **Muslims** overran the city.

The medieval impulse to collect relics was very different from the modern idea of collecting and preserving artifacts. People believed that the relics and anything that touched them had mystical powers, and they wanted to benefit from these powers. If a relic could be divided, it was. It was better to destroy a relic and put its power of sanctity in many places than to keep it whole, as in a museum. If the relic could be embedded in gold or transformed into another shape, they did that, too.

After its rescue from the Muslim invasion, the True Cross was split into pieces, and part of it was encased in gold and jewels and set in a chapel in Jerusalem. Another part went to Emperor Constantine. Its nails were removed; two went into a statue of Constantine on a horse. Other nails were said to be part of the Iron Crown of Lombardy or in as many as 30 churches across Europe. The silk that had wrapped the wood of the cross became a relic on its own and was divided into small pieces for many recipients. The portion of the cross that remained in Jerusalem became a prize for Christians and Muslims to capture and recapture over the years. When it finally came back to the Christians in 1221, it was sold to Venice for a large sum of money. Later, it was pawned for money and, finally, sold to King Louis IX of France, who laid it to rest with his other relics in a church. For years, many churches believed that they owned a splinter of the True Cross.

The Crown of Thorns had a similar treatment. It was kept in a **monastery** in Jerusalem for many years, and it steadily lost thorns, as they were plucked and given to kings or emperors. It went to Constantinople in 1063, and in 1261 it was sold by an emperor desperate for money to King Louis IX for his relics chapel. King Louis IX removed all the thorns as gifts to monasteries and churches around Europe. What remained of the crown went into a reliquary in a chapel of Notre Dame Cathedral.

The most famous relic of the Middle Ages is the Shroud of Turin, whose authenticity has been tested and questioned in modern times. The **cloth,** which bears a strange image of a man lying down, has a mysterious history. It may have been in Edessa, Turkey, in premedieval times, hidden in a box in the city wall. Emperor Justinian built Hagia Sophia Cathedral to house the shroud, and many Byzantine icon paintings of Jesus may be based on the shroud's image. The shroud was carried on devotional tours at times and then was returned to Constantinople. In the 13th century, it disappeared in the chaos of the **Crusades.** The shroud seems to have been purchased by Geoffroy de Charny, a French **knight,** and his family gave it to Louis of Savoy in the 15th century. From that time, it was housed in Turin.

Not only Jesus's burial shroud, but also any other piece of clothing supposedly belonging to Jesus or his mother became a valuable relic. Charlemagne believed he had the swaddling cloths of baby Jesus at the chapel of Aix La Chapelle in Aachen, his capital. Chartres Cathedral in Paris claimed to have the tunic worn by Mary when she gave birth to Jesus. In 911, when Vikings attacked Paris, the bishop displayed the tunic to the attackers

A proper house for a holy relic was most often shaped like a church, the house of God. In order to please the saint, churches ordered reliquaries that were extravagant works of art. The Eltenberg Reliquary, dated to the mid-12th century, is made of copper covered with gold. It is further decorated with enamel and carved ivory. (Ann Ronan Pictures/ StockphotoPro)

to make them abandon their **siege.** The relic later survived a fire that destroyed the old church, which convinced the people that Mary allowed the fire because she wanted a bigger cathedral for her tunic. The magnificent Gothic cathedral of Chartres was the result.

The disciples of Jesus became the source of many valuable relics of the Middle Ages. Christian tradition told what they had done in their lives and where they had died, and, in some places, their bodies may actually have been preserved. In other cases, it is highly unlikely that the bones revered as certain apostles in the Middle Ages were anything but fakes. The most important apostolic relics were those of Peter and James. Peter was buried in Rome, and a church was built over the grave site. The location may be authentic, since his followers began meeting at his grave soon after.

Tradition says that James (the brother of John) preached in Spain; he then returned to Palestine and was beheaded by King Herod. His relics, however, are in Compostela, Spain. A bishop at Compostela verified the bones of the saint, which were discovered along the coast of Spain in 813. It is very unlikely that the bones are really those of the Apostle James, but in the Middle Ages, they were never questioned. Santiago was difficult to reach, situated as it was on the Atlantic coast of Spain. A traveler from England or France had to cross the Pyrenees mountains or go by **ship** to the nearest port; either way, the traveler would be many days hiking through northern Spain, which was rugged. A pilgrimage could take four months, but it was still a very popular journey, and there were other relics shrines along the way where a pilgrim could increase the value of his or her trip.

The evangelists, the men who wrote the Gospels, were also revered saints. Mark's body was in Alexandria, Egypt, where he had died after founding a church. This is plausible, although the bones can't be authenticated. In the ninth century, two merchants from Venice bought the relic and smuggled the body past the Muslim authorities by packing pork products in the top of the box. Luke, another Gospel writer, was claimed by both Venice and Padua. Papal officials examined the bones and determined that Venice's bones were of a young man, so Padua's relics were authorized as authentic.

Early martyrs also left behind relics. Agatha, killed in third-century Rome, was housed in reliquaries at Catalonia, Sicily. Agnes, a young girl, was executed in Rome not long before Constantine declared the Christian religion to be legal. Constantine's daughter built a church over her grave site, and her skull is kept at the Vatican.

Not all saints were ancient, nor were all bodies dismembered. Benedict, the founder of the Western monastic tradition, remains buried at Monte Cassino. Anthony, a Franciscan preacher in Padua, has a revered shrine in Padua. Thomas à Beckett, the archbishop of Canterbury murdered at his cathedral, remains buried in the cathedral.

Other relics were too numerous to keep track of or authenticate. Vials of saints' tears or blood, and hair or bone shards from any number of disciples or martyrs, circulated widely during the Middle Ages. Their authenticity was never questioned. People also made their own relics by carrying cloth to a saint's tomb or collecting stone shards or dust.

Every church or monastery needed to claim it had relics. The monastery at Peterborough, England, believed it had the right arm of Saint Oswald, pieces of Jesus's manger and swaddling cloths, one bone of a child slain by Herod (in the "Slaughter of the Holy Innocents"), pieces of the miraculous five loaves, and relics of six apostles. Most cathedrals and abbeys had similar claims. One had the right arm bone of Mary Magdalene, while another had one of Saint Dunstan's teeth.

Relics began to shape church architecture. Pilgrims did not value relics as much if they were not housed in a grand way. They equated a noble building and gold trim with holiness. As a church obtained more relics, it had to build a larger basilica or cathedral, which it funded with the donations from pilgrims who came to see the relics.

Churches that held the relics had to be careful to protect them from theft or damage. Pilgrims were known to riot if they were not given adequate access. On the other hand, relics had to be stored in stone vaults just to protect them from fire, let alone theft. Where possible, stone vaults were designed to permit pilgrims to come close, but not to touch. Some churches with a large number of pilgrims displayed their relics in reliquaries that hung from a beam across the ceiling. It was high enough that pilgrims could not touch the relics, but they could see them.

Some churches were specially built to cope with crowds of pilgrims who came to see relics. They built crypts, rooms where visitors could sit near the relics. Some crypts, built underground so the relics were positioned beneath the church's altar, amounted to subterranean chapels with their own altars. They were designed with arched vault roofs and pillar supports. Canterbury Cathedral has an extensive crypt of this kind. As pilgrim crowds grew, churches began storing relics in special chapels above ground, encircled by walkways called ambulatories. Pilgrims could walk the ambulatory, which kept crowds orderly and moving. Relics were often in a large reliquary just behind the main altar. The typical Gothic floor plan of a cross was part of this design, since the top of the cross was usually the ambulatory around the relics.

Even with all these precautions, relics were frequently stolen. Although theft was a sin, even priests and monks did not feel guilty for stealing a relic because they believed the saint wanted the relics to be moved, or else he or she would have stopped them. The new owners could claim the old owners had not properly venerated the relics. Theft of a relic proved that the saint had chosen the new resting place.

See also: Cathedrals, Church, Jewelry, Pilgrims, Saints.

Further Reading

Bagnoli, Martina, ed. *Treasures of Heaven: Saints, Relics, and Devotion in Medieval Europe.* Baltimore: Walters Art Museum Press, 2010.
Cruz, Joan Carroll. *Relics.* Huntington, IN: Our Sunday Visitor, 1984.
Geary, Patrick J. *Furta Sacra: Thefts of Relics in the Central Middle Ages.* Trenton, NJ: Princeton University Press, 1991.
Geary, Patrick J. *Living with the Dead in the Middle Ages.* Ithaca, NY: Cornell University Press, 1995.
Manseau, Peter. *Rag and Bone: A Journey Among the World's Holy Dead.* New York: Henry Holt, 2009.
Stalley, Roger. *Early Medieval Architecture.* Oxford: Oxford University Press, 1999.

Roads

In the early Middle Ages, well-designed **stone** Roman roads were still very much in use. They were especially dense in Italy itself and in other regions that had been well developed by the Romans. Italy's road system was superior to that of Northern Europe all through the Middle Ages.

In Spain, France, and England, the Roman roads gradually fell into disrepair. Romans only built roads that linked their forts and towns, and Europe outgrew this infrastructure once the period of barbarian attacks ended. The last Roman-style roads were built in northern France around 600. Until very late in the medieval period, road building was not a priority. New **cities** grew where there had never been stone roads.

Roads were rarely built by planning but were developed when they led to a destination: **castle, monastery,** church, market, port, **bridge,** or cemetery. They were named according to where they went or what purpose they served. A road used to transport shipments of **salt** might be called Saltsway.

Medieval roads may be best considered as strips of land where private landowners gave people the right of way to walk and ride. In England, some statutes stipulated that travelers could travel next to a road without being charged with trespassing, if (and only if) the road had fallen into serious disrepair. Landowners had an incentive to keep the roads repaired if they didn't want **horses** and **wagons** to drive onto their land. Road repair in the Middle Ages generally meant leveling out the ruts and putting gravel into swamps or other depressions.

Some roads had been in use since prehistoric times. Some had served early medieval (such as Anglo-Saxon or Frankish) armies. Some were royal roads

By the late Middle Ages, cities had begun to pave roads with cobblestone or brick. Stone paving required men on stools to fit and pound stones into the dirt roadway, kneeling on stools and working inch by inch. It was a slow, expensive undertaking, so at first they paved only the main streets in the biggest cities. Paved streets remained a real mark of distinction until the modern age. (S. Greg Panosian/iStockphoto)

and were maintained to the king's standards: in England, wide enough for two wagons to pass. Wider roads developed along routes for driving cattle, and alternate roads developed in places where travelers wished to avoid tolls. Multiple roads developed on hills, so a traveler could choose which path looked least steep.

Kings and other noblemen traveled frequently as they moved from manor to manor. The English kings of the 13th and 14th centuries traveled almost continually, and they carried baggage in up to 20 wagons. Although the roads must have been difficult, they also must have been passable. We see glimpses into the difficulties of travel in kings' records: shortly before his death, King John's wagons had an unlucky ford crossing, and his crown and other **jewels** were lost.

The paving of town streets in Northern Europe came late in the Middle Ages. Large towns such as Paris and London wanted to improve sanitation and began to build cobbled streets with drains and gutters in the 12th century. It was slow and expensive, as workmen sat in the street on three-legged stools and pounded rocks or **bricks** into the dirt. The result was easier to keep clean, and it shed rainwater into the drains.

Italian towns tended to have more paved roads, perhaps because of their Roman traditions. Rome's streets had been paved since antiquity. In growing commercial towns like Bologna and Milan, many roads were paved with brick or stone. Property owners were responsible for paving the street in front of their buildings, and the city paved main streets and plazas.

See also: Bridges, Cities, Wagons and Carts.

Further Reading

Davies, Hugh. *Roman Roads in Britain*. Botley, UK: Shire Publications, 2009.

Harrison, David. *The Bridges of Medieval England: Transport and Society, 400–1800*. Oxford: Oxford University Press, 2008.

Hindle, Paul. *Medieval Roads and Tracks*. Princes Risborough, UK: Shire Publications, 1998.

Taylor, Christopher. *Roads and Tracks of Britain*. Worthing, UK: Littlehampton Book Services, 1982.

Roland, Song of

The "Song of Roland" was the most popular epic of its time. Composed by a Frankish **minstrel** named Turoldus, the poem first appeared in written form around 950. Its subject matter was Charlemagne's invasion into **Muslim** Spain in 778. The oral version may have been in circulation for years before it was written, but it was probably not composed close to the time of the events.

In the song, Roland is the Count of Brittany and Charlemagne's nephew. He is guarding the rear of a triumphant departure from Spain, after a military campaign of seven years in which the Christian Franks conquered almost all of Muslim Spain. The narrow pass over the Pyrenees mountains, from Spain into France, forces the huge army to travel slowly, and the baggage train at the back is miles behind. Roland's stepfather Ganelon has conspired with the Saracen ruler Marsile to attack Roland when he is isolated. Roland compounds this disaster by ignoring his friend Oliver's pleas to blow an ivory horn called the "Oliphant," which would summon help. When he finally blows it, help cannot arrive in time, and they are all slaughtered. While this is the most famous incident in the long epic, the story goes on to tell of Charlemagne's vengeance against Marsile, the burial of Roland and his companions, and an enormous battle between Muslims and Christians. The Frankish Christians win, and their Muslim enemies either die or convert.

In the historical events, Roland was a nobleman of Brittany, but he may not have been related to the king; little is known about him. He guarded the baggage in the rear, and the main army went ahead over the narrow pass of Roncesvalles. Charlemagne's campaign had not been long or victorious; his army had entered at the invitation of some rebellious Muslim rulers in northern Spain who wanted to rebel against the growing power of Abd al-Rahman of Cordoba, who had come to rule about two-thirds of Spain. The rebellion failed, and support melted away. A frustrated Charlemagne heard that the Saxons of Germany were rebelling against Frankish rule and headed back to the Pyrenees to cross into France. The city of Pamplona, home of Christian Basques, closed its gates to him, and his army destroyed it. As the army passed over the Pyrenees, vengeful Basques, and

The "Song of Roland" was the best-seller of its time as both a song and a storybook. This copy was lavishly illustrated, by 11th-century standards. This picture may show the knighting of young Roland. A bishop stands by to bless him as the king gives him a sword. Servants, possibly other knights, attach his spurs. Roland's minor defeat was turned into an epic of victory over the Saracens, medieval Europe's chronic foes. (The British Library/StockphotoPro)

probably some Muslims, attacked Roland and stole the plunder and other baggage the Franks were carrying out of Spain.

See also: Minstrels and Troubadours, Muslims.

Further Reading

Lewis, David Levering. *God's Crucible: Islam and the Making of Europe, 570–1215.* New York: Norton, 2008.

Merwin, W. S. *The Song of Roland.* New York: Modern Library, 2001.

S

Saints

Medieval Christians believed that among the perfect souls who went straight to heaven, some had been so good on earth that they had higher standing in heaven. These included monks who had done notable charitable works and many martyrs who had been killed for their faith. These holy ones, *sancti* in Latin and *saints* in English, could look down on earth and see what people were doing. They could hear prayers and work miracles.

Dead people were certified as saints if they had lived saintly lives, or if they did not smell rotten after their death (this was called "the odor of sanctity"), and if they appeared to work miracles after death. A miracle meant that God had listened to the saint when he or she spoke on behalf of a humble petitioner, and it certified the saint's position of influence in heaven. Medieval people had a low-threshold of definition for a miracle. It could be any improvement within a reasonable time frame, including natural recovery. It did not have to be immediate, and it was still a miracle if the person later became sick again.

During the 10th century, the **church** began to control the process of certifying dead people as saints. During the early years of Christianity, the test had been simple: a martyr's death. After there were fewer martyrs, saintly lives or evidence of miracles at a tomb made people saints. By 1215, the Fourth Lateran Council proclaimed that only the Pope could determine who was a saint. The process was called canonization, and the Papal Court needed evidence of a saintly life and detailed evidence of specific miracles. The petitioner who submitted the saint's name for consideration had to pay the costs of the investigation, so fewer saints were named in the later Middle Ages.

Many medieval people still venerated local, unofficial saints. As the canonizing process became more formal, some of these locally selected saints were called blessed, *beati*, rather than saints, *sancti*. The local people felt strongly about them, but they could not afford the sainthood process or perhaps the saint would not have passed Rome's stricter standards. One local French saint would never have passed the Pope's scrutiny. Saint Guinefort was a dog, killed by his master by mistake while protecting the master's baby son. The canine saint was venerated by the local people, who brought sick **babies** to the dog's grave.

Relics of saints were thought to have special power to work miracles in the saint's name. Most commonly these relics were slivers of bone, often said to be the finger of a saint. One saint's relic was his head, pickled in a jar. Other relics could include scraps of **cloth** they had worn or blessed or items they had used. Shards of a saint's tombstone could also carry the blessing of the saint. Many **monasteries** and churches built their fame around owning relics. The **Crusades** gave wide opportunity for relics real and false (and often stolen property) to be carried back to Western Europe. They were housed in elaborate boxes called reliquaries.

The foremost saint was Jesus's mother, Mary. During the 12th century, devotion to her as the *Mater Dei* (Mother of God) grew all over Europe. Many people believed Mary had been born without sin, and they revered her as the perfect woman. Many churches and monasteries were dedicated to Mary. Medieval art, both **painting** and **sculpture,** showed Mary with her baby son and with her son crucified. People prayed to Mary in the belief that if Mary asked Jesus to grant their petitions, he could not turn down his mother.

Other saints included the 12 disciples, Roman Christians who had died for their faith, and missionaries like the Anglo-Saxon Boniface. The most famous saint of the Middle Ages was Saint Thomas à Becket, the archbishop of Canterbury who was murdered at the altar of his **cathedral** in 1270. His tomb became a central place of pilgrimage in England.

Many people were named for saints; after the archbishop's murder, thousands of English babies were named Thomas. The **calendar** had saints designated for every day of the year, often more than one. Sometimes people were named for the saint on whose day they were born. Many regions had local saints, and those names were more popular.

Devotion to Mary, the highest saint in the hierarchy, increased during the Middle Ages. Her image in heaven was of a queen in a shining crown, but her image on earth centered on the sorrows she felt as a mother. Tradition said that the body of Jesus was taken from the cross and laid on her lap. A *pieta* was a sculpture of this scene. By the late Middle Ages and into the Renaissance, it was one of the most popular images of Mary. (Allan T. Kohl/Art Images for College Teaching)

People believed saints had particular concerns, based on what they had done while they were on earth. These saints became the patron saints for crafts or places or were called on for certain kinds of help. Sometimes, the link was direct and easy to understand, such as Saint Dunstan as the saint for English goldsmiths, since he had been a metal worker. Other times, the link was more obscure. Saint Barbara's father, who beheaded her, was killed by lightning, so Saint Barbara was the saint who could help with dangerous thunder and lightning, but she was also the patron saint of miners, who used explosives.

Many saints were designated as the helpers for various **medical** problems. Their link with these problems was sometimes connected to their lives and deaths. Saint Clair, who had her eyes put out, was the saint who helped with eye problems and blindness. Saint Agatha's breast was cut off, so she paid particular attention to prayers concerning breast cancer, breast injuries, and breast-feeding. The links with saints and their concerns were not even always known. For whatever reasons, Saint Sebastian helped with **plague,** Saint Osyth with fire, and Saint Oswald with sick **animals.** Saint Margaret was the helper of all midwives and childbirths.

Some saints resided at places, although they were, of course, in heaven. Mary's tunic at Chartres, and other relics of Mary in other places, allowed these places to claim Mary lived with them. Saint Denis had been buried at the abbey named for him in Paris, and Saint Martin's tomb in Tours fixed him there. Saint Anthony of Padua and Saint Francis of Assisi were considered to have lived in their burial locations. When a saint was definitely buried at a place, his favor surely could best be gained by going there to pray.

See also: Church, Medicine, Pilgrims, Relics.

Further Reading

Abou-El-Haj, Barbara F. *The Medieval Cult of the Saints.* Cambridge: Cambridge University Press, 1997.

Bagnoli, Martina, ed. *Treasures of Heaven: Saints, Relics, and Devotion in Medieval Europe.* Baltimore: Walters Art Museum Press, 2010.

Cruz, Joan Carroll. *Relics.* Huntington, IN: Our Sunday Visitor, 1984.

Salt

Salt occurs in almost every environment on earth, either as seawater or **water** from a salt spring or as rock salt below the earth's surface. Since ancient times, people have known that salt is necessary for human life and for preserving **food.** Water that contains salt is called brine; as water evaporates, the brine becomes saltier. As salinity continues to increase, salt crystals gradually form and fall to the bottom of shallow water, where they can be raked up. During the Middle Ages, salt was both mined and harvested from salty brine.

In Europe, the premedieval Celts mined and sold large quantities of salt for several centuries. Their Roman conquerors also made large amounts of salt by boiling seawater in **pottery** until a solid block of salt was formed (they smashed the pot to get the salt) and by building shallow ponds along the Mediterranean to let the sun and wind evaporate seawater until salt crystals formed. At the start of the Middle Ages, people in Europe continued to use the many saltworks the Romans had established along the shores of the Mediterranean and Adriatic seas.

Venice became rich as a leading salt exporter, thanks to an important innovation. Instead of using a single pond, salt makers constructed a series of shallow ponds. The first was a large open tank into which seawater flowed. The tank had sluices that kept additional seawater from entering the pond while the sun and wind did the first part of the evaporation. When the brine reached a certain degree of salinity, pumps sent it on into a second pond for further evaporation, and the sluices were opened to allow more seawater into the first pond. When water in the second pond reached a higher level of salinity, the water went to a third pond, and the process was repeated, and so on, until coarse salt crystals formed and could be raked up and dried. Over the course of a year, this method produced a large quantity of salt while requiring very little manpower. The salt produced by this long, slow evaporation process was a coarse salt, very suitable for salting **fish,** which was an important local industry.

The amount of salt a **city** could make and sell was limited only by the space it had available. The Venetian method spread through the Mediterranean during the eighth and ninth centuries. The best salt came from the Bay of Biscay, where the Loire River empties into the ocean. It was called Bay Salt, and it commanded a high price in other parts of Europe.

The shallow pond method worked well in a warm, sunny climate but not in cooler and cloudier northern areas. In early medieval times, the English made salt by boiling brine in shallow **lead** pans laid over a fire—known as the open pan process. The temperature of the brine and the rate of evaporation could be controlled to produce finer or coarser salt for different uses. Salt makers also used the pot process, pouring brine into ceramic or metal pots hung over a fire. A saltwork was called a wich house, a term that persists in English place names. The brine came from lagoons or from the sea itself.

The English also used sand from the seashore. Waves washed over the beach, depositing salt in the sand. In a medieval technique called sleeching, sand was air-dried and put into a pit (a kinch). Water (either sea or fresh) was poured over it until brine flowed out. The process was repeated until

Salt was one of the few necessities of life that was almost always produced some distance away; even common people had to buy salt at times. A salt merchant sold it by weight; he probably measured it into a container that the customer brought from home. The cost per pound was greater for cleaner, purer kinds of salt. (Österreichische Nationalbibliothek, Vienna, Austria/Alinari/The Bridgeman Art Library)

the brine was salty enough that an egg would float in it. Then it could be used as brine or dried for salt.

Brine springs and brine wells were another source of salt. Springs flowed in areas that had rock salt or in underground streams. To access the brine, brine wells were equipped with machinery to haul bucketfuls up to the surface. Men (often prisoners) walked treadmill-fashion on a giant slatted wheel, which turned a shaft that wrapped ropes around itself, lifting buckets of brine to the surface. The brine was boiled to make salt.

Rock salt underlies much of central Europe. The ancient Celts dug long sloping tunnels into the mountain, used pickaxes to break up the salt, and hauled it to the surface in leather bags. In the late 700s, rock salt mining started again under the leadership of the Catholic **Church.** In the mid-13th century, removing salt from a mine was made easier when water was piped into the dug-out rock salt; the water quickly became brine and was piped out of the mountain to a village, where it was boiled down. Income from the salt helped support the church and many **monasteries** that were built over brine areas. Salt was shipped via riverboats to other parts of Europe.

Southern Poland has deep deposits of rock salt. In the middle of the 13th century, miners began to dig out the rock salt that had hardened at ancient brine springs. The first miners were prisoners of war who were literally worked to death. In the 14th century, free men began to do the mining. The mines became deep enough that the salt was hauled to the surface by a huge pulley system worked by teams of eight **horses.**

Salt crystallizes in various sizes, depending mostly on the rapidity of the evaporation process: the faster the evaporation, the smaller the crystals. The finest salt is called *fleur de sel,* a light salt that was skimmed off the water's surface during evaporation. The next finest crystals are salt for dairy use (making butter and cheese); then come common salt, a coarser salt for curing ham, and the coarsest grades for salting fish, one of the most important uses for salt. Coarser salt usually had minerals and dirt mixed into it.

See also: Fish and Fishing, Food.

Further Reading
Fielding, Andrew, and Annelise Fielding. *The Salt Industry.* Princes Risborough, UK: Shire Books, 2006.
Kurlansky, Mark. *Salt: A World History.* New York: Penguin Books, 2002.

Schools

While most medieval people did not learn to read, many did—more as the centuries passed. By the end of the Middle Ages, literacy was common, though not yet universal. England's literacy rate may have been higher from the start, since reading and scholarship were prized by some Anglo-Saxon kings, most notably King Alfred. Parents who could read were able to teach children, and many parishes had priests who could read and were willing to teach a few motivated pupils.

The children of country serfs met several obstacles to attending school. In the countryside, it was harder to find a teacher, let alone a school. If they did, they needed the permission of their feudal lords to learn to read; the feudal lord could even be the local abbot, if a **monastery** owned the land. Whether the lord was a **knight** or a clergyman, he often charged the peasant family a fee to let the boy go to school. It may be that this fee purchased the boy's freedom, allowing him to go to town not only to study, but also to stay there and find work.

Large towns had grammar schools for boys. In England, they were more common after about 1200. At first, most schools, whether run by a **cathedral,** monastery, or private master, charged fees. There were both day schools and boarding schools; in towns with day schools, some students who came from a distance boarded with families. These schools primarily taught Latin to prepare boys for careers in the **church** or as clerks. They varied in size; most schools were restricted in size by their charter, either to maintain quality of education or to protect the competition. A grammar school held in a learned man's home usually had no more than 6 pupils, but large town schools could easily have 50 or more.

The Lateran Council of 1215 mandated that bishops must maintain free schools for training future priests. After this, all cathedrals had schools attached, often coordinated with their need for a boys' choir. The cathedral school of Notre Dame in Paris became one of the leading schools of **music** where innovations were tested. Cathedral schools treated their pupils as

This picture decorated the cover of a 13th-century Latin book. It shows a small monastery school of the time. The teacher is seated on a stool, with a stand to hold his book. The students sit on the floor. Some have books, while others must gather around to look on a shared copy. If the students could read along after the teacher, memorizing what was on the page, the teacher believed that they could read it. The mechanics of decoding letters and sounds were not of interest in the Middle Ages. (Erich Lessing/Art Resource, NY)

though they were part of the monastic community; the boys were present at many church services, often singing, and they lived on the monastic schedule. Bishops usually required their pupils to be tonsured like monks, with their hair cut very short and a bald patch shaved on top. The students did not have to take monastic vows, but they were counted as minor clergy and often did become monks.

During the 14th century, some wealthy patrons endowed secular schools that did not charge tuition. A secular school still ran according to religious methods, but it was not formally under the oversight of the bishop. In England, Winchester College was endowed by a wealthy secular canon, William of Wykeham, who later became bishop, but the school was not a cathedral school. It was founded as a school, rather than as a charity or choir of the cathedral. King Henry IV founded Battlefield School in 1409 at the town of Shrewsbury, near where he had won a victory over a rebellious earl. This small college was typical of privately endowed secular schools. It supported a teaching staff of only six, and it included an almshouse to care for the poor, probably including its own poor students.

Next, town governments through Europe began endowing schools, especially in the Netherlands and Germany. Some of these secular schools were entirely tuition free, funded by tax money. By the 15th century, large **cities** like Paris had as many as 50 small schools, mostly for boys, but some were for girls. Towns in Italy were organized as self-governing communes, and, by the 14th century, the town governments ran more schools than the churches did. While most schools remained private and charged fees, some were directly supported by taxes. Higher-level schools were geared for the needs of the Italian commercial empires, emphasizing accounting and document writing.

The word *college* could mean either a preparatory school before **university** or a division within a university. A medieval English college was often a school for boys between the ages of 10 and 17. Students from all different social ranks met at the school to learn, but the school honored their ranks even as children. The sons of noblemen ate at a higher table than the sons of tradesmen, and the poorest charity students served at table and ate with the **servants.** It is likely that the difference in rank did not greatly bother the students; the poor boys were used to hard work, and their status was a kind of work-study program. In some schools, poor students who received full scholarships to study without working had a high status because it marked them as particularly intelligent.

Colleges that boarded a large number of students had to maintain a large staff. Staff positions were the warden and the headmaster at the top, with a team of instructors often known as fellows in medieval England and an usher, whose job it was to mind the door to catch latecomers and to instruct the youngest students. The college also needed support staff, beginning with a steward and the warden's clerk and descending through the barber, cook, brewer, baker, laundress, valet, and servant boy. The serving staff was, of course, supplemented by the poor students who worked for their tuition. They sang in the choir, served at table, and served the wealthier students in their rooms, and they were not fed as well.

Some students at colleges did not continue to a university; as many as half went into trades. Apprenticeships also seem to have included a fair amount of general business education, such as how to write letters and contracts and how to keep accounts. Some apprenticeship contracts stipulated that the master would send the boy to school for a year or two as part of his training. This was seen in trades that required some knowledge of reading and arithmetic.

The age that most people considered ready for school was seven years old. Before that, boys were considered **babies** and not fully male. For those who were not taught at home, the school day began early, at dawn. Like other medieval workers, teachers had to make use of daylight to save money on lighting. Students were not expected to have breakfasted before they arrived; in some schools, there was a meal break in the morning after the boys had studied for a few hours. Boarding schools served a noon meal, while schools in towns allowed the pupils to go home at noon. The boys returned to school by about two in the afternoon, and the school day continued until about six in the evening. The day was not devoted only to silent reading or class recitations. Teachers also led the boys in prayers, in some cases prayers for the souls of the men who had endowed the school or its individual scholarships in exchange for these prayers.

School facilities were simple; they were not always buildings devoted to the purpose. Sometimes they were rented from a **guild,** church, or tradesman. At the beginning level, they did not use chairs and desks. Students sat on the floor and learned their letters from wooden tablets with handles that resembled ping-pong paddles. Some illustrations show small children standing in front of either their father or their teacher, holding the **alphabet** tablet so the instructor could look over their shoulders and point to the letters as they read. Basic writing at this instructional level was often on wooden tablets or slates that could be rubbed down and reused.

Early reading began with the alphabet and syllables and proceeded directly to the most important text, the prayer book. These prayers were in Latin, and they were merely memorized by the pupils. Those who could continue education beyond this level turned next to the psalter, often learning to sing as well as read. In England, the first stage of real schooling was called "music school." Some young pupils never learned to understand what they were singing but could sing in the church choir. Learning to read in English may have been a lesser activity, a side benefit of learning to read Latin syllables.

The next step was to learn Latin by memorizing words, and then memorizing the ways words could combine. This was "grammar school," and most grammar schools required students to prove basic reading skills for entrance. Grammar schools were more likely to have dedicated classrooms; some were boarding schools with dormitories. Cathedral schools were usually boarding schools. The classrooms that grammar schools used were simple, with benches along the sides, an open area in the center, and a head desk for the teacher. Some had writing desks, but most required students to rest books and writing materials on their laps. Most schools had outdoor privies as **latrines,** but some expected students to use a nearby riverbank.

Students at a grammar school needed to have some basic equipment besides suitable clothing. They had their own **pens,** pen sheaths, penknives, and inkhorns. They had to buy **paper** notebooks, and, at higher levels of instruction, they also bought or rented a few hand-copied **books.** Their school fees also contributed to purchasing firewood, hay for the floors, and candles. Some schools required the students to bring a supply of beeswax candles.

Learning heavily emphasized memorization, so a student who had memorized a prayer was said to "read" it. Students memorized many things, including poems, speeches, and psalms. Older students who aimed at university study or clerical work learned to write at dictation; the teacher read out loud, and the students copied. From the 15th century, we still have paper notebooks students made as they learned Latin. They copied Latin texts, did translations between Latin and English, and composed narratives in Latin. Teachers seem to have used some riddles and rhymes, as well as texts about everyday life, to teach Latin vocabulary and keep the work interesting. Some of the extant notebooks suggest the teachers included vocabulary the boys were interested in learning, including insults.

Mid-level students studied Latin intensively and often "parsed" words. This meant that the teacher pointed out a word in a Latin text, and the student had to state its part of speech and everything else that could be known about the word's form and use. Upper-level students were expected to speak nothing but Latin in the classroom, since at the university, all classes would be conducted in Latin. A mark of having mastered Latin was the ability not only to read and speak it but to write verses in Latin.

The liberal arts, as defined in the Middle Ages, were grammar, dialectic, and rhetoric, and after these, the higher arts of arithmetic, geometry, music, and astronomy. While grammar schools often taught basic arithmetic, they were mostly expected to teach only the first three arts. An upper-level student at a large grammar school could expect to begin to learn dialectic and rhetoric in Latin. In dialectic, students posed questions to each other and answered them according to basic logical propositions provided by the teacher. Rhetoric was the art of composition and speaking (in Latin, of course).

Medieval treatises on mathematics required students to memorize tables of addition and multiplication. Once students had memorized multiplication tables through 20 times 20, they could learn to solve problems of applied mathematics that they might face in everyday life, having to do with prices, time, and distance. Arithmetic training also taught the use of the abacus. Arabic **numbers** did not become widely used until after the close of the Middle Ages, but especially within Italy's strong commercial tradition, 14th-century students were taught accounting using these much simpler numbers. In Italy, the abacus was the subject most taught after basic reading.

Grammar schools in England often taught French before 1350. French was the native language of the aristocracy for as long as 100 years after the Norman conquest in 1066. As long as the English kings still ruled sections of France, such as Aquitaine, they needed to speak French well, and sometimes they were raised on the Continent. They commonly married French princesses, which refreshed the supply of native French speakers at the English court. Boys who wanted to work in any capacity at court needed to speak French passably well. French teachers could be natives of France or Englishmen who had been taught in French monastery schools. Some later French teachers wrote beginning lesson books, perhaps as an advertisement for their services. But after the Black Death **plague,** teaching French fell off sharply. It became very difficult to find teachers, and all but the highest-class schools gave up.

Masters whipped boys for being late, not paying attention, or making mistakes. They used thin rods of birch and other pliant wood. Most schooling involved a great deal of whipping, although reformers like Saint Anselm wrote educational tracts that recommended kindness.

Schools, both grammar schools and colleges, observed the liturgical **calendar** with its many **holidays,** both **fasts** and **feasts.** English schools appear to have followed a schedule of four terms, modified to three by eventually dropping the summer term. The fall term began at Michaelmas, the winter term after Christmas, and the spring term after Easter. It is likely that boys went home for a few weeks between terms. Christmas included a holiday that was exclusively for the boys at cathedral schools. They elected a boy bishop and enjoyed making parodies of the church's rites and presiding over parties. Schoolboys were usually in school when Lent began and could celebrate Shrove Tuesday their own way. In England, in addition to eating up the meat and dairy, schoolboys held cockfights.

The image of the Virgin Mary as a child, learning to read at her mother's knee, was a popular devotional and domestic scene. Although the Bible story made it clear that Mary was not from a wealthy family, medieval people assumed that her mother, Saint Anne, must have been in the literate upper class. The mother and child were always shown wearing fine clothes and reading from a real book. As was typical in a time of limited seating, the little child Mary must stand while her mother sits. While it tells us nothing about the childhood of the historical Mary, it shows what an aristocratic medieval mother did to teach her daughter to read. Daughters rarely went to school, so learning was handed down within the family. (The British Library/StockphotoPro)

Schools frequently put on plays, especially in England, but also in other European countries. Since the schools were often under the oversight of the church, the plays were usually miracle or mystery plays. The most popular plays illustrated the lives or miracles of saints, particularly the patron saint of the church or town. These plays were often filled with gory martyrdom and could have been genuinely popular with the boys. Choirboys were also part of the liturgical **drama** of Mass on special holidays, acting parts like the **women** visiting the tomb of Jesus on Easter.

Girls did not as commonly learn to read their spoken language and even less commonly learned Latin. Nuns may have taught some girls, singly or in groups. Many convents had small schools for orphans under their care and for upper-class girls who were placed there for schooling or future entrance into the convent. Most English or French girls who learned to read were taught at home by their mothers. It was a mark of higher social class to have a mother who could read; in some medieval illustrations, the Virgin Mary is shown learning her letters with her mother, Anne, who is dressed as a noble lady. By the 15th century, a family of small landowners expected to teach their girls to read and write. The Paston family, whose collection of medieval letters is a resource for scholars, had several generations of women who corresponded in good English. The few women who could read and write in French and Latin were always from noble families. Italy's schools were an exception to this rule. Florence records schools for girls as well as for boys, and there are women teachers on the pay records.

Among **Jews,** there was a strong tradition of fathers teaching their sons to read Hebrew, which was used as a universal correspondence language among Jews in different countries. In a town with a significant number of Jews, the synagogue often sponsored a school. The records of Jewish synagogue schools show that they did not use punishment with young children, but rather gave out sweets as rewards for learning. Older students were subjected to beatings like their Christian peers. Some Jewish students learned Latin as well as Hebrew and the local language.

See also: Alphabet, Babies, Jews, Music, Universities, Women.

Further Reading
Cook, T. G., ed. *History of Education in Europe.* New York: Routledge, 2008.

Hanawalt, Barbara A. *Growing Up in Medieval London: The Experience of Childhood in History.* New York: Oxford University Press, 1993.

Miner, John N. *The Grammar Schools of Medieval England: A. F. Leach in Historiographical Perspective.* Montreal: McGill University Press, 1990.

Newman, Paul B. *Growing Up in the Middle Ages.* Jefferson, NC: McFarland, 2007.

Orme, Nicholas. *Medieval Children*. New Haven, CT: Yale University Press, 2001.

Orme, Nicholas. *Medieval Schools: From Roman Britain to Renaissance England*. New Haven, CT: Yale University Press, 2006.

Sculpture

In the Middle Ages, sculpture was the predominant art form. While **painting** appeared in **books** and on some walls, sculpture decorated nearly all public buildings. Like other visual arts, sculpture was seen mostly as a way to use a visible image to lead man to the invisible reality. Most sculpture was employed in making religious art. The next greatest use of sculpture was in making tomb effigies.

Italian sculptors worked most in marble; they often carved Roman pillars into new figures. Until the later Middle Ages, when Italian marble was shipped north, sculptors in Germany, France, and England had to work with their local **stone.** It was usually limestone; the softest form, alabaster, became popular for carving, but in outdoor sculpture it has not held up as well as harder stones. Although stone sculptures are more common, many medieval sculptors worked in wood, bronze, **copper,** and, in the 15th century, terra cotta, a form of **pottery.** Sculpture was often painted; if it was in wood, it was always painted, but even stone sculptures were frequently painted. Wood and stone were also gilded with gold-flecked paint or **gold** leaf.

Many medieval sculptures were destroyed in the Reformation, when they were called idols, rather than art. Painted wooden **saints** were pulled out of wall niches and thrown in bonfires. Some stone sculptures were smashed with hammers. During the French Revolution, even more figures were attacked. Statues of kings and queens, on outside walls and as tomb effigies in crypts, were broken to pieces. During Europe's wars, especially the two World Wars, aerial bombs destroyed more churches and palaces. There are still many unharmed **cathedrals** where the original sculptures are in good condition, and scholars have collected stone fragments in museums and pieced together statues and effigies where possible.

Sculpture was not done for its own sake, as a fine art; it was always made as part of a building. Moreover, the buildings were usually churches, since **castles** could expect to be battered and were kept plain and secure on the outside. Only in the late Middle Ages did secular buildings like town halls start to commission sculptures. Medieval sculpture falls into the same two general periods as architecture, since the two forms were so closely connected. Romanesque churches were called basilicas; they were based on a Roman floor plan and used Roman-style arches. In the 13th century, the style changed to incorporate pointed arches and outer buttresses so that churches could use larger windows and lighter stone supports. The new style, now called Gothic, permitted sculpture to become both more realistic and more ornate.

Romanesque Style

The Romanesque period of sculpture comprised the early medieval centuries when there were many church reform movements and the active founding of new monastic orders and **monasteries.** As the monasteries became wealthy, they turned to decorating their buildings for the glory of God. Sculpture's first use was in making bas-relief depictions of Bible stories and figures of the saints to decorate columns, capitals, and doorways. The entire front of a Romanesque church could be considered a display board for as many saints, angels, and Bible stories the sculptors could fit onto it. The tympanum, the arched area immediately over the doorway of a church, often displayed the Last Judgment, Christ's ascension into heaven, or some other grand Biblical scene. Some doors of wood or bronze also had scenes carved or cast on them.

Although the idea of a column with a carved capital came from Greece and Rome, the Romanesque sculptor did not always decorate capitals with classical scrolls or leaves. Some capitals had human or **animal** figures carved in bas-relief. They showed Bible stories or scenes of daily life. Some of these scenes were very intricate and complicated, while others were relatively simple.

Woodcarving was an important art form during this time; there were carved doors and altars, but, above all, every monastery and church needed a crucifix. The crucifix was a large cross with the body of Jesus nailed to it. This had to be a true three-dimensional sculpture, not a bas-relief. It was usually carved out of wood, though it could also be cast in bronze or silver.

Romanesque sculptors often signed their work. There are capitals and bas-relief scenes with letters carved into the design, saying "Gofridus made me," or "Simeon of Ragusa made me." Some even included boastful descriptions of the sculptor as well-known or glorious. Although they were carving for the glory of God, the sculptors were proud to sign their names.

Gothic Style

The Gothic period began with Abbot Suger's desire to make the new Abbey of Saint Denis taller with larger stained **glass** windows. New principles of architecture changed the style of buildings and permitted them to be both larger and more heavily decorated. Arches were pointed, not semicircular, and walls were held up by external buttresses. Interior ceilings rose into higher vaults, now freed from the need to create internal support. Very tall windows were broken into smaller sections with carved stone tracery. The tracery often broke up the expanse into diamonds, roses, circles, and arches.

Gothic cathedrals left few spaces unadorned. Pulpits, which were raised on legs or pedestals so that the preacher could stand high above the congregation, were heavily carved with biblical scenes. Saints stood in every possible niche, inside and outside. Scrolls and geometric designs decorated every edge. Capitals on columns grew ever more elaborate and showed faces, birds, trees, saints, battles, and **cities.**

The more widespread use of imported marble permitted fine detail. Gothic sculpture shows greater sophistication than the older style, and figures were emerging from bas-relief into almost freestanding figures. A façade of Reims Cathedral displays figures of Mary with an angel and her friend Elizabeth, and all the figures are nearly freestanding, though still connected at the back. It was carved around 1270, the height of the Gothic.

During the 13th century, the people developed a cult of worship around Mary, the mother of Jesus. There was increased demand for statues showing Mary with the infant Jesus, Mary at the foot of the cross, or Mary in heaven. Mary often wore a large, ornate crown.

From the 14th century on, there was an increasing trend toward secular sculpture. The Black Death **plague** of 1348 was one factor. There was an increased emphasis placed on tombs, public statues, and other memorials. Kings and nobles commissioned more tomb effigies in wood or stone, instead of statues of saints. Lesser nobility and wealthy merchants commissioned brass memorials that were either etched or cast in a mold. Patrons who built chapels wanted their likenesses carved into biblical scenes or just included as memorials of the builder. The church was still important in civic life, but its importance decreased after the plague. Towns decorated not just their churches but also their public buildings. Wealthy cities, particularly in Italy, wanted public fountains and monuments. Italian city fountains, the source of public **water,** were often magnificent pieces of sculpture that symbolized the city's history, industry, and leading families. City monuments showed kings and other heroes on horseback, without any religious meaning.

In the 15th century, visual art became increasingly sophisticated and realistic. Sculptors were memorializing life, not just creating conventional images of heaven. Figures stood in natural poses and had fresh, smiling faces; they were recognizable individuals. They were dressed in flowing robes with highly detailed, natural folds and elaborate decorative bands.

In Italy, some sculptors were working in terra cotta, the ceramic technique of glazing pottery with tin and firing it several times to get a high luster. Lucia della Robbia made "The Visitation," showing the Virgin Mary and

At Reims Cathedral, the figures of the angel Gabriel with Mary and Elizabeth decorate the west facade. Medieval sculptures have often suffered some damage over the years. Particularly in France, some cathedrals were deliberately damaged in the revolution; statue arms and heads were targeted as symbols of the corrupt church. Originally, such figures may have been brightly painted, as wooden statues inside the church were. (Allan T. Kohl/Art Images for College Teaching)

her cousin Elizabeth, in several pieces. The lower and upper body parts were sculpted carefully, fired, and then cemented together and painted. Terra cotta sculpture could be completed much more quickly than marble carving.

Gothic Grotesque

The most famous Gothic sculptures are the gargoyles. The word *gargoyle* comes from French *gargouille,* "gargle." Latin *gargula* means "throat." Gargoyles are decorative spouts on rain gutter systems. In German, they are called water-spitters, *Wasserspeiers,* and in Dutch, *waterspuwer.* The stone supports for the roof had carved water channels, and the rainwater had to be projected out away from the building. A pipe could project out, but masons decorated everything, so they became an occasion for a grotesque, humorous joke.

Most gargoyles depicted winged monkeys, lions, bats, dogs, griffins, dragons, and demons. These creatures appeared to grip the wall with their

A medieval gargoyle on Milan's cathedral was shaped like a small dragon with a duck-like head. Rainwater poured out of its open beak. Every medieval gargoyle is a unique creation of monster, demon, animal, or human. Most of them show an irreverent and vulgar sense of humor that contrasts with the dignity of the same building's carved saints. (Allan T. Kohl/Art Images for College Teaching)

feet and lean out to fling the water several feet away from the wall. Many laugh or grimace or use their hands to pull their mouths open. When they are human figures, there is often some twist, such as a hand on the stomach, vomiting the rainwater, or even the figure turned around so the rainwater comes out of its bottom. Some Italian gargoyles are less grotesque: human figures that pour from pitchers or hold spouting animals.

The grotesque style of sculpting was different from the style on other building elements. Not only did all the figures have wide-open mouths, but they also were carved in an exaggerated way to make them visible from the street. Their features are cut unusually deep to create shadows to outline the features. Their wings, long ears, and claws are big and obvious. It is likely that many gargoyles were originally painted, but they were exposed to the weather and the paint did not last long.

People have long wondered why gargoyles were comic or wicked creatures, instead of abstract flourishes, angels with pitchers, or something similar that would seem more in keeping with the rest of the cathedral art. Some speculate that the gargoyles represented demons threatening the people below with danger if they fell into temptation or demons pressed into God's service. Some have wondered if the wicked-looking beasts were intended to frighten away evil spirits. There are no medieval writings that discuss them. On the other hand, as the Gothic style became standard on all buildings, gargoyles decorated public buildings made of stone. They can be found on late medieval and Renaissance hotels, mansions, and town halls in Northern Europe. They may not have had an explicitly religious purpose.

In the margins of illuminated manuscripts, artists drew similar grotesque creatures—some were half one animal and half another, some had more than one head, and some had wings. The Bayeux Tapestry, embroidered long before the period of Gothic art, decorated its top and bottom margins with birds, animals, and other figures that do not seem to bear any direction relationship to the story of the Norman conquest. It is possible that the gargoyles represent a medieval tradition similar to modern comicbook art.

The same art style can be seen on some other grotesque decorations that did not serve as rain spouts; some churches and even cloisters are decorated with comic, ugly heads of apes or men. Corbels, wall projections that helped carry the weight above them, often had a grotesque or comic face. Misericords, small projections hidden in the choirs that could support benches to help a priest or monk stand or kneel, showed scenes of daily life or animals and sometimes had grotesque faces or monsters. They were usually carved from wood and were not seen by the public, only by the clergy. It is possible that gargoyles, corbels, and misericords were a chance for sculptors to kick up their heels and have some fun, making whatever struck their fancy. Formal religious sculpture had to be done perfectly, but these informal pieces allowed for artistic freedom.

See also: Cathedrals, Painting, Pottery, Stone and Masons.

Further Reading

Benton, Janetta Rebold. *Holy Terrors: Gargoyles on Medieval Buildings.* New York: Abbeville Press, 1997.

Coldstream, Nicola. *Masons and Sculptors.* Toronto: University of Toronto Press, 1991.

Duby, Georges. *Sculpture: The Great Art of the Middle Ages from the Fifth to the Fifteenth Century.* New York: Rizzoli International Publications, 1990.

Little, Charles T, ed. *Set in Stone: The Face in Medieval Sculpture.* New York: Metropolitan Museum of Art, 2006.

Nees, Lawrence. *Early Medieval Art.* New York: Oxford University Press, 2002.

Petzold, Andreas. *Romanesque Art.* Upper Saddle River, NJ: Prentice Hall, 1995.

Sekules, Veronica. *Medieval Art.* New York: Oxford University Press, 2001.

Stoksad, Marilyn. *Medieval Art.* New York: Westview Press, 2004.

Toman, Rolf, ed. *Gothic: Architecture, Sculpture, Painting.* Cologne, Germany: Ullmann and Konemann, 2007.

Toman, Rolf, ed. *Romanesque: Architecture, Sculpture, Painting.* Cologne, Germany: Ullmann and Konemann, 2004.

Welch, Evelyn. *Art and Society in Italy 1350–1500.* Oxford: Oxford University Press, 1997.

Seals

In ancient times, documents were authenticated by means of a seal that made an impression in clay or wax. The custom of signing a document with an autograph began during the Middle Ages, and by the close of the period, seals were used only in some official capacities, such as customs or government certificates. Through most of the Middle Ages, though, seals were the most common means of authenticating a document, perhaps accompanied by a cross and the person's name. Unlike the crudely stamped **coins** of the time, seals could make a fine, detailed impression. They carried the owner's name and a design similar to a coat of arms. In some cases, the seal needed to have a date on it, so it carried letters around the rim specifying the year of the king's reign.

Although at first only kings had seals, by the 13th century, anyone who wanted to sign a document needed a personal seal. Anyone who entered a contract, bought or leased land, made treaties, or made proclamations had to own a seal. **Monasteries** and bishops had seals, as did companies, **guilds,** and every aristocrat. Kings had personal seals, and their households and departments (exchequer, navy, army, customs) had seals for conducting business. Judges, courts, towns, and counties had seals. When poor people needed to sign a contract but did not own a seal, they had to impress a **key** instead.

Aristocrats' seals had their heraldic arms as well as some personal marking, including their name. Guilds and tradesmen used symbols of their craft, while bishops and monasteries used religious symbols. People who did not have a right to **heraldry** used designs with **animals,** birds, hearts, letters, and mottoes. In a late medieval city, seal makers sold generic (but unique) seals for common people, and they cast seals with a few ready-made design elements that could be engraved with personal details for a particular customer. If a seal was lost, unauthorized parties could use it for forging. The owner had to get a new one made immediately.

Seals were usually made of metal, most often brass or bronze. Royal ones were often **gold,** and common ones used for business were base metals such as pewter. They could also be carved from ivory, jet, or even soapstone. Signet rings were not often used until the 15th century, although King Richard the Lionheart had one. Then, the design could be cut into

By the late Middle Ages, anyone who did business—buying or selling land or entering into other contracts—needed a seal to serve as verification of agreement. Guilds were among the first nonaristocrats to design seals. The butchers' guild of Bruges, like most other guilds, based its seal on its business. With a cow on one side and a hog on the other, an illiterate person could not doubt which guild had sealed a contract. (Paul Lacroix, *Moeurs, Usage et Costumes au Moyen Age et a l'Epoque de la Renaissance*, 1878)

the gold ring itself or into a stone such as jasper or onyx. Gems could also be cut as seals, but not set in rings. Gems made very fine aristocratic seals when set in handles of silver or gold.

The carved impression is called the matrix or the die. The seal could be large, with a carved handle, or it could be only a flat disc to hold the matrix. A common handle shape was six-sided, with a decoration at the top, particularly with some kind of ring or loop. Another common shape was round and flat, with a ridge on the back to hold between finger and thumb and a hole for a string or ribbon. A 14th-century design placed the center of the die on a screw in the handle so that it could be used in two levels, either the whole die or just the central design. Some seals had a second die to go at the back of the sealed wax, in which case it had pins to align it to the front die.

The usual way of signing a document, until the late Middle Ages, was to cut a slit in the **parchment** and loop a strip of parchment through it. Some drops of hot wax sealed the parchment strip, and the seal was pressed into the wax. A document with many signatures had many parchment strips hanging off the bottom, each with a little round piece. Each strip could have more than one wax seal, too, depending how long the tag was. Pieces of cord could also be used, instead of parchment, or the main parchment itself could have a flap hanging down to be sealed. Seals could also be pressed right onto the parchment.

The English kings began using a two-sided seal when they marked documents. The seal was a lump of wax impressed along a strip of parchment on both sides. Each side had a portrait of the king on his throne or in other regalia, but the images were different. Other English seal owners copied this practice; some even used a three-piece seal, in which, after impressing the front and back, the sealer added a tiny bit more wax and a third impression on the back.

Most documents were sealed with beeswax. In the later Middle Ages, resin was added to strengthen the wax, and sometimes even a few hairs were laid into the wax. The wax was usually natural colored, but verdigris green and vermilion red were also used. Colored wax could have been reserved for certain official uses, and some lords could have devised a particular color to be used with their seal. The most famous user of another material was the Pope, who used a sealed lump of **lead** called a bulla to authenticate his proclamations; this led to their modern name, "Papal bulls."

For most documents, the die was pressed onto the wax by hand, but for two-sided seals, they had to use a small rolling pin or a seal press. The seal press was made of oak, with an **iron** screw. Dies used in the seal press had to be flat, without handles. One piece had two or three holes, and the other had pins to fit into the holes to align the dies properly. The dies were placed into the press, and then the strip of parchment was attached to the document and the wax. The iron screw pressed both dies into the wax evenly for a clear impression on both sides.

Seals were also used to close letters and for some other purposes. When people borrowed or lent money, a tally stick was the earliest type of record of the loan, before accounting books came into use. Tally sticks were marked with notches to show the sum of money, and then with a wax seal along the same edge. When the tally stick was split vertically, the notches and seal were both broken, and each party had a matching half.

Customs officials used seals to mark goods after the import tax had been paid on them. They were required to inspect a wide range of goods, from spices and dyes to furs, rice, cotton, olive oil, turpentine, and whalebone. Some goods, such as **cloth,** were certified by attaching a piece of lead with the seal.

See also: Heraldry.

Further Reading

Harvey, P.D.A., and Andrew McGuiness. *A Guide to British Medieval Seals.* Toronto: University of Toronto Press, 1996.

Milne, Gustav. *The Port of Medieval London*. Stroud, UK: Tempus Publishing, 2006.

Williams, David H. *Catalog of Seals in the National Museum of Wales: Seal Dies, Welsh Seals, Papal Bullae*. Cardiff, UK: National Museums and Galleries of Wales, 1993.

Servants and Slaves

During the Middle Ages, several new social classes came into being. Although nobles had always kept servants, the new class of free townsmen, mostly craftsmen and merchants, began to keep servants. Every home and business had repetitive, unskilled, heavy work, and where possible this was put out to servants. They cut wood, tended fires, carried **water,** and washed laundry. Skilled maidservants put in long hours helping sew **clothing** and household linens, and, in humbler places or earlier times, they also helped spin thread and weave.

The poorest freemen had no servants, but most people had between one and four. **Records** do not distinguish between servants who helped strictly in the house and those who also helped with businesses attached to the house. In many cases, perhaps most, they helped in both places, for the distinction between work and home was not rigid.

The cheapest servants were children. There are records that in some Italian **cities,** little girls worked as servants with a contractual stipulation that their masters would provide them dowries when they were old enough to marry. The household would have a very inexpensive servant for five or seven years, with a lump sum payment due at the end. There was a gamble involved, because if the girl became unhappy with her place and left before she was old enough to marry, the master did not need to pay the dowry. The girl only got paid if she completed her term.

In England, there were also many child servants, usually at least 10 years old. For some, service in a noble household was a way to make connections and rise into a better station of life than their parents. If a child did well, he would be placed in a good job when he was grown. Children in rural villages eagerly sought positions as servants in cities. It was better to learn a craft, but for those who could not afford an apprenticeship, service was a stable line of work with opportunities to rise by promotion or marriage.

During the early Middle Ages, slavery was a common state of life. Slavery was not racial; it was the result of conquest. When a city was captured, its **women** and children were usually taken or sold as slaves, and its men were also pressed into hard slavery in mines or on **ships,** if they were not killed.

The Catholic **Church** disapproved of slavery and, in particular, banned the use of a fellow Christian as a slave. The economy of Europe did not require foreign slaves, and their use was never firmly established among the

Franks and Anglo-Saxons. The peasants in Northern Europe were often unfree, tied to the land they were born on. They needed permission to leave that land or marry. They were a kind of slave labor, but they were not foreign slaves, and they had a degree of freedom within their bondage to the land. They owed the lord labor, but they also worked for themselves. Most lords did not control their lives beyond demanding the required days of work.

Slave labor was normal both in the Byzantine Empire and in **Muslim** Spain. They owned both African and European Slavic slaves. These slaves served in the house, predominantly women but also men, and they worked in businesses. Some slaves worked in government offices, and some traveled with their merchant masters. Many worked on farms, especially Africans who were used to hot climates.

In medieval Western Europe, the slave trade dwindled, but it was still justified in some places as the sale of unbelievers. The wills of 13th-century Genoa mention slaves a number of times; they appeared to work in the house most of the time but were also owned by artisans who made them do heavy work in manufacturing. The slaves of Genoa probably came mostly from Spain and North Africa. The wills that mention slaves are most often written by people going on pilgrimage who provide for their slaves to be freed if they should die on pilgrimage.

The Italian settlements on the eastern coast of the Adriatic Sea were major slave-trading ports, since they had access to both the inland Slavs and the Mediterranean. They also had to import many basic necessities, which was labor intensive. They could not make a profit if they paid all workers. The word *slave* comes from the ethnic term *Slav*, because from Roman times into the Middle Ages, Yugoslavia and Russia were the main sources of captured laborers. The Slavs were Eastern Orthodox Christians, so they were not really unbelievers.

In Ragusa, the medieval forerunner to the modern city of Dubrovnik, rural Slavic women were trained in households and then sold abroad to other coastal cities such as Venice. These women were taller and stronger than the Italian-ancestry citizens. They could do manual labor of all kinds, from helping process exports to cooking and cleaning. Some were nurse-maids, and they were often freed upon the death of their masters. They may have looked like servants, but they were not paid, and if they ran away, they could be captured for a reward. Slavic men were not favored as household slaves because they were so much taller than the citizens, and they could create an uprising. Many of the slave women bore children for their masters but were not permitted to marry. The children remained slaves, in most cases.

The slave trade in Ragusa came to an end in the 13th century because slave prices ran so high that they began using indentured servants instead. A Slav's labor for a set number of years was purchased with an initial payment

Servants were the great invisible presence in medieval history. They are rarely mentioned in histories, although they have a place in court records. For the most part, they were a vast middle layer of society that owned little but kept everything moving. As in this image from the Luttrell family psalter, large numbers of servants kept all kitchen preparation going. (The British Library/StockphotoPro)

to the parents, with a final payment to come when the time was up. Although these people lived like slaves, they received training on the job and sometimes became skilled artisans, and they could not be sold abroad. They could expect to be freed after 5 or 10 years, and the owner was saved the expense of keeping them into old age.

In the 15th century, the Portuguese and Genoese began trading in West Africa. Portuguese settlers founded **sugar** plantations on islands in the Atlantic Ocean, such as Madeira and Cape Verde. By the close of the medieval period, black slaves were working in the labor-intensive sugar process. Sugar was a highly profitable trade in Europe; a block of sugar was worth as much as a block of silver. By 1500, the Atlantic island plantations exported enough sugar to bring the price to less than half of its previous levels, and the connection between sugar and African slavery was well established.

See also: Cities, Spices and Sugar, Weddings.

Further Reading

Blumenthal, Debra. *Enemies and Familiars: Slavery and Mastery in Fifteenth-Century Valencia.* Ithaca, NY: Cornell University Press, 2009.

Hanawalt, Barbara A. *Growing Up in Medieval London: The Experience of Childhood in History.* New York: Oxford University Press, 1993.

Hanawalt, Barbara. *Women and Work in Pre-Industrial Europe.* Bloomington: Indiana University Press, 1986.

Hunt, Edwin S., and James M. Murray. *A History of Business in Medieval Europe, 1299–1550.* Cambridge: Cambridge University Press, 1999.

Orme, Nicholas. *Medieval Children.* New Haven, CT: Yale University Press, 2001.

Wyatt, David. *Slaves and Warriors in Medieval Britain and Ireland, 800–1200.* Leiden, Netherlands: Brill, 2009.

Ships and Boats

Ships and boats were both crucial to travel in medieval Europe, since there were no good methods of land travel. As cities grew all along the coast, so did the need for ships that could transport large quantities of goods. When the Middle Ages opened, Mediterranean boats were built like the Greek and Roman galleys and cargo ships of earlier years. By the end of the Middle Ages, men had developed true ships, three-masted vessels fully equipped with billowing sails, in which they explored the coasts of Africa, India, and Central and South America. The development of boats and ships in the Middle Ages followed different paths in Northern and in Southern Europe because of differences in **climate,** natural resources, and the nature of the waters where the boats were used.

The Mediterranean is a very deep sea; it is more than a mile at its deepest. It has a very narrow passage out to the Atlantic, so there is virtually no tide. However, navigating the Straits of Gibraltar, only eight miles wide, is very difficult, so Mediterranean vessels needed good maneuverability. The galley and carrack were developed under these conditions. By contrast, the Norse and the Franks sailed the Baltic Sea, the rivers of Germany, the Barents Sea, the North Sea, and the North Atlantic. Most of these waters are relatively shallow along the coastlines; the Baltic itself is only about 1,000 feet in depth at its deepest. The North Atlantic waters are subject to violent winds and storms. Viking longships were well suited for maneuvering shallow rivers and coastlines and narrow, rocky fjords; Baltic cogs were wide and sturdy in storms.

Boats

Inland rivers were the highways of early medieval times, when **roads** were too poor for dependable travel. Many villages and towns were situated along streams that flowed into the larger rivers. In the Mediterranean region, there was a long, unbroken boat-building tradition that continued into the Middle Ages. Their **fishing** boats were like the open wooden plank boats of Roman times. In Northern Europe, however, there were not long traditions of boats, and at first they were very primitive.

The simplest kind of boat was a dugout canoe made from a large log; they were more common in the north, where there were forests of tall trees. These boats were among the most common riverboats for individuals and families, and they remained in use all through the medieval period. They were between 6 and 12 feet long and were carved to be wide and shallow. They sat low in the water but were very stable; they were often propelled by a pole. Large dugouts may have had a small sail.

The other primitive northern boat was the currach (or curragh), made from animal hides that were sewed together and then stretched over a wooden frame. To make a watertight surface, the strips of hide were overlapped along the sides of the boat. This method of overlapping layers of hide or planking on the side of a boat is called lapstrake construction. The currach had a planked floor and was propelled with oars; it was usable in rivers and along the coast. Currachs are still in use today in some remote areas of the British Isles. By the seventh or eighth century, there was a larger version of the currach, still constructed with overlapping pieces of hide but big enough to have four oars on each side and a steering oar in the back. These boats were sturdy cargo carriers capable of carrying a few cattle or a small flock of sheep.

Fishing boats in estuaries and along the seacoast needed to be larger and deeper, although some dugout boats may have ventured on the waves. The standard fishing boat of Northern Europe used lapstrake construction with curved wooden planks to build the craft up from its keel. In larger form, the same methods made seagoing vessels, but they were shallow and small for rivers. Most of them were rowed with a pair of oars, and some had a single sail. They were open and were usually filled with cargo or fishing nets. Their construction was not much different from the traditional Mediterranean fishing boats.

As shipping increased along the rivers, there were barges for goods and ferries for passengers. Barges and ferries were usually wider and flatter than other boats. Some were rectangular, rather than pointed at the prow. On small rivers, the ferry at a crossing was often attached to a rope that went from bank to bank, so the ferryman and the passengers could pull themselves across and not drift downstream.

In towns along the rivers, the shores and beaches were at first good enough for docking the early shallow boats. As boats grew larger, and as seagoing ships came up rivers to the city ports, a better system was needed. The earliest wharves seem to have been causeways of dirt built out into the water, shored up with wooden planks. The wharf jutted into the water with spaces between for the boats to tie up and unload. A harbor with wharves also allowed royal officials to inspect, regulate, and tax incoming wares. Every century, the wharves grew farther out into the water. Customs houses, shops, and warehouses were always built on the wharves until they were too crowded, and new wharves were built. In a large town, the riverbanks were no longer sloped, but walled.

Baltic and North Atlantic Ships

The classic Viking boat, the longship, was built by the same basic method as the currach but with long overlapping oak planks instead of hides. Using an iron ax or adze, the builders split tree trunks into long planks and shaped them to construct the hull. They laid a flat keel plank, added a garboard plank on each side of the keel, and then began building upward. The lapstrake planking that ran the length of these long boats was made of shorter planks notched at the ends (scarphed) and joined to make the required length. The planks were overlapped, sewn, or lashed together and then fastened with iron nails.

The interior framework was put in place only after the hull was built. This included the ribs and, in later years, wooden braces to stiffen the hull and allow the addition of a mast step to support a mast. A boat built this way is called clinker-built because the nails were clinched. Clinching or clinking a nail means using a hammer to bend the head of the nail against the wood, or against a small metal ring or plate (a rove), to hold better. Oakum caulking, which is woolen twine soaked in tar, was tucked into the cracks and edges. The steering oar of these boats was customarily hung on the right-hand side of the boat, the steerboard side. Loading was done on the left side of the boat, the ladeboard side. (This is the source of the terms *starboard* and *larboard* for the right and left sides of a boat.)

Norse ships in general were comparatively light; the oarsmen could move the boat along at a speed of three knots an hour (about 3½ miles per hour). Under sail, a Norse ship moved rapidly before the wind. The flexibility of a clinker-built hull made it possible to sail the boat in the open ocean, as the hull flexed with the waves.

Some key archeological finds have permitted archeologists to examine longships first hand and trace their development. Illustrations such as the Bayeux Tapestry are rarely accurate as to size, so it is difficult to know how large these ships were without firsthand examination. Three longships were preserved in the acidic bogs of Denmark, and five more were discovered under water, having been sunk deliberately to form an undersea wall. Some have been recovered from graves. Archeologists have dated these ships using dendrochronology, the analysis of tree rings in the wood.

The oldest ships, found in a Danish bog, had flat bottoms so that they could be easily drawn up on a beach. These ships dated back to Roman times. Only one had a real keel, and none showed evidence of a mast for a sail. One had rowlocks for oars lashed to the gunwale (the upper rim of the boat's body). They were steered with oars.

The ship burial at Sutton Hoo, in southeastern England, preserved a longship in a different way by building a wooden roof and earth mound over it. The Sutton Hoo boat was built during the sixth century and buried around 625. By the time it was discovered under its tumulus, the wood had rotted away, but the planks left clear impressions in the sandy soil, with some remnants of the iron nails. The ship was almost 90 feet long; the hull was about 4½ feet deep, and the keel was three inches deep. Each side was made of nine narrow strakes (planks), one inch thick and joined end to end by scarphing. The ship was propelled by 28 oarsmen and a sail. There were no benches; oarsmen in these boats probably sat on the sea chests that held their belongings.

The Oseberg ship is one of the few medieval vessels preserved intact. Most of what we know about the ways these ships were made and how they handled sailing conditions comes from careful study of the Oseberg ships and a few like it. One of the structural surprises was how close to the water the gunwale rode, compared to the high, curved prow. The design has proven surprisingly practical and stable in stormy conditions. (Werner Forman Archive/StockphotoPro)

By 700, nearing the heart of the Viking Age, some new building techniques had made the ships even stronger. Boats that were built for use in Norway's fjords and in the narrow and stormy sea between Norway and Denmark were made bigger and stronger, with their hulls braced so the ships could carry a mast and rigging. They had deeper hulls and massive keels for better stability in rough seas. Boatbuilders also developed vessels for different purposes, including cargo ships, fishing boats, and warships. Several of these types of boats were found in Denmark, in a narrow fjord at Skuldelev, where five vessels had been intentionally sunk in about 1050 to make a barrier against invasion by the Norse. The warship was the largest known Norse boat, at 118 feet long. It was probably built around 1030, and it could carry 100 men.

Another warship was a type called a drakkar; it was the classic Viking ship, able to carry 80 men. Drakkars were the pride of their owners, who adorned them with carvings of dragon heads, snakes, and birds of prey. The Skuldelev drakkar was built of wood from Ireland; the tree rings indicate the wood was cut in 1042. Dublin was a Norse settlement at the time, and the ship may have been built there. William of Normandy used drakkars to conquer England in 1066, as shown on the Bayeux Tapestry. The Vikings also preyed on cargo ships and were dreaded as raiders and pirates, especially in the Baltic.

The other three boats were not warships. One was an ocean-going knarr. It had decks fore and aft, with an open hold for cargo amidships. It could carry a crew of five to eight and a cargo of around 24 tons. The square sail would have been made from about 100 square yards of woven homespun strengthened with criss-crossed strips of leather. A knarr was more rounded than other Viking ships, with a deeper hull for cargo. It was mostly sail propelled, with just a few oarsmen to adjust the direction during tacking. Knarrs were very similar to another sort of fishing boat, the ferja, which also have been found sunken. It had an extra plank around the sides to make it deeper to carry more fish. There was also a small trading boat, a byrding. The deck was planked at the front and at the back, with an open hold for cargo. This boat moved along the coasts, carrying people and goods.

The cargo ship most widely used on the Baltic was the cog, termed a "round ship" because its width was fully half its length. Authorities disagree about the origins of the cog, some believing it to be a development of the longship but longer, heavier, and wider of beam to support sails. Others hold that the cog's ancestor was the logboat of the Frankish people who lived in that area during Roman times. A cog was found as wreckage in a river near Bremen, and it confirms that the pictures on the **seals** of some of the cities in the Hanseatic League were correct. The early cog was a round ship with a flat bottom and a single mast that carried a square sail. The cog curved up at the ends and was equipped with a broad right-side steering oar.

Shortly before 800, the emperor Charlemagne chose the cog as the best ship to ward off the Viking piracy that continually preyed on the rich ports and monasteries along the Baltic coast. He ordered a whole fleet to be built and also brought an army by land, an army that built **bridges** as they came to cross some of the rivers that were the inland transportation system under Charlemagne.

By around 1200, the cog had been further developed for carrying large amounts of cargo. It was the workhorse ship for cities of the Hanseatic League, a cooperative trading league organized in 1159 to facilitate the shipping of goods in Northern Europe and to ward off the constant Viking piracy. Eventually there were 84 cities in the Hanse, with Lübeck as its headquarters. Boats traveled the Baltic and North seas and the Atlantic Ocean and also worked inland on the Rhine River. Some voyaged southward to trade with people along the English Channel and even with cities along the Mediterranean.

The cog's height indirectly brought about a major design advance: a steering rudder hung on its straight vertical sternpost. It was a welcome change from the use of the steering oar; steering from up on the deck had become more and more difficult as boats got taller. Height also gave it an advantage over the Viking pirates, whose longships sat very low in the water. The Vikings' answering move was to add open wooden structures called "fighting castles" to the front and back of their longships to provide temporary platforms for archers and for hand-to-hand battle. Quickly, fighting castles were added to the cogs. Forecastles and sterncastles became standard parts of ships, though their use changed over the years. The right-side steering oar had to be much longer and was therefore harder to use.

Several other improvements in the cog were using the yard arm of the mast as an early crane for hoisting cargo in and out, adding bulwarks to protect the working area of the deck, using shingles on the sterncastle to enclose the tiller and provide a sheltered place, and adding hatches and a windlass. The cog also became larger; by the middle of the 13th century, some carried as much as 240 tons. Around 1400, some cogs became warships, armed escorts for valuable cargo. During the Hundred Years' War between England and France, cogs served as military transport or armed escort ships.

Two other northern ships deserve mention. One is the hulk, which was developed in England, probably in the late 13th century, as a hulk is pictured on the 1295 town seal of Hulksmouth. It displaced the cog as the main ship of the Hanseatic League. A Danzig town seal shows it as a large cargo carrier, flat-bottomed and equipped with a single mast and fore, stern, and top castles. The hulk could be towed on inland rivers. Its sterncastles and forecastles were actually part of the boat, not added-on platforms. The earliest known hulk dates from the late 700s. By around 1450, the hulk had largely replaced the cog. The other form of northern ship is the nef, a transitional form of the longship, the first northern hull with differences between the bow and the stern. The bow was more rounded than the stern, and the boat was fitted with a second mast (mizzen mast) that carried a triangular lateen steering sail to help keep the boat on course.

Mediterranean Ships

The Romans had used two basic kinds of ship. Galleys were their warships, and they used cargo ships known as round ships. During the Middle Ages, both types were adopted and improved on century by century. Early Byzantine dominance was challenged by new **Muslim** navies in the seventh century. Although the Arabs had been sailing the Indian Ocean in Indian-style ships, their Mediterranean fleets were in the same style as the Roman and Byzantine ships, since they bought surplus ships and hired local crews.

Roman warships were galleys that moved by means of both sail power and the muscle power of dozens of men at the oars. The basic Roman galley had been developed into larger versions—the bireme and the trireme—that used two or three levels of oarsmen, with several men on each oar. An even-larger galley had used five levels of oarsmen. Throughout the Middle Ages and even into the 18th century, Mediterranean warships continued to be galleys, most of them using both oars and sails.

One important development formed the principal warship of the Byzantine Empire—a dromon. There were three variations of the dromon. The smallest, the ousiakon, carried a company of 100 men (an *ousia*). It was a two-banked galley. The men on the lower bank only rowed; the men on the upper bank rowed but were also the fighters in battles with other ships. The pamphylos was a little larger; it carried a crew of more nearly 150. The true dromon carried a crew of about 200, with 150 oarsmen on two banks of oars and 50 marines (fighting men). These larger dromons had a raised tower near the mast, where the marines could stand to shoot arrows or throw spears or other projectiles. Most dromons also carried either a powerful catapult, which could throw a 20- or 25-pound object more than 250 feet, or a pressurized siphon flamethrower that propelled liquid Greek fire onto the enemy ship's deck. Greek fire was an incendiary substance that continued to burn even when it hit water.

Venice created its own version of the dromon while it was under Byzantine rule. It was called the *galeagrossa,* and it was put to both commercial and military use. In the Mediterranean, the two purposes ran together. Merchant ships needed defense, and navies had to carry cargo. Sailors learned to fight. Venice's Arsenal built galleys that eventually challenged the cogs' dominance in bringing Flanders wool to the Mediterranean.

648

Mediterranean ships, beginning with Greek fishing boats and including the massive dromon, developed a new type of sail during the Byzantine era. Roman sails had been square, but square sails moved a ship only in the direction the wind was blowing; adjustments allowed some variation but not much. Lateen sails were triangular, not square. They were hung from a yard (crossbar) that was fixed partway up the mast at a slant. A long, narrow triangle of sailcloth hung down almost to the deck. This shape creates a baggy lower part of the sail that traps the wind and funnels it up to the narrow top, creating a substantial amount of lift when a ship is sailing with the wind. It could be angled to let a ship steer a course that was not directly with the wind or almost against the wind. By the ninth century, the ships of the Mediterranean were generally lateen rigged and capable of working their way windward. The triangular sails were huge, and the yards they were fastened to were made of large tree trunks. The square sail eventually made a comeback around the 1300s, partly because of the amount of manpower needed to swing lateen rigging around. The square sail caught more wind and enabled the ship to move faster.

Mediterranean ships were not only different in having galleys of oars and lateen sails; they were constructed in a completely different manner from Baltic and North Atlantic ships. Viking ships and the cogs of northern waters were clinker-built: outer shell first, with overlapped strakes, and then construction of the inner framework. The method of construction in southern waters was just the opposite. They built the framework first, with beams and ribs, and then covered the framework with planking. Boats built this way are called carvel-built. Three medieval shipwrecks show advances in construction methods over several centuries.

A carvel-built hull from the seventh century found in the eastern Mediterranean, off the coast of Turkey, shows the basic construction method. The builders laid the keel first, then added high, curved endposts. They fastened planks alongside the keel, joined by mortise and tenon and pinned by trenails (wooden pegs that swell when wet to tighten the construction). They added planking up to the waterline, nailed to a framework, and set crossbeams from side to side to bind the hull together. These crossbeams protruded through the hull. At the stern, the crossbeams were a good place to hang a steering rudder on each side of the hull. In the middle of the ship, crossbeams helped support the mast. This particular ship was about 67 feet long and could carry more than 65 tons of cargo. When it sank, it was carrying 900 containers (amphorae) of wine. It also carried 11 anchors.

Another wreck along Turkey was dated by coins to the 11th century. The cargo was mostly glassware, and this ship also carried a large number of anchors. The carvel construction was more advanced by the 11th century. The framework was laid out, then curved timber ribs were added and planking was nailed on with iron spikes. The alternating of the scarphed joints contributed to the strength of the hull, as there was no continuous line of joints across the ship. A third wreck from the estuary of the Po River was dated to about 1300 and was 65 feet long. A new method made the ship strong enough to hold two masts. They used frames attached to floors that crossed the keel and were then secured to a timber bolted to the keel for extra strength.

In the years after 1000, the role of the ship changed dramatically. Commerce was increasing, merchants were becoming wealthy, and ships were increased in size to hold more cargo. After Crusaders set up a Christian kingdom in Jerusalem, there was a great surge of Christian **pilgrims** wanting to visit Jerusalem. All these factors created demand for larger ships.

The **Crusades** spurred a great deal of shipbuilding to transport **knights** and **horses** from Marseille or Venice to the Holy Land. At first, Crusaders rented any ships they could find, but by the Third Crusade of the 13th century, more were required. King Louis IX of France contracted with merchants in Genoa, Venice, and Marseille to provide custom-built ships for his two Crusades, in 1248 to 1254. These were substantial vessels, several with three decks. The horses were led into the ship through a door that was then caulked shut to keep water out when the ship went out to sea.

In the 15th century, the Baltic and Mediterranean traditions began to mix. The Hanseatic League had extended its reach into ports in the Mediterranean, and Venetian galleys were trading directly in Flanders. One early hybrid was the buss, a wide, carvel-built cargo fishing ship built in the Netherlands. Using the buss, Dutch sailors could stay out at sea longer. The buss sailed with the fishing boat; it was a floating fish-processing plant. The pair of vessels could stay out for several weeks and return with its catch salted while fresh.

The ultimate round ship of the late Middle Ages was the three-masted, full-rigged, ocean-going carrack. The carrack's precursor was the cog, the clinker-built cargo carrier of the Hanseatic League. In Mediterranean shipyards, the cog had been modified and refined; it was no longer clinker-built but was now carvel-built. Its sails also blended the best of north and south.

The carrack was large and heavy. Huge ribs formed the hull and supported multiple decks, a high sterncastle, and an even higher (though smaller) forecastle. The ship's tiller passed through a port to move the sternpost rudder. The edge-to-edge planking of the ship was caulked with oakum and tar or pitch to help keep seawater out. For the same reason, the ship was constructed with few hatches and no companionway (a stairway leading from the deck to the cabins below). Its three masts were the main mast and foremast, both square rigged, and the lateen-rigged mizzenmast, which rose from the sterncastle. Later versions of the carrack included another small sail—the spritsail on the bowsprit. Improvement in managing

Ships were integral to the Crusades. Most Crusaders gathered on the coast of southern France and embarked at Marseilles. Since their warfare was dependent on horses and they could not easily buy or train them on the other side of the journey, they had to get ships with stables built below the deck. Travel was uncomfortable; knights traveled with retinues of servants and squires, and the ship was too crowded to afford sleeping quarters for all of them. Although this 15th-century painting imagines the voyages in a cheerful way, the actual conditions must have been squalid. Horses needed some rest periods on islands in order to regain their health. (The British Library/StockphotoPro)

the ropes made the huge sails easier to handle, and multiple sails gave versatility to managing the course of the ship.

A large merchant carrack could carry 1,000 tons of cargo in its hold as it moved around the whole length of the Mediterranean and to and from the Baltic. Its great size made it an expensive ship, and it was expensive too in that it required a large crew. There were smaller carracks, too, such as the 100-ton *Santa Maria*, the ship that carried Christopher Columbus to the islands of Central America.

Columbus's other ships, the *Niña* and the *Pinta,* were caravels, not carracks. The caravel was a fast sailing ship developed in Portugal around 1440. It carried two or three masts, with either lateen sails or a mixture of square and lateen. The caravel had excellent sailing characteristics and did not need the large crew that was necessary on a carrack. It could move at a relatively fast pace; records show that on the return trip from America in 1493, the *Niña* and *Pinta* had at least one day when they covered nearly 200 miles of ocean. Caravels were generally the ships of choice for the voyages of exploration that marked the end of the 15th century and continued into the 16th century.

War at Sea

Ships were at times used for direct warfare, not just for military transport. Naval warfare was most important in the Mediterranean; both Muslim and Christian kingdoms kept naval fleets of galleys. Northern Europe's foray into naval warfare was delayed, although merchant vessels began carrying crossbows to defend against piracy. Piracy was the first reason to create military vessels to support merchant shipping, more than foreign warfare.

In the Mediterranean Sea, Egypt, Constantinople, Venice, Genoa, and other regional powers maintained galley fleets with both rowing benches and a lateen sail. The galleys were armed with a platform that ran the length of the vessel—so that men could pass easily from end to end—and with freestanding pavises (shields) and crossbows. Some had a forecastle, perhaps armed with small catapult **weapons.**

A naval battle typically began with distance shooting. Crossbows were increasingly the largest part of naval battles. As the ships rowed closer, each crew would try to board and master the other. Ships usually had a boarding platform of some kind, something that stuck out and could be touched to the other ship. They also threw grappling hooks out, attached to iron chains. Poleaxes could reach out to cut the enemy's rigging. Some crews threw soap on the other ship's decks to make fighters slip. Others threw lime at the enemy to blind them. Most devastating, those who had access to its formula flung Greek fire, catching the enemy's ship on fire. Nothing but ammonia, in the form of stale urine, could douse Greek fire. There was a great deal of hand combat, although crews were lightly armed. Plate **armor** had no place at sea, but hardened leather or light chainmail could help in close combat.

During the 14th century, the countries of the North Atlantic built up their stock of fighting ships. France and England both acquired some galleys. During the Hundred Years' War, French galleys harassed English shipping and attacked English ports and English-owned ports in France, such as Bordeaux. English galleys, often hired as Spanish or Italian mercenaries, tried to defend shipping. Germany's Hanseatic League was often armed, and there was an order of oceangoing Crusaders in Germany to protect shipping against infidel attacks.

See also: Fish and Fishing, Sieges, Weapons.

Further Reading
Fagan, Brian. *Fish on Friday*. New York: Basic Books, 2006.

Grohskopf, Bernice. *The Treasure of Sutton Hoo: Ship-Burial for an Anglo-Saxon King*. New York: Atheneum, 1970.

Hattendorf, John B., and Richard W. Unger. *War at Sea in the Middle Ages and the Renaissance*. Woodbridge, UK: Boydell Press, 2003

Haws, Duncan. *Ships and the Sea: A Chronological Review*. New York: Thomas Y. Crowell, 1975.

Haywood, John. *Dark Age Naval Power: A Reassessment of Frankish and Anglo-Saxon Seafaring Activity*. Norfolk, UK: Anglo-Saxon Books, 1999.

Hutchinson, Gillian. *Medieval Ships and Shipping*. London: Cassell, 1997.

Konstam, Angus. *The History of Pirates*. Guilford, CT: Lyons Press, 1999.

Lewis, Archibald R. *European Naval and Maritime History, 300–1500*. Bloomington: Indiana University Press, 1985.

Meisel, Tony. *To the Sea: Sagas of Survival and Tales of Epic Challenge on the Seven Seas*. New York: Black Dog and Leventhal Publishers, 2000.

Milne, Gustav. *The Port of Medieval London*. Stroud, UK: Tempus Publishing, 2006.

Morrison, John. *Age of the Galley: Mediterranean Vessels since Pre-Classical Times*. London: Conway Maritime Press, 2004.

Pryor, John H. *Geography, Technology, and War: Studies in the Maritime History of the Mediterranean, 649–1571*. Cambridge: Cambridge University Press, 1992.

Rose, Susan. *Medieval Naval Warfare 1000–1500*. New York: Routledge, 2001.

Unger, Richard W., and Robert Gardiner. *Cogs, Caravels, and Galleons: The Sailing Ship 1000–1650*. Seacaucus, NJ: Chartwell Books, 2000.

Woodman, Richard. *The History of the Ship*. London: Conway Maritime Press, 1997.

Shoes

By the Roman era, shoe making had the basic elements we recognize: soles and uppers that tied or buckled around the foot. In places with greater traditions of craftsmanship and more wealth, shoes were made by professional shoemakers using lasts—carved wooden models of feet. Medieval shoemakers worked within an unbroken tradition from Roman times.

As with other aspects of European culture, the Roman traditions were best retained in the Mediterranean region, while the Franks and other northern peoples began with their own methods, usually more primitive, and gradually adapted to blend the northern and southern styles. Careful excavation in London, in recent decades, has amassed a large collection of shoe styles from the Middle Ages. Since styles in the north usually lagged behind styles in Italy, innovations in the Italian cities probably took as long as 25 years to catch on in England.

Goatskin was called cordwain, and shoemakers were commonly called cordwainers. This was true even in England, where goats were a less important part of the economy than they were in the Mediterranean countries. Goatskin must have been one of the most common shoe materials in the early Middle Ages. After cow and sheep leather replaced it in England, cordwain continued to be the most common shoe leather in Italy, southern France, and Spain. Late medieval shoes for the wealthy were made of the most delicate calfskin or various kinds of woven fabric.

Although shoe styles changed from century to century, and different kinds of fasteners were developed, some general principles were constant. There was always a great difference in footwear between rich and poor, court and country. In every time, shoes were used by nobility at court to convey their status and wealth. Shoes wear out, and they are in contact with the floor, often with dirt. Anyone who can afford to have tooled leather, **embroidery,** or silk velvet even on his (or her) shoes must surely be wealthy.

Men's and **women**'s shoes did not look much different, if at all. In any given century, illustrations show us the same shapes, colors, and decorations. When rounded toes were fashionable, both sexes wore them, and when pointed toes came back in, both followed. In modern times, when shoes, especially men's, are relatively plain, the elaborate and gaudy styles of medieval men's court shoes make little sense. In Constantinople, fashionable shoes could show the toes or sides of the feet, as women's dress shoes do today. They could have embroidered bands around them or include sections of silk. When they laced, they usually laced along the side, leaving the top plain. These styles were all copied at European courts during the Middle Ages.

Boots came up around the ankles, while shoes ended at the anklebones. Some boots came up to the knee, while others enclosed the ankle and no farther. High boots were too expensive for common people, and most images of shoes show low-cut shoes or ankle boots. Boots to or above the knee were not much used until the Renaissance period, following the Middle Ages.

In all times, the poor were lucky to have shoes at all, and theirs were patched and plain. They kept to old, practical styles and often wore rags wrapped around their legs instead of hose. They used sturdier, thicker leather when they could afford it. Peasants' shoes were made from rough or untanned leather. If they were working in the fields, they often removed their shoes to keep them from getting too muddy.

People of all classes wore wooden platform sandals as a type of over-shoe to lift the leather shoe up from rain and snow. These were variously called clogs, pattens, or galoshes. They typically had a leather band the shoe slipped through, and some had a sandal-like strap at the back. The sole was made of wood, and it had arched pillars to support it. In some cases, the thickness was built up from layers of leather, but most often the whole clog was carved from wood. During the time that long points, called poulaines, were in fashion, these pattens or galoshes had extensions in front to hold the points up. In England, pattens were only in fashion during the 14th and 15th centuries, so many of them did have poulaine supports.

Shoe Styles

The story of shoe fashions in Europe seems mostly to be about the toes' points growing and shrinking. The earliest Viking Age shoes found in graves were simple shoes or boots with round toes, no decoration, and flat soles. The soles were made of thick leather and wore out quickly. They were cut off and replaced as long as the upper shoe lasted. By the 11th century, just before the Norman conquest of England, some shoes had pointed toes, but not as extreme as they became later.

Shoes found in excavations of Norman London in the 12th century mostly have drawstring ties around the ankle. The slots for the drawstrings were made of small parallel slits in the leather. The upper part of the shoe, the vamp, was cut from a single piece of leather. The shoes were simple, more like moccasins than like modern shoes. Some had a triangle of leather attached inside, at the heel, to stiffen it. They opened at the front, with overlapping tabs.

A common way of embellishing shoes for well-to-do townspeople was to sew a band of embroidery on the top of the shoe, from the toe to the shoe's throat. Most often, it was a stripe of plait stitch, an overlapping series of X's that formed a solid, smooth, thick line. Colored silk stood out from the leather with a high sheen. Many illustrations show **saints** and kings wearing shoes with these vamp stripes.

The 12th century brought many new fashions as Crusaders and their retinues traveled and observed each other. After a distinguished Crusader wore shoes with elongated, pointed tips to hide the corns on his toes, a new fad caught on in France. Shoes were made with impractically long pointed tips, and sometimes they were shaped like tails of fish or scorpions. Aristocratic shoes were often heavily embellished with gilding and embroidery. As wearing hose caught on, hose could sometimes replace shoes. Some pictures show men wearing hose alone; they may have been reinforced with a leather sole stitched to the cloth.

Shoe construction slowly became more sophisticated. Instead of large single pieces being cut and wrapped, moccasin like, 13th-century shoes used more separate pieces of leather. The heel sections, called quarters, were cut separately, and the vamp came in several pieces. It was more work for the shoemaker, but it used leather more efficiently and controlled the shape. The upper part of the shoe, the vamp, was more often made of fine calfskin in the 13th century. Shoes often had a cord stitched on the inside of a cut edge, to reinforce it. This permitted finer, softer leathers to be used. Most shoes came only to the top of the foot, but some had flaps that extended partway up the ankle.

Shoes in 13th-century London began to have side laces, as Byzantine shoes had for some time. The shoe opened only at the outside; it was solid across the top of the foot and on the instep. At the side slit, the shoemaker bored a set of holes similar to modern shoelace holes. They did not have metal grommets like modern shoes, but sometimes they were reinforced with a cord stitched around the inside of the hole.

In the mid- to late 13th century, shoes in London were often closed with buttoning toggles. The opening was again at the front. At that opening, a leather thong came about an inch or more out of the tongue. It had been folded back through a slit in itself, to make a knot, and then its free end was stitched inside the vamp. Around the ankle, two straps came to meet this toggle, with slits for it to button through. In shoes where the toggle has survived, some appear to be so long that they did not fasten the shoe tightly. There were fancier variations on the toggle fastening. In some cases, leather toggles came out of one of the straps and buttoned through slits in the other.

Toe points were not extravagant during the 13th century, but shoes for the wealthy were often embroidered and styled in various ways. One technique was to make decorative slits and cutouts in the leather so that the colored hose would show through. Since the slit was often at the side, the top of the foot was available to be decorated. The cutwork could be very elaborate, and it often covered most of the surface of the shoe. Excavated shoes have patterns of stamped circles, diamonds, squares, slits, and combinations of stars, triangles, and diamonds.

There were some tall boots that had pairs of straps up the ankle; one side had a toggle, and the other had a buttonhole slit. Other boots laced up the outside, with a side slit. The boots did not go up to the knee, but stopped just under halfway up. Boots were not fashionable; they were worn in certain professions, such as hunting. Royal huntsmen needed to wear fairly tall boots to protect their clothing and legs from brambles as they rode through **forests** and parks.

During the 13th century, the most popular kind of shoe decoration was a fine repeating pattern cut out of the leather. The design allowed the wearer's hose color to show through. Such shoes were only for indoor use; they were impractical outdoors or in muddy weather. (James Robinson Planche, *An Illustrated Dictionary of Historic Costume*, 2003)

Children's shoes were similar to adult shoes, but they tended to come higher up the ankle so that they could be laced securely. They more often had front fastenings, whether toggles or ties. They did not have pointed toes, but were practical and simple.

The 14th century was a time of rapidly changing fashion in clothing and hairstyles. In shoes, it was the age of pointed toes, sometimes to an extreme. The pointed tip was called a poulaine. It was usually stuffed with moss or fur to make it stand out or up stiffly. Most illustrations of 14th-century shoes show poulaines that were between two and six inches long.

London shoes were either very low-cut shoes or very tall boots, with little in between. Shoes were fastened with toggles, and boots laced at the side. Shoe construction was more standardized, probably reflecting the better organization of the cordwainers' **guild.** The top of a 14th-century boot was higher at the front, forming a point. A leather band was folded and sewn around the top to strengthen it. It was made of three or four pieces of cut leather, in addition to the sole. In some late 14th-century shoes, the sole was made in two pieces, with a separate heel. Soles had to be replaced and patched frequently, so perhaps this made it easier to replace a worn heel.

By the late 14th century, shoe styles became fancier and more extreme. They were cut low, and the area of the shoe's tongue was cut away to expose the colored hose. The shoe's tip became more extravagantly pointed. The shoe was held by a thin strap that came from the inner side and fastened on the outer side. There were two ways to fasten this strap. One was the buckle, the newest and most expensive fastener. The other was the latchet, in which the strap split into two thinner thongs at the end and tied through holes at the strap on the shoe.

Expensive 14th-century shoes had decorated leather. The leather was engraved with a sharp tool so that its top surface was scraped away to expose a different texture and color. Shoes had a wide variety of finely engraved geometric or floral patterns. Since more and more of the vamp had been cut away to show the colored hose, the long poulaines had to carry on the decorative patterning.

Shoe buckles became almost universal during the 15th century. The price of buckles must have come down as the craft became more widespread. Shoes were often fastened with straps and buckles, either at the side or in the front, and sometimes a shoe style used more than one buckle. Boots opened at the front, fastened with buckled straps, and had a tongue.

Shoe points were modest at the beginning of the century, but by the later years, they had become so excessively long that the English Parliament made a proclamation forbidding cobblers to make points longer than two inches. Citizens with long, padded poulaines, especially when wearing wooden pattens with poulaine extensions, were tripping other people in the streets.

Shoe Making

Shoemakers were a skilled craft from early times and an organized guild in the 12th century. Originally, cobblers were a separate trade; they fixed old shoes and sold them at a discount. Cordwainers made new shoes, but they also repaired these shoes for customers. The trades gradually blended until *cobbler* became the standard word for a shoemaker. Around 1300, shoemakers developed a means of measuring shoe sizes. In England, the measurement was the barleycorn, about one-third of an inch. A system of measurement allowed merchants to sell shoes at fairs, ready-made.

Shoemakers worked at a bench and used special leather-cutting **tools.** One was a curved half-moon knife with a sharp point; it resembled the top of a pike, and it was often stuck in the bench by its point. Another was a large pair of shears that had long blades and were formed from a single piece of metal. Shoemakers used awls to punch holes and long needles to stitch together multiple layers of leather. To size and shape their shoes, they had carved wooden feet called lasts. In a time when pointed shoes were fashionable, the lasts were also pointed. Shoemakers also had patterns, probably made of cloth, to guide their cutting.

Soles were cut from the toughest leather, usually in one piece. The shoe's upper pieces were cut from finer leather or cloth, and the shoe was stitched on the wooden last, inside out. This kind of shoe construction was called

A late medieval woodcut shows the look of a shoemaking workshop. As in most medieval shops, customers could stand outside in the street and look into a window. One shoemaker could tend the counter, working as he waited for customers. The others sat close enough to the window to have some natural light. On the table, their cutting and stitching tools are piled up; they are stitching soles and uppers on their apron-covered laps. While some shoes were made to order, others were made in advance and hung for display in the window. By the late Middle Ages, there was a rough standard for sizing shoes, so that peddlers could take shoes out to distant fairs. (Paul Lacroix, *Moeurs, Usage et Costumes au Moyen Age et a l'Epoque de la Renaissance*, 1878)

"turn-shoe" because the shoe then had to be turned right side out. Specialized stitches had to be used to attach the sole to the upper so that the stitches weren't exposed to the friction of wear and tear. Some shoes were lined with cloth.

When a shoe's sole wore out, it was repaired with patches called clumps. These were stitched onto the outside of the shoe and often had separate heel and foreparts. Cobblers had methods of stitching these clumps on so that the stitches were entirely on the inside of the leather's layers. A repaired medieval shoe more closely resembles a modern shoe with its hard sole and separate heel.

Heavily embroidered shoes often had cloth uppers, since it was difficult to embroider on leather. Shoes could also have embroidered cloth strips stitched onto them. Embroidery on shoes was always in silk and used bright colors. The designs ranged from animals and flowers to decorative scrolls and moons. Leather strips could be gilded and stitched onto shoes, in combination with embroidery.

See also: Clothing, Embroidery.

Further Reading

Brooke, Iris. *English Costume from the Early Middle Ages through the Sixteenth Century*. Mineola, NY: Dover Publications, 2000.

Grew, Francis, and Margrethe de Neergaard. *Shoes and Pattens.* Woodbridge, UK: Boydell Press, 2006.

Norris, Herbert. *Ancient European Costume and Fashion.* Mineola, NY: Dover Publications, 1999.

Norris, Herbert. *Medieval Costume and Fashion.* Mineola, NY: Dover Publications, 1999.

Scott, Margaret. *Medieval Dress and Fashion.* London: British Library, 2007.

Singman, Jeffrey. *Daily Life in Medieval Europe.* Westport, CT: Greenwood Press, 1999.

Sieges

In ancient times, **cities** often had strong walls around them, and warfare against these cities had always involved the basic tasks of breaking the walls, going over or under the walls, or starving the defenders into surrender. In the Middle Ages, Europe's decentralized political structure put a new twist on the siege by planting heavily fortified **castles** all over the landscape. Constantinople's thick city walls were similar to the fortresses of Roman, Greek, and more ancient times. Northern Europe, on the other hand, had several hundred small fortresses that were designed to hold off disproportionately larger attackers. In order to capture a region, an invader would need to besiege more than one fortress.

After the period of the First **Crusade,** knights returned with much grander ideas of defensive fortification. They had seen Byzantine fortress designs and had participated in attacks on Antioch, Acre, Jerusalem, and Tyre. Crusaders had built their own fortresses to hold the new territory, and they had used local engineering and labor to build much larger stone fortresses than Europe had at the time. When they came home, many rebuilt their family castles to incorporate the new defensive features. Castles became harder to capture by direct assault.

Sieges, attacks that stretched out over a long period of time, were the only way of capturing a castle unless it was taken by surprise. Sieges were expensive for both sides. The attackers had to sustain an army in hostile territory for a number of months, while the defenders had to make their **food** and **water** last. Both sides worked hard to attack or defend the walls. Walls could be broken down or surmounted by going over or under the walls. Siege machinery falls into three basic types. Catapults threw projectiles over the castle walls, either into the castle or from the castle toward the attackers. Rams battered the walls to make them fall down. Siege towers lifted attackers to the top of the wall so that they could enter.

Because of the high stakes and expense, sieges were not governed by the polite rules of chivalry. No trick was too dirty, gross, or savage. Treachery was one of the best ways of breaking a siege, if an insider could be bribed to open the gates or tell of a secret weak point. **Poison** or bacterial contamination of food or water was a popular way to break a siege.

Climbing, Ramming, and Digging

The simplest siege weapon was the ladder. The attackers wanted to get into the fortress, and one way was to go over the walls. Siege ladders had been used against city and fortress walls since ancient times. Basic facts that governed the construction of siege ladders began with length: if a ladder was too short, it would not allow the attacker to go over the top, but if it was too long, its top would stick up where defenders could shove it away. The ladder had to lean enough to be stable, but it had to be vertical enough to be strong. The ideal siege ladder came to just below the top of the wall, and its foot was placed at a distance from the wall equal to about half its length. Since the walls of a town or castle were of varying heights, and were surrounded by varying terrain, the attackers had to build custom siege ladders for each position.

A refinement on the simple ladder was a ladder with a bridge. The bridge was a sturdy plank hinged at the top of the ladder, raised by ropes. The ladder had to be somewhat freestanding, like a platform, since it could not lean against the wall. Some engineers designed folding ladders that could be made in advance and carried with the army or ladders that could be assembled from short sections. Some sieges also used ladders made of rope or leather, with hooks at the top. These ladders were for quiet night attacks, when the ladders could suddenly appear hooked on top of the walls by long poles without the defenders having seen any ladders.

Defenders tried to repel attackers on ladders by using the force of gravity. Standing at a higher level, they could drop harmful substances on the climbers. Most often, they threw large rocks to knock the attackers off the ladders or force them to cover their heads. Sometimes they threw or poured boiling water, oil, or any other hot substances they had on hand, such as tar. They could also throw quicklime, a highly caustic, alkaline material that burned on contact. In sandy places, they could heat sand to red-hot and fling it down. In some cases, they could fling nets onto the attackers when they reached the top and trap them.

To protect against all these defenses, attackers used heavy shields. Since classical times, there had been siege shields made tall, curved back, or with a small roof, and at times on wheels. Many shields were large enough for more than one man. Medieval sieges used all forms of wooden shields, covered with leather. In the 15th century, the tall siege shield was called a pavis. It often had a spike to drive into the ground and a pole to hold it up.

Of course, the first defense against siege ladders had been put in place before the siege began, when the fortress was designed. Most fortresses

Ant ala loft de france quil vint
par mionau si se consesla le roi

If a city or castle were not heavily defended, attackers could directly assault the walls
with ladders. Ladders were a quick way to get to the top and over the wall, but in
most sieges, the defenders were able to push the ladders back or drop stones on the
men climbing up. A slower method was to dig under the wall, assuming it was not
built on bedrock. In this scene representing a French assault on Genoa, an archer is
working to keep defenders on the run, allowing the attackers to work freely.
Normally, the city's walls were equally crowded with archers returning fire.
(The British Library/StockphotoPro)

used a ditch or moat that came as close as possible to the outer walls. Attackers had to fill in the ditch with sacks or barrels of rocks and earth. In some cases, they resorted to using catapults to land rocks and dirt in the moat. Unless the ground was reasonably level approaching the wall, their use of siege machines would be limited.

If the attackers continued to try to go over the walls, but needed more than ladders, the next logical step was to make portable sheds. Sheds could be made fire resistant with water and fresh skins. Sheds could also disguise or protect structural attacks, such as digging or battering rams.

The purpose of a ram is simple. It is a strong tree trunk that hits a wall, gate, or door repeatedly until the object is smashed. The design of a battering ram had three aims: to strengthen the ram itself, to increase its force, and to protect its operators from counterattack.

The end of the battering ram was strengthened by a metal tip. Sometimes this was actually in the shape of a ram's head, invoking the ram's butting strength and using the ram's extended snout as the focal point of the battering force. More often, it was a blacksmith's **iron** binding so that the wood did not shatter as easily from the force put on it. The ram's bulk was suspended by ropes that could swing it, so the operators of a battering ram did not need much human power to strike with it. Longer ropes, of course, gave it more swinging power. The frame that suspended the ram was usually roofed so that its operators were protected from arrows or stones. Finally, the roof was often covered with damp **animal** skins as fire prevention.

Defenders dropped projectiles and hot liquids on the operators of battering rams. They could also try to disrupt the action of the ram, if the ram's housing was too well defended to be vulnerable to rocks or fire. When the ram struck the wall, they could try to hook it and pull it up, either deflecting its blow or flipping its shed over.

Battering ram technology had been well explored during classical times, and, although rams were still used, castle designers built walls to withstand them. The thickest parts of the walls were at battering level, and gates, the main target of rams, were protected by gatehouses and moats. Attackers had to find new ways to use rams during the Middle Ages. Small rams could be mounted on ladders and lifted up to smash parapets. Attackers could build an earth ramp to a higher point in a wall, where it was likely to be thinner.

Attackers could also try to drill holes in the walls. Borers, too, had to work in the shelter of sheds and shields. It was not easy to drill holes in **stone** walls, so borers were more commonly used against **brick.** They were not a large feature of Northern European siege warfare, since most French and English castles were made of limestone and granite. A strong brick wall could be sufficiently weakened by holes that a ram could bring it down.

Holes could have wood pushed in and set on fire, and the heat further weakened the walls.

By the 14th century, castle walls were built to be too high and thick for ladders and rams to be effective. If ladders and rams could not boost attackers over or batter walls down, a more elaborate machine could be built. A siege tower was a heavy, cumbersome machine, not designed for a lightning attack or for secrecy. It was part of an all-out assault on a weakened castle. The tower was a tall wooden structure on wheels; it was sometimes called a castle or a cat. It had protective walls and a roof and was fireproofed if possible. Inside, it had wooden floors as stories where attackers could stand. A ladder led from bottom to top, so each layer of attackers could climb the ladder in turn. A top floor allowed archers to give further defensive cover to the attackers. The siege tower also had a bridge to cross to the top of the wall. This bridge could be a drawbridge, operated by a windlass in the bottom story.

Certain engineering issues governed the construction of siege towers. They had to be tall enough to reach the walls and stable enough not to tip when loaded with climbing soldiers. They also had to be portable, usually on wheels. Medieval siege towers were as tall as 75 feet high, but they were often shorter. Designs in medieval illustrations appear to favor a small fortress on a rolling platform, reached by one or more ladders. The attackers expected a tough fight before they could cross a bridge, and they designed it to have walls or even a roof. Other siege towers were more like rolling platform ladders with bridges. The builders had to think about fire, since the most common way to defend against a siege tower was to set it on fire. In the Byzantine region, siege towers became obsolete when it became clear the defenders would hurl Greek fire at them. Northern Europe was able to use siege tower tactics longer, since it was easier to defend wood against ordinary fire. The tower could be roofed with fresh turf or newly skinned wet hides.

Siege towers were heavy and could easily tip over. It was difficult to move them into position from the safe distance where they had been built. The ground had to be level, and many teams of oxen were needed to move them. They also needed to be moved close to the walls, which normally meant that pushing, not pulling, force was required. One way to move a very heavy siege platform was to sink one or more posts into the ground by the castle walls and loop heavy pulleys and ropes around them. The platform was then attached to the ropes, and it could be moved forward by oxen walking away from the battle. The siege tower inched closer to the fortress walls, but the muscle power moving it only moved farther out of range. The tower could come right up to the pulleys, if the defenders had not disrupted them. Towers could also be moved with levers, but, in any case, they moved very slowly because of their great weight.

One of the oldest methods of carrying out an attack on high walls was the siege tower. The siege tower had to act as a covered ladder that also defended its passengers from fire. When it had been moved close enough to the wall, the siege tower dropped a drawbridge and the attack began. (Duncan Walker/iStockPhoto)

Undermining a wall could be the most successful attack, and there were fewer ways for the defenders to work against it. Ideally, the defenders would not know that sappers were digging a tunnel under the walls. The first somewhat successful underground attack in medieval times was carried out by the Vikings when they besieged Paris in 885. After the Norman conquest of England, mining was part of many sieges. The siege of Rochester Castle in 1215, when King John of England was putting down a rebellion, was one of the few times when mining was a key factor in the castle's surrender. Miners dug under two outer walls so that the defenders were trapped in the keep. Château-Gaillard, built by King Richard I of England, was designed to be impregnable, but miners collapsed its walls twice. Mining was a large part of Crusader warfare, on both sides.

The best location to begin a sapping operation was in a place where the defenders could not observe what was going on without leaving the fortress. Sappers sometimes needed to start some distance away, on the other side of a hill. The attackers could put up a wooden palisade so that the defenders could not see what they were doing on the other side. If the diggers had to start in a place where the defenders could observe them, they needed a strong shed to protect them. The shed was sometimes nicknamed a "tortoise" or a "sow."

An attacking army drafted industrial miners to dig their siege tunnels. Since stone was tunneled from deep underground, even from under the city of Paris, miners knew how to dig any length of tunnel required, through any materials. Beginning in a safe place, they dug underground and moved in a carefully planned direction toward the walls. Sometimes, two tunnels were dug as parallel galleries. As the miners tunneled, they shored up the walls of the mine with strong timbers. Mining was an operation that required a large number of laborers, which made it difficult to carry out deep in hostile territory.

When a tunnel successfully reached a point under the defensive wall, the miners nearly always started a fire. The intense heat caused the ground to expand, which cracked the walls and collapsed the tunnel. Added to the wood carried into the tunnel, oil and fat made the fire burn hotter; one mine fire, in the siege of Rochester, used 40 pigs as sources of fat. The wood props securing the tunnels also burned, allowing the tunnels to collapse faster.

Once **gunpowder** was in use, it was even easier to produce a hot blast. It was harder to get away safely, since the combustion happened so quickly and the blast collapsed the tunnel. The best way was to approach the wall with snake-like curves and then use the curved passages to set a long fuse, out of sight and reach of the blast. As the fire crept along the fuse, the miners could escape out the end of the tunnel. Since gunpowder came into use at the end of the Middle Ages, it did not become a major force in siege mining until the Renaissance period.

Most walls collapsed when the ground supporting them caved in. There were few ways to build walls that were not vulnerable to sapping. One way was to reinforce the walls with stone columns laid like pegs through holes in the building stones. Places with ruined Roman or Greek columns could use them this way, but most places did not have ruined columns. The fortress design could also use very deep digging to place a moat or a wall in vulnerable places.

Defenders tried to detect tunnel digging when they could not see it. A bowl of water, set over an area being mined, quivered with the vibrations of the tools. If they could tell where the miners were approaching the wall, the defenders could dig down to meet and surprise them with combat. They could sink a hole nearby and try to set the attacking tunnel on fire, or they could flood it if they had a moat or river inside the walls. The attackers tried to make their tunneling less predictable by making decoy tunnels or by making the tunnels take unexpected paths. Tunnels could branch out, or they could zigzag or curve.

Ballistic Machines

Machines that threw projectiles were known by many names in their time, although today we refer to them all as catapults. There are a few simple forces that can provide ballistic power without explosives or motors. Levers and gravity can be harnessed to provide flinging power. The power of both tension and torsion derive from a material being bent so that it will spring or unwind back to its original state.

Tension engines worked by bending wood; it would spring back to shape when the tension was released, thus flinging a projectile with the force of its movement. Crossbows and longbows work on this principle, and some larger forms of crossbows could act as siege weapons, throwing larger projectiles. These great crossbows were built on a frame and used a windlass at the back of the frame to wind the bolt on its string far back. When the windlass was released, the wooden bow's tension thrust its heavy bolt forward with speed and great force. But wood's ability to bend and snap back is limited by its tendency to crack. Wooden bows could not throw anything larger than a bolt and could not take aim at walls, but only at people.

Torsion is the force exerted by a rope that has been twisted tightly and tries to untwist. It is the principle of a child's toy boat or airplane that uses a rubber band wound up tight to drive paddles or propellers as it unwinds. Torsion had been used to drive throwing machines since ancient times. The Romans had a throwing machine called an "onager," a wild donkey. It used a very thick band of rope, highly resistant to being twisted, as the torsion spring. When a lever was inserted into the torsion spring and cranked back so that the rope was forced to twist, on release it sprang into the air. The lever had a sling on the end with a heavy stone. As it sprang into the air, it struck a bar that stopped its movement, and the stone flew out of the sling. The onager's simple torsion spring provided great velocity and force.

Medieval uses of the torsion spring are not as clear. There is evidence that torsion machines of this kind were known in the time of Charlemagne. Artists' illustrations show a machine similar to the Roman onager, but instead of a sling at the end of the lever, there is a spoon-shaped cup for the rock to be placed in. It was probably called a mangonel. Turkish medieval sources picture a device similar to the Roman one, called a *manjaniq,* used by **Muslim** armies.

In the 14th century, there were large crossbows that did not use bent wood, but rather had two separate arms with torsion springs. Different types were known variously as ballistae and espringals (and in other languages, *springarda* or *springolf*). They were more often used by a fortress's defenders, since they shot bolts at individuals, rather than rocks at walls. The espringal was built into a wooden frame, mounted on a tower. On each side, the frame had a torsion spring made of very thick horsehair rope that was resistant to twisting. Levers inserted into each spring were pulled back by ropes attached to the firing mechanism. The espringal's firing system was like a crossbow, with a long groove for a bolt. The operator cranked the bolt back, pulling on the levers and the torsion springs. Released, the torsion springs untwisted and the levers shot the bolt forward, through the groove and out toward the target. The bolts were long and heavy. They could be expected to pierce wooden shields, steel armor, and sometimes more than one body.

The third type of throwing machine used levers and gravity. Since ancient times, people had known that if a lever is put over a fulcrum, like a seesaw, and the lengths are not equal, it takes a much heavier weight on the short end to balance a lighter weight on the long end. If the short end is suddenly weighted, the long end will fly into the air very fast. Unlike tension and torsion, which depend on the strength of bent wood or twisted rope, lever-based machines can throw very heavy objects with relative ease. As long as the lever's arm and the stand with the fulcrum hinge are strong enough, there is no load limit.

The perrier used only the lever to fling large stones. The perrier depended on a sudden downward pull by men or horses. Its frame lifted the lever's short arm above the men's heads, with a rope dangling down, and the long end rested on the ground with a sling. They could load a heavy rock into the sling. When the payload was in place, men with ropes pulled the short end down, as hard as they could, and the long arm with its rope swung upward suddenly, flinging the projectile into the air. In order to achieve significant force, the pull had to be both sudden and hard. Many ropes attached to a bar allowed many men or horses to pull. Sudden pull could be achieved by having the throwing arm restrained by a latch as the men began pulling, so the latch could suddenly be released. The perrier may have been in use by the 11th century.

The trebuchet used a lever with a very heavy counterweight on its short end. The long arm, with a sling on the end, was winched to the ground, forcing the boxy counterweight to lift into the air. Men loaded a large stone into the sling as the long end was held down firmly. When the long arm was released, the counterweight fell to the ground, suddenly lifting the long throwing arm and releasing its sling-propelled payload into the air. Because the machine's power depended on gravity to pull the counterweight down, not on men or horses to tug it hard, the trebuchet was the strongest of the throwing machines.

Trebuchets could be built larger and stronger to throw ever-larger payloads. Instead of a windlass, the winching could be accomplished by one or two wheels, the way the tallest cranes raised loads. Several men stood inside the wheel and walked on its steps, using their weight and a pulley system to magnify the force. The counterweight, perhaps by now a large wooden bucket filled with many large stones, slowly lifted into the air. The throwing

A wall painting shows an elegant view of a castle siege using a trebuchet. Just as the defenders are out of proportion to the size of the castle, the trebuchet shown is far too delicate to handle the real work of a catapult. The artist has captured the basic essence of a trebuchet, though: a weight (shown as a square against the dark diapering design of the wall) will suddenly drop, and this momentum will fling the other arm into the air. The stone, shown cradled in a basket, will gain extra force from the additional swing of its rope. A succession of stones might succeed in damaging the wall sufficiently to pull it down. (The British Library/ StockphotoPro)

arm was lashed down, the men got out of the wheels, and the counter-weight could be released.

Rocks are the best-known catapult payload, and they were the most commonly used. A machine could deliver a series of rocks to the same spot on a wall if the rocks were the same weight and the machine had not been moved. This pounded the wall over and over, increasingly weakening it. Iron shot was even better than stone shot, but it was more expensive.

As a siege went on, trebuchets were loaded with new payloads that were intended to frighten or harm the people inside. The trebuchet was now aimed to fling over the wall, not at it. Most often, armies threw dead animals or even dead human body parts. Severed heads were a common payload. Corpses spread disease, a deadlier attack than any rock. An assault with corpses was also a psychological terror weapon, especially if the heads or other body parts belonged to the targets. Trebuchets could also fling manure.

A shrapnel effect came from "beehives"—clay pots packed with rocks. They burst open on contact, and the rocks flew into the town to smash windows and injure people. Armies also threw incendiary mixes, such as hot tar and quicklime. Incendiary mixes were often called *naphtha;* there are a few existing recipes. Quicklime was the key ingredient, because water causes combustion on contact. Other ingredients were flammable substances: pine pitch, tar, oil, animal fat, and dung.

Greek fire was the most famous incendiary compound of the time. The name "Greek fire" caught on because it was invented in Constantinople, after they had lost territory to the invading Muslims. Byzantine soldiers used catapults to fling pots of Greek fire at besieging Muslim armies. It caught fire on contact, and even water did not put it out. They could pump it at attacking ships and burn up whole fleets; in this way, they saved Constantinople in the seventh century when other cities were conquered by the invading Arabs. The secret composition of Greek fire was carefully guarded for a long time, but eventually first Muslims and then Christian Europeans learned how to make it. It became a component of trebuchet attacks during sieges. However, there is no surviving account of what was in Greek fire. Many scholars speculate that it must have contained quicklime or saltpeter, and others believe it had to use petroleum as a main ingredient. The use of petroleum in some form seems very likely, since Greek fire was described as a liquid that burned even on top of water.

After the introduction of gunpowder, cannons became the main siege-breaking weapon. The largest cannons, called bombards, required large trains of horses and oxen to move their parts and heaps of stone shot. They had to be moved off their wagons with large cranes, and they were fired either from heavy wooden frames or from trenches dug into the ground. The idea was not to fire the stones or iron balls into the fortress, but to fire them straight at the defensive walls. A bombard that was placed lower to the ground could aim right at the ground level. It was most effective when it was close to the wall, its operators defended with wooden walls.

See also: Armor, Castles, Gunpowder, Weapons.

Further Reading

Bennett, Matthew. *Fighting Techniques of the Medieval World: Equipment, Combat Skills, and Tactics.* New York: Thomas Dunne Books, 2005.

Carey, Brian Todd. *Warfare in the Medieval World.* Barnesly, UK: Sword and Pen, 2006.

Donnelly, Mark P., and Daniel Diehl. *Siege: Castles at War.* Dallas: Taylor Publishing, 1998

Keen, Maurice. *Medieval Warfare: A History.* Oxford: Oxford University Press, 1999.

Nossov, Konstantin. *Ancient and Medieval Siege Weapons.* Guilford, CT: Lyons Press, 2005.

Partington, J.R. *A History of Greek Fire and Gunpowder.* Baltimore: Johns Hopkins University Press, 1999.

Payne-Gallwey, Ralph. *The Book of the Crossbow: With an Additional Section on Catapults and Other Siege Engines.* Mineola, NY: Dover Publications, 2009.

Rihll, Tracey. *The Catapult: A History.* Yardley, PA: Westholme Publishing, 2010.

Wiggins, Kenneth. *Siege Mines and Underground Warfare.* Princes Risborough, UK: Shire Publications, 2003.

Silk. *See* Cloth

Silver. *See* Gold and Silver

Slaves. *See* Servants and Slaves

Spices and Sugar

Medieval cooks considered anything used for flavor to be a spice. Their spices included the ones we are familiar with: cinnamon, nutmeg, ginger, cloves, and pepper. They also included what we call herbs: thyme, sage, mint, and parsley. But medieval spices included a range of ingredients that we would not think of, such as dates, figs, almonds, and even grape juice. Sugar was a spice. Anything that could change the flavor of a meat dish was a spice, and medieval cooks used all these ingredients in all dishes on the table.

The use of spices was often a matter of conspicuous display of wealth. Imported spices were in the top rank, because they were the most expensive. Imported sugar may have been the most expensive of all. Saffron, a spice native to Europe, was also extremely expensive, so it too was favored by cooks for the aristocracy. Herbs native to Europe were considerably down the scale of fashion and did not figure much in the most luxurious recipes. Cooks knew that their diners wanted expense and display.

The spices imported from the Far East were pepper, cloves, nutmeg, mace, cinnamon, cardamom, and ginger. These had been imported since Roman times, shipped to Middle Eastern ports and then into the Mediterranean Sea, but the supply dwindled to an expensive trickle during the years of barbarian invasions. After **Muslim** Arabs conquered most of the Mediterranean, shipping and travel became more dangerous, and spices were scarcer and more expensive. Only the richest could afford the few spices that still entered Europe. But in 1099, the First **Crusade** set up a kingdom in Palestine and its surrounding fortress cities, such as Antioch. For the next 200 years, knights, **masons,** merchants, and other workers flowed back and forth to support this kingdom. Trade in spices soared. Venice, Genoa, and other maritime cities obtained exclusive trade contracts for certain routes and places, while those places became wealthy by charging fees. Alexandria, Egypt, was one of the main hubs of the spice trade.

The most popular imported spice of the Middle Ages was pepper, and Europe was never entirely without pepper even during the years of most privation. Pepper's use was restricted to the aristocracy, though. It took a greater supply and a lowered price for pepper and other spices to become part of commoners' lives. When the spice trade was reestablished following the Crusades, spices became more common and were available to some well-to-do merchants and craftsmen. In the later Middle Ages, after 1350, as pepper became more available to the common man, it lost fashion among the rich. Fewer recipes used pepper. By the close of the Middle Ages, pepper was viewed as the spice of the poor.

Medieval recipes were generously spiced. Sauces for meat included not only salt and pepper, but also ginger, cinnamon, cloves, mace, cardamom, and saffron, and often all at once. The wealthy, whose households kept **records** still in existence today, purchased spices in staggering quantities. Their cooks used upward of a pound of assorted spices a day to make their stockpots of stews and sauces for the castle's household. While some meat and fish were eaten fresh, much of it had been salted, and this saltiness was probably the driving force behind recipes that chopped meat fine, mixed it with other ingredients, and drowned its taste in spices. Fresh meat, too, such as venison or pork, was stewed or dipped into sauces seasoned with cinnamon and ginger.

Many history books say spices were used to cover the taste of spoiled meat or fish, but this does not hold up in a closer examination. Medieval cooks and diners were aware that eating spoiled meat made people sick, although their ideas of the mechanisms of food spoiling seem quaint and were too heavily focused on the smells and bad air. Spices were probably used as preservatives, and spoiled meat could be a problem, but merchants

A 15th-century painter imagined the pepper harvest in the exotic, distant, unknown East Indies. To the right, natives were hard at work picking pepper corns from bushes. To the left, a merchant offered the results to a European king. Trade in pepper and other Indian spices drove Europeans to explore the oceans, each trying to find a way to corner this lucrative market. (Bibliotheque Nationale, Paris/The Bridgeman Art Library)

who sold spoiled meat were subject to harsh punishment, such as time in the public stocks.

A wide variety of herbs and spices were native to Europe. Some were very common and were used only by the poor, who might gather them or buy them for pennies at the market. Mustard grew wild all over Europe; the yellow condiment we call mustard today began as a medieval sauce made from vinegar, honey, and mustard seed. Sage, basil, fennel, mint, parsley, rosemary, cumin, coriander, and thyme grew wild in various regions. Crab apples, too, were gathered for their sour flavor. Garlic, chives, and onions were the most common seasoning for the poor.

Saffron is made from the dust on the stamens of crocus flowers. These flowers, imported from Persia, were grown all over Europe, but it took hundreds of crocus stamens to make any amount of saffron. The sheer time and work required to make an ounce of saffron made it one of the most expensive spices, and therefore it was much valued for its bright color and distinctive taste. Other flowers had scents valued as flavoring in confections: roses, violets, and the flowers of the elderberry bush and hawthorn trees.

Spices also formed the basis of many **medicines.** Physicians believed that the four humors of the body—hot, cold, wet, and dry—must be kept in balance. They believed that disease was an imbalance of these humors and that fever was the body's attempt to rebalance a system that had dropped toward being too cold and wet. The remedy was to ingest or apply something that was hot and dry. Spices like cinnamon and pepper were considered the hottest, driest substances, so they formed the basis of many medicines and poultices. Ginger was hot and wet, a rare combination, and a much-valued medicine for some diseases. Spices had the additional value of being expensive, so only the rich could have such medicine.

Sugar entered medieval Europe as an expensive import from the Middle East, although sugar cane had originally come from the Far East. Around the year 1000, the Arab empire set up a sugar refinery on the island of Crete, which they called Qandi, meaning "crystallized sugar." The English word *candy* clearly comes from this Arabic word.

Crusaders withdrawing from Palestine in 1291 established a kingdom in Cyprus and grew sugar there. The republic of Venice shipped sugar from Cyprus to the rest of Europe; so did Genoa and the Hanseatic League. As the distance from sugar producers grew, the price went up, because each port it passed through imposed a toll or tax. The price of a loaf of sugar in France or England was as much as its weight in **silver.**

The most common "candy" was candied whole spice, whether ginger, nutmeg, or even pine nuts. Nougat, a confection of sugar and nuts, was invented during the Middle Ages, probably in Spanish-Arab Andalusia. The Arabs also invented caramel, *kurat al milh,* meaning "ball of sweet salt." Caramel was sometimes used to remove unwanted hair, the way we now use wax. Ordinary medieval Europeans never saw or imagined these sweets; their availability to the public would only come with the New World trade in the next era.

Very few sweet desserts were part of the medieval European table. Almost all the cookies, cakes, and pies that we consider part of traditional European cuisine were developed later. However, toward the end of the Middle Ages, some cooks developed gingerbread. The earliest gingerbread was millet gruel boiled with honey, with spices added. Poured into a mold, it cooled and solidified, then was baked. The first true gingerbread came from Reims in the 1420s, when a bakery invented a spice bread made from rye flour, dark buckwheat honey, and spices. Sometimes this bread was cut into cubes and dipped into the spicy meat sauces at dinner.

See also: Food, Gardens, Medicine.

Further Reading

Adamson, Melitta Weiss. *Food in Medieval Times.* Westport, CT: Greenwood Press, 2004.

Freedman, Paul. *Food: The History of Taste.* Berkeley: University of California Press, 2007.

Freedman, Paul. *Out of the East: Spices and the Medieval Imagination.* New Haven, CT: Yale University Press, 2009.

Tannahill, Reay. *Food in History.* New York: Three Rivers Press, 1988.

Turner, Jack. Spices: *The History of a Temptation.* New York: Knopf, 2004.

Stained Glass. *See Glass*

Stone and Masons

Stone was the high-tech building material of the Middle Ages. Wooden buildings predominated in the early centuries because stone was so expensive. Only palaces and churches were stone, at first. By the 12th century, **castles** had to be stone, as did **city** walls. By the end of the Middle Ages, many **bridges,** some **roads,** and many **houses** were stone. Estimates suggest that more stone was quarried in medieval France than in ancient Egypt to build the pyramids.

Stone was used for other purposes than just building blocks. Italian marble was carved into monuments; marblers were very specialized stonecutters. Slate broke into flat slabs to make roof tiles. Limestone and chalk were burned to produce quicklime, an element of mortar. Large limestone kilns used acres of **forest** as fuel; they were among the first to convert to **coal** when it was discovered in the 13th century.

Stone building was planned and overseen by master masons, the architects of the Middle Ages. They signed a contract with the owner and acted as general contractor to hire other skilled workers to carry it out, under the stipulated budget. They drafted the plans and drawings, inspected buildings, and supervised stonecutting and actual building. Other masons were rough masons who hacked out rough shapes at the quarry, stonecutters who made precision blocks, and freemasons who could carve anything in stone, including window tracery and other sculpture.

Some stone quarries were owned by the king or by **monasteries,** others by private owners. France was the region most heavily quarried for building stone; much of it came from Caen, in Normandy. It was fantastically expensive to have stone moved far, so builders usually searched for places to quarry it locally. When only Caen limestone would do, the stone had to be moved by **boat.** In a few cases, it was best to dig a canal just to transport the stone to the building site.

Medieval quarries tunneled into the hillside, creating long galleries that ran parallel to each other or branched off in mazes. The tunnels were propped up with rock pillars, or the stonecutters left natural pillars. Paris has tunnels where the stone quarries dug down under the city. There are more kilometers of medieval quarry tunneling than of the modern Paris subway.

A 15th-century artist represented the importance of stone by showing masons towering over their building project. Each is working with typical masons' tools on a different phase of cutting, shaping, and placing blocks. In the far upper left corner, there is a windmill against the horizon. (The British Library/ StockphotoPro)

Rough masons used stonecutting **tools** in the quarry, such as picks, mallets, and chisels. These had to be sharpened frequently. When possible, stones were cut to order at the quarry. Master masons sent written orders with sticks marked to the size of the stones to be cut or canvas cut into patterns. In the quarry or in their lodge workshops, the rough masons cut the stones of a building to precise patterns. Sometimes stone pieces interlocked to form a weight-bearing pillar. Many stones had carved patterns; dressed stone like this was called ashlar. The stones were marked to show where they fit into the finished wall.

After 1300, architectural drawings were more common, and many have survived into the present. The earliest are on **parchment,** later ones on **paper.** Some were very large, drawn on several parchments stitched together. Some show several elevations superimposed on each other, in two dimensions. A tower that grew narrower at the top could be drawn as if it were a series of walls inside each other, showing their relative size and shape. Much of the mason's art and training was in understanding these drawing conventions and knowing how to interpret them. By the master mason's directions, the patterns were drawn full-size on a tracing floor that had a fine plaster coating that was easy to mark. Carpenters used the shapes on the drawing floor to make wooden forms that the stonecutters used to shape the stone pieces into replicas of the shapes laid out by the master mason. Accurate replicas were especially important in assembling Gothic arches and tracery.

Foundations were laid out with pegs and strings, and until the 11th century, walls were not always perfectly straight or perpendicular, but from the 12th century on, they were very geometrical. Master masons were very aware of the importance of good foundations and shored up soft ground with driven piles.

To build a wall, masons used only the classic trowel, identical to those used by bricklayers today, and a simple level. The level consisted of a flat piece of wood with a triangle built onto its surface; from the apex of the triangle hung a short line with a weight. When the base was on a perfectly level surface, the weight hung down to point at a mark directly under it. Any deviation from this level caused the weight to hang to the right or left of this central mark.

Builders used scaffolding similar to the modern kind, consisting of strong but temporary poles and shelving. The shelves in a medieval scaffold were made of wattle (woven branches) rather than solid boards, and the frame was tied together with rope. Builders often built round towers by inserting poles into holes built into the wall as they went and raising a spiraling walkway as they built. Ladders often connected levels, but they also made walkways by weaving flexible splints into the ladders' spaces.

See also: Cathedrals, Tools.

Further Reading

Coldstream, Nicola. *Masons and Sculptors.* Toronto: University of Toronto Press, 1991.

Gimpel, Jean. *The Medieval Machine: The Industrial Revolution of the Middle Ages.* New York: Penguin, 1976.

Harvey, John. *Mediaeval Craftsmen.* New York: Drake Publishers, 1975.

Hislop, Malcolm. *Medieval Masons.* Botley, UK: Shire Archaeology, 2009.

Sugar. *See* Spices and Sugar

T

Tapestry

Tapestries are among the first things people think of when they picture Europe in the Middle Ages. However, they were really an art form of the later Middle Ages and were only found in churches and **castles.** The most famous tapestry, the Bayeux Tapestry, is not even a tapestry. It is an **embroidered** linen wall hanging. True tapestries were decorative cloth wall hangings; the picture was woven into the fabric, not stitched onto it. They were made on very large looms, with painstaking care, by trained professionals.

Tapestries before 1300 are scarce and primitive, perhaps produced in home workshops or convents. Tapestry became a guild craft during the 12th century, and the 15th and 16th centuries were the peak of the tapestry industry's art. The workshops clustered in the **cloth**-producing regions of Flanders and northern France. Paris and Arras led tapestry weaving in France, and in Flanders, the most famous tapestry cities were Bruges, Ghent, Lille, and Tournai. The trade spread into places like Italy only by the emigration of Flanders-trained weavers.

Only the wealthiest patrons could afford tapestries. The price of a tapestry varied with the materials used (wool was the least expensive) and the level of detail desired. When finer threads were denser, more detail was possible, but the weaving slowed, and the tapestry's cost soared. On average, a tapestry weaver did very well to produce 10 feet per year. The price of a very large tapestry was astronomical. Less wealthy patrons had small tapestries or mere imitations—fabric with painted pictures.

The **church** may have been the greatest customer for tapestries. A long tradition going back into the early church of Roman times specified that on special **feast** days, churches had to hang decorative fabrics. Popes gave silk and **gold** hangings to churches, and local donors gave money to be used for hangings in their memory. Many of these altar cloths and banners were embroidered, but as tapestry craftsmanship spread, large churches collected woven hangings. Church officials such as wealthy canons, or royalty on the church's behalf, commissioned large tapestries to hang in the choir stalls, completely covering the space. Some of these tapestries were very long, close to 100 feet. They were usually about 6 feet tall, so they formed very long strips of pictures.

Liturgical tapestries usually illustrated the lives of a church's patron **saints,** and they usually included text that explained the action. The scenes of action were divided by decorative pillars or walls. As in other medieval art, the costumes and buildings depicted in the saint's story were contemporary; Roman guards wore 15th-century hats and doublets, and every town had a crenellated wall around it. The medieval love of the exotic brought unicorns, lions, and monkeys to the death of Saint Stephen or a newly invented late medieval **clock** tower into the buildings of Rome.

Tapestry designs were busy. A picture for a tapestry had many human figures, many animals, and wildflowers scattered across the grass. Not all designs were liturgical, of course. Secular tapestries showed **hunting** scenes and **gardens;** men blew horns and tended dogs, while groups of ladies walked, read, and sang in gardens. Some tapestries had **ships,** heraldic animals, kings, or castles. Unicorns were always popular.

The millefleurs style was characteristic of 15th-century tapestries. They displayed many small flowers scattered on a solid background. The flowers are always shown as whole flowering plants, with as much variety as possible. In the famous Unicorn Tapestry at the Cloisters of New York's Metropolitan Museum of Art, the white unicorn sits in a small enclosure, surrounded by more than 80 different types of flowers, most of which can be identified by naturalists: orchid, Chinese lantern, carnation, Madonna lily, thistle, columbine, pansy, marigold, and many more. A millefleurs tapestry typically had a central design—often an enclosure with an animal, but sometimes a group of other figures. The background color was most often green, to represent grass and make the tapestry appear to be a natural garden, but some tapestries used other colors to good effect.

Making a Tapestry

The making of a tapestry began with sketches and proceeded to a full-size cartoon. Sometimes the tapestry was first painted onto a large piece of cloth to see the full effect. Professional artists, not weavers, made these drawings and cartoons. When the patron had approved the design, the cartoons went to the weaving shop, where they became the shop's property. Unless the patron bought the cartoon or painted fabric test piece, the weaving shop was free to make a copy and sell it. Sometimes the patron used the painted fabric as a wall hanging while the tapestry was in production; the less wealthy used nothing but painted fabric hangings.

The warp was a strong wool thread in a plain color. Weft threads were usually fine wool and sometimes silk. Silk had a sheen that could be used for a lightening effect. Gold and **silver** threads also were used for effect. Wool dyes were simple, compared to artist's painting tints. Using madder or brazilwood for red, weld for yellow, and woad or a type of indigo for blue, dyers created the secondary and tertiary colors and many shades. Dyers added a mordant, a chemical that fixes the dye to the yarn; it was often a metal such as aluminum or zinc. Even the most colorful medieval tapestries appear to have no other substances but these few dyes and mordants.

Tapestry weavers worked on both upright and horizontal looms. The vertical loom is called high warp, and the horizontal loom is low warp, but the tapestries they produced were identical. The high warp technique came first. The weavers stood in front of a beam that wound up the finished fabric as they worked. The warp was stretched tightly to an overhead beam that unrolled the length of warp as the weavers moved upward. A simple draw-string system, connected to a bar, lifted alternate threads to create a shed, a space where the bobbin could be passed. On the low warp loom, the arrangement was similar; a beam at the front rolled up the fabric as it was produced, and the warp was stretched and rolled around a back beam. With a low warp loom, the drawstrings that raised or lowered alternate threads were connected to overhead pulleys and foot pedals, leaving both hands free to weave.

Up to six weavers, but on average three, worked side by side at these large looms. On a low warp loom, each controlled a section of warp with a set of foot pedals. The width of the tapestry was the desired height as it hung in the room, and if a tapestry was not designed to be square, it was designed to be longer against the wall than it was high. For this reason, the weavers worked on the pattern sideways; the warp threads that stretched in front of them would run horizontally when the finished tapestry was mounted on a wall.

They worked with their fingers, pushing a bobbin of colored thread up and down through the warp threads. Small details would use the width of only a few warp threads, while large colored areas, such as blue sky, would carry the bobbin across many warp threads before it came to another color zone. Bobbins not in use hung or laid at rest on the finished fabric. At any given stretch across the piece, anywhere from a few to a hundred different bobbins could be in use. As they wove, the weavers used combs to pack the weft to a tight, even density.

Sometimes, the artist's cartoon was stretched under a horizontal loom so the weavers could look down and see it. If they were working on a vertical frame, the cartoon hung on a wall, but not immediately behind the vertical loom. Weavers had to turn and look at the cartoon, then turn back to the warp. They used charcoal or chalk to sketch the design onto their warp threads. The design was worked facing away from the weavers, who saw only the back of the tapestry picture. This way, they could secure threads in ways that could not be seen from the front. On a high warp loom, the weavers could walk to the back to see the front. On a low warp loom, they needed a mirror on the floor to see the front as it developed. Weavers never saw the whole picture until it was cut from the loom.

At points where colors joined, the weaver could wrap both colors around a warp thread that formed the boundary, a technique called dovetailing. Since two colors shared that thread, one to the left and one to the right, the boundary was slightly blurred. Weavers could also interlock the colored weft threads around each other as each color turned back; the join was invisible at the front. At points where the design required a crisp line between colors, the weaver would leave a slit between them; one color turned back the way it came, not touching the other, which also turned back. Slits had to be small because they weakened the fabric's strength. The weaver then stitched the slits closed on the back of the tapestry. The last step in finishing the tapestry was to stitch on a protective linen backing.

Tapestry weaving was very dense; the weft threads were packed hard against each other. Especially in late medieval tapestry technique, the patterns were extremely detailed and used many shades of color. A man's **hair** was not a single brown; it was a fine pattern of dark and light browns that created an illusion of hair strands with sun shining on them. Robes required many colors to form the shadows and folds of cloth. Skies were not purely blue but had shades of blue and white cloud. At the horizon, tiny **houses** and castles were worked against the sky.

See also: Cloth, Embroidery, Painting.

Further Reading

Broudy, Eric. *The Book of Looms*. Lebanon, NH: University Press of New England, 1979.
Freeman, Margaret B. *The Unicorn Tapestries*. New York: Metropolitan Museum of Art, 1983.
Quye, Anita, Kathryn Hallett, and Concha Herrero Carretero. *"Wroughte in Gold and Silk": Preserving the Art of Historic Tapestries*. Edinburgh: National Museums Scotland, 2009.
Weigert, Laura. *Weaving Sacred Stories: French Choir Tapestries and the Performance of Clerical Identity*. Ithaca, NY: Cornell University Press, 2004.
Woolley, Linda. *Medieval Life and Leisure in the Devonshire Hunting Tapestries*. London: Victoria and Albert Museum, 2002.

Taverns and Inns

Taverns were a natural outgrowth of the ale home-brewing industry. Many women in the town and the country brewed ale in quantities greater than their families could drink before it spoiled. The simplest kind of tavern was a private house that permitted customers to sit at a table in the front room and drink the ale they had purchased. The traditional English symbol for a public house was a pole, broom, or branch posted above the door.

As **cities** grew, some taverns became businesses separate from home brewing. They named themselves "The Cock" or "The Vine" and had colorful pictorial signs. Taverns that did not brew their own ale or beer became tied to certain brewers with whom they kept purchasing accounts, especially in Germany and the Netherlands. Taverns in wine-growing regions sold only wine, but since wine was widely imported, London customers at large taverns could buy sweet Greek malmsey or any of 50 French or Italian wines.

Some taverns sold **food,** although many did not. When a tavern did sell food, the fare was likely to be simple and not likely to spoil, such as salted **fish.** Tavern keepers could also buy bread from a nearby bakery. Many taverns were prevented from cooking on the premises, since **guild** regulations did not include cooking. They could buy salted beef, bacon, pies, or other food from cookshops; customers could also buy from cookshops or street vendors and carry the snacks in. Cookshops sold small meat pies, often in trays carried by street criers. They also offered pieces of roast meat (hot off the spit or griddle) and hard-boiled eggs. Street vendors made some things right on the street, over a small charcoal fire. One such treat was the wafer, something like waffles, pizelles, and the funnel cakes of modern carnivals. Some vendor foods were not cooked, such as cheese and apples or pears sold from trays.

Taverns flourished because they filled a community need. Because housing was so cramped, it was almost impossible for many medieval men or women to invite friends to their **houses.** Wealthier people had larger homes, so taverns belonged to the poorer classes. Neighbors and students gathered in taverns regularly to meet each other. Many business transactions among the middle and lower classes were settled at taverns. In some places, taverns

By the close of the Middle Ages, travel was fairly common, and inns had become important hubs. In this Italian inn, the travelers appear to be storing their weapons on wall and rafter hooks. A long table at an inn offered many places for strangers to meet and mix, but at the same time, it mimicked feast tables where sitting in a certain place indicated a man's social importance. Some inns ordered round tables to keep guests from arguing. (Castello di Issogne, Val d'Aosta, Italy/Giraudon/The Bridgeman Art Library)

were also tax-collecting stations; in Poland, some taverns were managed by law courts.

Because taverns were transient meeting places, they were frequented by troublemakers. Fights broke out in taverns, sometimes spilling into the streets and turning into riots. Students in **university** districts were infamous for tavern fights and riots. Playing **games,** with or without gambling, was very common at tavern meetings; medieval people played dice, and cards came into use by the 15th century. Public houses were good places to meet and re- main anonymous, so prostitution was always close by a tavern, if not oper- ating out of the tavern itself. Some tavern keepers were accused of hiring out their servant girls as prostitutes.

Cities took an interest in regulating the tavern business. Paris imposed a curfew on taverns to keep fighting and prostitution in check. London regu- lations declared that tavern keepers had to permit customers to inspect their **barrels.** Wine and ale sometimes soured or were served in dirty containers. Even home-business taverns were inspected for fair prices. There were reg- ulation quarts and gallons, and every alewife, even in small towns, had to bring her containers in for inspection periodically. Even so, taverns remained crowded, dirty places of very dubious reputation.

Taverns did not offer lodging. In the early Middle Ages, few people trav- eled. Aristocrats stayed at friends' castles and manors, and lodging for poor people was very limited. In some places, private houses offered lodging for a fee but either did not mark their buildings as inns or used a simple signal like the branch that indicated a tavern. The lodgings in these early inns varied greatly, but most travelers could expect nothing better than a cot or a shared space in bed with other travelers or family members. Some monasteries of- fered guest lodgings, especially for pilgrims.

The 12th century saw an increase in **pilgrim** traffic, after the **Crusades** established hostels to protect pilgrims. **Roads** improved during the 12th and 13th centuries. The first real inns were along international pilgrim routes, but as more regional and local shrines developed, more inns devel- oped. The medieval term for a place of lodging was more often a hostel or hostelry. Some hostels rented **horses,** and others just provided a stable for a traveler's horse. A full-service, large hostelry on a pilgrim route required a large house with a hall for communal dining, chambers and beds, a courtyard with **latrines,** and a stable.

An innkeeper lived in the same house and literally shared his rooms, beds, and supper with travelers. Most inns were run by a married couple with a small staff of servants. Supper was a communal affair, as depicted in the *Can- terbury Tales.* The host ate with the clients; he had a legal interest in remain- ing with them as much as possible. An English law of 1285 made the hosts of taverns and inns responsible for what their clients did. It was in the inn's interest to keep everyone calm and friendly, to see that everyone was in bed at a good hour, and to watch for suspicious behavior. Robbery, especially of horses, was common at inns.

When the guests went to bed, they were still in communal quarters. While some inns had private rooms, many medieval inns expected guests to share beds. A traveler could expect to sleep with at least one other person, and some inns prided themselves on very large beds that could be packed with whole groups. Some guests could even sleep crosswise along the feet. Since discrimination on the basis of wealth and social standing was normal in the Middle Ages, a higher-status traveler could expect the only private room, while a poor man was lucky to have space at the foot of a crowded bed.

The character of the host made the inn's reputation. The Host in the *Canterbury Tales,* Harry Bailly, was a respectable man who knew how to size up the needs and social standing of each guest. He took a leading role in directing conversation and preventing fights. An inn was considered good if it had no more fleas than usual, provided decent food, and still had the same number of horses stabled in the morning. In a bad inn, the food was dirty or spoiled, the beds were obviously dirty, and the innkeeper worked with a theft ring to make the better horses disappear.

See also: Beverages, Cities, Food, Games, Pilgrims.

Further Reading

Hanawalt, Barbara A. *Of Good and Ill Repute: Gender and Social Control in Medieval England.* New York: Oxford University Press, 1998.

Henisch, Bridget. *The Medieval Cook.* Woodbridge, UK: Boydell Press, 2009.

Reeves, Compton. *Pleasures and Pastimes in Medieval England.* New York: Oxford University Press, 1998.

Roux, Simone. *Paris in the Middle Ages.* Philadelphia: University of Pennsylvania Press, 2009.

Thatch. *See Houses*

Tools

Basic hand tools have not changed much since antiquity. A few new tools were invented during the Middle Ages, and all were improved and specialized for various crafts. European workmen liked to tinker with and improve their traditional tools.

The development of tools followed the development of the blacksmith's art. Most farm tools were made of wood during the Carolingian era; only cutting blades were **iron,** because it was still very expensive. Iron-edged tools included spades, axes, scythes, and plowshares. Blacksmiths were generally located on estates, where they made **weapons** and horseshoes for the

knights. Making tools was a sideline. During the 12th century, there was a growing demand for tools as population and **cities** grew. Blacksmiths set up in towns and began focusing on civil uses of iron. In the later Middle Ages, iron became more plentiful, and more common tools, such as rakes, pitchforks, and shovels, could be metal.

Every profession had its specialized tools, and some tools, such as **embroidery** scissors, have left little evidence in the archeological or pictorial record. Scissors were in use, along with other specialized cutting tools like surgeon's instruments. Pictures of shoemakers and goldsmiths show some of the specialized knives, scales, and chisels particular to each profession. The greatest number of pictures through several centuries was devoted to the tools of the building trade. Many Bibles and prayer books chose to illustrate the story of how the Tower of Babel was built, and these pictures always showed lively construction sites filled with contemporary workers. Because of this, we have detailed knowledge of the tools used in construction.

Ditches, foundations, and all kinds of earth barricades and mounds were dug with shovels and spades. This was unskilled labor and could be done by peasants hired as day laborers. They used simple baskets and wheelbarrows to cart away the earth. Wheelbarrows shown in 13th-century pictures are similar to modern ones; they have a platform with a slight basket shape, a single wheel, two handles, and legs to rest the barrow on when stationary. Another carrying device was the pannier, which consisted of two long bars with a sheet of leather fastened between them. Two men carried the pannier heaped with stones or earth. For the heaviest loads, they used **carts** with two or even four wheels.

The signature building material of the Middle Ages was **stone,** although relatively few buildings actually used stone. **Castles** and **cathedrals** aimed at permanency and could afford the expense in materials, workmen, and time. **Masons** were general contractors for working with stone, from architects to rough-hewing in quarries.

Masons in quarries mainly used heavy mallets and hammers with strong chisels. The chisels were tempered by being reheated many times so that they would be stronger than any material they came against, but, even so, they had to be sharpened daily. Hammers could be pointed, a cross between mallet and ax. There were also stone axes, used to smooth rough-cut stone. Mallets and mauls beat against iron chisels and could have beechwood heads. Punches were like smaller chisels with pyramidal ends and were used to cut stone into finer shapes. For finer stone carving, masons used a variety of chisels, punches, and hammers.

Masons used squares and plumb bobs to make sure that lines were straight and edges were truly vertical. The plumb bob was a piece of lead shaped with a point and hung from a string; it always pointed to the earth and created a perfectly vertical line. Masons used compasses to draw true circles on the stone and measuring staffs to get the correct rough sizes. They often sat on three-legged stools, measuring stone and fitting it with their wooden templates to get the right shapes.

Next to stone, **brick** was a favored material for castles, churches, guild-halls, and town buildings. Bricklayers relied even more heavily on the plumb bob to keep their wall straight; they also kept a straightedge and a level. A medieval level was a flat board with a wooden triangle built over it. A plumb bob hung from the apex of the triangle. When it pointed straight down at the mark, the level was sitting perfectly horizontal; if the plumb bob pointed to either side of the mark, the wall was not level. The bricklayers' other tools were for applying mortar between bricks. They had a mortar-mixing bin and a pick for mixing the mortar, a shovel, and a smaller bin for carrying the amount needed to the wall. Bricklayers used a trowel that was identical to modern mortar trowels and a hammer for knocking the bricks into better alignment. For carrying bricks, mortar, or stones, a carpenter's helper used a hod. The hod was a shallow wooden dish with handles; because it was carried on the shoulder, it was often filled while placed on a tall stool so that the carrier could easily stoop under to lift it up.

Although castles and cathedrals were usually built of stone, most **houses** and other buildings in England and France were made of timber. Carpentry was skilled work and was carried out with hand tools similar to those in modern times, before the use of electric tools. One notable omission is the screwdriver; screws were not yet in use.

Carpenters used at least four different axes, beginning with the basic ax for felling trees and a hatchet for smaller cutting. Broad axes were slightly curved and set their blades perpendicular to the handle, like hoes; they were used for shaping trees into square beams. Roofing axes were similar but smaller and were used to cut gutters into roof beams and do other tasks that required gouging out a hollow. The smaller adze resembled these but was used to cut mortices into beams.

Drills were also called augers or bores. They were operated with a long cross bar at the top, so the carpenter could turn the drill bit with two hands. A cranked drill brace was not invented until the 15th century.

Blacksmiths made saws by cutting teeth into a plate of hot metal. There were handsaws, chiefly with thin blades held in tension in a frame, with a torsion rope at the top to keep the blade taut. These came in small or large versions for two men to use. Carpenters often used very long two-man saws with handles on both sides, especially when cutting a log into boards. Sawhorse trestles were part of their usual sawing kit.

Carpenters used a few more miscellaneous tools. Planes smoothed the square beams after they had been rough shaped by broad axes. There were files, made by striking a stick of iron with a sharp hammer to create ridges. Mallets and other hammers could be made of all wood or could have iron heads. They used square iron nails and long iron staples made from thick bent wire.

The boom crane evolved from the simple use of pulleys to raise heavy materials to the level where builders were working. The simplest kind was a pole with an arm bearing two pulleys; a rope went over the pulleys and dropped to the ground. A simple lifting device like this was called a falcon or hawk. The real breakthrough in raising heavy blocks of stone came with a giant treadwheel. This large wooden wheel fit several men inside, and they walked to move the wheel; its power could lift much larger loads. To strengthen the frame, instead of a vertical pole with a horizontal arm, builders leaned a stout log against a shorter pole, forming a triangle on the ground with a tall diagonal arm leaning out. The windlass, or crank, came into use in the 15th century. Used with simple cranes, a windlass could lift heavier loads than a man's arms could pull on their own.

The crane could be used for lifting or pounding. It could be a pile driver that pounded logs into soft ground like nails to create a firmer foundation. In this case, the crane lifted a very heavy block of wood and then let it drop

Basic carpentry tools have not changed much over time. Even in a time of power tools, carpenters still depend on L-squares like the one sitting on the ground. These medieval carpenters are using axes and saws to square off tree trunks as usable lumber. While the building in the illustration is too small to be a real building, house size was limited by the length of local tree trunks. (Paul Lacroix, *Moeurs, Usage et Costumes au Moyen Age et a l'Epoque de la Renaissance*, 1878)

on top of the log. For lifting building materials up to masons, bricklayers, or carpenters, they used a basket or tub with handles, tied to a rope. Stone blocks were lifted with a clamp called a lewis. In some cases, the stone had a set of depressions chiseled into the top so that the tongs of the lewis would fit into them. In other cases, the lewis was shaped like scissor tongs and suspended from a rope. When it was clamped around the stone block, the pull on the rope exerted more pressure on the tongs to remain closed, thus gripping the block securely.

Workmen had to go up and down the unfinished buildings using ladders and scaffolding. The standing platform of scaffolding was usually made of wattle (pliant branches woven together) because it was lighter and cheaper. Scaffolding could be built up from the ground in the form of poles lashed together to support the platforms. Castle building tended to use built-in scaffolding, particularly for round towers. As the tower rose, poles were built into the walls going upward in a spiral. When the tower was complete, the scaffolding was removed, walking backward down and pulling the poles out of the wall. Some towers still have these holes, and some still have pegs or poles that were left in case they were needed later for repair. The least common kind of scaffolding that was necessary in some cases was a hanging wattle platform, suspended from a crane or tower to lower workmen to the building site.

Medieval workmen used only one kind of safety equipment. When they were working at great heights, installing stone blocks for a vaulted ceiling, some tied a rope around their waist and secured it to a column. Not everyone did this, and it was the only safety measure known. Work accidents were as routine as accidents in other areas of life.

See also: Castles, Cathedrals, Forests, Houses, Iron, Stone and Masons.

Further Reading

Binding, Gunther. *Medieval Building Techniques*. Stroud, UK: Tempus Publishing, 2001.

Coldstream, Nicola. *Masons and Sculptors*. Toronto: University of Toronto Press, 1991.

Harvey, John. *The Master Builders: Architecture in the Middle Ages*. New York: McGraw Hill, 1971.

Harvey, John. *Mediaeval Craftsmen*. New York: Drake Publishers, 1975.

Hislop, Malcolm. *Medieval Masons*. Botley, UK: Shire Books, 2009.

Tournaments

The festival war games called tournaments first appear in the written records of Northern Europe around the year 1100. Real wars were at a lull;

the barbarian Vikings and Huns were no longer a problem, and the Hundred Years' War between England and France had not yet begun. The First **Crusade** had been launched in 1095, but many **knights** had returned home, bored. Tournaments provided employment and entertainment for those not on Crusade. The object of a tournament was to capture, not kill, the opposing fighter. Losing knights paid ransoms to winning knights, which made tournament skill a possible source of income.

Since the time of Charlemagne, knights had sometimes staged mock battles for training. When there was no war, young knights had to be toughened up by facing danger and being injured. Tournaments made training into a sport. During the 12th and 13th centuries, the main feature was a large mock battle, the melee. Far more than any other sport, tournaments were violent and caused severe injuries. Knights went into the field as well armored as they were in battle, and although they often used blunt **weapons,** the violence was still savage.

Tournaments, unlike war, had strict rules. There were judges and heralds to register (or disqualify) all invited and uninvited participants. There were fenced zones where injured knights were safe from attack in a melee. These may have been originally called the *lists,* a word that later came to apply to the jousting field itself. It was a foul to aim for the other knight's horse; the result was disqualification. One knight was chosen as a field referee, called the chevalier d'honneur. His lance had a headscarf pinned to it, and he could go to any knight in distress and touch him with it, disallowing any further attacks. A melee could continue only until the president of the tournament, the official in charge, decided to throw down his warder as a signal to the heralds. Then the heralds' trumpeters sounded retreat, and the fighting had to stop.

When a knight unhorsed his opponent, he claimed the loser's **armor** and **horse.** The loser nearly always ransomed them back; if not, the winner could keep or sell the equipment. Ransoms were fixed in advance; the price rose with a knight's rank. In this way, a poor but talented knight could become wealthy by playing the tournament circuit. Knights errant, who came from noble families that had lost their wealth and land, earned a living by jousting. Tournaments were a very expensive game for those who were not as talented; the average knight only entered the lists to the point that he could afford the losses. The biggest loser in a tournament would be a high-ranking nobleman, such as a count or even a king, who was a poor contender and only incurred losses that cost him high ransoms.

Tournaments always offered prizes, paid for by the sponsor or by aristocratic spectators, usually ladies. The most common type of prize was an **animal,** such as a dog, a falcon, a bear, or even a sheep or a large **fish.** Tournament **records** also tell us that some prizes were gilded statues of animals

By the 15th century, tournaments had become more sport than war training. Everything was formalized: the spectators had sheltered seats and included fine ladies, and the joust only took place in a guarded area called the lists. Each contestant and some of the spectators can be identified from his heraldic symbol; the artist did not need to add names. Although the lists were enclosed with a low fence, the area must have been much larger than shown here. In many later tournaments, the jousting knights were separated by a low wall that kept them in lanes. (Royal Armouries/ StockphotoPro)

like deer, falcons, or horses. It is possible that the ladies who sponsored the prizes acted as judges. The tournament always closed with a **feast** at which the winners were honored at the high table.

Knights who made a habit of attending most tournaments in a circuit across France, Flanders, and England traveled many miles with large retinues of **servants** and horses. When a band of knights traveled together, each with his spare horses, pack animals, squire, and other servants, the group was not only large but also rowdy. They were a notorious roadside hazard to other travelers, with whom they were too eager to get into quarrels. At times they robbed less powerful travelers. This tendency of knights to use their power too freely was a primary motivator of the code of chivalry, which insisted that they must never rob, rape, or bully a weaker party.

During the 12th century, the kings of England and France, and some other ruling lords, opposed tournaments as violations of their decrees of peace. Counts and princes who liked the danger and excitement of tournaments continued to sponsor and organize them, often at outlying fields on the border of two realms. The "Young King" Henry, son of Henry II of England and Eleanor of Aquitaine, was a big sponsor and participant in international tournaments. He kept a team of knights as paid staff to fight in melees and paid the ransoms when they lost. Aggressive, free-spending aristocrats of this type made the tournament the first-ranked interest all across Northern Europe. There were cases of bored knights in besieged towns or castles challenging the besieging army to a tournament outside the walls. In most cases, both sides respected the rules, and then went back to their war stations when it was over.

The **church** at first opposed tournaments as festivals of pride and vice and as opportunities to sin by killing, even accidentally. If a man died in a tournament, he was considered a suicide, since he had put himself in harm's way. Some bishops excommunicated tournament participants, but wealthy knights bought their way back into grace by giving alms or donating land to the church. Tournaments were so popular among the nobles of England, France, and Germany that the church's opposition made no difference. People loved tournaments, where courage and skill could be seen close up without the danger and confusion of a real war. By the time minstrels were circulating stories of the Virgin Mary disguising herself as a knight, moral opposition had no effect, and the church stopped opposing tournaments.

Aristocratic **women** came to tournaments as spectators. By the 12th century, their role in public had changed, and the new spirit of courtly love encouraged knights to fight better to impress the women. Ladies chose champions and gave favors and were prominent guests in the viewing stands. Some ladies learned to joust, and by the 14th century, when knights began to come in costumes, some ladies came costumed as men. Their **clothing** fashions were also influenced by **heraldry**; the cotehardie often bore embroidered heraldic arms so that the ladies could attend the games dressed like modern sports fans, in team colors. A few bold ladies grew so infatuated with tournaments that they began traveling from one to the next, instead of attending only those closest to home.

Tournaments filled nearby towns with participants, spectators, merchants, craftsmen, and horse thieves. When a knight could find a **house** to rent, instead of staying in the field in his tent, his squire hung his banner or shield in the window of the rented rooms. Local **castles** and manors permitted friends and other participants to stay, and visiting kings generally stayed at these castles, rather than in tents. In the tournaments where towns served as headquarters for regional teams of knights, halls and kitchens were rented for receptions and feasts. There was usually a trade **fair** associated with a tournament, and merchants and craftsmen for tournament-related business set up booths. Some armor makers became itinerant armor menders, following knights on the circuit. The event was also a big opportunity for local merchants to sell more **food** and other provisions.

The nature of tournaments changed during the five centuries when they were popular. Early tournaments of the 12th century had both single-combat challenges and a mock battle—the melee. In single-combat challenges, un-horsing the opponent meant victory and the right to claim a ransom. In the melee, the knights were assigned to opposing armies, and they charged each other at a given signal. Although the object was to capture opponents, many knights were seriously injured or killed in melees. In early tourna-ments, the mock battle was not formalized or confined to the field at hand. A group of knights could veer off the field and chase into nearby woods or fields. These large mock battles brought out hundreds of knights, and some large 12th-century tournaments claimed to have more than 1,000 participants.

The 13th century may be considered the height of the tournament. Each event, now formalized with traditional rules, lasted about a week. The knights began with some days of practice jousting, and then held for-mal jousting challenges. While the original meaning of a joust was any kind of single combat with any weapons, by the 13th century it meant only the combat when knights rode against each other with lances. Fights could be to the death (or until injury or surrender), or they could be just for points, like a game. If the lances and swords were blunt, they were called "arms of courtesy." After a day of rest and paying ransoms, the knights chose sides for a melee. The mock battle was held in a more restricted area, a field rather than the general countryside as in the previous century. The last day was for feasting, dancing, and **minstrel** performances.

In the late 14th century, tournaments began to have as much pageantry as warfare. In some English tournaments, the knights wore costumes onto the field. They fought as monks or even as cardinals. At the opening day of another tournament, the knights paraded onto the field, each held with a **silver** chain and led by a lady on a horse. In a French tournament of the middle 15th century, the participants dressed as shepherds. There was a trend away from full armor and real weapons; some places ruled that only partial armor could be worn, and even squires could not bring so much as a dagger.

By the 15th century, tournaments had completely changed. There were no dangerous melees, and the single combats were very formal and styl-ized. Battlefield fighting no longer used lances, so training with a lance was only for a tournament. Armor had become very heavy, as it was made entirely from plates of metal. It was less necessary and more ceremonial, often covered with decorative etchings and used mostly in parades. Horses were larger and slower, and saddles were improved to the point that knights could not always be unhorsed. Knights rode against each other with a low wall, called the tilt, between them. Contestants won on style points given by judges.

Tournament Equipment

During the height of the tournament's popularity—the 12th and 13th centuries—chainmail hauberks were the usual armor. There were also tournament-specific fashions. Some knights wore peacock feathers or fluttering ribbons or straps on their armor, and knights at tournaments always wore the most colorful fashions in surcotes. Squires wore lighter armor, such as padded tunics and lighter hauberks called haubergeons. During the 13th century, squires began to dress more like knights, and knights wore ever more elaborate attire.

In the 14th century, the development of plate armor for the battlefield brought it into the tournament. From that time, tournaments drove the development of armor as much as war. Horses did not need armor in a tournament, but plate armor for the horse's chest developed in response to pike warfare. Equine armor looked impressive and was very expensive, so in the later tournaments of the 15th and 16th centuries, it was often used.

By then, the knight's tournament armor had diverged from war armor. It had lance rests built in, and the side turned toward the oncoming lance was more heavily padded and plated. Special plates deflected lance blows at points of frequent contact. Some regions developed padded leather shock absorbers. Tournament armor by the end of the 15th century was not unlike a heavily padded football uniform. German armor makers had become dominant in Europe at this time, so the German tournament style also became dominant. It was heavy, expensive, and extensively decorated and gilded. By the 16th century, tilting armor had become highly specialized.

The helm developed for tournaments by the 15th century was impractical in war. It was pointed in front to deflect lances, and the entire face was covered. A slit permitted the knight to see only in front of him, and only when his head was tipped forward. In a single-combat joust, the knight could focus only on the threat in front of him.

A lance used in a tournament was different from a lance used in war. It had no sharp point; instead, it had a blunt end with three iron fingers sticking out to allow the knight to push on the other knight's armor and throw him from his horse. Originally, the shaft of the lance was just a 14-foot pole, but by the 15th century, the grip end had been specially designed for tournament use. The knight's breastplate had a bracket riveted to the right side to help hold the heavy lance. The lance was thicker at the handle end to transfer the center of gravity back toward the knight's hand. The handle had been carved out of this thick end, so the thicker part formed a guard for the hand.

The lance was held under the right arm, against the body, which made it cross over to the left side of the horse's neck, sticking out in front. The knight aimed at his opponent's head or body, and he had to hold the lance

The late-developed helmet for jousting was very impractical for real warfare. In a tournament, the knight knew exactly where his attacker was and could sacrifice visibility to face protection. He could only see out through the slit when his head was lowered to charge. (Royal Armouries/StockphotoPro)

as firmly as possible, pointing straight forward. At the moment of impact, he rose in his stirrups and pushed forward with his body's weight. At the same time, he had to duck or deflect his opponent's blow.

The knight's tournament saddle had a high back and a high, wide pommel called a burr plate. Even more than in battle, in a tournament the oncoming lance could slip and strike the knight's saddle or leg. Since the point of jousting was to remain in the saddle, it held the knight with great stability. Stirrups had to be very strong, and they were designed to avoid trapping a knight's foot, in case he did fall.

Tournament weapons became increasingly ceremonial as the Middle Ages passed. Blunt swords used as arms of courtesy could still hurt someone; at times, whalebone swords were used. With whalebone swords, leather armor was adequate. A combat of this type was truly sport, rather than war.

With the increase of pageantry and show over the centuries, tournament equipment included heraldic flags, caparisons for the horses, surcotes, and tents. A knight needed many wooden lances and at least two swords and shields. He needed at least one spare horse. His squire stayed in the tent with him and helped him dress, and they needed their supplies for the week. Additionally, both knight and squire needed fine clothes for the final banquet.

See also: Armor, Feasts, Heraldry, Horses, Knights, Weapons.

Further Reading

Barber, Richard, and Juliet Barker. *Tournaments: Jousts, Chivalry, and Pageants in the Middle Ages.* Woodbridge, UK: Boydell Press, 2000.

Barker, Juliet. *The Tournament in England, 1100–1400.* Woodbridge, UK: Boydell Press, 2003.

Charny, Geoffroi de. *Jousts and Tournaments: Charny and the Rules for Chivalric Sport in Fourteenth-Century France.* Highland Village, TX: Chivalry Bookshelf, 2003.

Clephan, R. Coltman. *The Medieval Tournament.* Mineola, NY: Dover Publications, 1995.

Crouch, David. *Tournament.* New York: Hambledon, 2006.

Oakeshott, Ewart. *A Knight and His Horse.* Chester Springs, PA: Dufour Editions, 1998.

Oakeshott, Ewart. *A Knight and His Weapons.* Chester Springs, PA: Dufour Editions, 1997.

Toys. *See* Games

Troubadours. *See* Minstrels and Troubadours

U

Unicorns. See Monsters

Universities

In medieval times, a center for advanced study was called a studium. Students, who already could read and write Latin, listened to lectures in Latin. The entrance exam was typically a test of ability with Latin. Students studied the liberal arts curriculum of rhetoric, mathematics, and grammar. Rhetoric was the main field of study, as they studied arguments and philosophical questions. After the main course of study had been completed, students could choose to study **medicine,** law, or theology, depending on the strengths of each university.

The first university was at Bologna, Italy, and its specialty was the study of law. Next were Paris and Oxford, both centered originally on theology as well as law. Paris and Oxford were under **church** oversight, while the university at Bologna was independent. Medical schools could be independent of universities, as at Salerno, or they could be part of a larger institution, as at Pisa and Milan. By the 14th century, most **cities** had a university.

The bedellus in a medieval university was the official responsible for keeping classes running, like a modern dean. In Paris, a teacher was called magister, while in Bologna, he was called doctor. Although university scholars did not have to be ordained clergy, they were often in orders. If they were not, they were expected to live as monks and devote themselves only to learning. The Dominicans and Franciscans came to dominate teaching in the universities during the 13th century.

Lecturers at early universities were paid directly by students, who contracted to hear them lecture on their specialty subject. The word *university* came from the Latin expression for associations of students and teachers, *universitates scholarium* and *universitates magistorum,* who used collective bargaining to negotiate the terms of study. Students demanded that teachers meet certain standards, such as being in class on time and not lecturing past quitting time. At Bologna, they forced the masters to promise to start and end their lectures on time or pay fines. Instructors were required to cover the promised curriculum, and they could not be absent without permission from the students. On their side, teachers demanded standardized fees. These collective-bargaining associations became the name of the institution whose customs they shaped: the university.

General university subjects were logic, rhetoric, **music,** astronomy, arithmetic, and geometry. Logic received the most attention; it expanded to include all the works of Aristotle, which included studies of science and ethics. A standard method of teaching was an oral debate over a question proposed by the teacher. The students took part in the debate and based

University lectures were often given in much simpler rooms than this fine paneled hall at the Sorbonne in Paris. The format was generally the same all over Europe: a lecturer spoke in Latin as students studied the text and took notes. Debates provided the only variety. (© Glasgow University Library, Scotland/The Bridgeman Art Library)

their arguments on their reading. An opening topic might be, "Whether lightning is fire descending from a cloud." The first stage consisted of arguments to the affirmative, called the principal arguments. Then other students (or the teacher) provided arguments to the negative, contradicting one or more of the principal arguments, and usually citing an authority such as Aristotle. The format allowed university students to hear their study put to use and to sharpen their wits about how to reason and debate.

In order to produce textbooks for the students, the university sent work to outside copyists. After the professors created an exemplar of a short text, private copyists, including educated women, made copies by hand. These simple copies, called in Latin *pecia*, could be made quickly and inexpensively. Students could buy or rent them. Because these short **books** were intended for student use, they were unlike any other medieval books and much more like modern ones. They had wide margins for taking notes in class, and they divided the text into paragraphs and red letters (rubrics) that broke up the text. They also put spaces between words to make them easier to read.

Completion of the general university course took between 4 and 6 years. After this, students could study law, theology, or medicine. Each university developed a specialty. Theology was the specialty of Paris, to the deliberate exclusion of other graduate studies, so that theology students would not be distracted. The university at Bologna had a medical school that allowed students to witness the dissection of cadavers, but medical students at Oxford did not witness dissections. Many medical faculties at universities did not incorporate patient care, but required only memorization of standard texts. A medical degree might be earned in 8 years, while a theology degree required at least 12.

On completing the degree, the student had to apply to actually receive it, and this application cost a substantial fee that provided a great part of the university's funding system. Some students could afford to attend the university, but they could not afford to graduate. The most common title granted on graduation was "master." This title permitted the graduate to teach. "Doctor" also indicated "teacher" and was used in some universities as the teaching title. It was gradually applied to physicians, since they were very learned.

The organization of colleges within a university came about as a solution to housing for students who were often as young as 15 and were far from home. A college was a small community to support these students' living needs. Many of the first colleges were endowed by a patron so that the students enrolled there would say prayers for the patron's soul; the college provided room and board in exchange. These early colleges often gave preferential acceptance to poor relatives of the founder, and some began to require work, as partial payment, from the poorest students. The Sorbonne began as a charitable boarding house for poor theology students and only later added teachers to become a real college. The colleges of Oxford began similarly.

By the late Middle Ages, colleges maintained a cook and a laundress. A maniple oversaw the college's operations, and larger colleges began to employ tutors to help their resident students. As books were donated, colleges built up **libraries.** College rules helped regulate student behavior; since most students lived at the college free of charge, the college could require attendance at Mass or at university lectures, and it could expel those who were too unruly. Students who lived on their own could easily turn into petty criminals or vagabonds, so the college system of organization helped make university study respectable again. By the end of the period, some students were paying to live at colleges, but it was considered more of an honor to have been admitted for free, on merit. The colleges were the first real dedicated buildings at most universities, which generally rented their lecture halls and only built or purchased buildings after the Middle Ages.

Students were typically unruly. They considered themselves to belong to the university, rather than to the town. They insulted students or travelers of other nationalities and got into violent fights. They gambled and drank. It was unclear whether they had to obey the town's laws or whether they were answerable only to the university. When a student occasionally committed a violent crime, the town and university came into conflict. At Oxford in 1355, a fight at a tavern led to a riot the following day in which some students and townspeople were killed, and some college buildings burned. The usual redress for these riots was in favor of the university, since the kings had a keen interest in keeping the universities open. It was easier to discipline the town.

During the medieval period, many masters and lecturers began to wear distinctive robes and **hats** to show their academic status, just as other professions and **guilds** had distinctive clothing. The robes and beret-like caps were originally identical or similar to the robes and caps of the clergy, since many of the lecturers were monks. The variations on these robes and caps through the late Middle Ages and Renaissance became the modern cap and gown of graduation. At the University of Paris, by the mid 14th century, doctors of theology wore black robes, often with matching hoods. Doctors of law wore red robes with wide sleeves. At the Italian universities, scholars wore red robes edged with miniver fur.

See also: Books, Medicine, Music, Numbers, Schools.

Further Reading

Frugoni, Chiara. *Books, Banks, Buttons, and Other Inventions from the Middle Ages.* New York: Columbia University Press, 2003

Gordon, Benjamin L. *Medieval and Renaissance Medicine.* New York: Philosophical Library, 1959.

Grant, Edward. *Science and Religion, 400 B.C. to A.D. 1550: From Aristotle to Copernicus.* Westport, CT: Greenwood Press, 2004.

Haskins, Charles. *The Rise of Universities.* Piscataway, NJ: Transaction Publishers, 2001.

Newman, Paul B. *Growing Up in the Middle Ages.* Jefferson, NC: McFarland, 2007.

Ridder-Symoens, Hilde, ed. *A History of the University in Europe.* Vol. 1, *Universities in the Middle Ages.* Cambridge: Cambridge University Press, 2003.

Wagons and Carts

The most ancient form of **animal** transportation, which was used all over medieval Europe, was the pack. **Roads** were often no better than narrow paths, and where **bridges** existed, they were rarely wide enough to allow a wheeled vehicle to pass. Most farm products and peddled goods were moved in packs on oxen or mules. Wheeled vehicles had been used in Europe since Roman times, but they only expanded in use as roads improved. During the early Middle Ages, the old Roman roads decayed; new towns and **cities** did not build good roads, but allowed paths and tracks to widen into dirt roads. Wheeled transportation increased, but it was never as important as shipping by water during the period. Its importance was mostly local and personal, in the form of simple carts. There were always places where wheels were impracticable. In winter, or in very steep places where more friction with the ground was helpful, sledges were also used.

By the Middle Ages, the wheel had developed into the stable form still in use today for many farm carts. Spokes made of oak attached to an elm hub, also called a nave or stock. The spokes were hammered into curved beech or ash pieces called felloes, which fitted like puzzle or arch pieces into a wheel shape. In the earliest wheels, thin wood pieces called strakes were nailed around the outside of the felloes to form the rim. Additional nails, left sticking out a bit, could give the wheels more traction. After **iron** technology became common, iron rims were standard. A band of iron ran around the outside rim; it was applied while hot so that it would shrink as it cooled and create a very tight fit. All through the Middle Ages, the earlier technique of nailing wooden strakes around the wheel remained very popular. A farmer or carter could repair this wheel himself if needed.

Wheels properly attached to a cart or wagon were set at an angle, called dishing, to counterbalance the swaying of the animal's movement, the shifting of the load, and especially the uneven road surface. The axles were set so that the top of the wheel leaned away from the cart. Early axles were made of oak and attached the wheel with a wooden linchpin. Iron axles were stronger than wooden ones and replaced wood in more expensive and durable carts in the later Middle Ages.

Harnesses for both carts and wagons were most often made of leather, but they could be made of **cloth.** The most expensive piece of the harness was the **horse's** collar, which had a wooden framework inside the padded leather covering. Halters, traces, girth straps, and occasionally saddles made up the rest of the kit.

The first form of wheeled vehicle was a two-wheeled cart. During the Middle Ages, the two-wheeled cart was much more common than the four-wheeled wagon. Two wheels sufficed to carry the load, and a two-wheeled cart was easier to maneuver on a deeply rutted road or track. They could be used with an ox, a donkey, a small horse, or even the peasant's own muscle power. Additionally, a two-wheeled cart easily acted as a dump truck. Carts could haul manure, hay, or wood, and if the cart was unhitched from the animal at the destination, it tipped back to dump the load. No medieval carts have survived into contemporary times; the cart was a working piece of equipment that remained in service until it fell apart.

Two-wheeled carts were able to manage all but the heaviest farm loads. For hauling hay or grain at harvest, a large cart could be loaded heavily and hitched to more than one ox or horse. The cart's shafts connected to the closest horse, with one or two horses in front, their heavy collars connected by ropes to the shafts. The heaviest, largest carts were called *plaustra* in Latin and may have been used primarily with oxen. They were heavily loaded with hay but still had only two wheels.

Carts acted as common transportation not only within farms and villages, but also from the farm or village into the market town or city. Two-wheeled carts carried the majority of goods to and from the point of sale. Carts carried into cities loads of charcoal, cheese, bread, nuts, **pottery** jugs, candles, firewood, and flour. It is hard to name any commodity that was

Two-wheeled carts carried most farm products around Europe, since they were cheaper to make and easier to maneuver on turns. The picture shows a heavy covered cart turning to go up a hill. The horsepower is not quite sufficient and a team of farmhands must help push it and keep its load from falling out. (The British Library/ StockphotoPro)

not carried by carts, which hauled **water,** manure, rubbish, gravel, chalk, lime, building **stone, brick,** timber, and all kinds of produce and manufactured goods.

Carts were as often hired as owned. Farmers owned carts, as did manufacturers who used them for transport every day, but most people in a town did not. Just as horses could be hired, so could a cart and ox. Royal officials could often press private carts into service at a moment's notice. Some carters also made regular journeys between large towns and cities, carrying packages and goods for people who did not transport things enough to warrant the use of a whole cart. These private carriers operated as a regular parcel delivery service.

Carts required frequent upkeep. Wheels and other parts had to be lubricated regularly, and about every year, the axle wore out and had to be replaced, particularly if it was an old-fashioned wooden axle. A heavily used cart ran through two or three sets of wheels in a year. Depending on its use, the body of a cart lasted a year or two before it needed to be replaced or fixed.

A wagon is, by definition, a box with at least two axles and four wheels. Wagons were common on the European continent during the Middle Ages, but not in England. Many of England's roads were inadequate for wagons until the 16th century. Wagons were a greater financial investment; a wagon cost more initially than a cart, and it required the upkeep of four wheels and two axles. It was used to pull heavier loads and usually needed multiple oxen or horses, a further expense. Wagons were used for heavier, longer distance transport, such as moving household goods over long distances. When nobles traveled between their **castles** and manor **houses,** they used wagons to move their **furniture** and supplies. They were called *currus* in Latin household **records,** which became *car, char,* and *charet* in 15th-century English. Wagons were more expensive and less common and were less likely to be worked until they fell apart, so a few old wagons have survived.

During the 12th century, wagon technology took some steps forward. First, the oxen or horses were connected with a set of double shafts (wooden poles) around the animal's body. The double shaft attached to the horse collar or oxen yoke so that the animal's shoulders pulled equally on the load. In the next stage, the shafts were connected not to the wagon directly, but to a whippletree. The whippletree was a bar in front of the wagon; it received the direct pull of the animals and was connected to the wagon at only one point. It was mounted on a pivot so that the animals could turn and the wagon would follow.

Next, the development of an undercarriage that could turn the front wheels made wagons much easier to use but harder to build. The front axle had to be mounted on its own framework that was independently attached to the wagon, although the rear axle could still be attached directly to the wagon. The front axle's assembly pivoted on a tough oak or iron pin.

It is unclear whether the pivoting front axle was in use all through the Middle Ages. Some scholars suggest it was an innovation around the 13th century, while others believe it had been a standard part of wagon building since Roman times. Pictures are ambiguous; when a shaft or rope in an illustration is attached to the base of the wagon (or more clearly to the axle, not the wagon box), it is possible it is showing a pivoting front axle. Some illustrations portray a wagon with both axles fixed and the horse's shafts directly connected to the wagon's box. It may be that both kinds of wagon were in use.

Manuscript illustrations that show carts and wagons rarely show them with solid wood bodies. Wood was expensive, so it was only used for the parts that had to be structurally sound. The sides of a typical cart were often made of wattle: vertical poles, with flexible branches woven between them. The sides could also be made of vertical poles held together at the top by a horizontal bar, like a cage. Solid wood boxes were only built if the load was heavy, such as root crops, stones, or **coal.** Taller poles could be added to transport a tall load, such as hay.

Kings and queens traveled from manor to manor either on horseback or in coaches. Some records tell the splendor of these specially crafted wagons. They were roofed with rounded hoops supporting a canopy, and they had seats with cushions. The walls were covered with linen at the least, and more often with silk. The rainproof covering was sometimes made of canvas coated with wax. The interior was as splendid as the royal family's status and wealth could manage: silk velvet cushions, **embroidery,** diamonds, and gilding. The exterior was brightly painted, with heraldic coats of arms.

By the 14th century, and perhaps earlier, some wagons had frames that suspended the covered box on leather straps or chains so that it swayed instead of jolting with the rough road surface. In Latin household records, this was a *currus mobilis,* a "moving" (swaying or swinging) car. French records call these vehicles chariots. An even-gentler way to travel was the litter, a carriage box without wheels that was suspended between two horses. Litters were used only for royalty.

The wagon's most unusual use was in the seasonal dramas put on by English city guilds. Specially designed wagons served as portable stages that moved through the city and stopped at scheduled intersections and squares. The wagons had platform stages, walls to serve as backdrops with painted scenery, and special features like trapdoors, curtains, and upper stories. Some even had lights or fireworks. Each guild that put on a stage of the larger drama invested a lot of money and work in their unique stage wagon; the wagons were used only once a year and lasted for many years'

Aristocratic women on long journeys used covered wagons pulled by a team of horses. These wagons were padded and decorated to make them clean and comfortable for the ladies, but little could be done to improve the wagon's suspension and the bad roads. During the Middle Ages, some wagons began to have simple suspension systems so that the wagon box rocked instead of jarring, and most had wooden shafts to hitch the teams to. It is hard to tell if the harnessed horses were sometimes attached to the wagon box with only ropes, as in this painting, or if such drawings showed the artist's ignorance and lack of a real-life model. (Paul Lacroix, *Moeurs, Usage et Costumes au Moyen Age et a l'Epoque de la Renaissance*, 1878)

use. It seems likely that some traveling jongleurs had similar wagons for their shows, but only the city guild wagons have survived in historical records.

See also: Agriculture, Bridges, Drama, Horses, Roads.

Further Reading

Bork, Robert, and Andrea Kann, eds. *The Art, Science, and Technology of Medieval Travel.* Burlington, VT: Ashgate Publishing, 2008.

Langdon, John. *Horses, Oxen, and Technological Innovation.* Cambridge: Cambridge University Press, 1986.

Piggott, Stuart. *Wagon, Chariot, and Carriage: Symbol and Status in the History of Transport.* London: Thames and Hudson, 1992.

Vince, John. *An Illustrated History of Carts and Wagons.* Bourne End, UK: Spurbooks, 1975.

Viner, David. *Wagons and Carts.* Botley, UK: Shire Books, 2008.

Washing. *See Hygiene*

Water

Most human settlements are planned around a water supply; people settle at the mouth of a freshwater stream flowing into the sea or at a good ford across a river. Some settlements are not made with regard to water, or, as they grow, they outstrip their local water supply. The problem of finding enough clean water began to be a pressing problem for medieval settlements in the 11th century.

Although medieval people had inaccurate ideas about what caused disease, they felt strongly that bad odors were unhealthy and that cloudy water could not be good to drink. They did not think of boiling water as a way to purify it, even if boiling water was their normal cooking method. Water was not a chosen drink; monks only drank it to mortify the flesh, and it was too often impure to be considered a good drink. It was also the drink of **beggars**; drinking water was a social shame. Water could be improved by adding wine, vinegar, or **spices,** but it was still barely acceptable. But water had to be used in cooking, brewed as ale, and mixed into wine, so it had to be pure.

Former Roman provinces often had aqueducts to bring water from mountain springs. In the fall of Rome, many aqueducts were torn down, but some continued to bring water into the city. Aqueducts in Britain fell into disrepair quickly, but some in France, Spain, and Italy continued to function for several centuries. These communities had an advantage in developing new water systems, but water technology spread through Europe mostly through **monasteries.** Benedictine and Cistercian monasteries developed most water-system technology.

Monastic Water Systems

Medieval European monasteries were known for their well-planned water supply systems. Some monks altered a river channel to bring water to their compounds. They usually had to line such channels with **stone,** and some channels were covered in stone to keep the water clean. Many monasteries dug deep trenches and laid up to three miles of pipes to bring water from a nearby river or spring. Springs were preferred, and usually a springhouse was built over them to keep them clean. Usually several water sources had to be tapped and collected into the main pipeline.

Italian monasteries could sometimes make use of old Roman aqueducts, but in Northern Europe, they had to use underground pipes. The pipes were most often made of **lead,** but some were made of **pottery,** and a few were hollow tree trunks. Since Roman pipes had all been lead, nobody yet suspected that lead was poisonous.

Bringing water from afar was not a simple task. The water had to flow steadily downhill, since gravity was the only engine for water flow. When a stream or spring at a higher elevation had been located, it was often on someone else's land, and the proposed conduit would cross many lands. These conduits could have been entirely in rural land, or they could have crossed under a town wall, under streets, and into the friary or abbey. Monasteries had to get permission or buy the strips of land they needed to dig. In order to maintain the conduit's steady downhill gradient, ditches to bury pipe varied from a few inches to 24 feet. The ditches had to be lined with stone or clay and the pipes carefully joined with molten lead, tow, or **iron** collars. When conduits came to other ditches, creeks, or **roads,** they had to go over or under; some pipes ran along **bridges.**

When the pipeline came to the monastery, there was sometimes a series of settling tanks to allow dirt in the water to settle before the water was ready for drinking. The water system brought supplies into many of the buildings. If the pipes were narrow and watertight, there was often enough water pressure to feed a fountain. Fountains were the preferred water distribution method in the Middle Ages. They looked and sounded beautiful and peaceful, and they made water available to many people at once. A monastic lavatory station could be a water fountain with a dozen spouts so that many monks could wash at the same time. Other fountains were set up for filling jugs by dipping them into the reservoir.

The reservoir of the fountain drained into pipes that carried the water away to other buildings and rooms. Monasteries without fountains had cisterns and reservoirs filled by the pipes that formed an underground river. Pipes went to the dormitories, the kitchen, the workshops, and the washing stations. Washbasins, called lavers, were made of stone, bronze, or lead. The water came into laver stands through pipes with **copper** taps on the end, which were sometimes shaped like animals' heads. The water could be turned on and off by a stopcock faucet in a circular socket. Water flowed if the hole in the stopper aligned with the hole in the pipe but was stopped if the stopper was turned so the holes did not align.

Secular Water Systems

In rural places, springs, wells, and rivers supplied water. Medieval wells were nothing more than holes dug down to the water table. Later wells had walls around them, roofs, and windlasses to pull buckets up. In the Middle Ages, most did not, and many accidents occurred. Older children and **women** were the most common water carriers. They could lose their footing at the well's edge and fall in, and many drowned. By late medieval times, many **cities** passed ordinances that wells needed walls, windlasses, and clean **buckets.** In the country, they rarely did. Some wells were not clearly visible, and strangers fell into them in the dark. Without protective walls, wells could be contaminated by spring flooding, and they also became even more invisible.

In medieval Italy, rural cisterns were more common than wells. Rain fell, but it had to be collected for later use. The roof channeled water through the gutters into the cistern. Cisterns were stone lined, and some were large enough to serve several families. In particularly dry places where spring or cistern water was scant, dirt or sand could be used to clean dishes or tools.

Castles always had wells as part of their defensive planning. In case of a **siege,** the castle could not be left without water; piping water from the outside was not an acceptable solution. Typically there was a well in the courtyard and another within the keep itself. This well had a shaft built over it so that a bucket could be lowered into the well from any floor of the keep. As castles modernized and became less centered on the keep, the well was often built into a building that served to pump the water into a high tank, where it supplied pipes going to different buildings. Many castles were near

Perugia's medieval fountain still stands in its old public square, although it is now fenced off. It was the main water source for most of Perugia's residents in its time. The round design allowed many people to dip pitchers into the fountain's basin or hold them under one of its many spouts. Italian cities had the best public water systems of the Middle Ages. (Francesco Remolo/Dreamstime.com)

larger water supplies like rivers or lakes; barrels could be filled there for large-scale water uses.

Medieval **cities** usually grew around a water supply, most often a river or large stream. The river allowed the people to travel easily, often to the seacoast for trade, and it also gave them a supply of water. Within the city walls, there were sometimes natural springs with public wells built over them. Citizens and neighborhoods also dug wells all over the city so that they could get their water nearby. As long as the towns were relatively small, they could count on their water supply. The problem was that as they grew, they also used the rivers for carrying away waste of all kinds. When there were more cities along the same river, the water became polluted. Within the city, the wells could not always stay clean, since latrine cesspits allowed sewage to leak into groundwater.

Industry increased the need for water. Some industries, such as ale brewing, were inherently water based, while others, such as tanning, dyeing, and laundering, depended on water for large-scale washing. These tradesmen needed **barrels** full of water, and while some could use polluted water, many could not. Other industries used the river heavily for sanitation; this was especially true of butchers, who wanted the river to carry away the blood of the animals they slaughtered. Tanners also were among the heaviest polluters. Cities began to face water shortages for both businesses and residents.

The problems were compounded by the never-ending need to build new housing and workshops. Many cities that originally had tributary streams feeding their major rivers needed to build over them. Smaller streams silted up, and others were encased in underground pipes so that whole streets could go over them. When a city had a great river flowing through it, over the years its embankment became a solid wall of docks, wharves, and houses. Cities like London and Paris built public access points, wide stairs that permitted the public to access the river. People drew water for their cooking and washing, and nearby there was usually a public **latrine.** It was an outhouse that dropped waste directly into the river.

By the 13th century, medieval cities needed to bring in a lot of water from outside the city. The countries in the old Roman Empire, particularly in Italy, inherited aqueduct systems and even some city sewers and plumbing. Public fountains were standard in Italian cities from an early time. Northern Europe's cities had no existing infrastructure for water. They used lead pipes and the hollowed trunks of hardwood trees like elm to channel river and spring water from outside the city walls. In some cities, the local monastery's system provided the basic piping, and the town used its overflow capacity. When a city's water needs outstripped its supply, the city or private vendors brought water in casks and carts from rural springs.

Italian towns had at least one large fountain, and often several. The water fell down in multiple spouts into a reservoir, so users could fill pitchers at a spout or dip buckets into the basin. The fountains were built and maintained with great pride by each city and were often elaborately carved and decorated with symbols of the city and its leading families. Families had to walk to the fountain to fill pitchers and casks, but businesses were supposed to find another water source. In the 14th century, Perugia enacted statutes to make sure water would remain clean in the public fountain. Jugs dipped into the fountain's pools had to be washed first, and small bronze jugs were chained to the fountain so that they never touched the ground. Some towns appointed a warden to watch over the fountains to keep people from dumping trash or dirt into them or from taking too much water. Washing clothes and personal bathing were strictly forbidden and carried heavy fines. The fountains had to be scrubbed out periodically, even so.

Water for industrial and large-scale use had to be obtained somewhere else. Siena had industrial fountains throughout the town that were assigned to certain trades. The guilds maintained them, and they had to be cleaned much more often than the public drinking fountains. Some had pools where businesses were permitted to wash wool, meat, **fish**, or **cloth.**

Some Italian cities, such as Bologna, used a system of small canals that flowed through city neighborhoods and could be controlled by gates. Neighborhoods knew which days they would have water for washing and also were expected to keep their streets clean. In Italian communal towns, neighborhood wells were regulated and cleaned frequently; they had to be walled and provide a windlass and a clean bucket.

London's Chepe market had a public water system called the Great Conduit, built in the 13th century. It was a large system of pipes that brought water chiefly to the main fountain in Chepe but also to the side markets of East and West Chepe. It also provided water to households and neighborhoods in other parts of London. The water came from springs in Tyburn and other streams as far as three miles away. In a city system like this, the main pipes were five or six inches wide, but pipes bringing water into a house or business were supposed to be only a finger's width, and sometimes no thicker than a goose quill. This limited a house from using more than its share of water. Most houses did not receive water privately, but instead contributed to maintaining the neighborhood fountain. Some public water supplies were placed inside a building that could be locked up for the night.

The Conduit required a fair amount of upkeep and policing. Brewers, who used water in very large quantities, were not supposed to use the Conduit water freely. Other business uses that would use up or foul the water had to be watched. Some butchers and fishmongers washed their meat in the fountains, leaving blood and pollution behind. The pipes and tanks needed constant maintenance, with dues paid by residents and businesses. By the 14th century, the aging water mains burst at times and flooded Fleet Street.

Other medieval cities had similar systems, but water supply remained a constant problem. Springs ran dry, and cities had to find new sources. People dirtied or damaged the fountains, and everyone accused others of taking more water than their share. Paris forbade professional water carriers from filling their casks at public fountains during the night; they had to fill their buckets as quickly as possible, and only if the reservoir was full. Some people stood in line many times a day to get public water, and as the population rose, the lines got longer.

See also: Beverages, Cities, Hygiene, Latrines and Garbage.

Further Reading

Cosman, Madeleine Pelner. *Fabulous Feasts: Medieval Cookery and Ceremony.* New York: George Braziller, 1995.
Dean, Trevor. *The Towns of Italy in the Later Middle Ages.* Manchester, UK: Manchester University Press, 2000.
Kucher, Michael P. *The Water Supply of Siena, Italy: The Medieval Roots of the Modern Networked City.* London: Routledge, 2005.
Magnusson, Roberta J. *Water Technology in the Middle Ages.* Baltimore: Johns Hopkins University Press, 2001.
Squatriti, Paolo. *Water and Society in Early Medieval Italy, AD 400–1000.* Cambridge: Cambridge University Press, 2002.
Wright, Lawrence. *Clean and Decent: The Fascinating History of the Bathroom and the WC.* Toronto: University of Toronto Press, 1967.

Weapons

Personal weapons were very important during the Middle Ages, since during most of the period, there were not only invasions and foreign wars, but also civil wars, uprisings, and robbers. Everyone carried at least a knife, and many men tried to have better arms. The trend during the 1,000 years of the Middle Ages was toward more steel and more machinery. Weapons achieved a certain amount of art and beauty during the golden age of the **knight,** but as **gunpowder** was introduced, the Middle Ages closed with the new use of primitive handguns.

Weapons varied not only by time but by region. Some regions were conservative and relatively primitive, such as Scandinavia's tendency to continue using Viking-style weapons to a late date. Some regions were more in contact with foreign cultures and were influenced by them to use different weapons and tactics. Spain's **iron** deposits put their smiths at the forefront of developing swords and steel. Italy was ahead in war machinery, such as crossbows and guns.

At any given time, the greatest difference in weapon use was by social class. The arms that an aristocrat could carry were very different from the arms of a peasant. Only nobility could use swords; at the height of the Middle Ages, most people lived their lives without ever touching a sword. Peasants used spears and bows. Mercenaries used machinery that required technical ability.

Spears

The spear was the primary weapon in early medieval Europe. Every Anglo-Saxon and Frankish warrior had at least two spears, a throwing spear and a longer lance. The right to carry a spear went with freedom; a **slave** caught with a spear was severely punished under Charlemagne's laws. Anglo-Saxon and Frankish lances had broad, flat, very sharp heads and were attached to strong ash poles about eight feet long. Throwing spears, called darts, often had barbed heads. The barbs were not small, as on a fishing hook; they were large and long. The spearheads, however, were not large, and they could be mass-produced inexpensively on early forges. Darts were mounted on lighter, shorter shafts. Warriors probably considered them throwaway weapons, while their lances were expected to survive the battle or be reparable.

Hunting spears continued to be used all through the Middle Ages, especially for fighting **animals** that were too dangerous to encounter at close range. Wild boars rushed at their attackers, and boar spears had to be about nine feet long to spear the boar when he was not yet close enough to bite.

Spears were always primary weapons in war. The Bayeux Tapestry shows them used on both sides, Norman and Anglo-Saxon. Lances on the Bayeux Tapestry are about nine feet long and seem to be used for thrusting and stabbing, not for throwing. Lances often had a relatively long spearhead, similar to a bayonet.

The lance also developed as the mounted knight's spear, held in front during a charge. These lances were up to 14 or 15 feet long, since they had to reach in front of the **horse.** In war, they had real spear points and were used by a line of knights charging at a gallop. For **tournaments,** the lance lost its point and became blunt. It underwent more changes as tournament jousting became a sport. The jousting lance was thicker at the handle, in order to move the center of gravity toward the knight's hand. Its purpose in a tournament was to knock the other knight off his horse, not to pierce his armor.

The lance of the foot soldier developed into a variety of forms of special spears with ax heads. These are generally called polearms; they were developed to allow foot soldiers to fight against mounted knights. Polearms were

A cavalry charge with lances was an unstoppable war machine until the development of polearms. Knights practiced constantly to maintain their skill in unhorsing opposing riders while ducking oncoming lances. Once a line of knights had unhorsed their opponents, smaller weapons were used to fight on foot. (James Robinson Planche, *An Illustrated Dictionary of Historic Costume*, 2003)

all basically a long pole with a complex blade mounted on the end, a blade that was designed to do several different tasks. A good polearm could cut, stab, bludgeon, and hook. It is likely that they began as peasant or towns-man innovations for making weapons using farm or craft **tools**. Laborers in an orchard had to use a blade mounted on a pole to cut tall tree branches, and the blade could be like a saw, a knife, an ax, or a hook. All these blades were useful against mounted knights.

Names for these weapons varied, since they were developed and used by untrained local fighters. They did not develop international terminol-ogy the way knights' weapons did. This makes it difficult to know exactly what the kinds of poleaxes were. In 14th-century England, poleax weapons could be called godenac, croc, faussa, pikte, guisarme, or vouge. The dif-ferent names could have signified technical differences among these weap-ons, or they could have been just different slang words for essentially the same poleax.

The 12th-century gisarme (or giserne) usually had a hook on the end of the pole. It may often have used a broad, curved ax blade, as well. It was similar to the earlier medieval bill and the later pike and halberd.

The pike was a very long, two-handed weapon used after the 12th cen-tury. The shaft of a pike could be as long as 18 feet, while the spearhead was short and sharply pointed. Pikes were used in a block, with the pikemen

Polearms combined spear and ax, then added hooks that could pull a man from the saddle. There were many variations and names; pike and halberd are among the best known. Halberds like these pictured were used in decisive battles around 1300, when private citizens defended themselves against attack by knights. (Dreamstime.com)

standing behind each other in rows in the formation of a square. When a pike's end was jammed into the ground, it was strong enough to impale a charging horse.

In the 14th century, the halberd was developed in Switzerland as a spear with a unique defense against knights on horseback. In addition to a long spearhead, the halberd had an ax blade and a hook for pulling men off their horses. In two key battles, the halberd was able to defeat knights in chainmail. In Flanders (1302) and in Switzerland (1315), peasants and town citizens with halberds used terrain conditions to defeat larger forces of knights. The development of the halberd was one reason plate **armor** began to replace mail.

Swords

The sword was always the weapon of the aristocracy. Commoners were allowed to have long knives, but the true sword was forbidden, as well as too expensive. European swords were sharpened on both edges, whereas the swords used by Arab and Turkish armies were curved and only sharp on the outer edge. Sword design evolved during the Middle Ages as metal-working improved and fighting conditions changed.

Early medieval swords were very flat and had elaborate pommels and guards to block the user's hands from blows. We have many swords from pagan graves, in Sweden, Denmark, and England, from early Anglo-Saxons and from later Vikings. The wood and leather handgrips on these swords have rotted away, so the remaining grip is just the tang, the iron bar between the blade and the hammered-on pommel. The guard is a short bar at the end of the sword's blade, but the pommel is often enameled, jeweled, or **gold.** Naturally, common warriors had less interesting swords, but the sword was always viewed as the king of weapons, and craftsmanship was lavished on it. Only aristocratic Frankish, Anglo-Saxon, and Swedish warriors carried swords, so swords tended to be expensive and elaborate.

During the 11th, 12th, and 13th centuries, swords came in many sizes but were basically grouped into war swords, used with one hand, and very long swords called two-handed swords. War swords were not small; they averaged about 36 inches long and weighed about three pounds. The grip added another 7 or 8 inches. A war sword like this was used most often when fighting on horseback, since it was long enough to reach away from the horse but light enough to use in one hand.

Two-handed swords had blades averaging 50 inches, and the grips were 12 inches, allowing room for two large hands in armored gloves. The two-handed sword could be used to cut and stab, but also to block an opponent's blows. Its pommel could be used as a small club. Although the sword was so heavy, it was carefully balanced to make it easy to wield. The

Swords were the highest-class weapon in early medieval Scandinavia. The pommel and hand guard were usually decorated. The pommel's elaborate designs could include enamel, engraving, and inlaid precious metals or stones. The end of the tang that formed the hand grip was encased in wood and leather handles that have broken and decayed over the centuries. (Statens Historiska Museum, Stockholm/Werner Forman Archive/ StockphotoPro)

heavy pommel acted as a counterweight to the blade. Knights had trained with these weapons since they were young and could handle them with dexterity.

In the late Middle Ages, swords to fight against plate armor had to be shorter, thicker, and reinforced. They were used more for thrusting than for slicing. Slicing swords tended to be long and heavy. The 14th and 15th centuries saw a trend toward smaller, lighter swords in many parts of Europe.

Sword construction was basically the same for all types. A sword's blade was made with a long tang—that is, the end of the blade sticking down to where it will become part of the grip. A guard for the hand was slipped over the tang, and then a wooden grip, and then the end pommel was hammered into place, holding it together. The wooden grip was often wrapped with **cloth** or leather, sometimes decorated in ornate ways.

The steel used for swords was very hard and not easily scratched. The sword's blade was kept razor sharp. Although steel making had not yet been fully developed, blacksmiths had learned how to use charcoal and a second firing to add carbon to the iron as an outer coating. This case-hardened steel was stronger than wrought iron, and it could be polished to mirror smoothness.

Swords were hung from a girdle, a belt around the waist, or a baldric, a strap over one shoulder. In battle, swords may have been hung with bare blades, ready to pull, but in training and for travel, scabbards protected the blade from rust or from hurting anyone. Scabbards were sometimes attached to the leather belt directly but also could be clipped to it with rings and hooks. The sword was not carried high on the waist or strapped tightly. Sword belts hung lower so that the sword's handle hung at the upper thigh, not the hip. The sword's pommel could also have a chain or leather strap that wrapped around the knight's wrist.

The early medieval Saxons had been named for the characteristic long knife they carried, which they called a seax or sax. From this long knife, a humbler sword developed, called the falchion. It was only sharp on one edge of the blade, which was curved. The other side was straight and dull. It was more like a kitchen knife.

Daggers were long knives that were more like small swords. The Latin word for a dagger was *cultellus,* from which the word *cutlass* developed. Some daggers had both edges of the blade sharp, like a sword, and others had only one edge sharp, like a falchion or saber. While daggers were widely used, knights did not carry them until the 14th century. Until then, they were the weapons of peasants. Daggers were also easier to hide and were more often used for assassinations than the great long swords.

In the **Muslim** regions, swords had always been curved; they are known to us as scimitars or sabers. They were sharp only along the outer curve of the blade and were used for slashing. They were used somewhat in European areas that had greater contact with Muslims, such as in the Byzantine regions, and among the Huns who had migrated from Central Asia with sabers. The Huns became westernized and stopped using sabers during most of the Middle Ages.

Axes and Clubs

The Franks were named for the throwing ax they used when they first invaded the Roman Empire. The Romans called the throwing ax a *francisca*. The Franks also carried larger axes for fighting at close range. These axes must have been similar to what they used to cut wood and were about the same size and shape as a full-sized modern ax.

Battle-axes were a main weapon for the Vikings who invaded England, France, and Russia in the ninth century. The ax heads were not broad, and they were forged to have a hole through the back so that a wooden handle could be attached. By the 11th century, their axes blades were broader and were known in Anglo-Saxon records as "Danish axes"—the largest kind.

During the Middle Ages, some knights used axes while on horseback. The axes were not large and could be carried easily as an adjunct to other weapons. By the close of the Middle Ages, these horsemen's axes often had a sharp pick on the other side.

Axes developed into longer and shorter variants. The long ones, pole-axes, merged with spears. Another ax development was the war hammer, which had a short shaft closer to the size of a modern hatchet. The war hammer had a point on the end, a pick at the back, and a two-pronged hammerhead.

The mace was a club, sometimes with a rounded end and sometimes with short blades or prongs. A mace with sharp spikes could put a hole in a knight's armor, but it could also get stuck. However, there were maces with sharp spikes all around an iron ball, and some maces had the ball attached to a chain for greater force. Maces were knights' weapons, although they were less elegant and chivalrous than the sword.

Bows

The longbow was originally from Wales but was adopted as the national weapon by the English during the Hundred Years' War with France. Longbows had been the chief hunting weapon of early medieval Europe. They became weapons of war during the 10th century. Hunters did not use barbed arrowheads, but otherwise their bows were the same as those used for war.

Longbows were sized to each individual archer and were around six feet long. They were either straight or somewhat curved forward. They were most often made of yew wood, and the strings were hemp or flax, rubbed with beeswax. Arrows for a longbow were about three feet long. The wooden shafts were made of aspen, ash, and other woods and were carefully cured so that wetness in the wood would not cause warping. They had forged-iron arrowheads, and different types were used for different military purposes. Many arrowheads for war were barbed. Goose feathers were glued and sewn onto the notched ends by professional arrow makers, called fletchers. Three rows of feathering, each six to eight inches long, constituted typical fletching.

The secret of the longbow lay in the bowmen's lifelong training to use the weight of their bodies, not the strength of their arms, and to shoot quickly and accurately without needing to take visual aim. Boys were trained with small bows from the age of seven. A good archer could shoot a dozen arrows in a minute, and all would hit their target, at 400 yards. Bowmen went into battle with only helmets and swords, sometimes shields, and sometimes with less. Some bowmen fought in bare feet so that they could better grip the ground. Because bowmen shot so fast, they needed to carry many arrows into battle. At a rate of 12 arrows per minute, 60 arrows would only provide five minutes of shooting.

In the Mediterranean and Byzantine regions, bows could have been shorter and more like Roman bows. They were composite bows made of several materials laminated together, perhaps wood strengthened with bone. They were probably recurve bows, in which the wood curves away from the archer and stores more tension than a single piece of wood that has been bent into a longbow. Short bows were more useful for fighting on horseback, so they were also used by invading Mongols, Huns, and Turks.

The crossbow, also called the arbalest, had been used in Roman times, and it continued to be used as a hunting weapon in some places. During the 11th century, it appeared again as a weapon of war. The Bayeux Tapestry records crossbow use at the Battle of Hastings in 1066. Although the Normans used it in their conquest of the English, the crossbow was never as popular in England as the native Welsh and English longbow. The crossbow was most popular in Germany and Italy, where it was used for hunting as well as for military purposes. In some German and Italian cities, crossbowmen formed shooting **guilds.** After the 13th century, its use spread north again; the crossbow began to be used by even the primitive warriors of Scandinavia.

Crossbows were powerful, but slow, compared with the longbow. The crossbow was often used by the defenders in a **siege,** since they could slowly pick off attackers at a distance while staying out of sight behind a parapet. Crossbows were made larger, and sometimes stationary, for siege defenses. Personal, portable crossbows continued to be very numerous and were always being improved.

The crossbow was a short, powerful bow mounted on straight wooden stock with a tough bowstring pulled back and locked with a latch that had a lever trigger under the stock. The bowman did not have to pull the string and aim at the same time; he could span (load) the crossbow, take aim, and fire a trigger when ready. The arrows were short and were called bolts. They fit into a groove on the wooden stock in front of the bowstring. Early crossbows required the user to put his feet on the bow and pull hard on the string to put it into firing position, and later crossbows added a stirrup to the end to make this easier.

During the 12th century, crossbows were made with composite materials such as horn, sinew, and wood. As crossbows became more powerful, they required a mechanism to pull the bowstring back. At first, this was a hook that required powerful body strength to use, but in the 14th century, crossbows used a windlass and ratchet to crank the bowstring into place.

See also: Armor, Gunpowder, Hunting, Knights, Sieges.

Further Reading

Clements, John. *Medieval Swordsmanship: Illustrated Methods and Techniques.* Boulder, CO: Paladin Press, 1998.

Edge, David, and John Miles Paddock. *Arms and Armor of the Medieval Knight: An Illustrated History of Medieval Weaponry.* New York: Crescent Books, 1993.

Fliegel, Stephen. *Arms and Armor.* Cleveland, OH: Cleveland Museum of Art, 2008.

Nicolle, David. *Arms and Armour of the Crusading Era, 1050–1350.* 2 vols. Mechanicsburg, PA: Stackpole Books, 1999.

Nicolle, David. *Medieval Warfare Source Book: Warfare in Western Christendom.* London: Brockhampton Press, 1999.

Oakeshott, Ewart. *The Archaeology of Weapons: Arms and Armour from Prehistory to the Age of Chivalry.* Mineola, NY: Dover Publications, 1996.

Oakeshott, Ewart. *A Knight and His Weapons.* Chester Springs, PA: Dufour Editions, 1997.

Payne-Gallwey, Ralph. *The Crossbow: Its Military and Sporting History, Construction, and Use.* New York: Skyhorse Publishing, 2007.

Pollington, Stephen. *The English Warrior: From Earliest Times till 1066.* Hockwold, UK: Anglo-Saxon Books, 2002.

Reinhardt, Hank. *The Book of Swords.* Riverdale, NY: Baen Publishing, 2009.

Weddings

European marriage customs differed less by region than by social class. All across the continent, the aristocracy who owned land followed customs of inheritance and family composition that were dramatically different from the peasants and artisans of country and town. Aristocratic families needed public, legally defensible weddings because large amounts of land and authority were at stake. Peasants and townspeople could form private marriages since their property was sometimes not more than a few **kitchen utensils.**

Marriage and Divorce

The heartland of Europe—France and Germany—was settled by the Franks during the early Middle Ages. After the Franks converted to Christianity, there was a long period when their marriage customs did not change and were in conflict with Christian teaching in Rome. Frankish kings had always been focused on producing an heir, whatever it took. They could be polygamous, or they could have a legal wife and concubines. Frankish kings could marry a pair of sisters, and some could have been in sexual relationships with their own sisters. Divorce was easy; a Frankish noble just had to repudiate a wife and send her home, and any reason would do: lack of children, illness, misconduct, or just changing his mind.

The traditional Frankish wedding ceremony began with betrothal and a formal agreement on terms of property transfers. The man gave the girl a ring when this was concluded, and he gave the bride's family a sum of money—a token brideprice. The wedding consisted of giving the bride to him with a public ceremony and feast, but we know little about the ceremony. The morning after the wedding, the man gave his bride an additional sum, the "morning gift." These gifts could be money or land. The custom of the morning gift persisted until the 12th century, when new inheritance laws made it impractical.

In Charlemagne's time, both boys and girls married in their early teens. However, even during that period, the normal age of marriage began to shift later for men. The marriage age for girls went up from 12 to 15, and some men were not married until their late 20s. This remained the average in Europe through the Middle Ages.

The **church** in the early Middle Ages viewed divorce as a real fall from the ideal of lifetime monogamy but did not forbid it. There were valid reasons to divorce, and, in some cases, remarriage was permitted. Those who divorced were given penances. Increasingly, as the church's power grew, not the secular nobles but the bishops ruled on contested divorce cases, and they were less and less likely to uphold the divorce. Since wives were often repudiated in an abuse of power by the husband, this protected the rights of **women** to some extent.

When Charlemagne became the Pope's military defender and was crowned Holy Roman Emperor, it became important to force the Franks to follow traditional Roman Catholic marriage customs. The church proclaimed stricter rules about marriage and divorce than they had previously enforced. No man could have more than one wife. That wife could not be a relative closer than a cousin in the seventh degree. No divorce was permitted, unless the wife had been grossly at fault, and that divorce must be approved by the church. Charlemagne himself set an example of following these rules. In his quest for heirs, he married five times, but never more than one woman at once. He repudiated one wife before he was crowned emperor, but he persevered as an example of fidelity after that.

When the church made these rulings, there was a cultural mistake that had grave results for centuries. Romans had counted degrees of relationship differently from the Franks and other Germanic nations. In the Roman system, a fourth-degree relative was a simple cousin; a seventh-degree relative would be a somewhat more distant cousin. But the Germanic method of calculating relationship was different: a cousin was only a third-degree relative, and a seventh-degree relative was anyone descended from the person's great-great-great-great-great grandfather. This degree of relationship often included everyone in a village, as well as most of the aristocracy. The church also barred people from marrying the widow of a blood relative or someone related to a godparent.

These consanguinity rules were so restrictive that most people had to ignore them, or else they would never marry. They provided a loophole for marriages to be annulled when divorce was not permitted. King Louis VII and Eleanor of Aquitaine had their marriage annulled after 15 years and two daughters because they were related to the fourth degree. The truth was that they had come to dislike and distrust each other, and Louis needed a son. Once their marriage was annulled, Eleanor married Henry of Anjou, who was related to her in the same degree as King Louis VII.

The Fourth Lateran Council of 1215 rolled back the consanguinity laws to forbid relatives of the fourth degree but permitted the fifth, sixth, and seventh degrees to marry. It maintained other aspects of these laws, and degrees of relationship continued to provide a means of annulment for the rich and powerful. Medieval Popes usually granted these annulments.

Before the Second Lateran Council of 1139, many priests were married. If a priest was elevated to a bishop, he was expected to set an example of celibacy, like a monk. Bishops had to place their wives in convents. It was not a period of strict enforcement, though. Some nobles and kings still had concubines, and unmarried men often kept a concubine they did not plan to marry. Since commoners could live together without any real ceremony and be considered man and wife, it was unclear what it meant to have a concubine. What rights did she have, when many legitimate wives did not have wedding ceremonies?

Church law, trying to grapple with what legal status to give a man's concubine, finally came to rest with the Fourth Lateran Council in 1215. Private weddings were no longer to be legally upheld. Weddings must be public, and they must be preceded by a priest's reading of the banns, the statement on intention to wed. The banns must be read on two successive Sundays, so anyone had time to object if the person was already married or if they were too closely related. From this time on, medieval weddings began to develop into a standard form all across Europe.

Difficulties of Consent

The primary concerns in weddings were personal consent, proper witnesses, and a proper distance of family relationship between the bride and groom. The community could ensure witnesses to the degree of relationship and to the ceremony itself. Ascertaining consent was more difficult. In a proper ceremony, both individuals had to say, clearly, that they consented to take the other person as a spouse. The two chief problems were child marriages and family coercion, when one party was forced to give consent that was not real.

Children of the aristocracy married much younger than commoners' children. Parents were concerned about establishing the correct family alliance in case they suddenly died and left the task to a guardian. Betrothals between small children took place, as did actual weddings; royal marriages could involve infants. Even when the marriages were arranged as though the individuals were adults, the girls were often no older than 13. It was not possible for such young children to give real consent. When small children were married, adults had to say the vows for them.

The church disapproved of child weddings, since the children could not consent. There were cases of young people who had been betrothed or married as small children but who refused to fulfill their obligation when they were old enough. The church upheld their right to refuse consent when they were of age. A general consensus developed in England, though it was not applied to royalty, that there should be no betrothals of **babies** under the age of seven. After the age of seven, betrothals could be contracted by the families, but the wedding itself must wait until the young people were fully of age to consent.

Commoners' children were traditionally well into their teens and 20s before they married. By the late Middle Ages, most marriages took place between young adults in their 20s. However, coercion could be just as much of a problem even when the property was relatively small. Many marriages were still more about money than about love. Love came after, if the couple treated each other well. Before the wedding, it was all about getting the best deal.

At the lowest level, even in the 13th century, English serfs who were considered unfree had to pay a fee, called the merchet, when a daughter married. The merchet was probably higher if the girl married a man outside the lord's manor, since he was losing a worker, so there was an incentive for the girl's family to persuade her to choose someone else. The fee was paid with goods such as chickens or bags of oats. A peasant girl's dowry at this time was her share of the inheritance and was usually household goods, **animals, clothing,** and, less commonly, money.

Middle-class marriages involved complicated negotiations over property, even if the property was not very valuable. Personal liking was a factor, but it was not the biggest one. The man's family was shopping for the best dowry they could find; they might have low-level negotiations with more than one girl's family. A girl with few siblings could receive a larger share of property and could make a better match. The families negotiated openly and bluntly, raising their requests on each side as they bargained for the present and future finances of the couple.

Because social hierarchy was such a very important part of the medieval world, young people often agreed with their parents' interest in the financial standing of the other families. If the young man or young woman did not know any of the individuals under discussion, or had only met them once, then the most exciting prospect of the match might be to live in a **stone house** or to have five cows. These advantages promised solid benefits of health and friendship in the future; girls married into a station in life, and this was the only moment of choice.

There were two halves to the negotiation, since both families were expected to contribute. The dower was the contribution of the man's family,

Until well after the close of the Middle Ages, a couple did not wear special clothes to their wedding. They wore the finest clothes they had, but expected the garments to be worn on many later occasions. This folk painting commemorates a medieval wedding in Sweden. (Uppsala University Collection, Sweden/Giraudon/The Bridgeman Art Library)

and the dowry was from the woman's family. The dower was a contractual amount of money or land that stayed with the woman if she became a widow and would then go to her children. In a simple family with a single husband and wife and children, this would not be a complicated business. But in some cases, a husband or wife married more than once, and there were stepchildren. The marriage contract specified what family property could go with her if she remarried as a widow and what property would stay in the man's family, perhaps reverting to his brother in the absence of sons. The dower was security for her future.

The importance of the dowry increased over the medieval period and became especially important in cities. In Italian **cities** like Florence, relatives left money to nieces, cousins, and granddaughters for their dowries, aware that even a small increase could make a big difference in a girl's future life. A dowry was one of the biggest investments a family could make in its posterity. By the 15th century in the cities, dowry amounts were highly competitive and took up much of a family's wealth. In rural places and in Northern Europe, dowries could be a mix of money, land, and possessions such as animals or **furniture.** It was also common to promise a girl a certain amount immediately and another portion on the death of her parents. Some women passed to their daughter items they had received in their dowries, like bronze pots or **silver** spoons.

Although families arranged marriages, the theory was that marriages were not to be forced, and both individuals were to be freely consenting. There was no way to inquire closely as to how free consent had been obtained, and in some cases, it was not completely free consent. Families often put heavy pressure on a girl to marry a man they preferred, even if he was much older than her. Some girls were pressured to marry a man as part of a deal to cancel a debt the family could not pay. Employers could put pressure on a man to marry a girl he had corrupted. Sometimes, even after a marriage contract was notarized, a relative or other party came forward to say that a prior marriage offer should prevent the wedding. Since verbal agreements were legally enforced, it could be difficult to disprove the truth of such a prior agreement.

Orphans posed a particularly difficult problem concerning consent, and it demonstrates why wealthy parents were so anxious not to leave unbetrothed orphans. Children of any social class who were wards of an individual, or of the town, could have their wardships bought and sold, even to strangers. Sometimes, a widowed mother had to buy the wardship of her own children to keep them with her. Sometimes a wardship was bought and sold several times, and the last one holding it when the child came of marrying age could determine the match. Men occasionally bought a wardship in order to marry the child to one of their own children. Sometimes the wardships were obtained solely for the fees associated with marrying the child off, if the child had no property. The wards themselves had no legal rights until they were of age.

In theory, an orphan had to consent to a match, but, in fact, orphans had no voice in the matter. Even aristocratic orphans, wards of a king or a bishop, were married off in a way that best profited the guardian. Poor orphans in a city, wards of the mayor, were married off for the sake of the fees paid for the wedding. Orphans with a small amount of property were desirable because the city released the property immediately, whereas living families might delay on the donation or change their minds.

Courtship was supposed to be the solution to these dilemmas. When a young woman, either a girl or a widow, was a desirable match, the man courted her to gain her consent. He met with her to talk and gave her gifts. Consent was the key point that made a marriage legal. In late medieval England, although marriages were supposed to be proclaimed in public, private marriages were still legally binding. The couple only had to say the words "I take you as my husband" or "I take you as my wife" before witnesses for the contract to be legally enforced. If either one could be temporarily swayed into speaking these words in a **tavern,** before witnesses, he or she would be in a legal, permanent union. Family consent was recommended as a protection; while families could be swayed by financial concerns, they often had good notions of how to protect a young person from a swindler. Girls were not supposed to allow a man's attentions until the family had screened him.

Wedding Ceremonies

Medieval weddings rarely took place inside churches. The banns had to be proclaimed in church, since it was a weekly public meeting. The ceremony, however, took place on a weekday, in the marketplace or on the church steps. It had to be in a visible place with witnesses and provide an opportunity for the general public to see.

Weddings could not take place during a major **fast** season. This ruled out the month of December, the season of Advent before Christmas. Lent, the 40 days before Easter, was ruled out, as was the period between Ascension Sunday and Pentecost, after Easter. Christmas and Easter were popular times for weddings, since they were **feast** seasons anyway.

The wedding ceremony in 14th-century England was typical of Northern Europe and only somewhat different from the Mediterranean region. The families and friends of the couple came to the church square; the couple wore their best clothes, but only royal weddings featured specially made garments. A priest usually officiated, although there was no church service unless the couple attended Mass afterward. (In upscale weddings, the family often paid for a celebratory Mass.)

Standing on the steps outside the church, the priest asked them both if they were legally free to marry. Were they both of age? Were they not within the forbidden degree of relationship? Were they both freely consenting to this union? Either before or after their vows, the priest joined the couple's hands.

A typical late medieval wedding vow said, "I take thee, Joan, to my wedded wife, to have and to hold, from this day forward, for better, for worse, for richer, for poorer, in sickness and in health, till death us depart, if holy church will ordain, and thereto I plight thee my troth." When both parties had spoken their vows, the priest blessed the wedding ring. Only the bride received a ring. The groom slipped it onto the bride's thumb, and then the first, second, and third fingers, saying, "In the name of the Father, the Son, and the Holy Ghost, with this ring I thee wed." The ring came to rest on the finger still known as the ring finger.

After their vows, the couple gave alms to the poor. Sometimes the priest delivered a homily on the meaning of marriage, and sometimes they went into the church for a celebratory Mass. Most weddings were followed by a feast as splendid as the family could afford. In the cases of **castle** families, the feast may have lasted more than one day. Entertainment by **minstrels** was customary. The guests also sang and danced to folk tunes.

The charivari was a folk custom that began in rural France but spread to other countries. Revelers wore masks and made loud noisy music to annoy a newly married couple. The revelers often ended up brawling, and they broke local noise ordinances. In some regions and social classes, the feasting guests also accompanied the bride and groom to their new bed.

In medieval Italy, dowries grew to be huge, and both betrothal parties and wedding feasts were expensive and showy. After the marriage contract had been notarized, the groom and his family made a procession through town to the bride's house. They made as much of a parade as possible, since it was a public announcement. There, they had a feast with entertainment, and it may have been the groom's first chance to meet the bride, who was often sheltered from public view.

As much as a year could pass between the betrothal ceremony and the wedding, also called the "ring day." On that day, the groom and his family came to the bride's house with a wedding ring. The wedding guests also attended, and the couple made public vows of consent to the marriage; they may have been in the public square, outside the bride's house, or on the church steps. The notary posed questions to ascertain consent, and then put the bride's hand toward the groom to receive a ring. If a priest were involved, he blessed the ring. The groom's party presented gifts to the bride, and the bride's family gave a feast. The bride's trousseau was delivered to the groom's home, but the bride did not go to his house yet. Gifts continued to go back and forth. Finally, the bride was transported to the husband's house, at night, with torches, on a white horse. In Rome, they stopped along the way at a church for Mass. With the bride at the groom's house, the marriage was finalized, but there could be feasts for several days.

Italian weddings were such displays of wealth that by the late Middle Ages, towns were passing sumptuary laws against the most conspicuous elements of the display. The wedding was an event for the community, and the family put on its best show. Even wealthy families borrowed or rented such luxuries as **tapestries,** a "cloth of gold" dress for the bride, drapery, vases, statues, and **paintings.** The bride's family courtyard was turned into a palace for a day.

Poorer families borrowed, rented, and displayed what they could; relatives contributed their finest things for the day. In a city neighborhood with cramped housing, the alley or street could be turned into the venue for the party. A 16th-century illustration of a poor man's wedding shows the neighborhood courtyard readied for the party. A sheet is suspended over a table that has napkins and pitchers of drink, and musicians play nearby for the dancing couple. Neighbors look out the window or stroll in. The **music** and dancing at an Italian wedding went late into the night.

In Christian Spain, during the era of Reconquest, girls had equal inheritance power and brought into the marriage a significant trousseau of household furnishings. The bride rode a horse in a public procession to the church, usually on Sunday, where the wedding was blessed by a priest. The groom's family paid for a feast.

See also: Feasts, Jews, Minstrels and Troubadours, Women.

Further Reading

Dean, Trevor, and K.J.P. Lowe, eds. *Marriage in Italy, 1300–1650.* Cambridge: Cambridge University Press, 1998.

Diehl, Daniel, and Mark Donnelly. *Medieval Celebrations.* Mechanicsburg, PA: Stackpole Books, 2001.

Gies, Frances, and Joseph Gies. *Daily Life in Medieval Times.* New York: Black Dog and Leventhal, 1990.

Gies, Frances, and Joseph Gies. *Life in a Medieval City.* New York: Harper and Row, 1969.

Gies, Frances, and Joseph Gies. *Marriage and Family in the Middle Ages.* New York: Harper and Row, 1987.

Hanawalt, Barbara A. *Growing Up in Medieval London: The Experience of Childhood in History.* New York: Oxford University Press, 1993.

McSheffrey, Shannon. *Love and Marriage in Late Medieval London.* Kalamazoo, MI: Medieval Institute Publications, 1995.

Newman, Paul. *Growing Up in the Middle Ages.* Jefferson, NC: McFarland 2007.

Orme, Nicholas. *Medieval Children.* New Haven, CT: Yale University Press, 2001.

Weights and Measures

Measurement standards varied regionally but were extremely important within each region and time. Merchants measured as accurately as possible, and cheating on a measurement was a crime. Prices were usually regulated by **guilds,** and this required them to have standard measurements. Although measures were determined locally, when international traders got involved, they developed tables of conversion. Weights and measures even differed depending on what goods were being measured. The Roman Empire introduced a standard weight, the libra, but in medieval Europe, standards varied across professions. Only in later times was there any attempt to unify these traditional measures.

Goods sold by weight came to be called avoirdupois, which means "having pounds" in French. Many common foodstuffs were avoirdupois goods. **Cloth** was sold by length and wine and wheat by volume. Officials at **fairs** and ports had to know how every trade measured its goods. They had to keep on hand the local, regional, or national standards of measurement and enforce their use. Weighing, taxing, and certifying were big business in the Middle Ages.

Weights

No situation could be as thoroughly confusing as standards of weight in medieval Europe. They varied both regionally and by trade. One medieval European weight was the centner, which was approximately 100 pounds. The centner's weight varied, though; some of these weights have survived into modern times and can be compared. A centner of **iron** or lard was heavier than a centner used in the **food** marketplace. A centner of yarn was different from a centner of silk. In medieval Paris, in the 12th century, there were two royal scales. One weighed only wax (in *poids de la cire*), and the other weighed everything else (in *poids-le-roy*). In England, weights were taken in stones, pounds, and ounces, but when weighing **silver** as **coins,** they were pounds, shillings, and pence. A stone of **glass** was much smaller and lighter than a stone of **lead.**

As Europe became more industrial and commercial, rulers stepped in to regulate the measurements in their territory. The English Magna Carta, in the 12th century, stated that the realm needed standard weights and measures, rather than local ones, but nothing was really enforced. At the close of the Middle Ages, many kings were still trying to outlaw local weights and impose their royal standards. In 1340, Edward III sent standard bushels, gallons, and pounds into each county so that they could regulate their weights.

When national weights were successfully imposed, their enforcement still depended on local officials. **Cities** had officially certified balances and measures. The mayor leased them to citizens who made a living charging fees for on-site measurement at markets and ports. (In London, the smaller balance was traditionally leased to a **woman** as a way of helping a widow make a living.) Businesses then used the official balances to calibrate and certify their personal ones. The weights that businesses used had to be marked with an official mark by the blacksmith or balance maker who cast them. In some places, these personal weights were shaped into figures such as a lion or a rider on a horse. This tended to be an early, primitive practice, persisting in Scandinavia after Southern Europe had standardized to square, disc, or bell-shaped weights. Large weights always had a ring on top so that they could be lifted with a lever, if needed.

Weights were used with small and large balances, also called beams. Small balances measured in pounds, while the great beam measured by the hundredweight. Great beams were used in wholesale and importation businesses. The counterweights for both sizes were carefully regulated by each city. They were made of metal and carried an official stamp. In earliest use, they were iron, but the standard became brass. Cheaper, less official weights were made of lead.

Balances came in the form of pan balances and steelyard balances. Pan balances had two arms with pans, balanced on a fulcrum, with individual weights to balance the merchant's goods. Steelyard balances may have been promoted by Hanseatic League merchants, who dealt in very large quantities. On a steelyard balance, the horizontal beam hangs from a fulcrum, but this ring is not placed in the center. It is closer to one side, which has a pan or hook for the load to be measured. The longer arm has a weight that can be moved closer or farther from the fulcrum to balance the load. The weight does not change, but its position on the arm tells the measurement.

A city market had an official great beam balance with an arm made of iron or heavy timber. Small balances that weighed pounds and ounces were usually of brass, while tiny jewelers' balances could be made of silver or ivory. Fine balances used silk strings, usually green, to hang the balance pans. The great beam often had no pans, but rather used hooks and chains to hang the heavy goods. Merchants' balances often had wooden or iron pans. The finest scales for apothecaries and jewelers used ivory, glass, or some other easily cleaned substance.

Merchants who sold underweight goods found the goods confiscated, and they were also fined. Confiscated bread and wine were used to supply the prisons and some public employees. In some periods, public pillories were used to shame dishonest merchants. They were displayed with their dishonest wares hung around their necks, and citizens could mock or pelt them.

The Port of London became a highly organized weighing station by the 13th and 14th centuries. It was the first point of contact for all inspection

Capan.

Most daily commerce depended on accurate weights and measures. Anything not sold by volume or length was probably sold by weight, so nearly every shop had a set of balance pans and weights. Here, cured meat such as sausage is being weighed for a customer. (Bibliotheque Nationale, Paris/Art Media/StockphotoPro) and taxation, as well as for regulating foreigners entering the city. The port dealt only in wholesale goods. As these goods came into the port, the customs officials were ready with a team of men and horses to move them straight to the weighing area. Grain kept busy a team of eight Master Meters, each with assistants, horses, and sacks. The measuring teams had official bushels and strikes (rods for leveling bushels). Bakers and brewers came to buy their grain as it was measured out. **Salt,** too, was measured in bushels by its own team of officials and then loaded into sacks. Buyers and sellers paid the meters directly for their services.

Not all weighing was avoirdupois, of course. Some professions depended heavily on being able to weigh goods accurately. Apothecaries and medical doctors prescribed small amounts of **spices** and other substances using a system of ounces and drams. The "Troy weight" was another system of fine measurement from Troyes, in Champagne. It stipulated 20 pennyweight to the ounce and 12 (not 16) ounces in a pound. The Italian spice trade had a sophisticated system of measurements. More than 200 different spices could be sold in very large amounts or in very fine measures.

A goldsmith's set of weights and balances was specialized. The weighing of **gold** and silver coins was the measurement demanding the most accuracy. The production of accurate coin scales pushed royal governments increasingly into the regulation of weights. Coin scales could be either pan balances or steelyard balances. Some were made to measure one type of coin alone; the other pan was a set weight, and an indicator at the fulcrum showed whether the coin balanced it and by how many grains of gold it was off. The traditional measure of gold, the carat, was at first a carob seed.

Volume and Length

Dry volumes were somewhat less trade specific than other measures. In England, at least, the basic dry measure was the bushel, the standard basket for a packhorse. The peck was a quarter of a bushel, while eight bushels made a quarter. Charcoal was always sold in quarters. By the 14th century, bushels were carefully standardized in terms of the basic English liquid measure, the gallon. One bushel was equivalent to eight gallons. Most dry goods sold by volume worked well with bushels, but hay required larger measures. Hay came in wagon- and cartloads, but also in half loads and quarters and in smaller bundles called boteles and fesses.

Liquid measures were not simple, although in theory they became standardized to the gallon. Ale came in **barrels,** but beer and ale barrels were not the same size. Beer barrels were larger, perhaps because they hewed to German standards. English coopers made most barrels to a standard of 30 gallons, which were used as ale barrels. Barrels were also used for soap, oil, and eels. Smaller English liquid measures went from gallon to quart to gill, which was about a modern cup. Large liquid measures included other kinds of containers, from tubs and **buckets** to various sizes of butts and casks. Ale in small quantities came in wooden quart containers made by turners, a special craft profession.

Wine was sold in special large barrels called tuns; tuns held 252 standard gallons of wine. At the Port of London, a team of 12 men had to be on hand to manage incoming tuns of wine. They had to be rolled into warehouses, sometimes near at hand and sometimes not so near.

The standard medieval lengths were the foot and the mile. A fathom was six feet, a mile was 5,000 feet, and a league was two miles. In England, land was measured chiefly with the furlong, the distance a peasant typically plowed in one direction. In modern times, the furlong is defined as 660 feet, one-eighth of a mile, but the medieval furlong was shorter. It was not related to the mile at all. The furlong was divided into 40 rods. When using a heavy moldboard plow, peasants always farmed in long strips, not square fields. For that reason, the acre was defined as one furlong (40 rods) by 4 rods. It was about how much land a yoke of oxen could plow in a day.

Cloth measurement was another regional jumble. Officially, all medieval cloth was measured in yards and ells, but the ell varied. Since the cloth industry was centered in Flanders, and its main selling took place at the Champagne **fairs,** these measures became the most international. In Troyes, a bolt of cloth was 28 ells, but in Ypres, it had to be 29. At the Provins fairs, cloth was measured by cords (12 ells) and lengths (12 cords). As if the bolts and lengths were not confusing enough, the ell varied. The Troyes ell was 3 feet, 8 inches, but the Provins ell was 2 feet, 6 inches. They used a system of feet and inches in which 12 inches made a foot, but the inches were also broken into 12 parts, called lines. Each fair had an official iron ruler, and merchants had wooden rulers that had to match it. The Champagne fairs came to an end before the industry could decide on a universal standard.

See also: Barrels and Buckets, Beverages, Cities, Coins, Fairs.

Further Reading

Egan, Geoff. *The Medieval Household: Daily Living c. 1150–c. 1450.* Woodbridge, UK: Boydell Press, 2010.

Gies, Frances, and Joseph Gies. *Life in a Medieval City.* New York: Harper and Row, 1969.

Graham, J.T. *Weights and Measures and Their Marks.* Princes Risborough, UK: Shire Publications, 2008.

Kilby, Kenneth. *The Cooper and His Trade.* Fresno, CA: Linden Publishing, 1989.

Kisch, Bruno. *Scales and Weights: A Historical Outline.* New Haven, CT: Yale University Press, 1965.

Milne, Gustav. *The Port of Medieval London.* Stroud, UK: Tempus Publishing, 2006.

Nicholson, Edward. *Men and Measures: A History of Weights and Measures, Ancient and Modern (1912)*. Whitefish, MT: Kessinger Publishing, 2008.

Wheels. *See* Wagons and Carts

Windows. *See* Glass

Wine. *See* Beverages

Women

The status of women in the Middle Ages varied with place, time, and social class. Of these three, social class was the most outstanding factor determining the role a woman could play in life. Changes in women's overall status came about partly because the middle class—merchants and craftsmen—grew during the later Middle Ages, and its treatment of women became more dominant. In each period, and in every place, we can distinguish three basic classes: the landowners, the townsmen who worked with their hands or as merchants, and the country folk who farmed. It was very difficult, if not impossible, to move up in class.

Land inheritance and dowries shaped the lives of girls in the upper class. They had no freedom to choose whom to marry and little freedom to decide even whether or not to marry. Parents or guardians chose husbands for girls, and if a girl married someone who was not approved, she could be (and often was) disinherited. In many parts of Europe, upper-class girls were married very young. Their parents could not be certain of living long enough to marry the girls at older ages and did not want the task to fall to a guardian, so they married off children as young as six. A child bride moved to her new husband's home and finished growing up there. Her husband was almost always a child, as well, and became a playmate.

In most parts of medieval Europe, the girl's dowry was a large determinant of whom she married. Girls from families that could not afford a large dowry could see their daughter slip into poverty by marrying badly or remaining single. In the later Middle Ages, as dowries skyrocketed, grandparents left money to girls in their wills, specifically giving to their dowries. Although the girls might never see a penny of this money themselves, it increased their chances of finding a respectable married home. Girls in the landowning class often had farms or manors as dowries, and in the highest-ranking families, they could bring small duchies or even kingdoms.

Married women of this class, the ladies of the **castles** and manors, had many responsibilities. They oversaw the household **servants,** and they

The castle lady lived a life of comfort and ease, but she also lived under very strict rules of conduct with little freedom of movement. The illustration is from a poem written by Christine de Pizan, one of the few successful women authors of the Middle Ages. A widow who had to support her children, she began writing poems, stories, and advice. The new availability of paper and secular copyists allowed her to sell enough books to become reasonably prosperous. (Paul Lacroix, *Moeurs, Usage et Costumes au Moyen Age et a l'Epoque de la Renaissance*, 1878)

often oversaw the education of girls from other families. Depending on the place and the era, many of these ladies kept busy with necessary crafts such as spinning, weaving, and **embroidery.** Some brewed medicinal potions or ale themselves. Each manor or castle was a self-sustaining farm, as much as it could be. A lady had to be at least somewhat familiar with farming, all the crafts, building repair, education, and buying and selling.

When the lord of the manor or castle was away from home, the lady took over all his oversight responsibility. She hired and fired, bought and sold, and even took over the defense of the castle or **house.** She was his representative in all matters. During the **Crusades,** husbands could be away for years, if they came back at all. There was a corresponding rise in the rights and freedoms of these ladies. In some places where women had been barred from directly inheriting land, laws were amended to permit widows or daughters to inherit.

The medieval lady's education varied in place and time. In the early period, while literacy was uncommon and while barbarian invasions kept survival as the primary focus, very few women could read. Only the daughters of some kings such as Charlemagne learned to read. By the 11th century, most upper-class girls were learning to read. They needed to read in order to amuse and educate themselves and to keep their husbands' accounts when they were in charge. Many girls learned some form of **music** and **dance.** They learned a strict code of manners: how to greet, converse, and eat, as well as how to handle difficult social situations. The lady's role in public was to appear beautiful and serene and to give no sign of trouble if she was anxious or unhappy. A lady's stressful face might give away her husband's secret troubles.

The condition of widows varied greatly. In some places and in some eras, a widow had few rights. In 12th-century England, unless a widow bought back the right to raise her children and give them in marriage, they were removed, regardless of age, and placed with a guardian. Guardianships could be sold several times until the child came of age, so many widows tried to buy back these rights. In England, they automatically received one-third of a husband's estate to keep, but no more. In other places, they could retain the whole estate and live with independence, or they could return to their family's home to be cared for or remarried.

The image we have of the medieval lady is a fairy-tale construction blended with truth. Most upper-class women led difficult lives, although they were surrounded by luxury. Their marriages were often unkind, since they were matched on the basis of land, money, or power. But they lived on a plane above the noise and dirt of the classes below them, and they left behind an impression of magical elegance. Some of this image comes from the romances and **troubadour** songs. Many romances told the stories of beautiful, refined, intelligent, sweet ladies who won the love of kings and **knights** and who suffered for this love. While some real ladies led such lives, most did not.

Women in towns had fewer restrictions than castle ladies. They worked hard, starting in childhood, but had more control over their own destinies. Some town girls became apprentices on their own, in some eras and places. More often, girls helped in the family trade and then helped their husbands in their trade. Wives worked next to their husbands in all kinds of crafts, and the craft **guilds** made exceptions for wives, daughters, and some female servants to work in trades that were generally barred to women. Widows often carried on a husband's craft or business.

Cities included a wide range of material wealth. Some women in town were servants, living in a back room of the house and never earning enough to move into anything better. These women tended (and breastfed) **babies,** cleaned, washed, sewed, and did all the laborious work of a house. Their wages went up and down as conditions changed. Sometimes their parents were paid for their labor so that they helped support younger siblings at home. Some worked to save for a dowry. Being a servant was still considered better than living in poverty in the country, and servants could move up to better employment if they had skill and good recommendations.

At the top of the urban scale were the merchants' wives, who might live with more luxury than castle ladies. By the end of the Middle Ages, merchants' town houses had every possible comfort. The sumptuary laws tried to prevent their wives from dressing like noblewomen, which shows that they could afford it, and many were doing so. Less wealthy crafts supported women and families on a more modest scale. They were busy and generally lived in financial security.

The trades of spinning and brewing were dominated by women. Many town women made and sold beer or ale out of their homes. Every woman kept a spinning distaff nearby and used wasted minutes to add to a growing spindle of thread. Some women spun for a living. Our term *spinster,* meaning an unmarried woman, comes from this large group of women who kept themselves alive without the support of a husband, industriously spinning yarn and thread at all hours. While weaving was a man's job, lace making and silk weaving were dominated by women.

Medieval farm workers formed the backbone of the economy. They were either free or unfree. Unfree peasants were not exactly **slaves,** but they did not have the freedom to move away or alter their terms of employment. They were born to live on a manor, and they stayed on that manor unless they were granted freedom or unless they paid an annual fee for permission to live in a town. We also call these unfree farmers "serfs." Free farmers were not necessarily better off financially, but they did not owe the same obligations to a landowner and could move if they chose.

The women of these farm families, both free and unfree, had very few options. They worked hard next to the men, helping sow and harvest and care for the **animals.** They cut firewood and hauled water. In addition, they cared for children and made as much as possible of what their family would need through spinning, weaving, and sewing. They cooked and brewed, and they gathered seasonal fruit and nuts. Most peasant families were very poor, and the lives of these women were hard. Some obtained permission to work in a nearby town as servants, but otherwise, they married locally and carried on with peasant farming life as they had always known it. Those who lived near a market were often able to earn extra money by brewing ale, like town women.

During the early 12th century, women began trying to join or imitate men's religious orders. Some of the **monastic** orders welcomed and protected them, and others did not. Throughout the 12th and 13th centuries,

Poor women generally had more freedom of expression and travel than castle women, but they also had ceaseless hard work. These women are helping with the daily task of milking the sheep. They also made the butter and cheese, spun the sheep's wool, and kept up innumerable other chores such as making ale, tending children, gathering wood, and sewing. (The British Library/StockphotoPro)

the attitude of the Popes changed. Some viewed women's vocations with suspicion, while others admitted that women, too, could be called to a religious life and were mainly concerned with their support, protection, and regulation.

Early orders of nuns were informal. Many wealthy young women in Flanders and northern France left their homes and refused marriages, instead choosing lives of complete poverty in the order of Beguines. The Beguines had no property and lived in huts of their own choosing, rather than in a convent. Saint Clare, their founder, was a friend of Saint Francis and considered herself personally to be under his pastoral care, although he resisted any oversight of women.

As more women clamored to join orders, the **church** had to make formal provision for them. The Cistercian order of monks admitted women's convents to its rule, provided that they follow the same rules of order and discipline. Cistercian convents multiplied in France and Spain, probably because the Cathar religious movement, which had been suppressed violently, allowed for religious vocations of women; the church needed to supply this need in order to rule out a Cathar revival.

By the later Middle Ages, many convents owned vast property, served as boarding **schools** to the children of the rich, or took in society women who did not have a serious vocation. Unwelcome daughters could be placed in a convent, without regard to their wishes. Poor and serious convents still existed, but there were many nuns who did not take the religious life seriously and who gave convents a bad reputation. They kept pets, visited men, and neglected chapel.

A few women lived unusual lives for their times. Some were religious—abbesses who wrote well-known books. Italian legend said that a woman taught at the **medical** school in Salerno in the 11th century. Her name was Trotula, and although a real person cannot be positively identified, medical books under her name circulated during the 12th and 13th centuries.

Two French ladies lived unusual, famous lives in the 15th century. Christine de Pizan was born in 1364. When her husband, a French court secretary, suddenly died, Christine turned to writing love ballads to support her family. In time she became one of the most successful writers in France. In 1405 she published *The Book of the City of Ladies* and later wrote *The Three Virtues,* both of which discussed the proper lives and roles of women. A famous illustration shows her offering her newest **book** to the queen.

Joan of Arc is perhaps the most famous medieval woman, although her life was very short. As a teenager, she saw visions of **saints** who urged her to go to the court at Chinon and present herself as a military commander. The uncrowned French king Charles VII was on the verge of losing his kingdom to combined English and Burgundian forces. Wearing white **armor** and urging confident, offensive action, Joan led the armies of France and Aragon to several victories. After King Charles VII captured Paris and was crowned, Burgundian forces captured Joan. King Charles did not ransom her, and she was sent to the English to be tried as a heretic for hearing voices and wearing men's **clothing.** Joan was burned at the stake in 1431.

See also: Babies, Beverages, Minstrels and Troubadours, Monasteries, Weddings.

Further Reading

Bennett, Judith M. *Ale, Beer, and Brewsters in England: Women's Work in a Changing World.* New York: Oxford University Press, 1999.

Bennett, Judith M. *Women in the Medieval English Countryside: Gender and Household in Brigstock before the Plague.* New York: Oxford University Press, 1989.

Gies, Frances, and Joseph Gies. *Daily Life in Medieval Times.* New York: Black Dog and Leventhal, 1990.

Hanawalt, Barbara. *The Wealth of Wives: Women, Law, and Economy in Late Medieval London.* New York: Oxford University Press, 2007.

Hanawalt, Barbara, ed. *Women and Work in Pre-Industrial Europe.* Bloomington: Indiana University Press, 1986.

Power, Eileen. *Medieval Women.* Cambridge: Cambridge University Press, 1975.

Singman, Jeffrey. *Daily Life in Medieval Europe.* Westport, CT: Greenwood Press, 1999.

Shahar, Shulamith. *The Fourth Estate: A History of Women in the Middle Ages.* New York: Routledge, 1984.
Stuard, Susan Mosher, ed. *Women in Medieval Society.* Philadelphia: University of Pennsylvania Press, 1976.
Wilson, Katharina M., and Nadia Margolis, eds. *Women in the Middle Ages: An Encyclopedia.* Westport, CT: Greenwood Press, 2004.

Z

Zoos

Many kings and noblemen (and even some Popes) kept menageries of exotic **animals,** following the example of Roman emperors. The Roman emperors used some of the animals for public displays at the Circus. Medieval monarchs rarely, if ever, had fighting exhibitions in the Roman style. Some had public parades of their animals to show their magnificence. A favorite theme was to have exotic animals paraded with foreigners from Arabia or Ethiopia in order to suggest that the king was dominant over these far-off regions.

The earliest medieval zoos were in **Muslim** Spain. The caliphs in Cordoba kept a large zoo of exotic animals, many imported from Africa and Asia. It was surrounded by a moat to keep the animals secure. In the ninth century, Charlemagne kept a menagerie at Aachen, in a **climate** colder than most of the animals were adapted for. The caliph of Baghdad sent an elephant for his collection, which had to make a long journey on foot over the Alps and only lived a few years. Charlemagne also kept camels, lions and monkeys, and a few bears.

Beginning with William I, the English kings kept a menagerie that was housed at the Tower of London by the middle of the 13th century. The records are not clear as to which animals lived there at which times, nor how they were fed or cared for. One chronicler stated that Henry I had a victory parade in Normandy that included a leopard riding a **horse** and a panther pulling a chariot. Another reported that King Henry II of England kept a menagerie of exotic animals at his palace at Woodstock. Reportedly, he had lions, leopards, camels, and a porcupine.

Henry III kept a pair of leopards or lions at the Tower of London, a gift of Emperor Frederick II of Germany. His son, Prince Edward, became known as the "Leopard Prince" in association with both the **heraldic** and the menagerie cats. Henry III added a polar bear, a gift from the king of Norway. The keepers allowed the white bear to swim in the Thames on a leash, catching its own **fish,** but kept it muzzled the rest of the time. In 1254, Henry's brother-in-law, King Louis IX of France, sent him an elephant. It lived in a special house in London and was eagerly viewed by the public, but it did not live more than a few years.

The Tower of London continued to have a royal menagerie, probably housed mainly in the gatehouse of the Lion Gate. As animals died, they replaced the lions, leopards, and bears, with at least one more polar bear making its appearance in the reign of Edward I. Tower records show that each lion ate one quarter of a sheep every day, making them very expensive pets. By the 15th century, the collection was not large, but it was still in existence. The Lion Tower began to admit some paying visitors to see the animals. King Henry VI decreed that in lieu of a cash fee, visitors could offer

Modern eyes, used to seeing African lions in films and at public zoos, would not consider Villard de Honnecourt's sketch of a lion very lifelike. Honnecourt was clearly working from a real lion, but his impression of the lion had been shaped by standard paintings that were not accurate. It was rare to have a chance to watch one long enough to observe the shape of its facial features, the way it moved, and its proportions. Private zoos offered the sole opportunity, but only on rare occasions. (Bibliotheque Nationale, Paris/Giraudon/The Bridgeman Art Library)

an animal, such as a dog, cat, or sheep, to feed the lions. In 1436, the lions died, presumably of an illness, and the collection had to be started again.

The largest royal menagerie on the European continent may have been the one owned by Frederick II of Germany in the 13th century. He kept it at his palace in Palermo, Sicily. Frederick was a highly educated, intelligent man with a keen interest in science. He kept lions, leopards, camels, elephants, and a giraffe and sometimes displayed them in parades. The kings of France also had menageries at some of their castles: elephants, bears, lions, and porcupines are among those recorded, as well as exotic birds. King Charles V kept a porpoise in a pool, and even the duc de Berry kept bears. The 14th-century Popes who lived in splendor at Avignon kept exotic animals, including peacocks, ostriches, and camels, as well as the common lions and bears.

Italian **city** menageries kept many lions. Medieval Rome, like ancient Rome, kept lions as a symbol of its dominance. Florence kept a pit of 24 lions and sometimes used them in fighting displays against other animals. Venice's lions were observed as the lioness gave birth to three cubs, and to everyone's amazement, the cubs were born alive. Bestiaries had explained confidently that lion cubs are born dead, and are licked back to life after three days, as a picture of Jesus's death and resurrection. Once

Europeans had even a limited opportunity to observe lions and other animals firsthand, they stopped trusting the ancient myths passed down by the bestiaries.

See also: Animals.

Further Reading

Hahn, Daniel. *The Tower Menagerie.* New York: Penguin, 2004.

Kisling, Vernon N., Jr., ed. *Zoo and Aquarium History: Ancient Animal Collections to Zoological Gardens.* Boca Raton, FL: CRC Press, 2001.

Resl, Brigitte, ed. *A Cultural History of Animals in the Medieval Age.* New York: Berg, 2007.

Bibliography

Aczel, Amir D. *The Riddle of the Compass*. Orlando, FL: Harcourt, 2001.

Adamson, Melitta Weiss. *Food in Medieval Times*. Westport, CT: Greenwood Press, 2004.

Amphlett, Hilda. *Hats: A History of Fashion in Headwear*. Mineola, NY: Dover Publications, 2003.

Andrea, Alfred J. *The Medieval Record: Sources of Medieval History*. Boston: Houghton Mifflin, 1997.

Arnold, Hugh. *Stained Glass of the Middle Ages in England and France*. London: Adam and Charles Black, 1939.

Aromatico, Andrea. *Alchemy: The Great Secret*. New York: Harry N. Abrams, 2000.

Asbridge, Thomas. *The Crusades: The Authoritative History of the War for the Holy Land*. New York: Harper Collins, 2010.

Ashe, Geoffrey. *The Discovery of King Arthur*. New York: Anchor Books, 1985.

Aspin, Chris. *The Woolen Industry*. Princes Risborough, UK: Shire Publications, 1982.

Aubrey, Elizabeth. *The Music of the Troubadours*. Bloomington: Indiana University Press, 1996.

Baines, Patrician. *Flax and Linen*. Princes Risborough, UK: Shire Publications, 1985.

Bayard, Tania. *Sweet Herbs and Sundry Flowers: Medieval Gardens and the Gardens of the Cloisters*. New York: Metropolitan Museum of Art, 1997.

Beadle, Richard, ed. *The Cambridge Companion to Medieval English Theatre*. Cambridge: Cambridge University Press, 2001.

Beech, George. *Was the Bayeux Tapestry Made in France? The Case for Saint-Florent of Saumur*. New York: Palgrave MacMillan, 2005.

Bibliography

Bennett, Richard. *History of Corn-Milling.* Vol. 2, *Watermills and Windmills.* Ithaca, NY: Cornell University Press, 1898.

Benson, Anna, and Neil Warburton. *Looms and Weaving.* Princes Risborough, UK: Shire Publications, 1986.

Benton, Janetta Rebold. *Holy Terrors: Gargoyles on Medieval Buildings.* New York: Abbeville Press, 1997.

Berger, Anna Maria Busse. *Medieval Music and the Art of Memory.* Berkeley: University of California Press, 2005.

Bergin, Thomas G. *Boccaccio.* New York: Viking Press, 1981.

Biddle, Martin, ed. *King Arthur's Round Table.* Woodbridge, UK: Boydell Press, 2000.

Binding, Gunther. *Medieval Building Techniques.* Stroud, UK: Tempus Publishing, 2001.

Binski, Paul. *Painters.* Toronto: University of Toronto Press, 1991.

Blackburn, Graham. *The Illustrated Encyclopedia of Ships, Boats, Vessels, and Other Water-Borne Craft.* Woodstock, NY: Overlook Press, 1978.

Bogin, Meg. *The Women Troubadours.* New York: W.W. Norton, 1980.

Bork, Robert, and Andrea Kann, eds. *The Art, Science, and Technology of Medieval Travel.* Burlington, VT: Ashgate Publishing, 2008.

Borst, Arno. *The Ordering of Time: From the Ancient Computus to the Modern Computer.* Cambridge: Polity Press, 1993.

Bouchard, Constance Brittain, ed. *Knights in History and Legend.* Buffalo, NY: Firefly Books, 2009.

Bouchard, Constance Brittain. *Strong of Body, Brave, and Noble: Chivalry and Society in Medieval France.* Ithaca, NY: Cornell University Press, 1998.

Brooke, Christopher. *The Age of the Cloister: The Story of Monastic Life in the Middle Ages.* Mahwah, NJ: Hidden Spring Books, 2003.

Broudy, Eric. *The Book of Looms.* Lebanon, NH: University Press of New England, 1979.

Brown, David J. *Bridges: Three Thousand Years of Defying Nature.* Buffalo, NY: Firefly Books, 2005.

Brown, Michelle P. *Understanding Illuminated Manuscripts: A Guide to Technical Terms.* Malibu, CA: J. Paul Getty Museum, 1994.

Brown, Michelle P. *The World of the Luttrell Psalter.* London: British Library, 2006.

Brown, R. Allen. *The Architecture of Castles: A Visual Guide.* New York: Facts on File, 1984.

Brown, R. Allen. *Castles: A History and Guide.* Poole, UK: Blandford Press, 1980.

Brown, Sarah, and David O'Connor. *Glass-Painters.* Toronto: University of Toronto Press, 1991.

Bruton, Eric. *The History of Clocks and Watches.* Edison, NJ: Chartwell Books, 2004.

Butt, John J. *Daily Life in the Age of Charlemagne.* Westport, CT: Greenwood Press, 2002.

Caldwell, John. *Medieval Music.* Bloomington: Indiana University Press, 1978.

Cameron, David Kerr. *The English Fair.* Stroud, UK: Sutton Publishing, 1998.

Campbell, James W. P., and Will Pryce. *Brick: A World History.* London: Thames and Hudson, 2003.

Campbell, Margaret. *Medieval Jewelry in Europe, 1100–1500.* London: V&A Publishing, 2009.

Cantor, Norman F. *In the Wake of the Plague: The Black Death and the World It Made.* New York: Simon and Schuster, 2001.

Cantor, Norman F., ed. *The Medieval Reader.* New York: Harper Collins, 1994.

Casson, Lionel. *Libraries in the Ancient World.* New Haven, CT: Yale University Press, 2001.

Chambers, E. K. *Arthur of Britain.* New York: October House, 1969.

Chambers, E. K. *The Mediaeval Stage.* 2 vols. London: Oxford University Press, 1903.

Charny, Geoffroi de. *A Knight's Own Book of Chivalry.* Philadelphia: University of Pennsylvania Press, 2005.

Cherry, John. *Goldsmiths.* Toronto: University of Toronto Press, 1992.

Cipolla, Carlo M. *Before the Industrial Revolution: European Society and Economy, 1000–1700.* New York: Norton, 1976.

Clark, John, ed. *The Medieval Horse and its Equipment.* Woodbridge, UK: Boydell Press, 2004.

Clutton-Brock, Juliet. *Horse Power.* Cambridge, MA: Harvard University Press, 1992.

Cohen, Mark. *Under Crescent and Cross: The Jews in the Middle Ages.* Trenton, NJ: Princeton University Press, 2008.

Coldstream, Nicola. *Masons and Sculptors.* Toronto: University of Toronto Press, 1991.

Coldstream, Nicola. *Medieval Architecture.* Oxford: Oxford University Press, 2002.

Cook, Martin. *Medieval Bridges.* Princes Risborough, UK: Shire Publications, 1998.

Cooper, Emanuel. *Ten Thousand Years of Pottery.* Philadelphia: University of Pennsylvania Press, 2000.

Cormack, Robin. *Byzantine Art.* Oxford: Oxford University Press, 2000.

Cosman, Madeleine Pelner. *Fabulous Feasts: Medieval Cookery and Ceremony.* New York: George Braziller, 1995.

Cosman, Madeleine Pelner. *Medieval Holidays and Festivals.* New York: Charles Scribner's Sons, 1981.

Crocker, Glenys. *The Gunpowder Industry.* Princes Risborough, UK: Shire Publications, 1999.

Crouch, David. *Tournament.* New York: Hambledon, 2006.

Crowfoot, Elisabeth, Frances Pritchard, and Kay Staniland. *Textiles and Clothing, 1150–1450.* Woodbridge, UK: Boydell Press, 2001.

Cruz, Joan Carroll. *Relics.* Huntington, IN: Our Sunday Visitor, 1984.

Cullingford, Benita. *Chimneys and Chimney Sweeps.* Princes Risborough, UK: Shire Publications, 2003.

Cummins, John. *The Art of Medieval Hunting: The Hound and the Hawk.* Edison, NJ: Castle Books, 1998.

Cunnington, C. Willett, and Phillis Cunnington. *The History of Underclothes.* London: Faber and Faber, 1981.

Cust, A. M. *The Ivory Workers of the Middle Ages.* London: George Bell and Sons, 1902.

Darr, Alan Phipps, and Tracey Albainy. *Woven Splendor: Five Centuries of European Tapestry in the Detroit Institute of Arts.* Detroit: Detroit Institute of Arts Founders Society, 1996.

Davidson, Audrey Eckdahl. *Holy Week and Easter Ceremonies and Dramas from Medieval Sweden.* Kalamazoo, MI: Medieval Institute Publications, 1990.

Davis, R.H.C. *The Medieval Warhorse.* London: Thames and Hudson, 1989.

De Courtais, Georgine. *Women's Hats, Headdresses, and Hairstyles.* London: Batsford, 1986.

De Hamel, Christopher. *Scribes and Illuminators.* Toronto: University of Toronto Press, 1992.

Dean, Trevor. *The Towns of Italy in the Later Middle Ages.* Manchester, UK: Manchester University Press, 2000.

Dean, Trevor, and K.J.P. Lowe, eds. *Marriage in Italy, 1300–1650.* Cambridge: Cambridge University Press, 1998.

Dennys, Rodney. *The Heraldic Imagination.* New York: Clarkson N. Potter, 1975.

DeWindt, Edwin Brezette. *A Slice of Life: Selected Documents of Medieval English Peasant Experience.* Kalamazoo, MI: Medieval Institute Publications, 1996.

Diehl, Daniel, and Mark Donnelly. *Constructing Medieval Furniture.* Mechanicsburg, PA: Stackpole Books, 1997.

Diehl, Daniel, and Mark Donnelly. *Medieval Celebrations.* Mechanicsburg, PA: Stackpole Books, 2001.

Diehl, Daniel, and Mark Donnelly. *Medieval Furniture: Plans and Instructions for Historical Reproductions.* Mechanicsburg, PA: Stackpole Books, 1999.

Diehl, Daniel, and Mark Donnelly. *Siege: Castles at War.* Dallas, TX: Taylor Publishing, 1998

Dodsworth, Roger. *Glass and Glassmaking.* Princes Risborough, UK: Shire Publishing, 1996.

Dohrn-van Rossum, Gerhard. *History of the Hour: Clocks and Modern Temporal Orders.* Chicago: University of Chicago Press, 1996.

Donaldson, Gerald. *Books.* New York: Van Nostrand Reinhold, 1981.

Drogin, Marc. *Medieval Calligraphy: Its History and Technique.* Mineola, NY: Dover Publications, 1989.

Duby, Georges. *Medieval Art: Foundations of a New Humanism, 1280–1440.* Geneva, Switzerland: Editions d'Art Albert Skira S.A., 1995.

Duby, Georges. *Sculpture: The Great Art of the Middle Ages from the Fifth to the Fifteenth Century.* New York: Rizzoli International Publications, 1990.

Duncan, David Ewing. *Calendar: Humanity's Epic Struggle to Determine a True and Accurate Year.* New York: Avon Books, 1998.

Edlin, Herbert L. *Trees and Man.* New York: Columbia University Press, 1976.

Egan, Geoff. *The Medieval Household: Daily Living c. 1150–c. 1450.* Woodbridge, UK: Boydell Press, 2010.

Egan, Geoff, and Frances Pritchard. *Dress Accessories, 1150–1450.* Woodbridge, UK: Boydell Press, 2002.

Ehrenberg, Ralph E. *Mapping the World: An Illustrated History of Cartography.* Washington, DC: National Geographic, 2005.

Ellenblum, Ronnie. *Crusader Castles and Modern Histories*. Cambridge: Cambridge University Press, 2007

Emery, Anthony. *Discovering Medieval Houses*. Princes Risborough, UK: Shire Publications, 2007.

Epstein, Steven. *Wills and Wealth in Medieval Genoa, 1150–1250*. Cambridge, MA: Harvard University Press, 1984.

Evans, Joan. *A History of Jewelry, 1100–1870*. Mineola, NY: Dover Publications, 1989.

Eveleigh, David J. *Candle Lighting*. Princes Risborough, UK: Shire Publications, 2003.

Fagan, Brian. *Fish on Friday: Fasting, Feasting, and the Discovery of the New World*. New York: Basic Books, 2006.

Fearn, Jacqueline. *Thatch and Thatching*. Princes Risborough, UK: Shire Publications, 1976.

Fielding, Andrew, and Annelise Fielding. *The Salt Industry*. Princes Risborough, UK: Shire Books, 2006.

Flegg, Graham. *Numbers: Their History and Meaning*. New York: Barnes and Noble, 1993.

Fletcher, R. A. *Moorish Spain*. Berkeley: University of California Press, 2006.

Foster, A. M. *Bee Boles and Bee Houses*. Princes Risborough, UK: Shire Publications, 1988.

Fox-Davies, A. C. *A Complete Guide to Heraldry*. New York: Skyhorse Publishing, 2007.

Freeman, Margaret B. *Herbs for the Medieval Household*. New York: Metropolitan Museum of Art, 1997.

Freeman, Margaret B. *The Unicorn Tapestries*. New York: Metropolitan Museum of Art, 1983.

Freese, Barbara. *Coal: A Human History*. Cambridge, MA: Perseus Books, 2003.

Frugoni, Chiara. *Books, Banks, Buttons, and Other Inventions from the Middle Ages*. New York: Columbia University Press, 2003

Fry, Plantagenet Somerset. *Castles: England, Scotland, Wales, Ireland*. New York: F+W Media, 2005.

Fry, Plantagenet Somerset. *Castles of Britain and Ireland*. New York: Abbeville Press, 1997.

Gale, W.K.V. *Ironworking*. Princes Risborough, UK: Shire Publications, 2002.

Gay, Ruth. *The Jews of Germany: A Historical Portrait*. New Haven, CT: Yale University Press, 1994.

Geltner, G. *The Medieval Prison: A Social History*. Trenton, NJ: Princeton University Press, 2008.

Gies, Frances. *The Knight in History*. New York: Harper and Row, 1984.

Gies, Frances, and Joseph Gies. *Cathedral, Forge, and Waterwheel: Technology and Invention in the Middle Ages*. New York: Harper Collins, 1994.

Gies, Frances, and Joseph Gies. *Daily Life in Medieval Times*. New York: Black Dog and Leventhal, 1990.

Gies, Frances, and Joseph Gies. *Marriage and Family in the Middle Ages*. New York: Harper and Row, 1987.

Gies, Joseph, and Frances Gies. *Life in a Medieval Castle*. New York: Harper and Row, 1974.

Gies, Joseph, and Frances Gies. *Life in a Medieval City*. New York: Harper and Row, 1969.

Gimpel, Jean. *The Medieval Machine: The Industrial Revolution of the Middle Ages*. New York: Penguin Books, 1977.

Gordon, Benjamin L. *Medieval and Renaissance Medicine*. New York: Philosophical Library, 1959.

Gottfried, Robert S. *The Black Death: Natural and Human Disaster in Medieval Europe*. New York: Free Press, 1985.

Grant, Edward. *Science and Religion, 400 B.C. to A.D. 1550: From Aristotle to Copernicus*. Westport, CT: Greenwood Press, 2004.

Gravett, Christopher. *The History of Castles: Fortifications around the World*. Guilford, CT: Lyons Press, 2001.

Grew, Francis, and Margrethe de Neergaard. *Shoes and Pattens*. Woodbridge, UK: Boydell Press, 2006.

Grohskopf, Bernice. *The Treasure of Sutton Hoo: Ship-Burial for an Anglo-Saxon King*. New York: Atheneum, 1970.

Hahn, Daniel. *The Tower Menagerie*. New York: Penguin, 2004.

Hallam, Elizabeth, ed. *Chronicles of the Age of Chivalry*. New York: Greenwich Editions, 2001.

Hallet, Anna. *Almshouses*. Princes Risborough, UK: Shire Publications, 2004.

Hanawalt, Barbara A. *Growing Up in Medieval London: The Experience of Childhood in History*. New York: Oxford University Press, 1993.

Hanawalt, Barbara A. *Of Good and Ill Repute: Gender and Social Control in Medieval England*. New York: Oxford University Press, 1998.

Hanawalt, Barbara, ed. *Women and Work in Pre-Industrial Europe*. Bloomington: Indiana University Press, 1986.

Hardin, Terri. *Forts and Castles: Masterpieces of Architecture*. New York: Todtri Productions, 1997

Harris, Jonathan. *Constantinople: Capital of Byzantium*. New York: Continuum, 2007.

Harrison, David. *The Bridges of Medieval England*. New York: Oxford University Press, 2004.

Harvey, John. *Mediaeval Craftsmen*. New York: Drake Publishers, 1975.

Haws, Duncan. *Ships and the Sea: A Chronological Review*. New York: Thomas Y. Crowell, 1975.

Haywood, John. *Dark Age Naval Power: A Reassessment of Frankish and Anglo-Saxon Seafaring Activity*. Norfolk, UK: Anglo-Saxon Books, 1999.

Henisch, Bridget Ann. *Fast and Feast: Food in Medieval Society*. University Park: Pennsylvania State University, 1976.

Henisch, Bridget Ann. *The Medieval Calendar Year*. University Park: Pennsylvania State University Press, 1999.

Henisch, Bridget. *The Medieval Cook*. Woodbridge, UK: Boydell Press, 2009.

Hill, Donald. *A History of Engineering in Classical and Medieval Times*. La Salle, IL: Open Court Publishing, 1984.

Hindle, Paul. *Medieval Roads and Tracks*. Princes Risborough, UK: Shire Publications, 1998.

Hindle, Paul. *Medieval Town Plans*. Princes Risborough, UK: Shire Publications, 2002.

Hopwood, Rosalind. *Fountains and Water Features*. Princes Risborough, UK: Shire Publications, 2004.

Howard, Nicole. *The Book: The Life Story of a Technology*. Westport, CT: Greenwood Press, 2005

Hunt, Edwin S., and James M. Murray. *A History of Business in Medieval Europe, 1299–1550*. Cambridge: Cambridge University Press, 1999.

Hyland, Ann. *The Medieval Warhorse from Byzantium to the Crusades*. London: Grange Books, 1994.

Innes, Miranda, and Clay Perry. *Medieval Flowers: The History of Medieval Flowers and How to Grow Them Today*. London: Kyle Cathie, 2002.

Jackson, Sophie. *The Medieval Christmas*. Stroud, UK: Sutton Publishing, 2005.

Jennings, Trevor S. *Bellfounding*. Princes Risborough, UK: Shire Publications, 1992.

Johnson, Hugh. *The Story of Wine*. London: Mitchell Beasley, 2004.

Kaeuper, Richard W. *Chivalry and Violence in Medieval Europe*. New York: Oxford University Press, 1999.

Keates, Jonathan, and Angelo Hornak. *Canterbury Cathedral*. London: Scala Books, 1994.

Keen, Maurice, ed. *Medieval Warfare: A History*. Oxford: Oxford University Press, 1999.

Kelly, John. *The Great Mortality*. New York: Harper Collins, 2005.

Kelly, Jack. *Gunpowder: Alchemy, Bombards, and Pyrotechnics*. New York: Basic Books, 2004.

Kendall, Alan. *Medieval Pilgrims*. New York: G. P. Putnam's Sons, 1970.

Kerr, Julie. *Life in the Medieval Cloister*. New York: Continuum Press, 2009.

Kieckhefer, Richard. *Magic in the Middle Ages*. Cambridge: Cambridge University Press, 2000.

Kilby, Kenneth. *The Cooper and His Trade*. Fresno, CA: Linden Publishing, 1989.

King, Ross. *Brunelleschi's Dome: How a Renaissance Genius Reinvented Architecture*. New York: Walker and Company, 2000.

Kisch, Bruno. *Scales and Weights: A Historical Outline*. New Haven, CT: Yale University Press, 1966.

Knighton, Tess, and David Fallows, eds. *Companion to Medieval and Renaissance Music*. New York: Schirmer Books, 1992.

Konstam, Angus. *The History of Pirates*. Guilford, CT: Lyons Press, 1999.

Kors, Alan Charles, and Edward Peters, eds. *Witchcraft in Europe, 400–1700: A Documentary History*. Philadelphia: University of Pennsylvania Press, 2001.

Kurlansky, Mark. *Salt: A World History*. New York: Penguin Books, 2002.

Lacy, Robert, and Danny Danziger. *The Year 1000*. New York: Little, Brown, 1999.

Laiou, Angeliki E., and Cecile Morrisson. *The Byzantine Economy*. Cambridge: Cambridge University Press, 2007.

Landsberg, Sylvia. *The Medieval Garden*. New York: Thames and Hudson, 1996.

Langdon, John. *Horses, Oxen, and Technological Innovation*. Cambridge: Cambridge University Press, 1986.

Launer, Donald. *Navigation through the Ages*. Dobbs Ferry, NY: Sheridan House, 2009.

Leigh, G. J. *The World's Greatest Fix: A History of Nitrogen and Agriculture*. Oxford: Oxford University Press, 2004.

Lewis, David Levering. *God's Crucible: Islam and the Making of Europe, 570–1215*. New York: W. W. Norton, 2008.

Lewis, Griselda. *A Collector's History of English Pottery*. Woodbridge, UK: Antique Collectors' Club, 1999.

Lilley, Keith D. *Urban Life in the Middle Ages*. New York: Palgrave McMillan, 2002.

Lindahl, Carl, John McNamara, and John Lindow, eds. *Medieval Folklore: An Encyclopedia of Myths, Legends, Tales, Beliefs, and Customs*. Westport, CT: Greenwood Press, 2000.

Lindberg, David C. *The Beginnings of Western Science*. Chicago: University of Chicago Press, 1992.

Little, Charles T, ed. *Set in Stone: The Face in Medieval Sculpture*. New York: Metropolitan Museum of Art, 2006.

Logan, Donald F. *A History of the Church in the Middle Ages*. New York: Routledge, 2002.

Lopez, Robert S. *The Commercial Revolution of the Middle Ages, 950–1350*. Englewood Cliffs, NJ: Prentice Hall, 1971.

Lovett, Patricia. *Calligraphy and Illumination: A History and Practical Guide*. New York: Harry N. Abrams, 2000.

Magnusson, Roberta J. *Water Technology in the Middle Ages*. Baltimore: Johns Hopkins University Press, 2001.

Manseau, Peter. *Rag and Bone: A Journey among the World's Holy Dead*. New York: Henry Holt, 2009.

Martin, G., and Ann Williams, eds. *Domesday Book: A Complete Translation*. New York: Penguin, 2003.

McKitterick, Rosamond. *Atlas of the Medieval World*. New York: Oxford University Press, 2004.

McLeish, John. *The Story of Numbers: How Mathematics Has Shaped Civilization*. New York: Fawcett Columbine, 1991.

McMurtrie, Douglas C. *The Book: The Story of Printing and Bookmaking*. New York: Oxford University Press, 1967.

McMurtrie, Douglas C. *Some Facts Concerning the Invention of Printing*. Chicago: Chicago Club of Printing House Craftsmen, 1939.

McSheffrey, Shannon. *Love and Marriage in Late Medieval London*. Kalamazoo, MI: Medieval Institute Publications, 1995.

Meisel, Tony. *To the Sea: Sagas of Survival and Tales of Epic Challenge on the Seven Seas*. New York: Black Dog and Leventhal, 2000.

Menocal, Maria Rosa. *The Ornament of the World: How Muslims, Jews, and Christians Created a Culture of Tolerance in Medieval Spain*. New York: Little, Brown, 2002.

Mentasti, Rosa Barovier. *Murano: The Glass-Making Island*. Treviso, Italy: Vianello, 2006.

Merrifield, Mary P. *The Art of Fresco Painting in the Middle Ages and the Renaissance*. New York: Dover Publications, 2003.

Milne, Gustav. *The Port of Medieval London*. Stroud, UK: Tempus Publishing, 2006.

Miner, John N. *The Grammar Schools of Medieval England: A. F. Leach in Historiographical Perspective*. Montreal, Canada: McGill University Press, 1990.

Monk, Eric. *Keys: Their History and Collection*. Princes Risborough, UK: Shire Books, 2009.

Montagu, Jeremy. *The World of Medieval and Renaissance Musical Instruments*. Woodstock, NY: Overlook Press, 1980.

Mortimer, Ian. *The Time Traveler's Guide to Medieval England: A Handbook for Visitors to the Fourteenth Century*. New York: Simon and Schuster, 2008.

Murray, Stuart A. P. *The Library: An Illustrated History*. New York: Skyhorse Publishing, 2009.

Musset, Lucien. *The Bayeux Tapestry*. Woodbridge, UK: Boydell Press, 2005.

Netherton, Robin, and Gale R. Owen-Crocker. *Medieval Clothing and Textiles*. Vol. 1. Woodbridge, UK: Boydell Press: 2005.

Newman, Paul. *Growing Up in the Middle Ages*. Jefferson, NC: McFarland, 2007.

Nicolle, David. *Arms and Armour of the Crusading Era, 1050–1350*. 2 vols. Mechanicsburg, PA: Stackpole Books, 1999.

Nicolle, David. *Medieval Warfare Source Book: Warfare in Western Christendom*. London: Brockhampton Press, 1999.

Norman, Edward R. *The Roman Catholic Church: An Illustrated History*. Berkeley: University of California Press, 2007.

Norris, Herbert. *Ancient European Costume and Fashion*. Mineola, NY: Dover Publications, 1999.

Norris, Herbert. *Medieval Costume and Fashion*. Mineola, NY: Dover Publications, 1999.

Norwich, John Julius. *A History of Venice*. New York: Alfred A. Knopf, 1982.

Nossov, Konstantin. *Ancient and Medieval Siege Weapons*. Guilford, CT: Lyons Press, 2005.

Oakeshott, Ewart. *A Knight and His Armor*. Chester Springs, PA: Dufour Editions, 1999.

Oakeshott, Ewart. *A Knight and His Horse*. Chester Springs, PA: Dufour Editions, 1998.

Oakeshott, Ewart. *A Knight and His Weapons*. Chester Springs, PA: Dufour Editions, 1997.

Olmert, Michael. *The Smithsonian Book of Books*. Washington, DC: Smithsonian Institution, 1992.

Orchard, Andy. *Pride and Prodigies: Studies in the Monsters of the Beowulf-Manuscript*. Toronto: University of Toronto Press, 1995.

Orme, Nicholas. *Medieval Children*. New Haven, CT: Yale University Press, 2001.

Orme, Nicholas. *Medieval Schools: From Roman Britain to Renaissance England*. New Haven, CT: Yale University Press, 2006.

Bibliography

Orme, Nicholas, and Margaret Webster. *The Medieval Hospital, 1070–1570.* New Haven, CT: Yale University Press, 1995.

O'Shea, Stephen. *The Sea of Faith: Islam and Christianity in the Medieval Mediterranean World.* New York: Walker and Co., 2006.

Pancaroglu, Oya. *Perpetual Glory: Medieval Islamic Ceramics from the Harvey B. Plotnick Collection.* Chicago: Art Institute of Chicago, 2007.

Parry, Stan. *Great Gothic Cathedrals of France.* New York: Viking Studio, 2001.

Partington, J. R. *A History of Greek Fire and Gunpowder.* Baltimore: Johns Hopkins University Press, 1999.

Pastoureau, Michel. *Heraldry: An Introduction to a Noble Tradition.* New York: Harry N. Abrams, 1997.

Pellechia, Thomas. *Wine: The 8000-Year-Old Story of the Wine Trade.* New York: Thunder's Mouth Press, 2006.

Pérez-Higuera, Teresa. *Medieval Calendars.* London: Weidenfeld and Nicolson, 1998.

Pfaffenbichler, Matthias. *Armourers.* Toronto: University of Toronto Press, 1992.

Piggott, Stuart. *Wagon, Chariot, and Carriage: Symbol and Status in the History of Transport.* London: Thames and Hudson, 1992.

Pirenne, Henri. *Medieval Cities: Their Origins and the Revival of Trade.* Trenton, NJ: Princeton University Press, 1939.

Pointer, Sally. *The Artifice of Beauty.* Stroud, UK: Sutton Publishing, 2005.

Pollard, A. J. *Imagining Robin Hood.* New York: Routledge, 2007.

Pollington, Stephen. *The English Warrior: From Earliest Times till 1066.* Hockwold, UK: Anglo-Saxon Books, 2002.

Pollington, Stephen. *The Mead Hall: Feasting in Anglo-Saxon England.* Hockwold, UK: Anglo-Saxon Books, 2003.

Pollington, Stephen. *Rudiments of Runelore.* Hockwold, UK: Anglo-Saxon Books, 1998.

Poole, Julia E. *English Pottery.* Cambridge: Cambridge University Press, 1995.

Posamentier, Alfred S., and Ingmar Lehmann. *The Fabulous Fibonacci Numbers.* Amherst, NY: Prometheus Books, 2007.

Power, Eileen. *Medieval Women.* Cambridge: Cambridge University Press, 1975.

Prache, Anne. *Cathedrals of Europe.* Ithaca, NY: Cornell University Press, 1999.

Prioreschi, Plinio. *Medieval Medicine.* Omaha, NE: Horatius Press, 2003.

Quye, Anita, Kathryn Hallett, and Concha Herrero Carretero. *"Wroughte in Gold and Silk": Preserving the Art of Historic Tapestries.* Edinburgh: National Museums Scotland, 2009.

Read, Piers Paul. *The Templars.* New York: St. Martin's Press, 1999.

Reeves, Compton. *Pleasures and Pastimes in Medieval England.* New York: Oxford University Press, 1998.

Reinhardt, Hank. *The Book of Swords.* Riverdale, NY: Baen Publishing, 2009.

Resl, Brigitte, ed. *A Cultural History of Animals in the Medieval Age.* New York: Berg, 2007.

Reyerson, Kathryn L., and Debra A. Salata, eds. *Medieval Notaries and Their Acts: The 1327–1328 Register of Jean Holanie.* Kalamazoo, MI: Medieval Institute Publications, 2004.

Richards, E. G. *Mapping Time: The Calendar and Its History*. New York: Oxford University Press, 1998.

Richards, Julian D. *Viking Age England*. London: English Heritage, 1991.

Richards, Peter. *The Medieval Leper*. Cambridge, UK: D. S. Brewer, 1977.

Robinson, Andrew. *The Story of Measurement*. London: Thames and Hudson, 2007.

Rock, Hugh. *Church Clocks*. Botley, UK: Shire Publications, 2008.

Rose, Carol. *Giants, Monsters, and Dragons: An Encyclopedia of Folklore, Legend, and Myth*. New York: Norton, 2000.

Rotberg, Robert I., and Theodore K. Rabb. *Climate and History*. Princeton, NJ: Princeton University Press, 1981.

Roth, Norman. *Daily Life of the Jews in the Middle Ages*. Westport, CT: Greenwood Press, 2005.

Rowe, Anne. *Medieval Parks of Hertfordshire*. Hatfield, UK: University of Hertfordshire Press, 2009.

Rubin, Miri, ed. *Medieval Christianity in Practice*. Trenton, NJ: Princeton University Press, 2009.

Sawyer, Birgit, and Peter Sawyer. *Medieval Scandinavia: From Conversion to Reformation, Circa 800–1500*. Minneapolis: University of Minnesota Press, 1993.

Schütz, Bernhard. *Great Cathedrals*. New York: Harry N. Abrams, 2002.

Scott, Margaret. *Medieval Dress and Fashion*. London: British Library, 2007.

Scott, Philippa. *The Book of Silk*. London: Thames and Hudson, 1993.

Scott, Robert A. *The Gothic Enterprise: A Guide to Understanding the Medieval Cathedral*. Berkeley: University of California Press, 2003.

Scully, Terence. *The Art of Cookery in the Middle Ages*. Woodbridge, UK: Boydell Press, 1995.

Seay, Albert. *Music in the Medieval World*. Englewood Cliffs, NJ: Prentice Hall, 1975.

Sekules, Veronica. *Medieval Art*. Oxford: Oxford University Press, 2001.

Sheingorn, Pamela. *The Easter Sepulchre in England*. Kalamazoo, MI: Medieval Institute Publications, 1987.

Singman, Jeffrey. *Daily Life in Medieval Europe*. Westport, CT: Greenwood Press, 1999.

Solomon, Steven. *Water: The Epic Struggle for Wealth, Power, and Civilization*. New York: Harper Collins, 2010.

Sorda, Enrique. *Moorish Spain*. New York: Crown Publishers, 1963.

Squatriti, Paolo. *Water and Society in Early Medieval Italy, AD 400–1000*. Cambridge: Cambridge University Press, 2002.

Stalley, Roger. *Early Medieval Architecture*. Oxford: Oxford University Press, 1999.

Staniland, Kay. *Embroiderers*. Toronto: University of Toronto Press, 1991.

Stark, Rodney. *God's Battalions: The Case for the Crusades*. New York: Harper Collins, 2009.

Staubach, Suzanne. *Clay: The History and Evolution of Humankind's Relationship with Earth's Most Primal Element*. New York: Berkley Books, 2005.

Staver, Ruth Johnston. *A Companion to Beowulf*. Westport, CT: Greenwood Press, 2005.

Stevens, John. *Words and Music in the Middle Ages: Song, Narrative, Dance, and Drama, 1050–1350.* Cambridge: Cambridge University Press, 1986.

Stuard, Susan Mosher, ed. *Women in Medieval Society.* Philadelphia: University of Pennsylvania Press, 1976.

Sunshine, Paula. *Wattle and Daub.* Botley, UK: Shire Publications, 2008.

Swann, June. *Shoemaking.* Princes Risborough, UK: Shire Publications, 1997.

Symes, Carol. *A Common Stage: Theater and Public Life in Medieval Arras.* Ithaca, NY: Cornell University Press, 2007.

Tait, Hugh, ed. *Five Thousand Years of Glass.* London: British Museum Press, 1991.

Thompson, Daniel V. *The Materials and Techniques of Medieval Painting.* Mineola, NY: Dover Publications, 1956.

Toussaint-Samat, Maguelonne. *A History of Food.* Cambridge, MA: Blackwell, 1992.

Toy, Sidney. *Castles: Their Construction and History.* Mineola, NY: Dover Publications, 1985.

Turner, Jack. *Spice: The History of a Temptation.* New York: Knopf, 2004.

Tuulse, Armin. *Castles of the Western World.* London: Thames and Hudson, 1958.

Tyerman, Christopher. *The Crusades.* New York: Sterling Publishing, 2009.

Unger, Richard W. *Beer in the Middle Ages and the Renaissance.* Philadelphia: University of Philadelphia Press, 2004.

Ure, John. *Pilgrimages: The Great Adventures of the Middle Ages.* New York: Carroll and Graf, 2006.

Villieus, Capt. Alan, et al. *Men, Ships, and the Sea.* Washington, DC: National Geographic Society, 1973.

Vince, John. *An Illustrated History of Carts and Wagons.* Bourne End, UK: Spurbooks, 1975.

Viner, David. *Wagons and Carts.* Botley, UK: Shire Books, 2008.

Volz, Carl A. *The Medieval Church.* Nashville, TN: Abingdon Press, 1997.

Waley, Daniel. *The Italian City-Republics.* New York: McGraw-Hill, 1969.

Walker, Ralph S. *Reading Medieval European Coins.* South Salem, NY: Attic Books, 2000.

Walther, Ingo F., ed. *Gothic.* Cologne, Germany: Taschen, 2006.

Warner, Philip. *The Medieval Castle: Life in a Castle in Peace and War.* New York: Taplinger Publishing, 1971.

Watts, Martin. *Watermills.* Princes Risborough, UK: Shire Publications, 2006.

Watts, Martin. *Windmills.* Princes Risborough, UK: Shire Publications, 2006.

Waugh, Alexander. *Time: Its Origin, Its Enigma, Its History.* New York: Carroll and Graf, 1999.

Weatherford, Jack. *The History of Money.* New York: Three Rivers Press, 1997.

Weigert, Laura. *Weaving Sacred Stories: French Choir Tapestries and the Performance of Clerical Identity.* Ithaca, NY: Cornell University Press, 2004.

Welch, Evelyn. *Art and Society in Italy 1350–1500.* Oxford: Oxford University Press, 1997.

Wescher, H. *The Cloth Trade and the Fairs of Champagne (Ciba Review 65).* Basle, Switzerland: Ciba Review, 1948.

Wheaton, Barbara Ketcham. *Savoring the Past: The French Kitchen and Table from 1300 to 1789.* New York: Touchstone Books, 1983.

White, Lynn, Jr. *Medieval Technology and Social Change.* Oxford: Clarendon Press, 1962.

White, T. H. *The Book of Beasts: Being a Translation from a Latin Bestiary of the Twelfth Century.* New York: Putnam's Sons, 1954.

Whiteman, Robin. *Brother Cadfael's Herb Garden: An Illustrated Companion to Medieval Plants and Their Uses.* New York: Bulfinch, 1997.

Wickham, Glynn. *The Medieval Theatre.* New York: St. Martin's Press, 1974.

Wiggins, Kenneth. *Siege Mines and Underground Warfare.* Princes Risborough, UK: Shire Publications, 2003.

Wilford, John Noble. *The Mapmakers.* New York: Random House, 1981.

Wilson, David Fenwick. *Music of the Middle Ages.* New York: Schirmer Books, 1990.

Wilson, David M. *The Bayeux Tapestry.* London: Thames and Hudson, 1985.

Wood, Melusine. *Historical Dances: 12th to 19th Century.* London: Dance Books, 1982.

Woodcock, Thomas, and John Martin Robinson. *The Oxford Guide to Heraldry.* New York: Oxford University Press, 1988.

Woodman, Richard. *The History of the Ship.* Guilford, CT: Lyons Press, 2002.

Woolgar, C. M. *The Senses in Late Medieval England.* New Haven, CT: Yale University Press, 2006.

Wright, Lawrence. *Clean and Decent: The Fascinating History of the Bathroom and the WC.* Toronto: University of Toronto Press, 1967.

Wright, Lawrence. *Warm and Snug: The History of the Bed.* Stroud, UK: Sutton Publishing, 2004.

Ziegler, Philip. *The Black Death.* Dover, NH: Alan Sutton Publishing, 1993.

Non-Print Sources

Architecture

Canterbury Cathedral. Architecture, Religion, Art, and Literature. http://www.canterbury-cathedral.org/history.html.

Castle. DVD. David Macaulay. Washington, DC: Corporation for Public Broadcasting, 2006.

Castles of Britain. Castles Unlimited. http://www.castles-of-britain.com/castle6.htm.

Cathédrale Notre Dame de Paris. http://www.notredamedeparis.fr/-Cathedral-for-art-and-history-.

Chartres Cathedral: A Sacred Geometry. DVD. New York: Janson Media, 2003.

Museum of the Opera del Duomo. http://www.mega.it/eng/egui/monu/but.htm.

NOVA: Building the Great Cathedrals. DVD. Washington, DC: Corporation for Public Broadcasting, 2010.

Virtual Abbey: A Medieval Tour. New York Carver. http://www.newyorkcarver.com/Abbey.htm.

Virtual Tour of Raglan Castle. Jeffrey L. Thomas. http://www.castlewales.com/rag_tour.html.

Art: Painting and Sculpture

Gallery of Medieval Europe. The British Museum. http://www.britishmuseum.org/explore/galleries/europe/room_40_medieval_europe.aspx.

Landmarks of Western Art: The Late Medieval World. DVD. West Long Branch, NJ: Kultur Video, 2006.

Madonna and Child & the Virgin Mary in Art. DVD. Dallas, TX: Swan-Jones Productions, 2008.

Medieval Art Gallery. The Metropolitan Museum of Art. http://www.metmuseum.org/works_of_art/medieval_art.

Medieval Art in Pisa. Il Museo virtuale di Pisa. Cooperativa Alfea. http://www2.alfea.it/.

Medieval London. The Museum of London. http://www.museumoflondon.org.uk/English/EventsExhibitions/Permanent/medieval/.

Medieval Salisbury. Salisbury and South Wiltshire Museum. http://www.salisburymuseum.org.uk/collections/medi.eval-salisbury/.

Musée des Augustins. Musée des Beaux Arts de Toulouse http://www.augustins.org/en/monument/accueil.htm.

Musée National du Moyen Âge. Réunion des musées nationaux. http://www.musee-moyenage.fr/ang/index.html.

Stained Glass Museum. Ely Cathedral. http://www.stainedglassmuseum.com/.

State Museums. Florence, Italy. http://www.uffizi.firenze.it/english/musei/musei.asp.

Daily Life

Guide to Medieval and Renaissance Instruments. Musica Antiqua. Iowa State University. http://www.music.iastate.edu/antiqua/instrumt.html.

Hill Museum and Manuscript Library. Saint John's University. http://www.hmml.org/collections10/collections10.htm.

Marriage During the Middle Ages. Medieval-Weddings.net. http://www.medieval-weddings.net/index.htm.

Medieval Games. Knight, Ron. http://www.modaruniversity.org/Games.htm

Medieval Life and Times. Alchin, L. K. http://www.medieval-life-and-times.info/.

Medieval and Renaissance Material Culture. Karen Larsdatter. http://larsdatter.com/index.html.

Medieval and Renaissance Woodworking. Gary R. Halstead. http://www.medievalwoodworking.org/links1.htm.

Schøyen Collection. 740 Manuscripts Spanning 5,000 Years. Martin Schøyen. http://www.schoyencollection.com/.

York Mystery Plays. DVD. York, UK: York Festival Trust, 2010.

Warfare

Arms and Armor. The Metropolitan Museum of Art. http://www.metmuseum. org/works_of_art/arms_and_armor.

Higgins Armory Museum. http://www.higgins.org/.

Medieval Castle Siege Weapons. Garfield Benjamin. http://www.medieval-castle-siege-weapons.com/index.html.

Mediaeval Sword Virtual Museum. Lee A. Jones. http://www.vikingsword.com/vmframe.html.

NOVA: Medieval Siege. DVD. Washington, DC: Corporation for Public Broadcasting, 2004

Medieval Warfare: Agincourt. DVD. West Long Branch, NJ: Kultur Video, 2007.

Index

Index

Bycocket hats, 330
Byrnies, 28, 30

Cabbage, 249
Caernarvon Castle, 99
Calendar, 87–91; church, 122; fasts, 232; feasts, 234; holidays, 340–41; pens and ink, 559; saints, 618; schools, 627. *See also* Holidays; Saints
Calends, 89, 90
Cancer, 481
Candle clocks, 140, 452
Candles, 450–52. *See also* Lights
Candlesticks, 452
Candy, 674
Cannons, 312, 313, 670–71
Canoes, 643
Canons, 118–19
Canterbury Cathedral, 608, 609, 618
Canterbury Tales, The (Chaucer), 72, 686, 687
Caramel, 674
Caravels, 652
Cargo ships, 646–47
Carité de Notre Dame des Ardents, 211–13, 498
Carmelite friars, 507
Carmelite Water, 187
Carnival, 123, 209, 346
Carolingian minuscule, 12, 13
Carols, 199, 202–3, 343
Carp, 243
Carpenters, 689–90
Carracks, 650–51
Carthusian monks, 504, 505–6, 507, 511
Carts. *See* Wagons and carts
Carvel construction, 649–50
Castle of Perseverance, The, 211
Castles, 91–102; bricks and tiles, 77; construction, 99–100; Crusades, 194; development, 93–97; food, 256, 257; houses, 375; inside a castle, 97–98; latrines and

garbage, 439–40; notable, 98–99; painting, 548; records, 601; sieges, 660; tools, 691; warfare, 100–102; water, 714–15; women, 739–40. *See also* Sieges; Stone and masons
Catalan Atlas, 475–76
Catapults, 667–71
Cataracts, 486
Cathar Inquisition, 602
Cathedral Basilica of Saint Denis, 298
Cathedral of Santa Maria del Fiore, 112–13
Cathedrals, 102–13; bells, 60; classical style, 103; funerals, 269; glass, 298–300; Gothic style, 108–12; Mediterranean style, 112–13; music, 521; relics, 607–8, 609; Romanesque style, 103–8; saints, 618; schools, 623–24, 626, 627; sculpture, 632. *See also* Church; Stone and masons
Catholic Church. *See* Roman Catholic Church
Cats, 20–21
Cattle, 18–19, 250
Cauldrons, 425
Causeways, 81
Caxton, William, 589
Cemeteries and graves, 122, 265, 269, 286, 571
Centner, 734
Cesspits, 440
Chainmail, 24
Chairs, 273
Chamber pots, 439, 441
Chapels, memorial, 269–70
Chaperons, 330, 331
Chapter houses, 509
Charcoal, 311, 550
Charlemagne: alphabet, 12; calendar, 87, 88; church, 116; coins, 174; food, 247; funerals, 270, 271; gardens, 289; knights, 427; libraries, 446; Roland, Song of,

Index

Index

About the Author

RUTH A. JOHNSTON is an independent scholar with a research specialty in medieval literature and languages. She is the author of *A Companion to Beowulf* (Greenwood, 2005).